The Beginner's Guide to Photographing Birds

I0729634

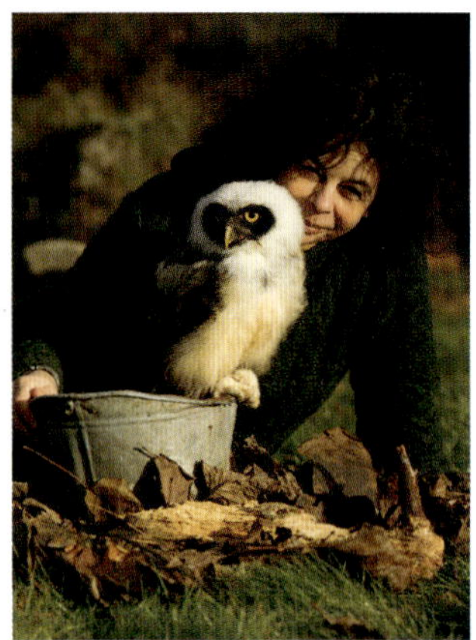

Rosl Rössner is an enthusiastic bird photographer as well as a falconer and has shared her knowledge in special photography workshops for many years. Her pictures stand out, not only because they are technically perfect but also because they always aim to show the bird as an individual with its own personality. Her photography is all about evoking emotions. You can look at her photos at *www.birdpictures.de,* and you can book her bird photography workshops at *www.fototrainer4you.de.*

Rosl Rössner

The Beginner's Guide to Photographing Birds

Essential Techniques for Hobbyists and Bird Lovers

rockynook

The Beginner's Guide to Photographing Birds
Rosl Rössner

www.birdpictures.de

Project editor: Maggie Yates
Project manager: Lisa Brazieal
Marketing coordinator: Katie Walker
Copyeditor: Maggie Yates
Layout: WolfsonDesign
Cover design: Aren Straiger

ISBN: 978-1-68198-935-8
1st Edition (1st printing, November 2022)
Copyright © 2022 by dpunkt.verlag GmbH, Heidelberg, Germany.
Title of the German original: Faszination Vogelfotografie
ISBN 978-3-86490-871-2
Translation Copyright © 2023 by Rocky Nook. All rights reserved.

Rocky Nook Inc.
1010 B Street, Suite 350
San Rafael, CA 94901
USA

www.rockynook.com

Distributed in the UK and Europe by Publishers Group UK
Distributed in the U.S. and all other territories by Ingram Publisher Services

Library of Congress Control Number: 2022939343

All rights reserved. No part of the material protected by this copyright notice may be reproduced or utilized in any form, electronic or mechanical, including photocopying, recording, or by any information storage and retrieval system, without written permission of the publisher.

Many of the designations in this book used by manufacturers and sellers to distinguish their products are claimed as trademarks of their respective companies. Where those designations appear in this book, and Rocky Nook was aware of a trademark claim, the designations have been printed in caps or initial caps. All product names and services identified throughout this book are used in editorial fashion only and for the benefit of such companies with no intention of infringement of the trademark. They are not intended to convey endorsement or other affiliation with this book.

While reasonable care has been exercised in the preparation of this book, the publisher and author assume no responsibility for errors or omissions, or for damages resulting from the use of the information contained herein or from the use of the discs or programs that may accompany it.

Printed in China

PREFACE

I am happy that you're interested in bird photography and that you have picked up my book. I wrote it to introduce you to the fascination of bird photography and encourage you to carefully analyze your own pictures as well as those of others. Perfect technical skills are not what makes a photo great. Rather it's so much else: framing, composition, colors, lines, and textures, to name just a few of the factors that play a major role in how we perceive photos and how we react to them emotionally. Whenever I photograph a bird I don't just want to do it technically correct but also show the bird's individual character. Because birds have personalities, too—feathered personalities!

This book is also very deliberately meant for people who find joy in admiring and photographing birds in zoos, bird parks, or falconries. Not everyone can afford the gear for good wildlife photography, and not everyone has the opportunity to go and see birds in the wild. But even under conditions of captivity, you can take impressive photos, once you've mastered a few rules and techniques.

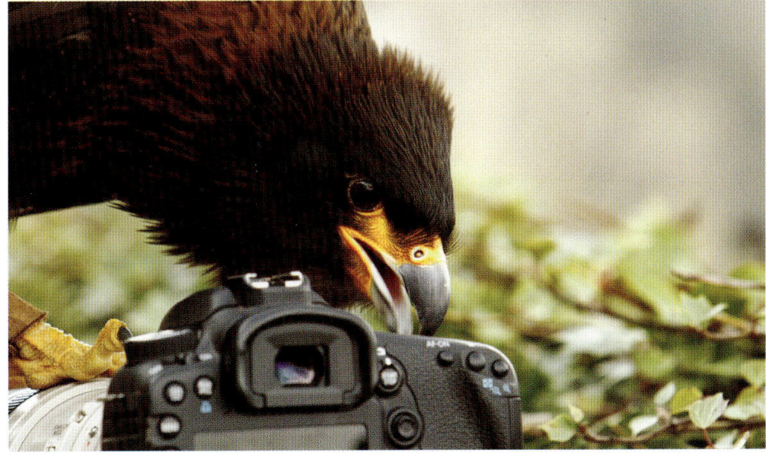

Striated caracara | German Raptor Research Center at Guttenberg Castle, Germany | 180mm, aperture 7.1, 1/250 s, ISO 1250

This book is less about cameras and equipment and more about image composition in bird photography. I want to give you tips and strategies to help you take pictures that truly catch the eye!

To do this, I'll introduce you to some rules and principles. Of course, you don't have to follow them at all times. But I think it makes sense to know these rules—and then decide if you want to honor them or deliberately break them.

One more thing is close to my heart: While practicing our hobby, we must always remember that it's our responsibility to not harm the animals. No picture is worth the price that a bird might abandon a clutch of eggs or that we alert a predator to the presence of chicks! It should be our top priority in bird photography to avoid disturbances as much as possible and show consideration to the birds.

▶
Little owl | Germany | In this book, I want to help you train your eyes: What are the strengths and weaknesses of an image? Is it a successful photo? | 135mm, aperture 2.0, 1/1250 s, ISO 1250, -1 exposure compensation

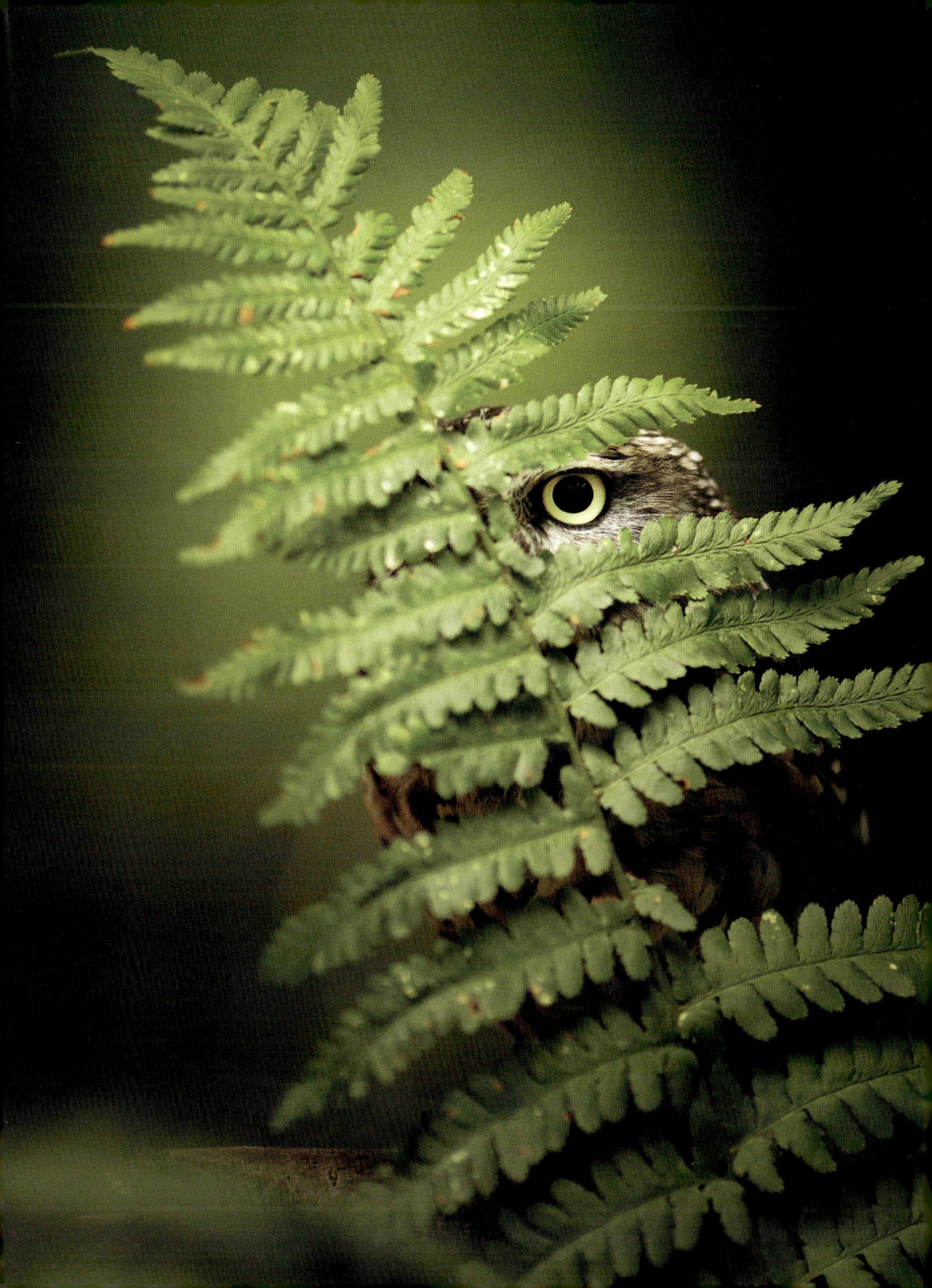

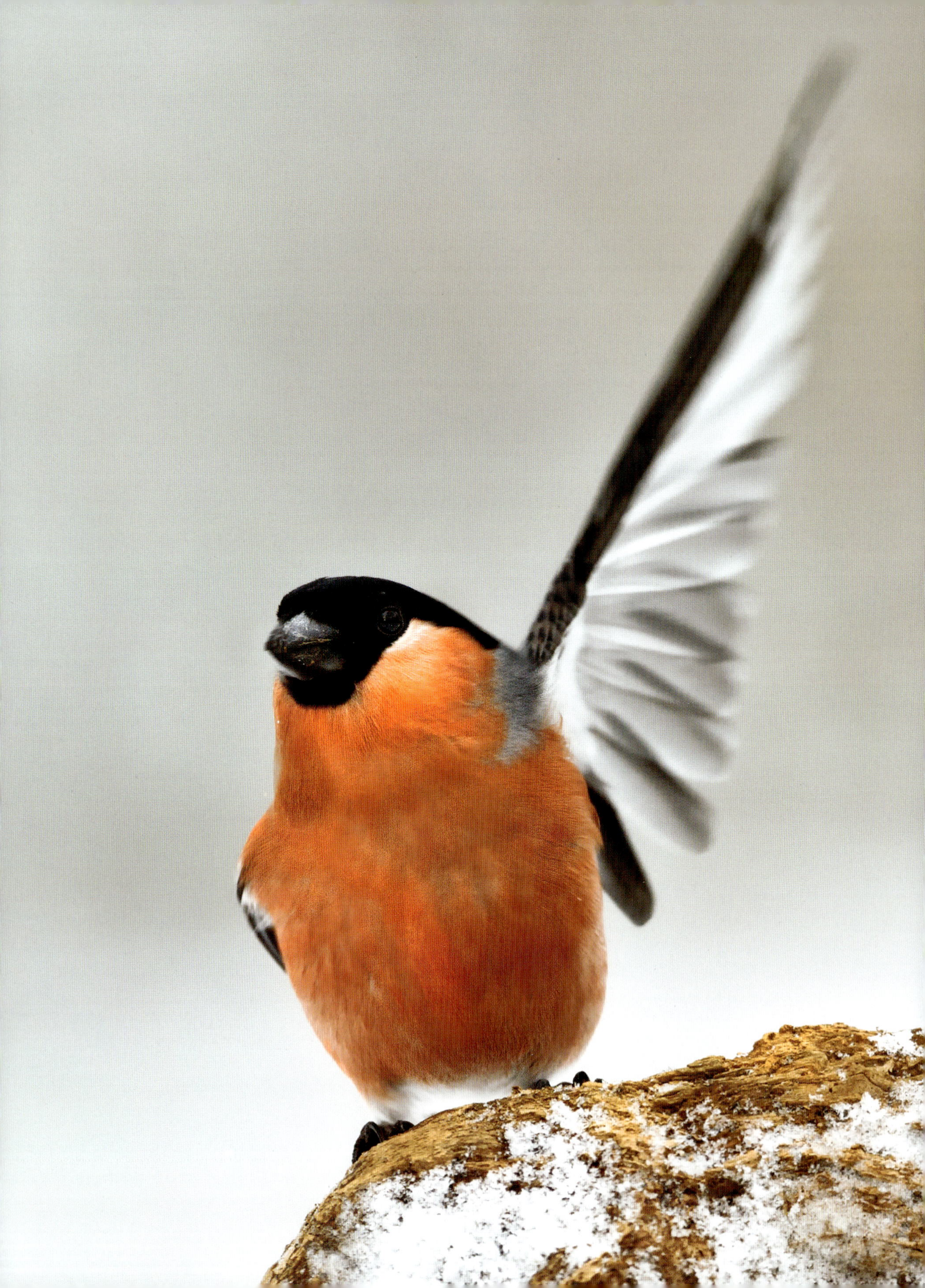

CONTENTS

◄

Eurasian bullfinch | Germany | "This way," the bullfinch
seems to say…. | 500mm, aperture 5.6, 1/8000 s, ISO 1000,
+2/3 exposure compensation

5   The Making of 25 Successful Photographs   169

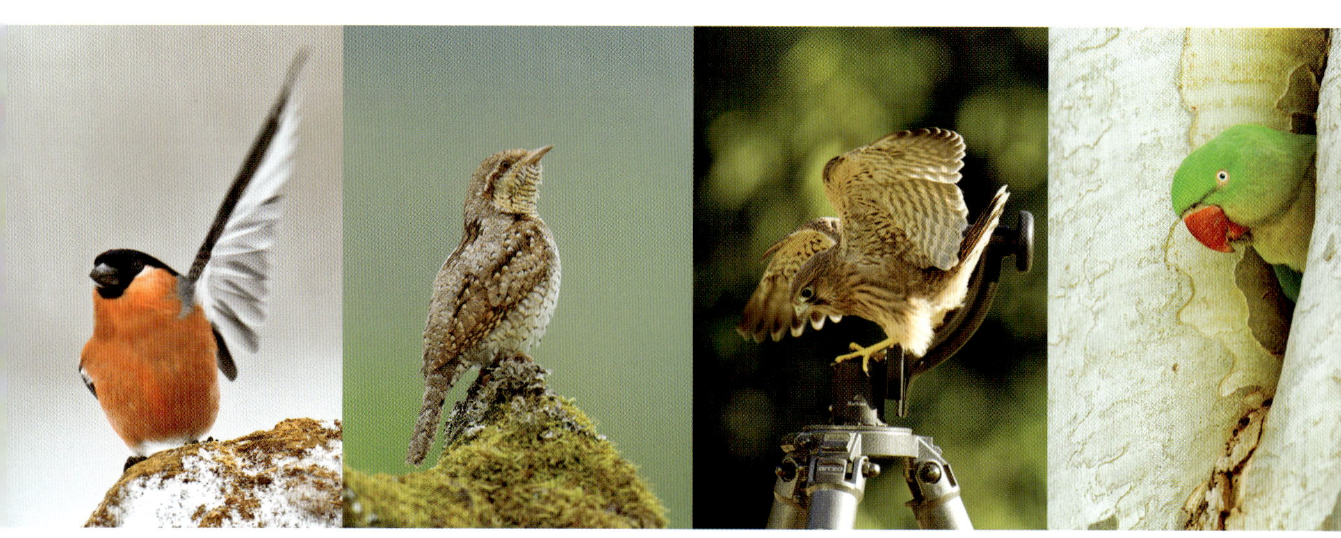

     CONTENTS

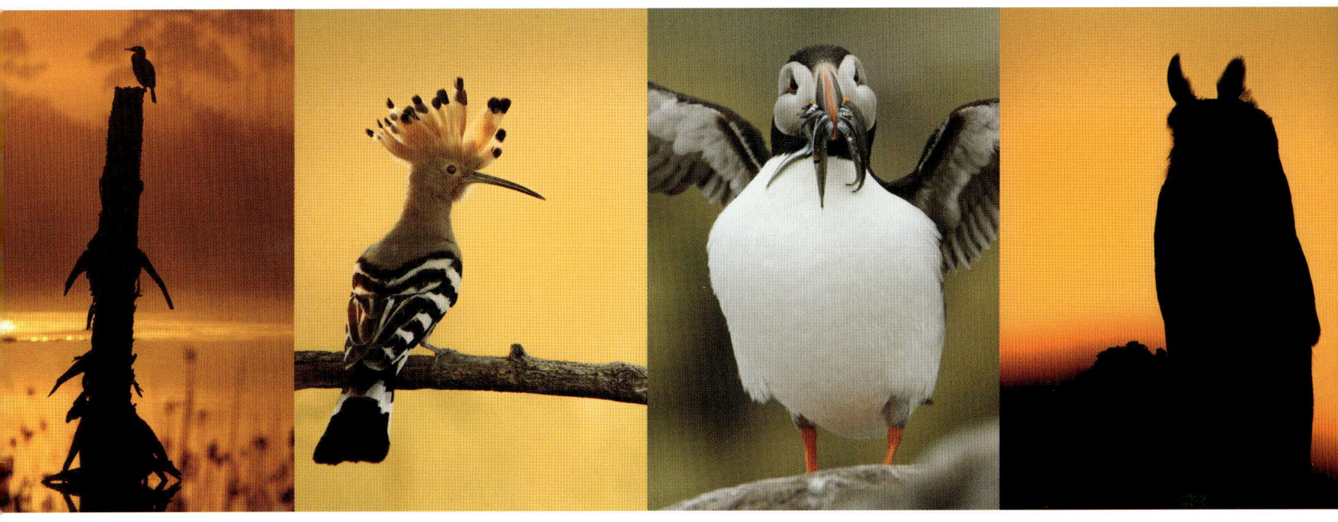

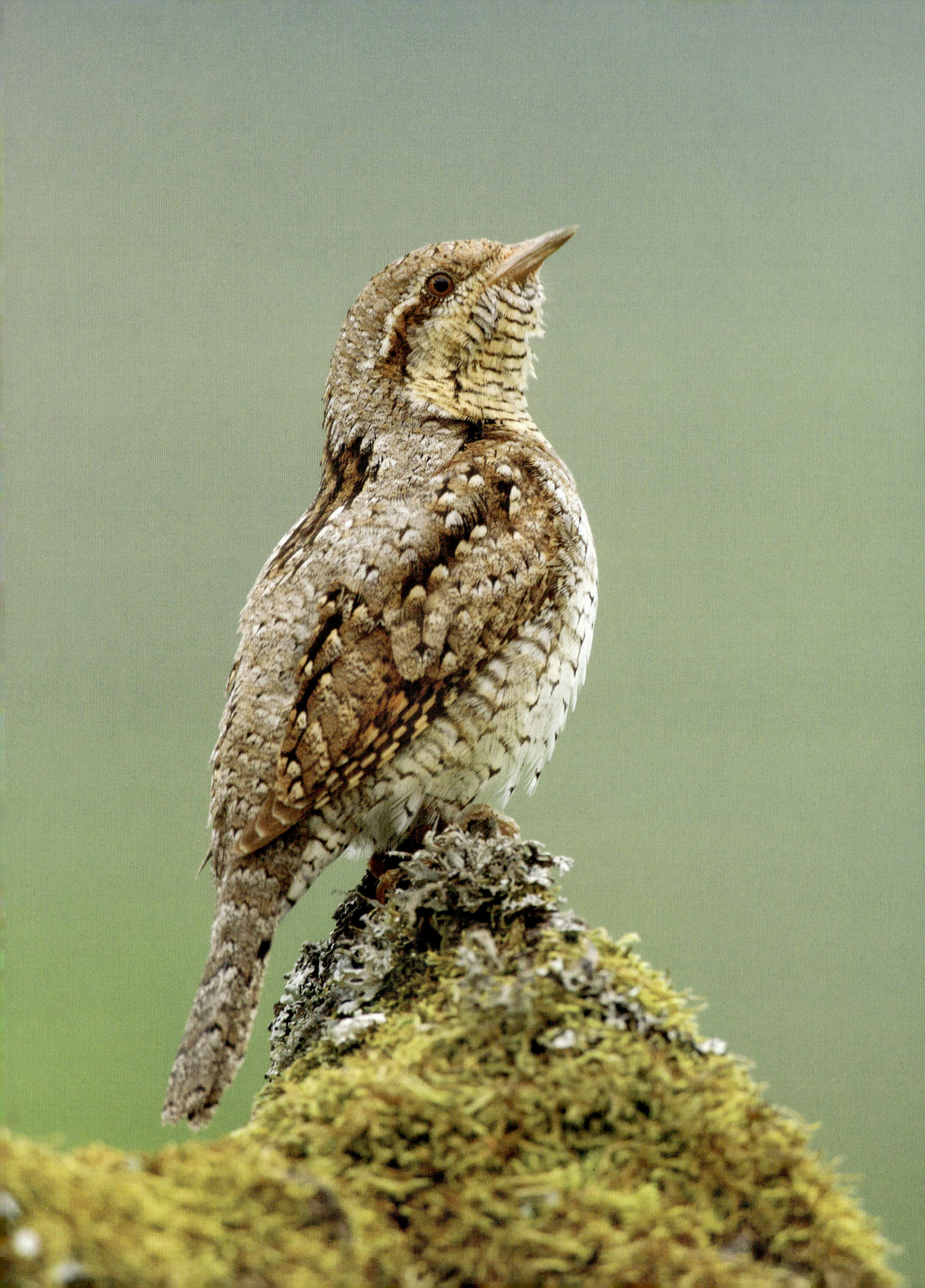

1 WHAT MAKES A GREAT BIRD PHOTOGRAPH?

Tastes differ. This is true for every art, including photography. But there are criteria for what makes a photograph successful, in the sense that most viewers will find it appealing. First, it must be technically adequate. Blurred eyes, camera shake, or the wrong shutter time immediately disqualify a photo from being good.

Wryneck | Germany | More than just useful for identification: The wonderful colors and the interesting pose of this bird make this photo appealing. | 500mm, aperture 5.6, 1/125 s, ISO 2000, -1/3 exposure compensation

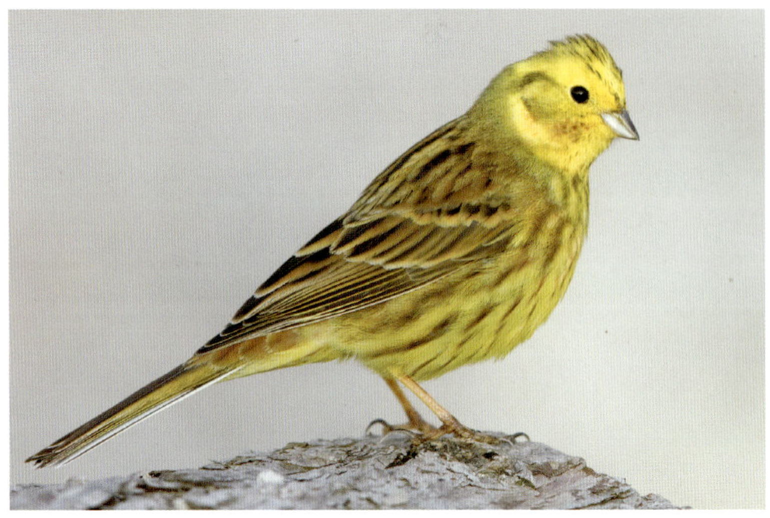

But apart from the technical skills that you simply have to master, other factors very much matter as well. I would argue that good technical skills are only the beginning when it comes to creating an effective image. This doesn't mean that it's impossible that a photo that is intentionally out of focus because of a long shutter time or motion blur can't be really good. What's important is that the rules were broken intentionally and that it enhances—rather than detracts—from the story the photo tells.

Much of what makes us decide if a photo is good or not, happens subconsciously. Our eyes and brain register and process things before we consciously perceive them. For example, colors trigger emotions: Red signals danger, excitement, and tension. Blue is a cooling and calming color. Yellow and orange communicate warmth and joy; green stands for nature, growth, and naturalness.

Of course, in bird photography, how you photograph can also differ with the intended use of the picture. I can try to get a photo that would be suitable for a bird guide. Such an image should show the bird in profile and in a posture that is typical for the species. The outline and colors of the plumage should be clearly visible and the whole bird should be sharp. Other times, I might try to show a bird as an individual with its own personality. Perhaps it's doing something that tells its own little story. For a picture like this I might shoot the bird in a completely different posture, and the technical side—i.e., sharpness, depth of field, and exposure—must fit that story. First and foremost, a good picture must do what it intends to do.

CHAPTER 1

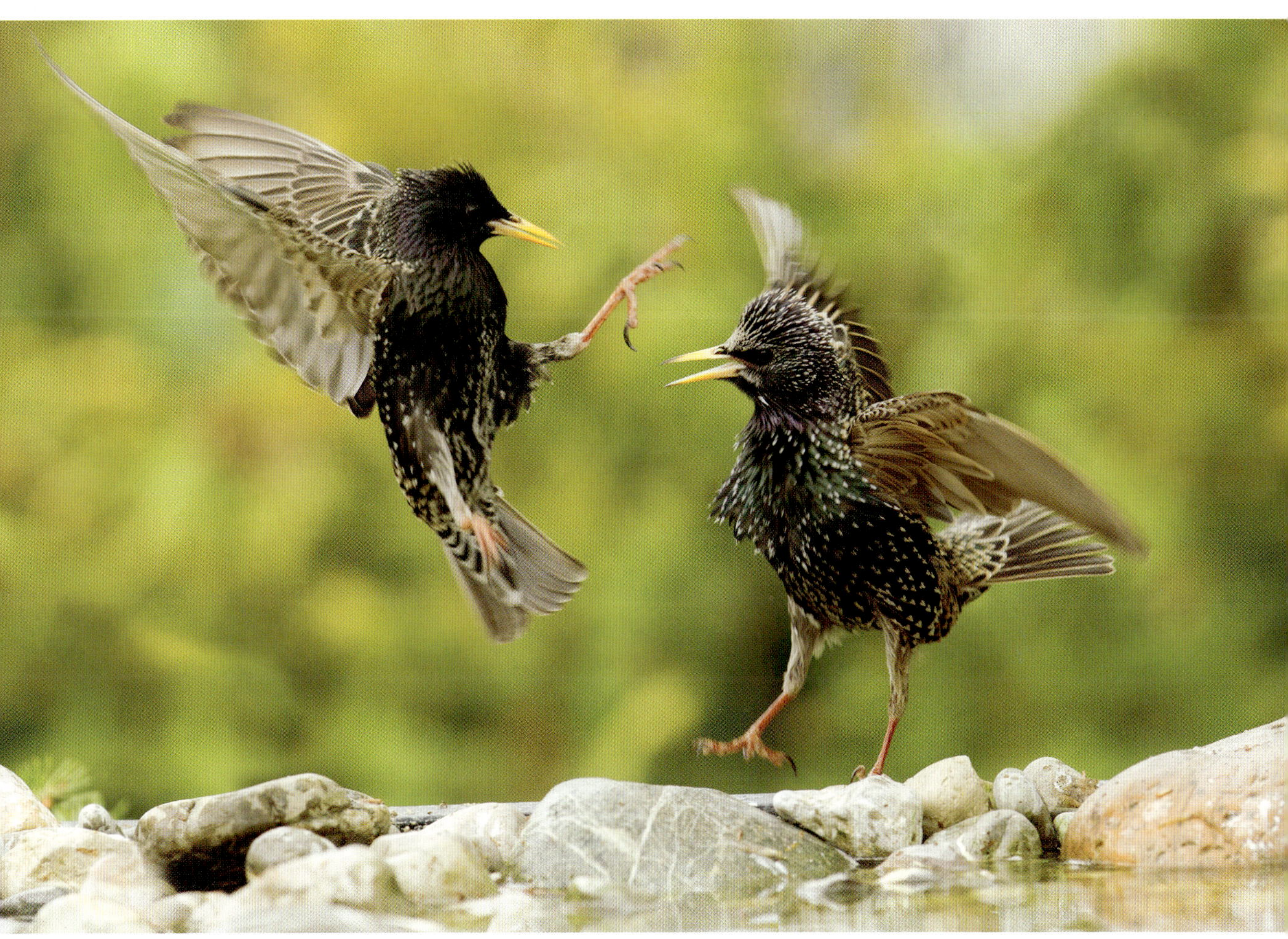

The way I see it, the most important thing that makes a photo work is that it evokes emotions. They can be positive or negative. However, in bird photography, we mostly work with positive emotions. A chick being carried through the water on its mother's back can evoke such positive reactions as can two birds in courtship. A puffin with a beak full of fish can elicit astonishment; a majestic eagle, admiration. The photo of a clumsy duckling might make the viewer smile, while an image of a sparrowhawk that has caught the prey it is named for will likely generate a feeling of pity for the sparrow but also admiration for the elegant hawk, that only wants to live, after all.

It doesn't really matter which emotion it ends up being—if your image evokes any reaction of this kind, you should be happy. You achieved what you wanted!

Starlings | Germany | This photo tells a story: The two starlings are fighting. | 300mm, aperture 4.0, 1/500 s, ISO 1250

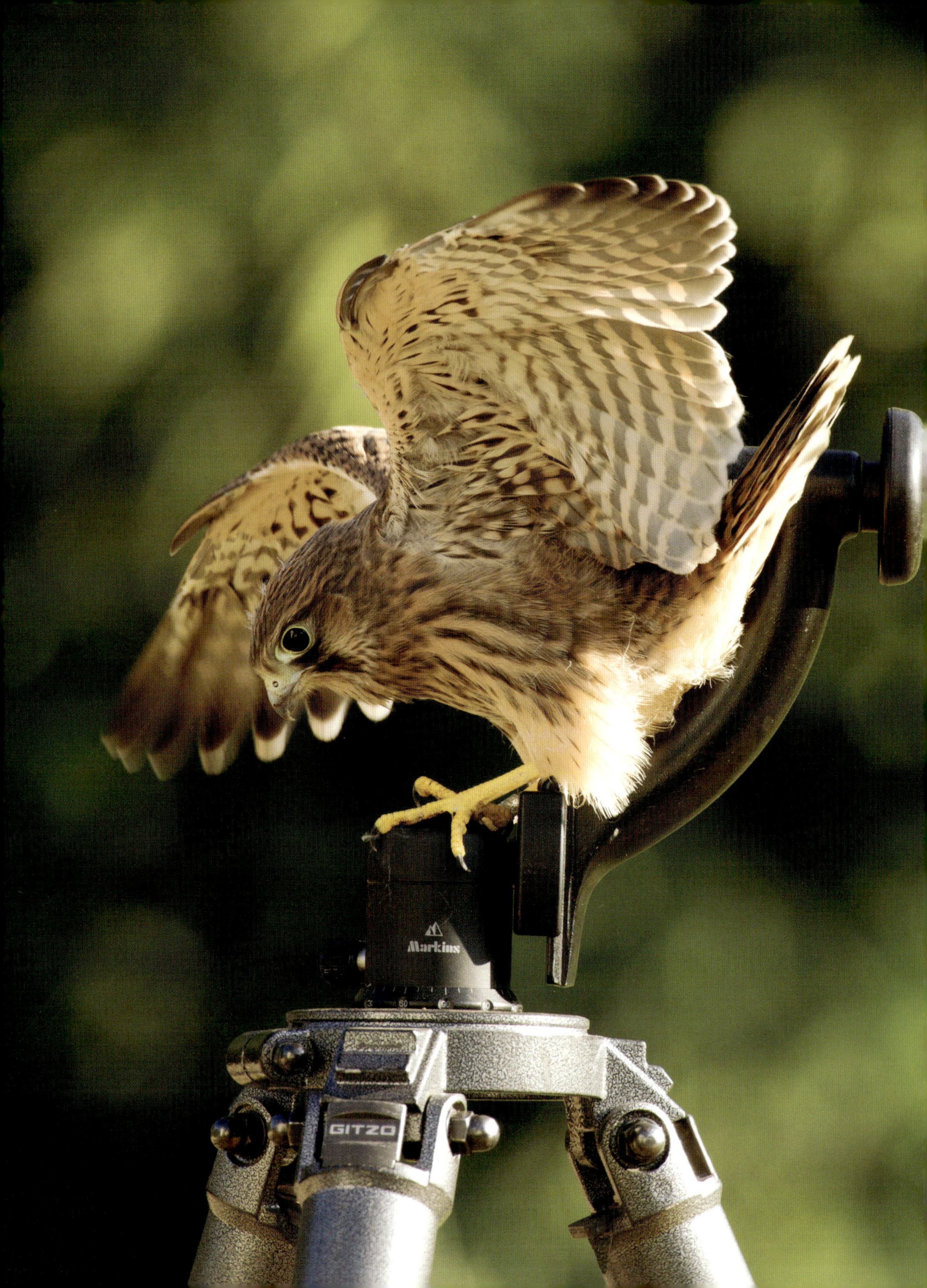

2 THE NECESSARY GEAR

Unfortunately, bird photography is something that requires relatively expensive equipment to achieve really good results. Generally speaking, you won't be able to avoid buying a high-quality camera and a telephoto lens with a relatively long focal length. In this book, I'll only discuss equipment that is absolutely necessary. If you want to dive deeper into what is available in terms of technology, there are a lot of books on that.

Common kestrel | Germany | A bird photographer's toolkit needs to include a stable tripod and a suitable tripod head. But occasionally, someone might misuse this piece of equipment…. | 500mm, aperture 6.3, 1/250 s, ISO 1000, -2/3 exposure compensation

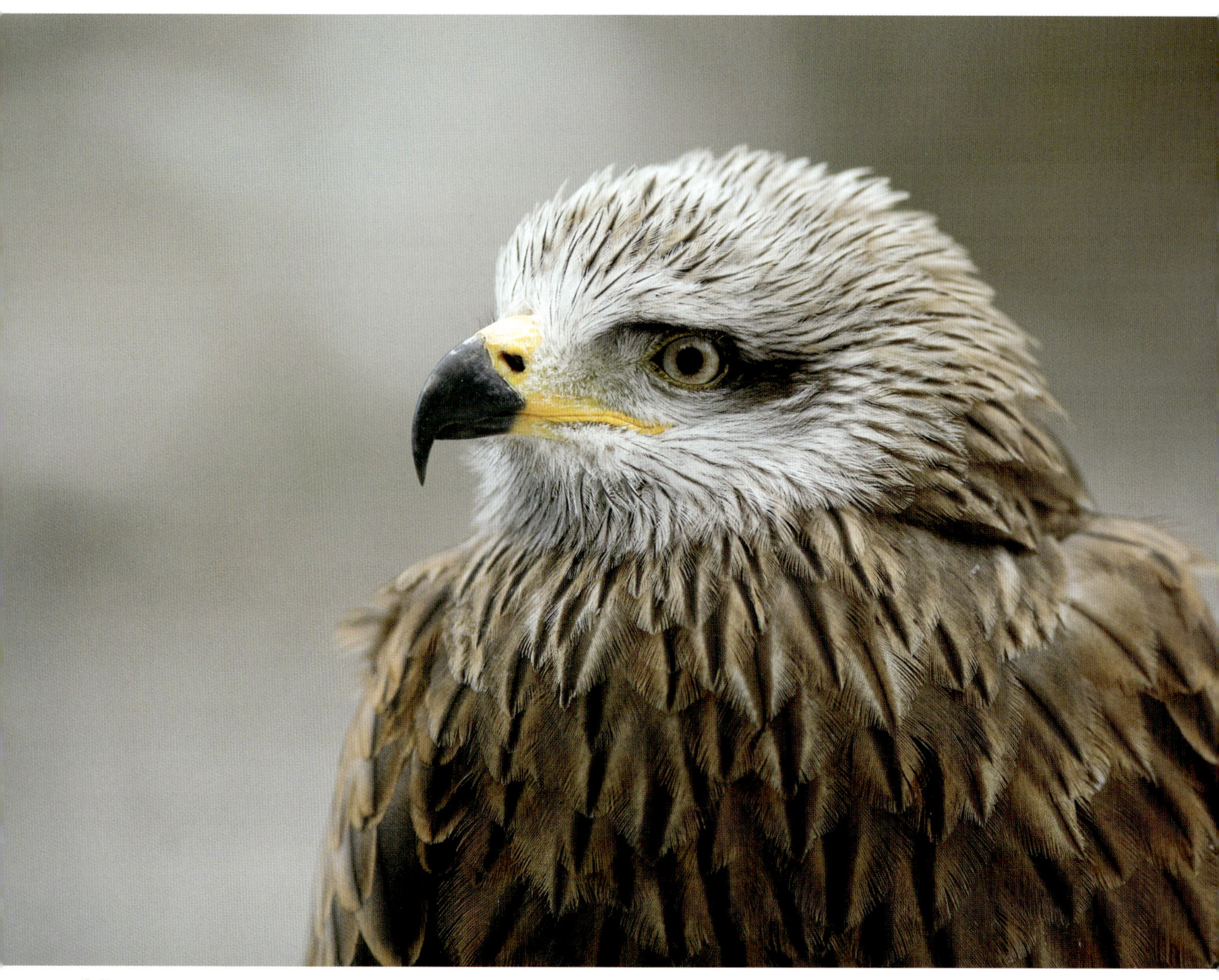

Black kite | Germany | In "aperture priority" mode, I select the aperture, here an open aperture of 2.8, to gently blur the background. | 300mm, aperture 2.8, 1/800 s, ISO 1000, +1/3 exposure compensation

2.1 The Camera

The camera needs to fulfill several requirements. Until not too long ago, SLR cameras were the only option, but mirrorless cameras are constantly getting better. So, you're faced with the decision: mirror or no mirror? Personally, I shoot with various SLR cameras but more and more photographers in my workshops rely on mirrorless systems, also because these cameras are a bit smaller and lighter than the larger versions with mirrors.

Regardless of what you decide: Your camera needs to be able to do various things. The most important ones are described below.

Shooting Modes

Cheap entry-level cameras often come with a lot of automatic settings and motif modes that you should mostly avoid when photographing birds. Yes, you could use the "portrait" mode to take a bird portrait or the "sports" mode to photograph a bird in flight. However, these automatic modes leave you little control over the final result. Therefore, I recommend photographing only in the semiautomatic modes "timer value" or "aperture value" or in "manual mode." These are three settings that you should be able to find in any model!

In "timer value" mode (S or TV), you select the shutter time and ISO value, and the camera calculates the appropriate aperture. On the other hand, in aperture value mode (A or AV), which I use almost exclusively, you set the aperture value and ISO, and the camera selects the shutter speed to achieve the correct exposure.

In "manual mode" (M), you set all three values yourself: the aperture, the shutter speed, and the ISO. Many photographers swear by this because it lets them control all the values themselves, leaving nothing to the camera's automatic system. Personally, I prefer the AV mode but that's a matter of habit. I like that with AV I don't have to pay as much attention to changes in the light as the camera responds to that automatically.

Photographers need to decide which file format they want for their photos. The options are RAW or JPEG files. RAW image files store raw data on the memory card without much processing. These files are often referred to as "digital negatives" because the data still needs to be "developed" and converted into other common formats before it can be printed or used online.

You can also save photos as JPEG files on the camera. In contrast to RAW image files, these have already been processed by the camera (you can usually set how) and are ready for use.

I always shoot using RAW image files, because it allows me to edit the images later without any loss of quality. I might adjust the white balance or exposure, for example. Then I'll convert the images that I need for a project into JPEG and leave the others as RAW image files on the hard disk.

A downside to RAW image files is that you'll need a photo editing software that can read and display them. If you are serious about bird photography, this is probably unavoidable.

2-2 ▶

Long-eared owl | Germany | If you take your photos in RAW, you can easily adjust some of the finer details, like the white balance, during photo editing. | 300mm, aperture 2.8, 1/250 s, ISO 1000

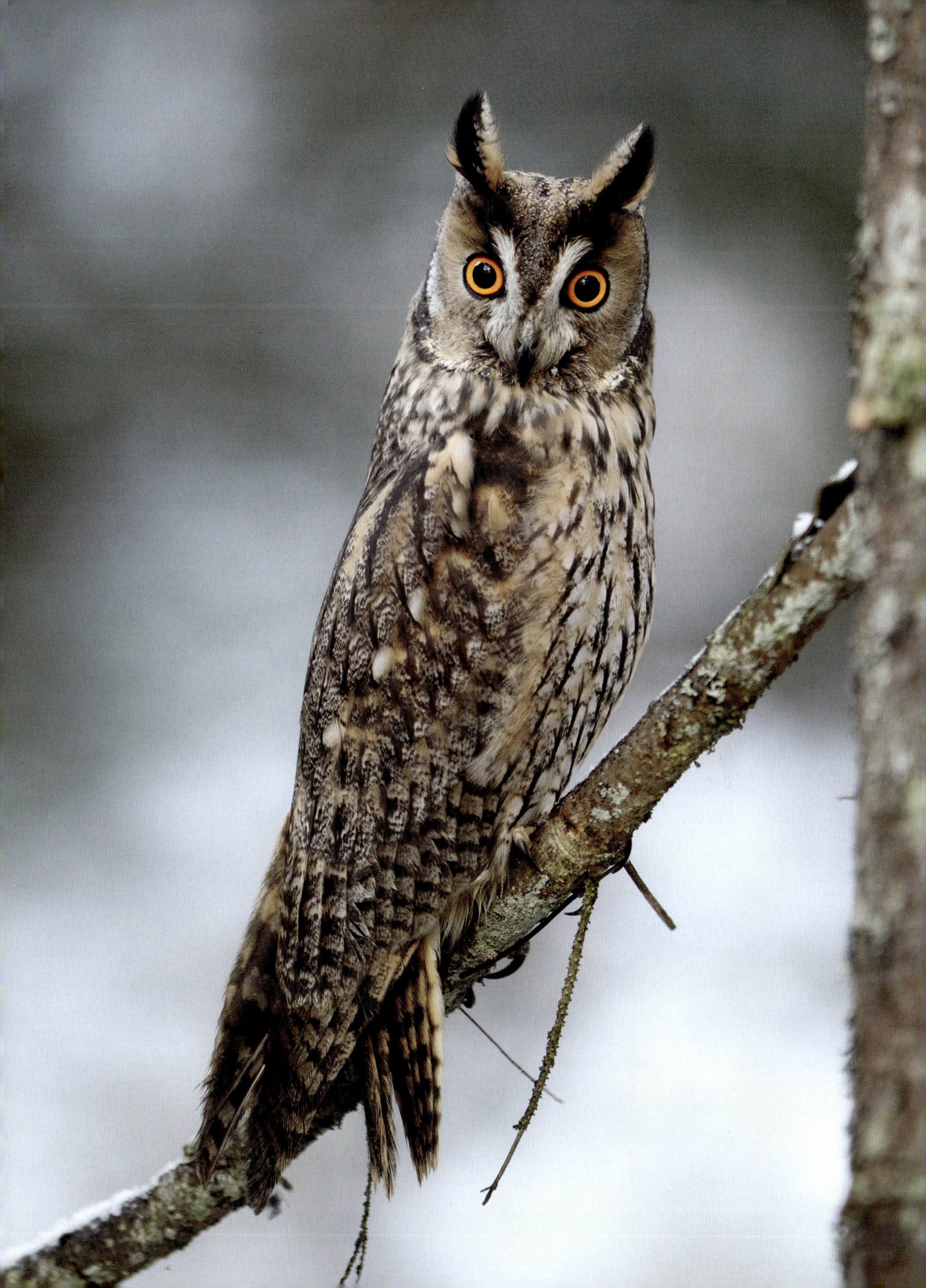

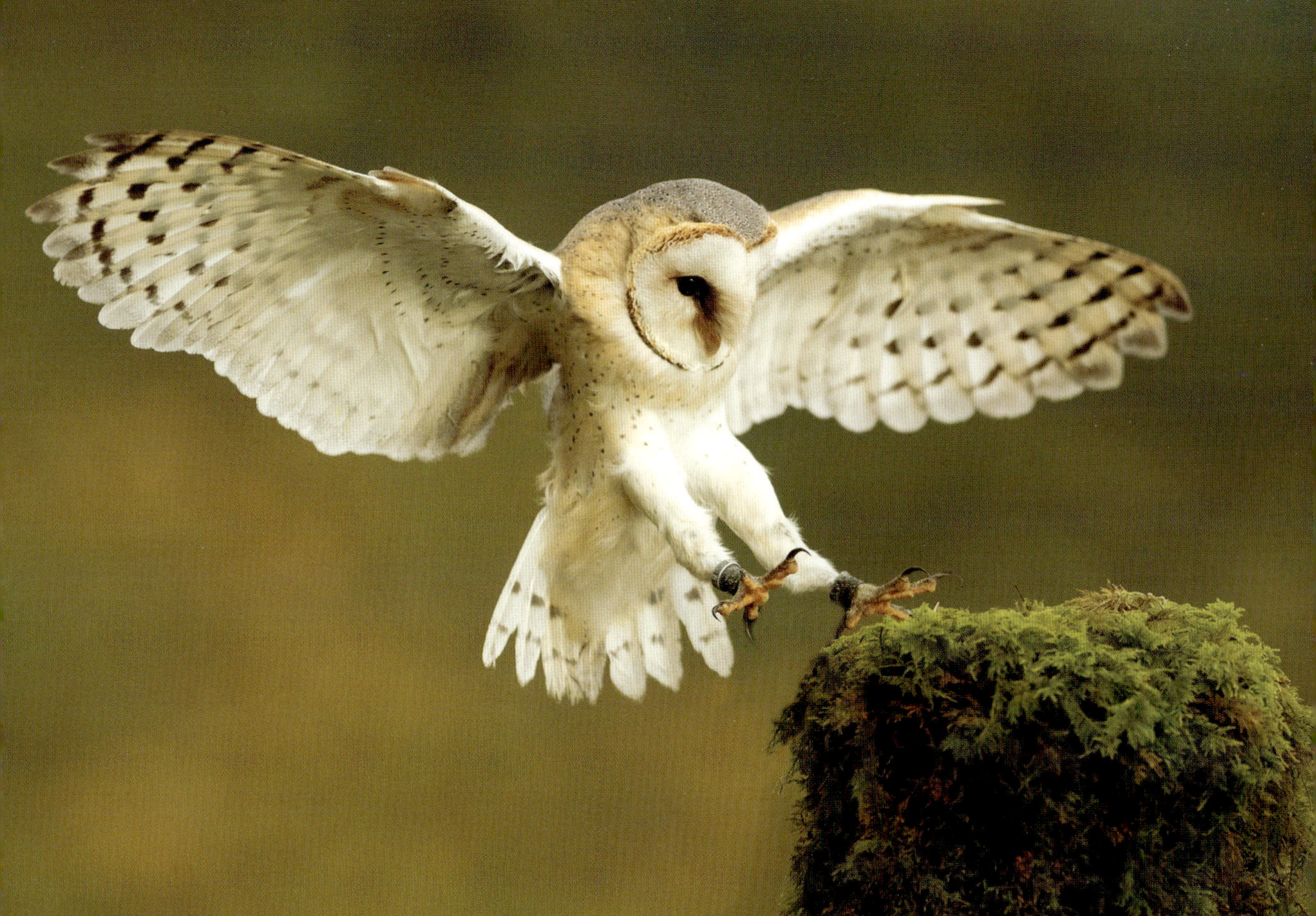

Continuous Shooting

The ability to take continuous shots—as fast as possible—is an important feature of your camera. My first digital camera managed a
maximum of three frames per second, but now I prefer cameras that
allow continuous shooting of 11 frames per second or more. That way,
when I'm taking action or flight shots, I'm able to select the ones with
the best wing position from a series, for example.

Autofocusing Points

When taking portraits, you should always put the focus on the eye.
That's why I think it's important that you can pick the point on which
the camera should focus. The more autofocusing points the camera

CHAPTER 2

offers, the better I can compose my image and the more precisely I can place focusing points. Cheap entry-level cameras may only have nine autofocusing points, which greatly limits composition and makes things difficult. With high-end cameras, on the other hand, you can choose between more than 60 autofocusing points. Mirrorless cameras usually have numerous autofocusing points distributed over the entire field of view.

Focus Tracking

One feature that every camera should offer is automatic focus tracking. It means the camera keeps the focus on a moving subject once the autofocus has locked on it. This mode is essential if you want to compose aerial shots or if a bird is moving on the ground. I always have this setting activated, even for simple portrait shots, because birds almost always move a bit. For example, if a bird turns its head slightly while I'm taking pictures, the autofocus will automatically track the movement and stay on the eye. All you need to do is activate continuous autofocus on your camera (AF-C). If your subject moves within the field of view as well, you may want to activate a metering control. It's often called "subject tracking." Your camera's manual is the best place to look for these terms.

▼ 2-4

Wren | Germany | As birds tend to move constantly, even if only a little, I always keep the setting on automatic focus tracking to make sure that the focus stays on the eye. | 700mm (500mm + 1.4x converter), aperture 6.3, 1/250 s, ISO 1000, -1/3 exposure compensation

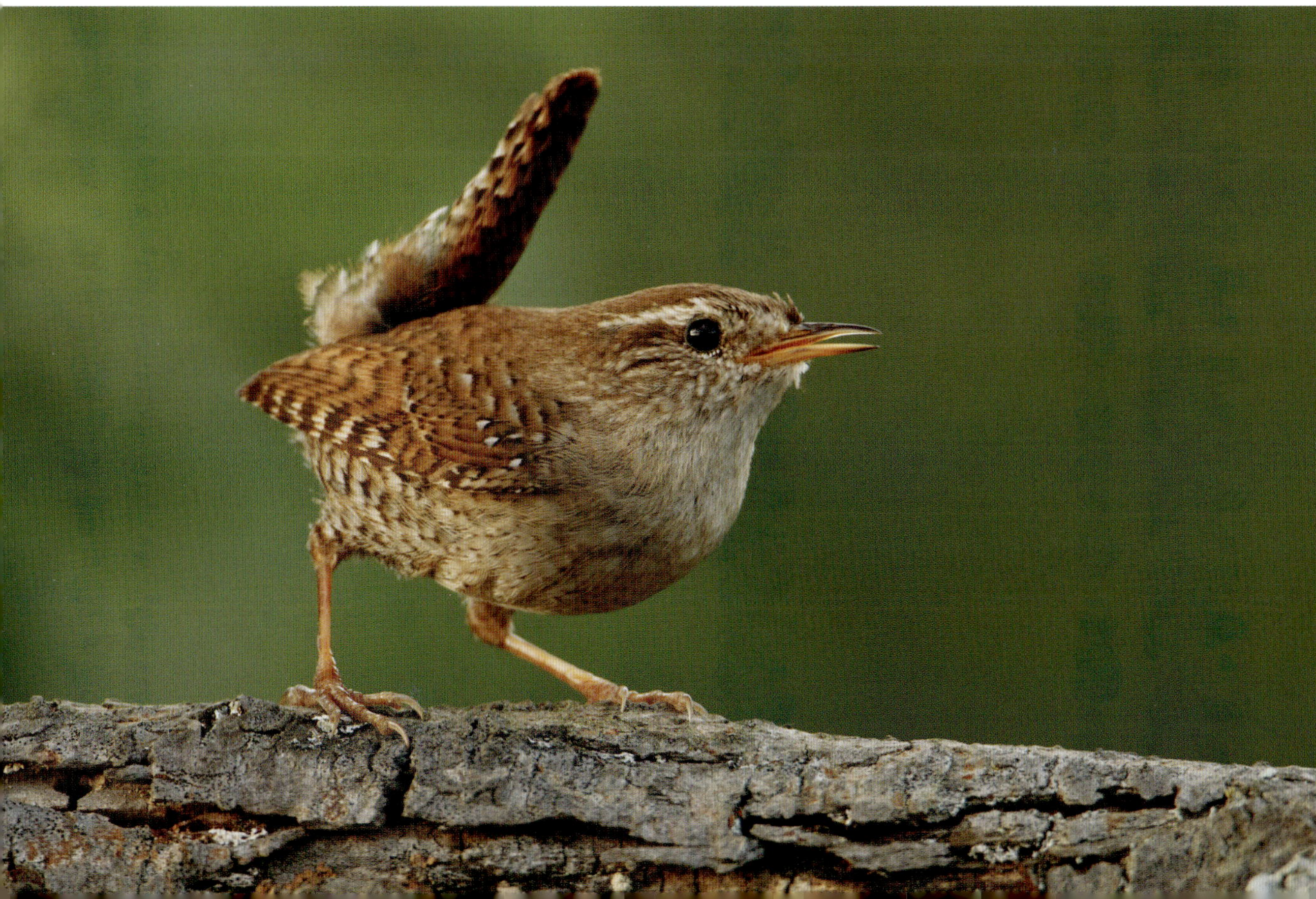

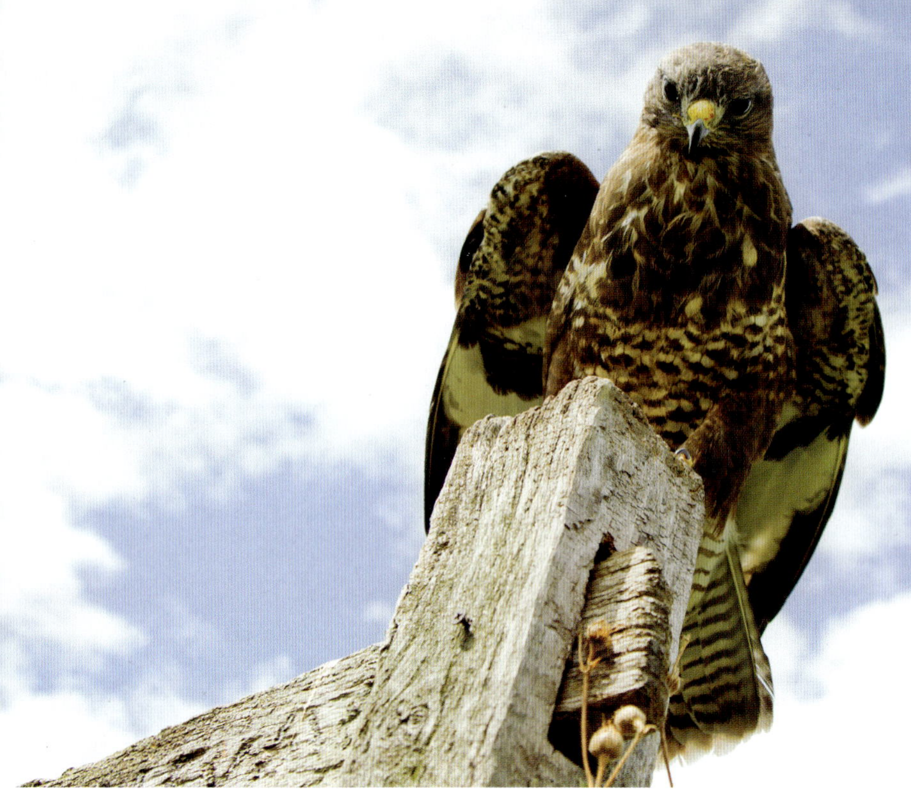

Common buzzard | Wales |
I photographed this tame
buzzard by laying on the ground
and pointing up with a wide-
angle lens. | 28mm, aperture
5.0, 1/1000 s, ISO 200,
+1 exposure compensation

2.2 The Lens

You can use most cameras to photograph birds but the same can't be said for lenses. In this section, I want to talk a bit about how I use my lenses. There's a fundamental difference between zoom lenses and fixed focal lengths. Often, fixed focal lengths take better pictures compared to zoom lenses. They are usually very fast and offer an outstanding autofocusing speed and imaging performance. Zoom lenses, on the other hand, give you more flexibility in how you frame the shot and let you react more quickly to a changing situation as there's often little time to change the lens on your camera in the heat of the moment.

The focal lengths below are for cameras with so-called full frame sensors (approximately 24×36mm), which is the equivalent to the old 35mm negatives or slides in analog photography.

Wide-Angle Lenses

A wide-angle lens is a lens with a focal length of less than 50mm. They are rarely used in bird photography, although I have photographed breeding colonies with them, like the northern gannets on Bass Rock in Scotland. They are also an exciting option for in-flight shots of many birds in one frame at once. And you can use a wide-angle lens if you want to include a lot of the bird's surroundings and can get relatively close. If the bird is far away, it will likely show up too small in a wide-angle lens picture.

Standard Lenses

A so-called standard lens covers a focal length of about 50mm. This focal length is roughly the same as the angle that the human eye can view and is commonly used in street photography, next to wide-angle lenses. If you buy a camera and it comes with a lens, it's usually one with a focal length in the 50mm range. For bird photography, these lenses are of rather limited use. Lenses that come bundled with cameras rarely do well in lower light and have a rather slow autofocus. Of course, some 50mm lenses are of high quality, but I have never found much use for them.

Telephoto Lenses

Most bird photography is done with telephoto lenses, meaning lenses with a focal length above 50mm. A telephoto lens can bring far-away subjects close. Some very good zoom lenses cover from 70mm to 200mm. I often use these in dog or horse photography. Occasionally, they are also handy when you are in a tree stand and the birds are relatively large and close. But as a rule, focal lengths in this range are still too short, although I have used such lenses when working with tame birds—in workshops, for example. My favorite lens when photographing my owls is a 135mm lens, f/2.0. The f/2.0 or 1:2.0 figure denotes the starting aperture or open aperture, in other words the shutter speed of the lens. The lower the number, the faster the lens and the better the back- and foreground can be intentionally blurred.

If you mostly take pictures in zoos, bird parks, and at your feeding station at home, it might be worth buying a zoom lens in the, say, 100mm-400mm range. You can often get affordable models that may not be particularly fast but are fast enough under normal light conditions. Alternatively, most manufacturers offer fast but very expensive versions of these lenses that can be used in many different settings. This focal length has the advantage that it's highly variable and excellent for photographing animals of different sizes, for example, on a safari.

In wildlife photography, you really can't ever have too much focal length and most bird photographers use lenses with focal lengths of up to 500mm or 600mm. These two fixed focal lengths are particularly popular if they also come with a high speed and great imaging performance. In photographs taken with an open aperture, these lenses usually separate the subject well from the background and produce exceptionally beautiful bokeh. We speak of "separating the subject"

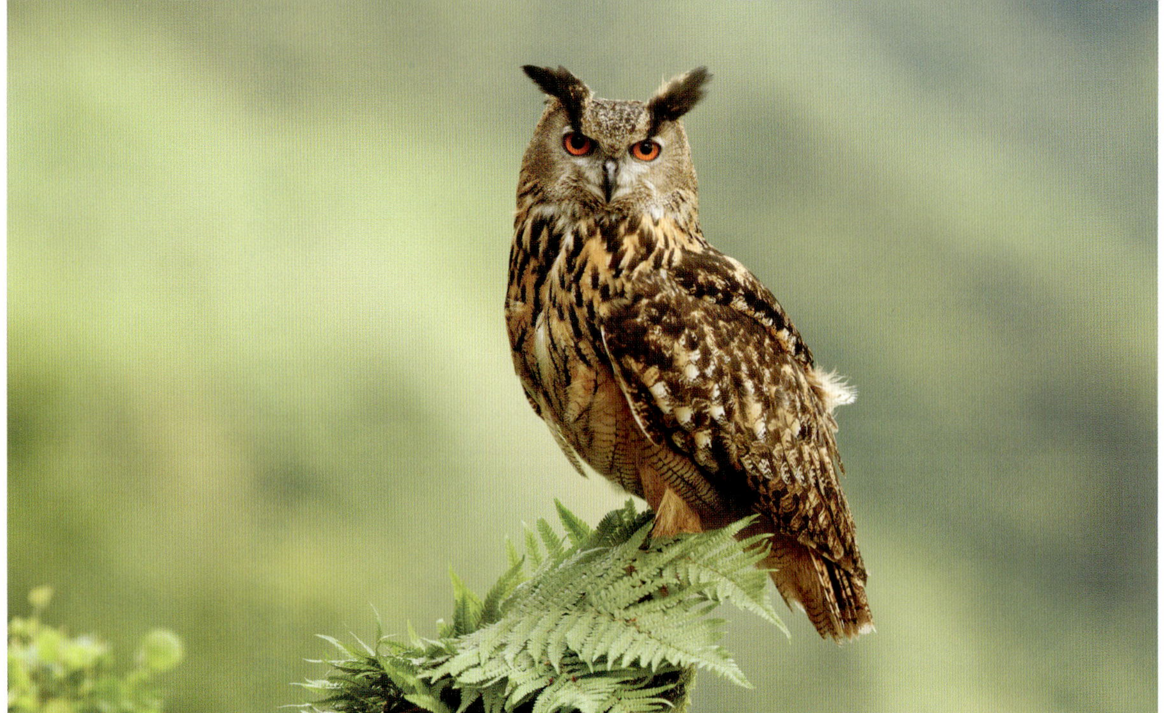

when the subject is shown in sharp focus against a background that is as blurry as possible. The blurrier the background, the clearer the subject stands out. Bokeh refers to the aesthetic quality of blurring (see section "Beautiful Bokeh" starting on page 56). A disadvantage of these lenses is their high price and that they are quite heavy. Generally speaking, you can't use them for freehand shooting, they need to be mounted on a tripod. I use four different prime telephoto lenses: 135mm f/2.0, 300mm f/2.8, 500mm f/4.0, and 600mm f/4.0.

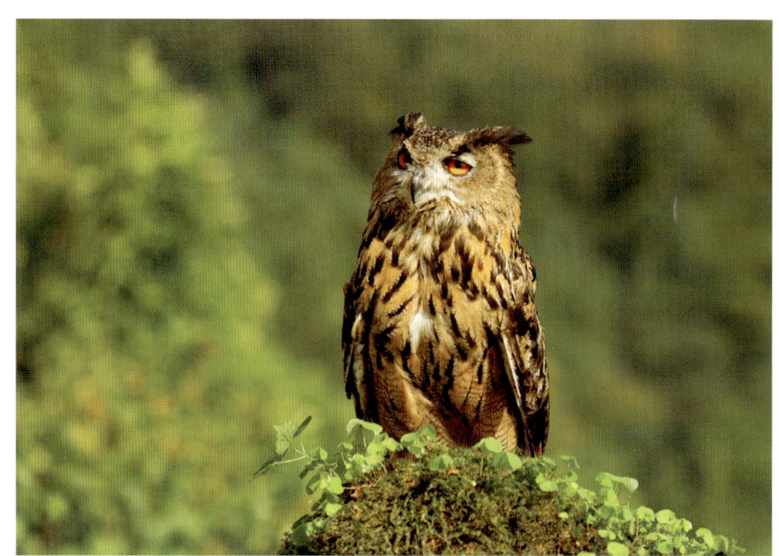

CHAPTER 2

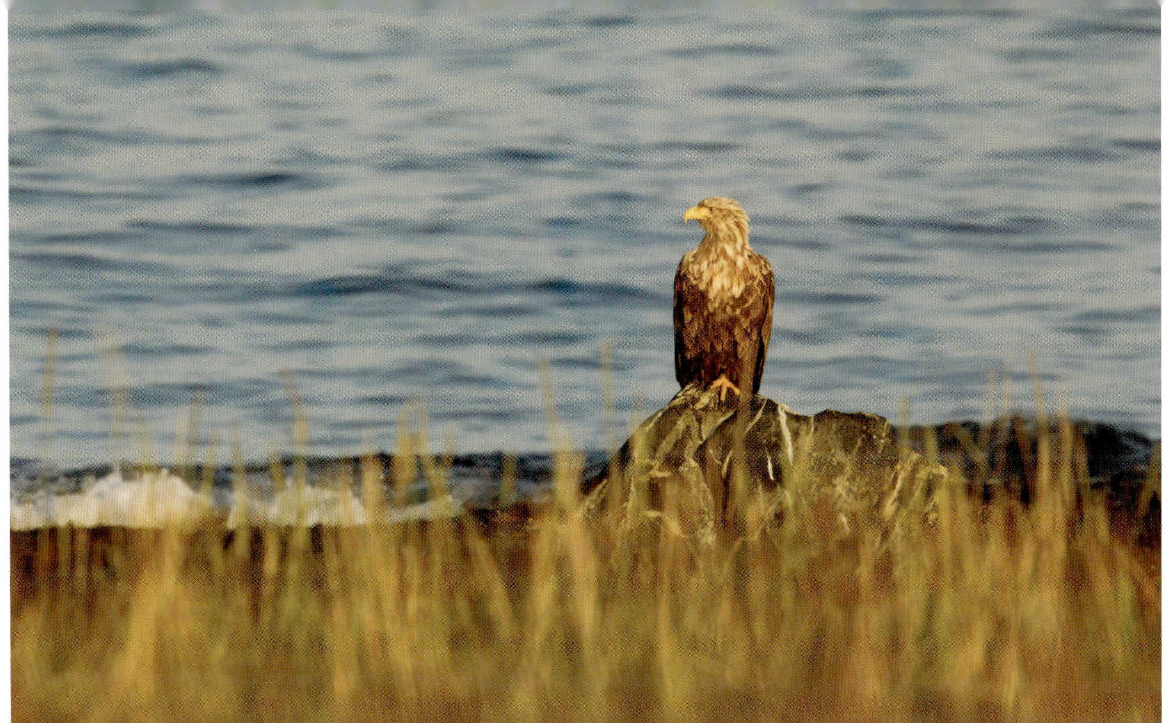

2.3 Converter

I always carry a 1.4x converter in my luggage. It's also sometimes referred to as an "extender." It's a small piece of equipment that can be mounted between the camera and lens to magnify a subject by 1.4. This lets you increase the focal length a bit more when the bird still shows up too small in the picture even with quite a large focal length. When using a 1.4x converter, you lose one f-stop of light, but it doesn't affect the quality all that much. Personally, I can't do without my converter, especially when traveling.

You can also get 2x converters that double the image size. I have tried these several times, but they don't work for me. I find that too much quality gets lost and the pictures lack sharpness. But I admit that I have seen other photographers achieve good results with them.

▲ 2-8

White-tailed eagle | Norway | One of the few pictures I have taken with a 2x converter. The shy sea eagle was just very far away. | 1200mm (600mm + 2x converter), aperture 14, 1/400 s, ISO 1600

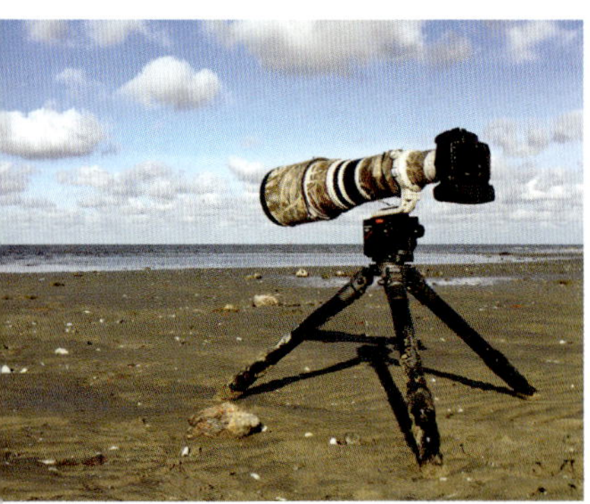

2-9 ▲

My set-up at Texel, The Netherlands | Tripod and tripod head must be able to handle heavy equipment and be robust enough for outdoor use. | iPhone 4, 28mm, aperture 2.4, 1/2100 s, ISO 50

2.4 The Tripod

If you use large telephoto lenses, you won't get around buying a sturdy tripod. It must be able to handle the weight of the camera and lens—a bit on the heavy side is better in a tripod than too lightweight and unstable. An important feature is that the tripod legs can be extended far enough to the sides to allow you to get down to the ground level with the camera and lens. Some tripods have a center pole that prevents this. I find these models less useful. It should be easy to extend or shorten the legs and the maximum height of the tripod must match the height of the photographer.

2.5 The Tripod Head

Picking the right tripod head is essential in bird photography. You must be able to pan and tilt the camera smoothly and feel sure that the heavy equipment stays stable at any given time. Personally, I don't think a ball head is good enough for this. I use various tripod heads, including a stable video head and two different gimbal tripod heads. All three let me balance the camera while keeping it stable at any tilt angle and I can move it effortlessly to change the framing without having to loosen or tighten screws.

Unfortunately, it'll be another chunk of money before you have gotten yourself a decent tripod with the right kind of tripod head. Skimp here and you'll find little enjoyment with bird photography.

2-10 ▶

Three of the different tripods and tripod heads I use for my work. | 85mm, aperture 2.5, 1/2000 s, ISO 800

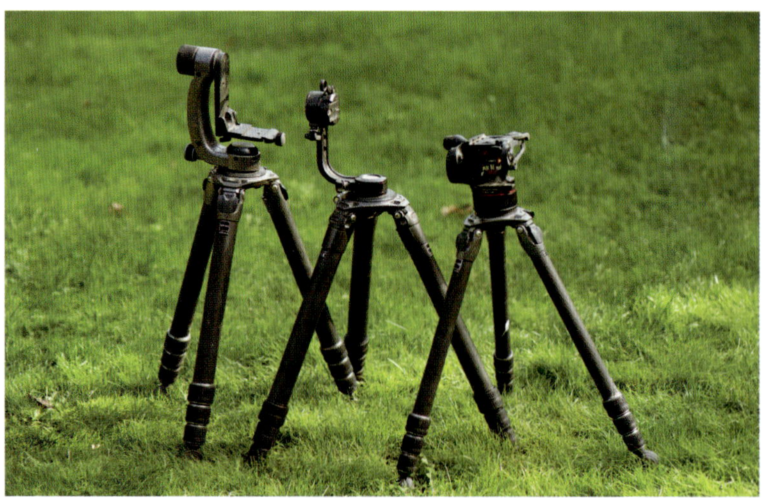

CHAPTER 2

2.6 Other Equipment

Bean Bag

When using my car as camouflage, I balance the camera on a "bean bag" on the rolled-down window. You can buy these beans bags at mail-order stores for nature photography supplies. I also use them when I'm on foot to rest the camera on rocks, for example, or even just on the ground.

Memory Cards

The fastest camera is no good if your memory card is slow. When buying memory cards, make sure they have a fast write speed so that you can use your camera's continuous shooting function to the fullest!

The Right Clothing

As a nature and bird photographer, you can't be too fussy about what you wear. Often, you'll need to sit on the ground or even lie flat on your belly. I find it highly inconvenient to always carry around a sleeping pad or such for this purpose. Instead, I wear sturdy clothing that is easy to wash. For nature photography, you should pick muted colors that help camouflage you a bit. Of course, your clothing should also be temperature appropriate. In winter, you'll want to be warm. A hat and gloves, in particular, are essential to avoid losing too much body heat.

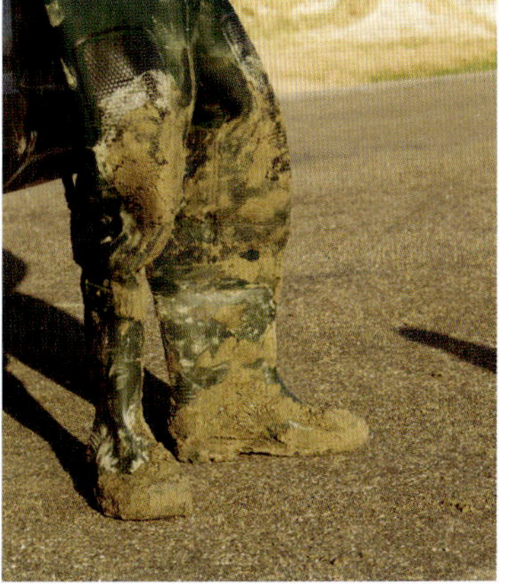

▲ 2-11

Fishing wader pants | I can't imagine doing beach shots without them: Waterproof waders that let you get down to the birds' eye level even in the thickest mud! | iPhone 4, 55mm, aperture 7.1, 1/1250 s, ISO 500

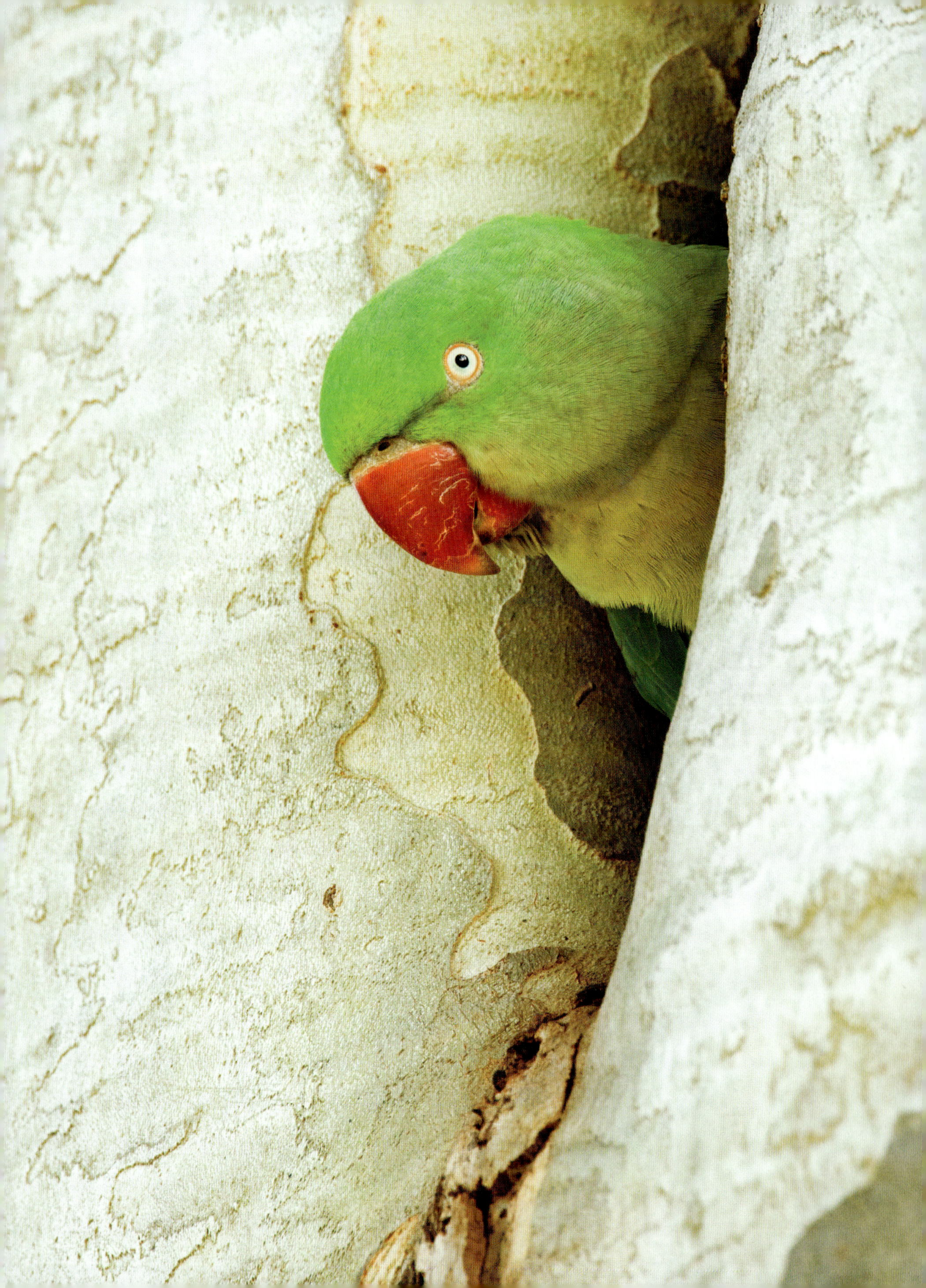

3 FINDING BIRDS TO PHOTOGRAPH

There are many opportunities to photograph birds: You can focus on taking pictures of wildlife or photographing birds wherever you find them. You can take photos at your own feeding site, visit zoos and bird parks, or put your skills to the test at falconry displays.

Alexandrine parakeet | Germany | If you know where to find certain birds and have a bit of patience, you'll find success in taking interesting pictures! | 700mm (500mm + 1.4x converter), aperture 8.0, 1/4000 s, ISO 800, +1/3 exposure compensation

3.1 Wildlife

Photographing birds in their natural habitat is the most difficult option. Most birds are quite shy and it takes a lot of patience to get attractive pictures. And the better you get, the higher your standards will be! Initially, you might already be happy if a bird is just sharp. But after some years, you'll only be satisfied if the foreground, background, and composition work, too. You'll find many tips in this book on how to analyze your wildlife photos, which will help you improve them.

So how do you go about finding find wild birds? Start by going to the right kind of place. If you live in a city, this may be a park where you'll often find a surprising number of wild birds that are relatively tolerant of humans. Walk through the park with your eyes open and listen for bird calls. It's helpful if you have some practice in recognizing the calls of certain species so that you can go and look for them. If you hear a woodpecker, search the trunks of trees and you might spot it. Should you hear the pretty melody of a robin, on the other hand, it's worth checking the treetops around you as that's where it might perch.

Parks that have a small lake or pond are often particularly rewarding. Its water birds are accustomed to people, which means that you can get quite close to them.

3-1 ▶

Approaching bar-tailed godwits | Texel, The Netherlands | Of course, photographing animals in the wild is a highlight in bird photography! | 300mm, aperture 7.1, 1/5000 s, ISO 1000

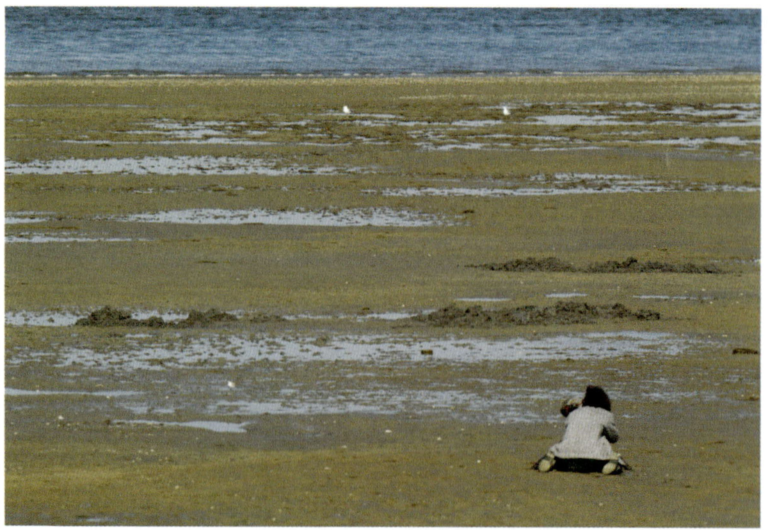

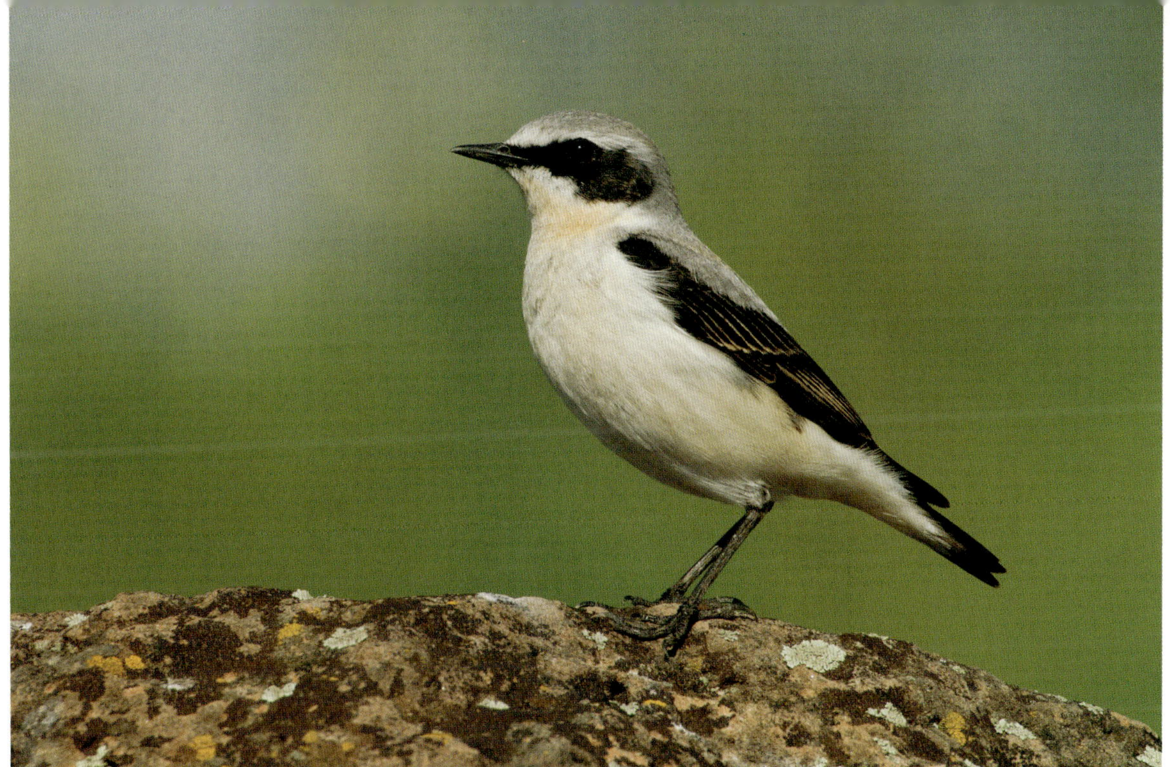

If that's not enough wildlife for you, head to the countryside. Unfortunately, the birds there often flee while you're still quite a distance away and you may need to use some sort of camouflage. These days, cars make for excellent camouflage. If you spot a bird at its singing perch, park nearby (make sure it's allowed) and wait. If you have enough patience, it'll most likely come back and get used to your car. But avoid quick movements or loud noises anyway so you don't scare it off. Many of my pictures have been taken from the car. I put a small bean bag on the rolled-down window, rest my lens and camera on it, and wait to see what happens. With a shy bird, it can be worthwhile to cover the passenger side window with a piece of fabric to hide your silhouette. Once you've found a convenient spot for your car, for example on a public road through a wild orchard, you might get to see quite a few birds that call that orchard home. Often, you start out watching one particular bird and unexpectedly get beautiful shots of a completely different species in the process. But it's important to have patience and not give up too soon or keep changing locations.

Northern wheatear | Germany | This pretty wheatear was photographed from the car. These days, cars make for excellent camouflage. | 500mm, aperture 6.3, 1/1250 s, ISO 500, -1 exposure compensation

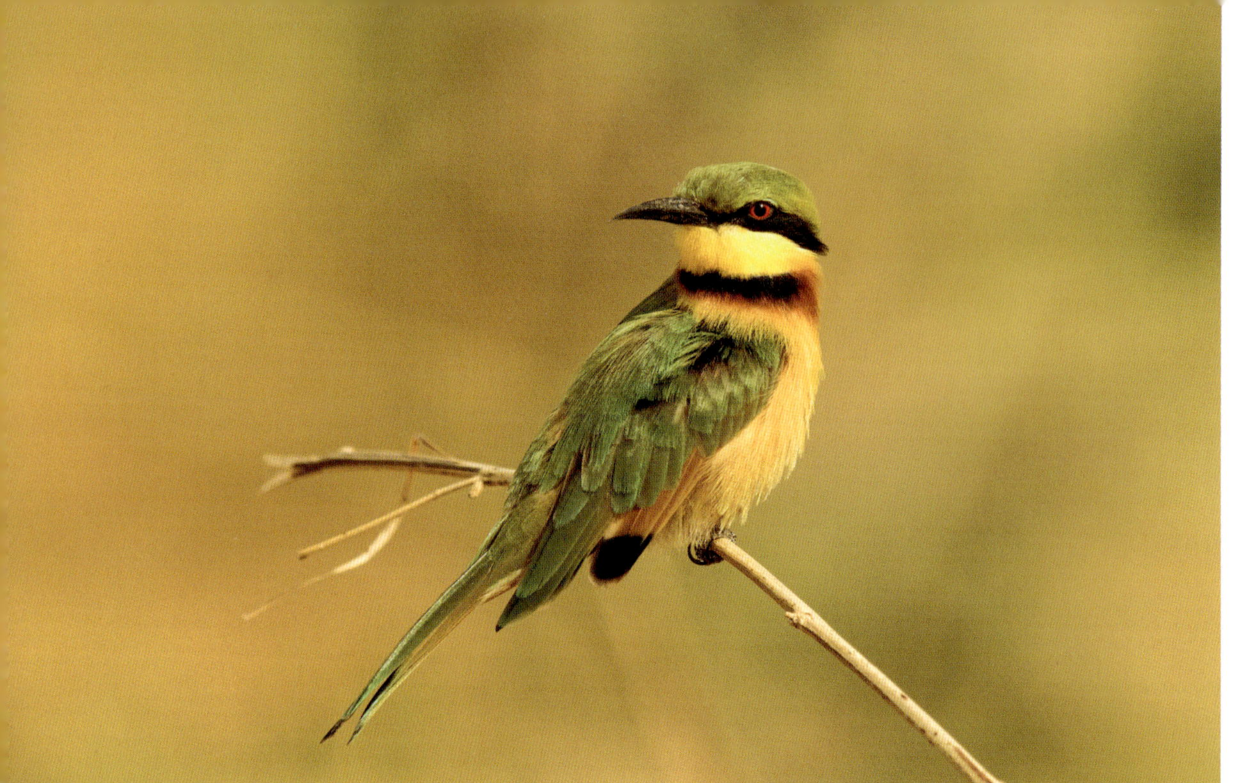

If you prefer to roam through nature on foot, protected areas are easy to find and are a good option. Unfortunately, it's often hard to get close enough to the birds for a good shot. In most wildlife refuges, you'll need a telephoto lens with a long focal length. Of course, that means that you have to carry around quite a bit of weight, especially if you're photographing with a tripod.

Useful Tools

There are various bird guides and identification apps that are almost indispensable. Not only do they describe the bird's appearance but they also give information about its distribution and habitat. On top of that, apps usually include the audio of bird calls, which you can compare to what you hear in nature. The *Collins Bird Guide: The Most Complete Guide to the Birds of Britain and Europe* is particularly commendable (as the book or app).

3.2 Photographing in Zoos

Most zoos are home to many different species and will offer excellent opportunities to photograph birds in a controlled setting. Getting close enough to the birds without having them fly off won't be a problem since they are used to people and cameras. Photographing in zoos also has the great advantage that you can take your time with each bird. You can freely move around to different backgrounds and, should a bird sit in a slightly awkward spot, you can easily wait until it has moved to a better one. I recommend focusing on a few animals and taking your time until you've captured some really good photos. If you just rush through the zoo trying to photograph as many animals as possible, you'll achieve little more than snapshots. Many zoos have walk-through aviaries where you can take pictures without any distracting barriers. Find a spot with a nice background and wait until a bird moves there. Observe how the birds behave. Many are faithful to their routines and keep frequenting the same locations. Find a spot nearby and move around until you've found the optimal frame.

▼ 3-4

Smew | Cologne Zoo, Germany | You can find beautiful subjects in the zoo, too! |700mm (500mm + 1.4x converter), aperture 7.1, 1/3200 s, ISO 1250, -1 1/3 exposure compensation

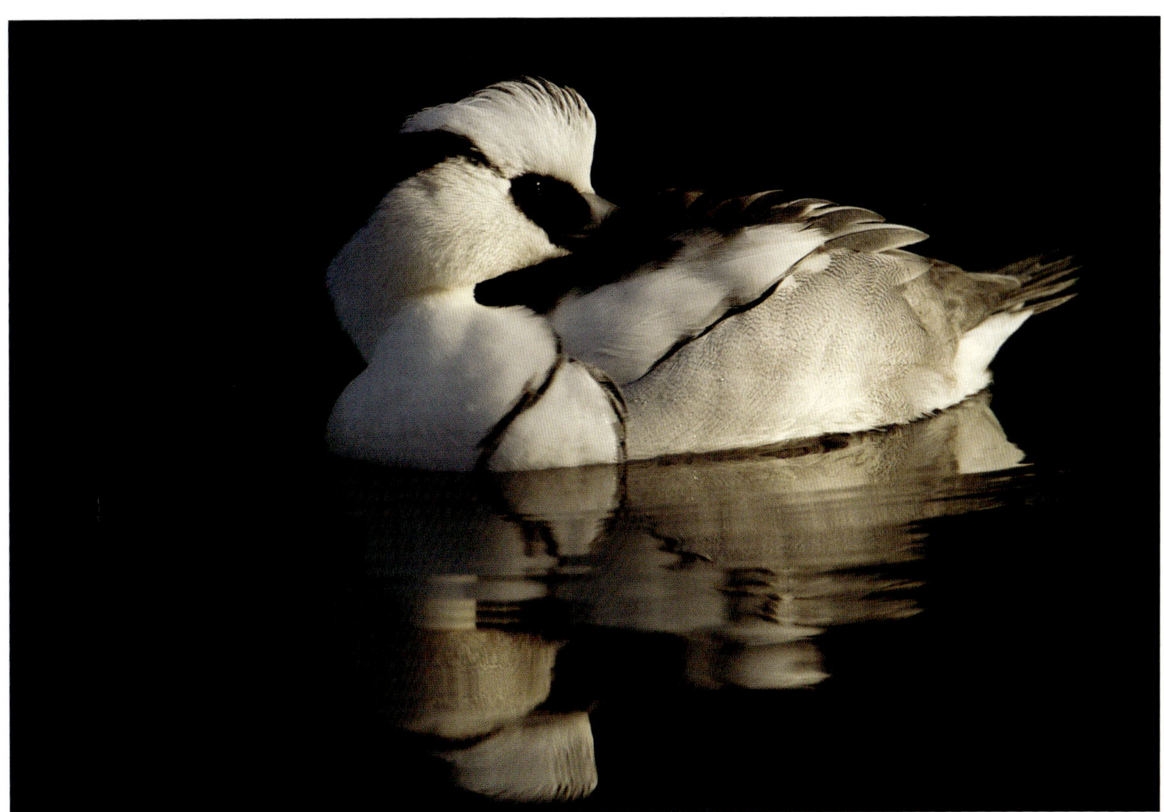

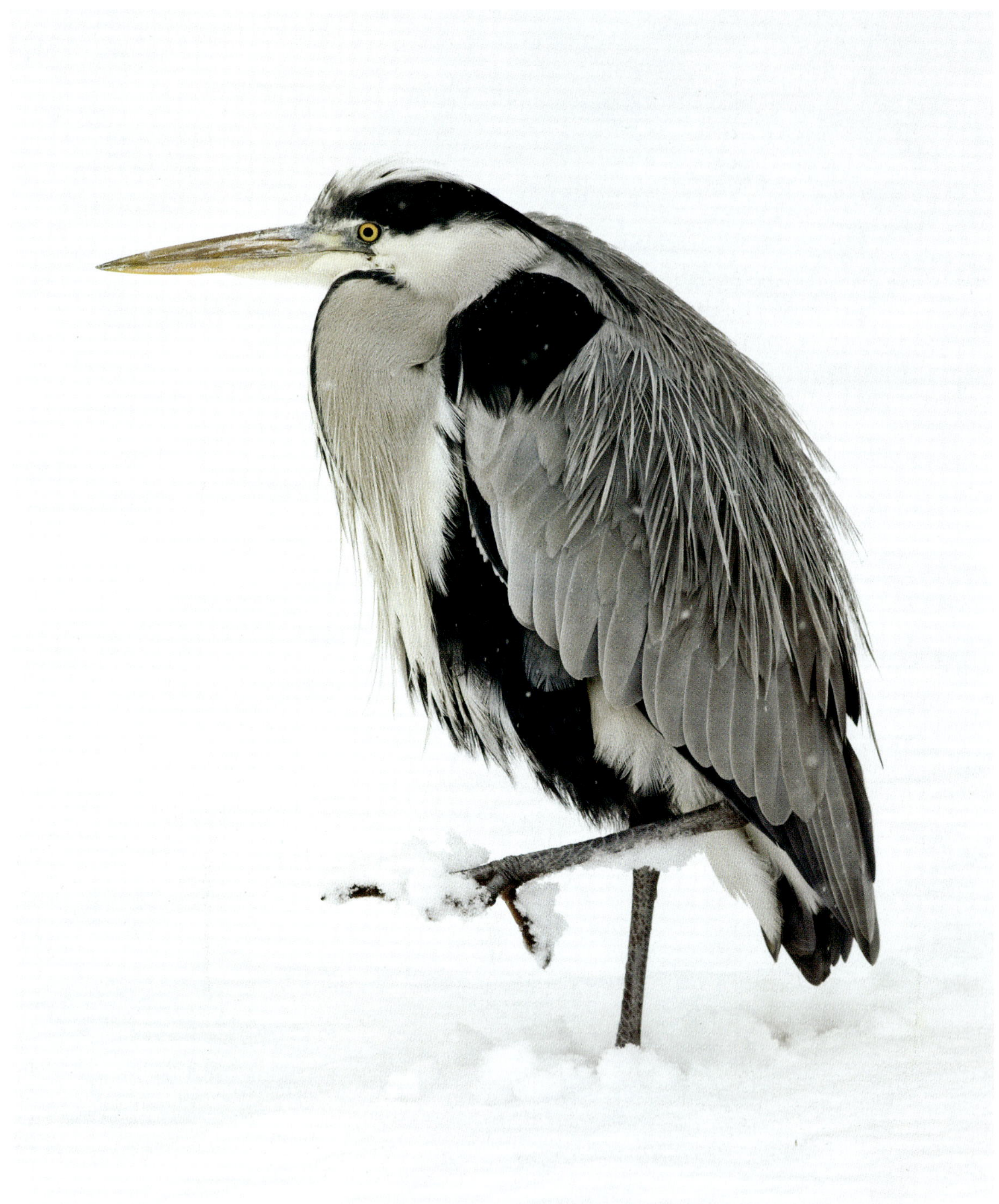

Gray heron | Karlsruhe Zoo, Germany | Very often you'll find wild birds at the zoo as well. They are used to people and can be photographed at one's leisure. That's how I took this picture of a gray heron in the snow with a 300mm lens. | 300mm, aperture 7.1, 1/400 s, ISO 640, +1 exposure compensation

Zoos are also great for really focused detail shots, such as close-ups of an eye or the plumage. You can get close enough to the animal to experiment with motifs of this kind.

Keep an eye out for wild birds at the zoo. There may be a few gray herons hanging around the penguin enclosure, for example. Or you may come across some crows near the food court. These birds tend to be markedly less shy than their counterparts in the wild, and you can get much closer to them.

If you want to photograph into an enclosure, here are a few tricks: Take off the hood of your lens—which should normally always stay on!—and carefully place the lens right against the wire of the fence. It will show up in the viewfinder as a bright, very blurry stripe. Move the camera around until you see as little of the wire as possible. Depending on the mesh size, you might not even see the fence at all later in the photos. Another good trick is to shoot with a wide-open aperture. This will make any mesh disappear almost entirely. And, if you're photographing through a pane of glass, it's best to put the lens (hood attached in this case) right against the glass to avoid reflections.

Yet another advantage of doing a day-long photo shoot at the zoo is that you can avoid the harsh midday light by spending that time in the comfort of the food court, enjoying a snack….

If you plan to publish any photos you've taken at a zoo or park, please note that some have rules about that, so make sure to contact the zoo management or press office beforehand!

▼ 3-6

Guira cuckoo | Heidelberg Zoo, Germany | I managed to snap this hilarious action shot of some cuckoos at the zoo. Unfortunately, these pretty birds are no longer housed there. | 500mm, aperture 8.0, 1/250 s, ISO 1250, -1/3 exposure compensation

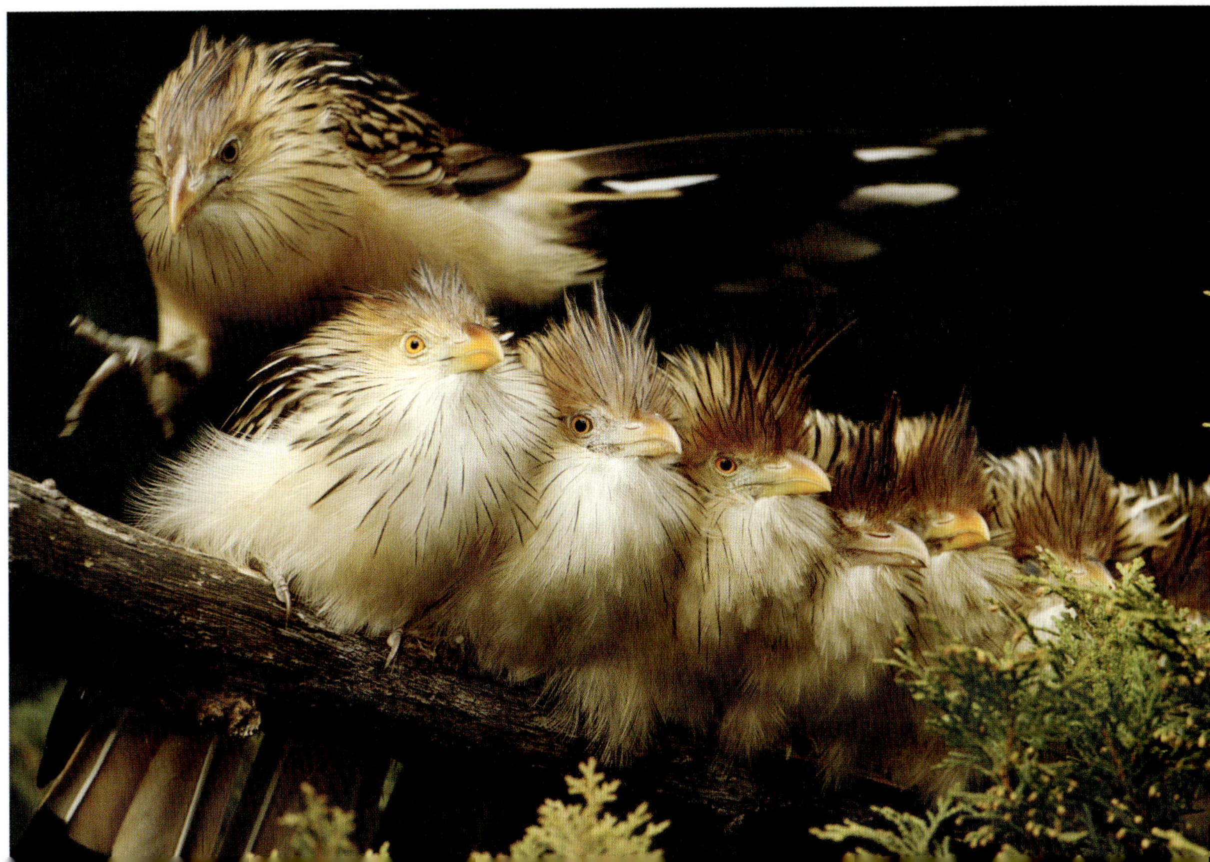

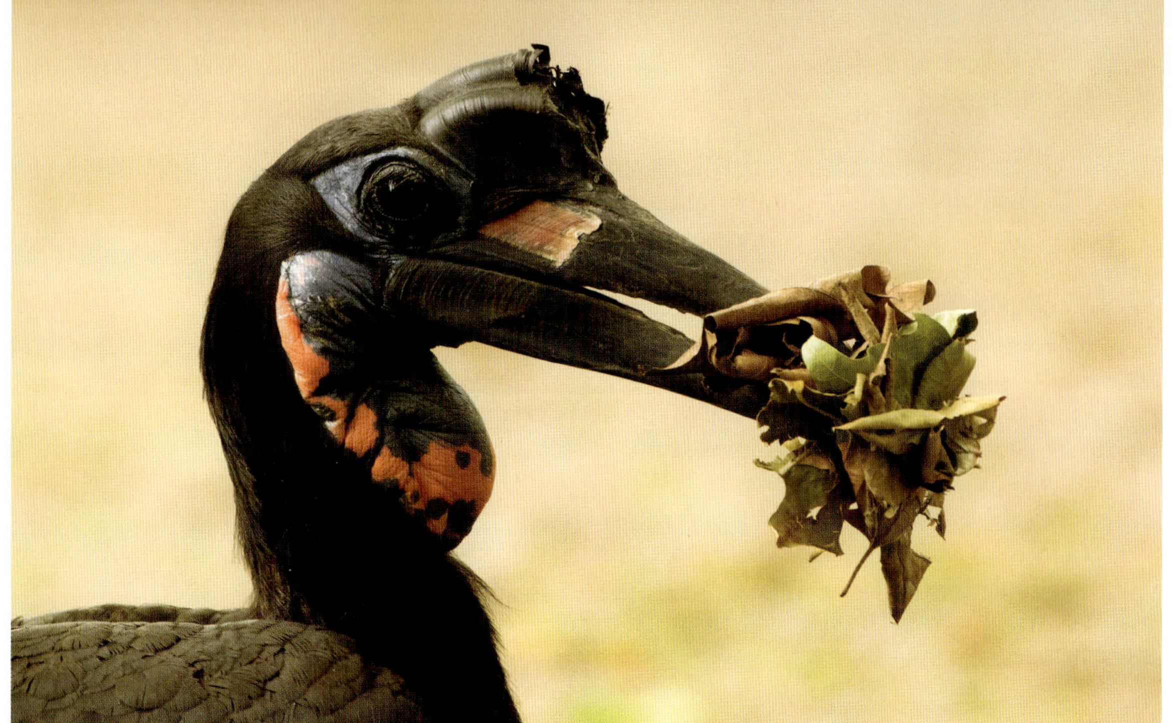

Ground hornbill | Hagenbeck Zoo, Germany | In bird parks, you often get to photograph interesting behavior up-close. This ground hornbill was gathering nesting material. | 400mm, aperture 5.6, 1/400 s, ISO 1600

3.3 Visiting a Bird Park

If you want to take photographs in a bird park, follow the same guidelines that apply to a zoo. If the park is large, you can ask at the ticket office about walk-in aviaries and head there right away to catch the best morning light. Or, you can focus on your favorite birds. Again, don't try to photograph all the birds in the park; instead, take your time at your individual stops until there are some really great pictures stored on your memory card.

Ruffed duck | Hagenbeck Zoo, Germany | Bird parks also give you the chance to portray rare bird species from a close distance. | 840mm (600mm + 1.4x converter), aperture 5.6, 1/500 s, ISO 800, -2/3 exposure compensation

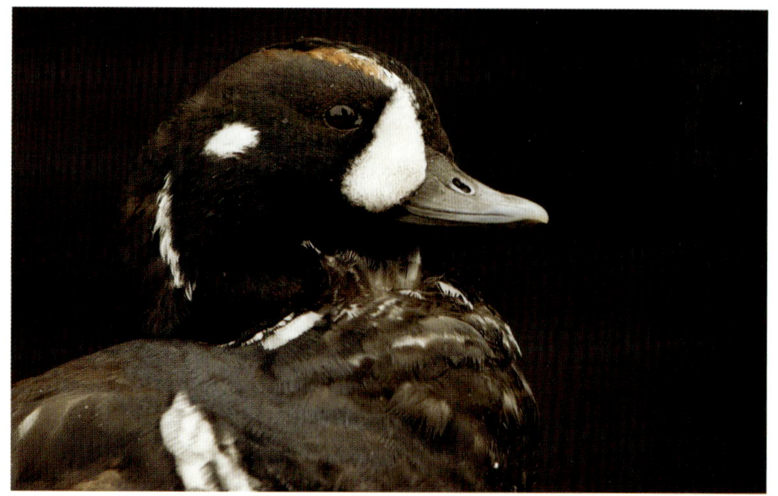

CHAPTER 3

Be sure to visit the waterfowl pond. Usually, there will be something happening there and you can play around with your camera settings. The birds are swimming and bathing, and there might be scuffles or interesting courtship and mating behavior. You might also find some young birds that will be great to photograph.

If an aviary turns out to be a bad choice for taking pictures, for example, because of an unattractive background or too many distracting elements, I tend to move on and look for other motifs. Evaluate your subjects and their surroundings carefully and don't waste too much time before deciding whether it is worth taking pictures of them.

Ask whether the park offers scheduled feedings or flying displays. If so, show up early and try to find a spot that will give you the most uncluttered background possible. If a flying display is scheduled twice a day, it is worth attending both. You'll get to see what is happening when at the first show and might be able to find a better spot for the afternoon one.

3.4 A Day at the Falconry

If you have the chance, make sure to visit your local falconry. This is probably the only place where you can get this close to majestic eagles, speedy falcons, and mysterious owls. At least during the day, many birds will be outside and away from their enclosures with their intrusive bars, allowing you to get wonderful portraits of these elegant birds.

▼ 3-9

Bald eagle | German Raptor Research Center at Guttenberg Castle, Germany | The shadowy background contrasts starkly with the bald eagle's bright head plumage. | 300mm, aperture 2.8, 1/2500 s, ISO 320, -1 exposure compensation

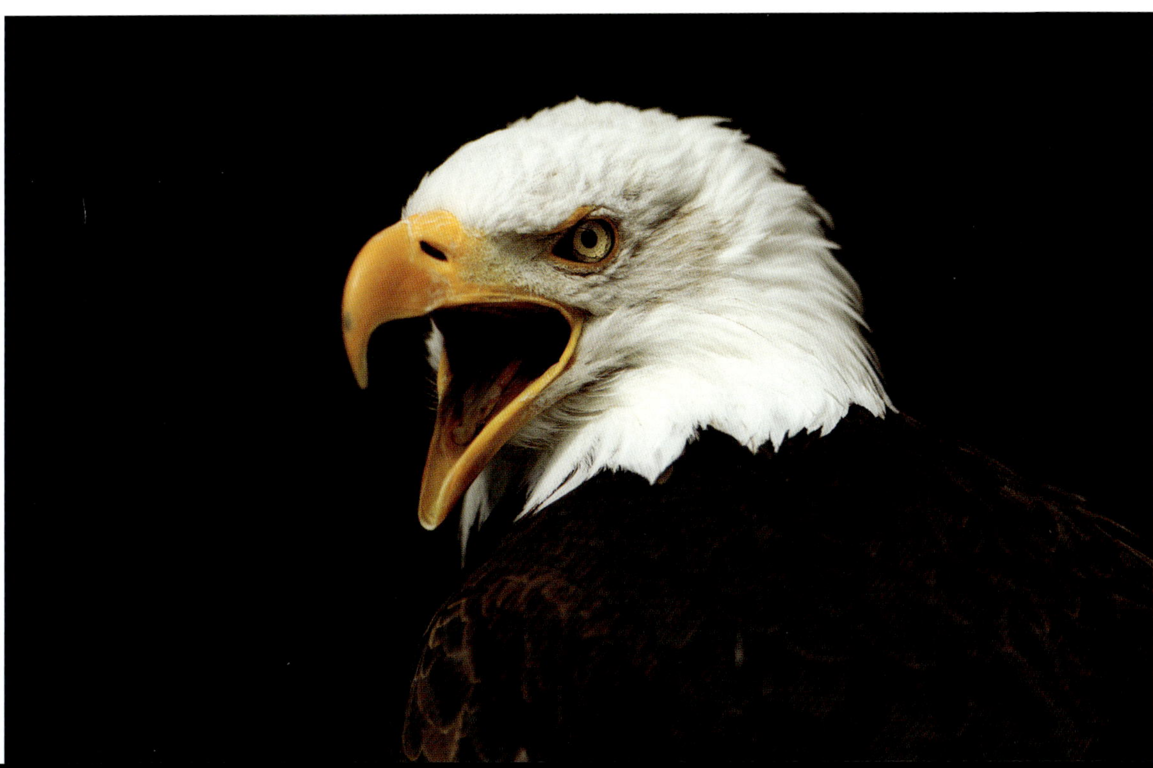

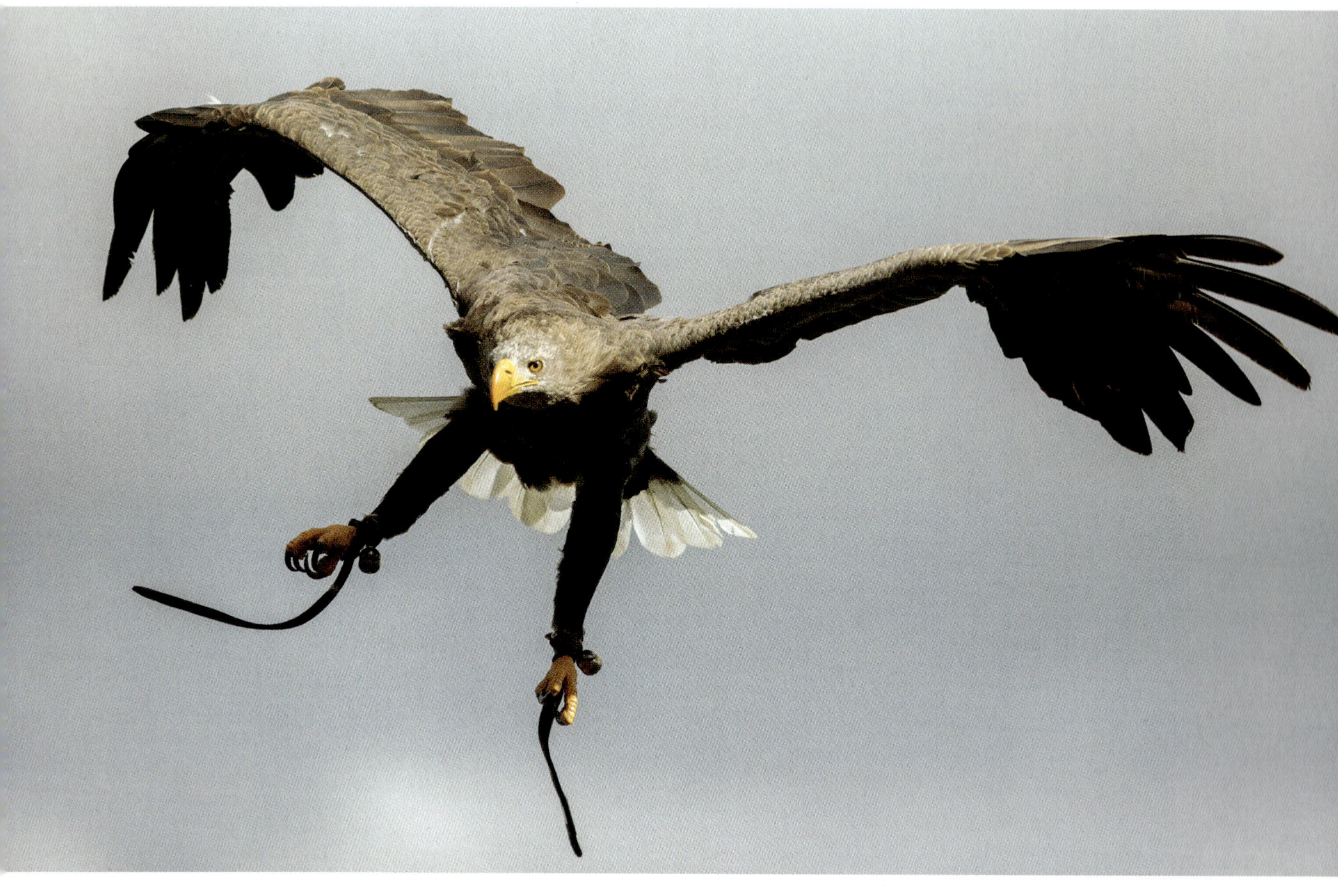

White-tailed eagle | German Raptor Research Center at Guttenberg Castle, Germany | Flying displays at a falconry offer wonderful opportunities to practice photographing birds in-flight so you'll be perfectly prepared for taking pictures of them in the wild! | 300mm, aperture 3.2, 1/8000 s, ISO 800

Visit the flying displays that are being offered and practice photographing these fast and agile birds in the air. Most of these shows will also teach you a lot about birds of prey, which will be a great help when you encounter them in the wild.

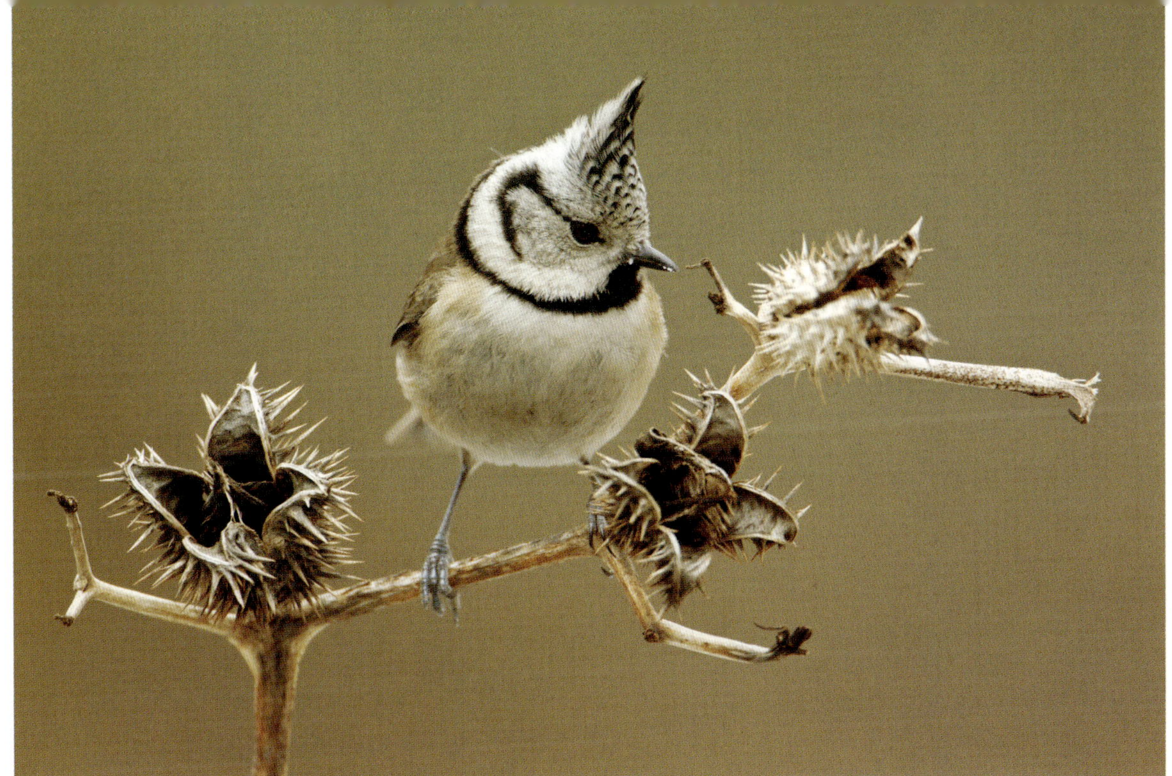

3.5 At the Feeding Station

If you have your own yard or even just a balcony, it is definitely worth-while to set up your own feeding station. It offers many great opportunities! You get to know the birds in your area, can observe them closely, and experiment with different perches that will result in very different photos. Even if no rare birds show up at your feed-ing station—it never gets boring to take pictures of common birds that do!

Offer various types of food for the different species and make sure there's always fresh water available at an easy distance. It's best to set up a small stand or camouflage tent close to the feeder. This will allow you to photograph the birds up-close without disturbing them. With some long-term planning, you might even be able to put in your favorite plants for the background.

▲ 3-11
Crested tit | Germany | You can always rearrange the perches at your feeding station, creating very different pictures. | 700mm (500mm + 1.4x converter), aperture 6.3, 1/500 s, ISO 1600

3.6 Workshops and Trips

You can find countless workshops and trips specifically for bird photography. But keep in mind that you'll need to book a real photography trip and not just a birdwatching trip. Most likely, a pure birdwatching trip will not get you close enough to the birds, and most birdwatchers don't spend as much time watching as you will need to photograph birds.

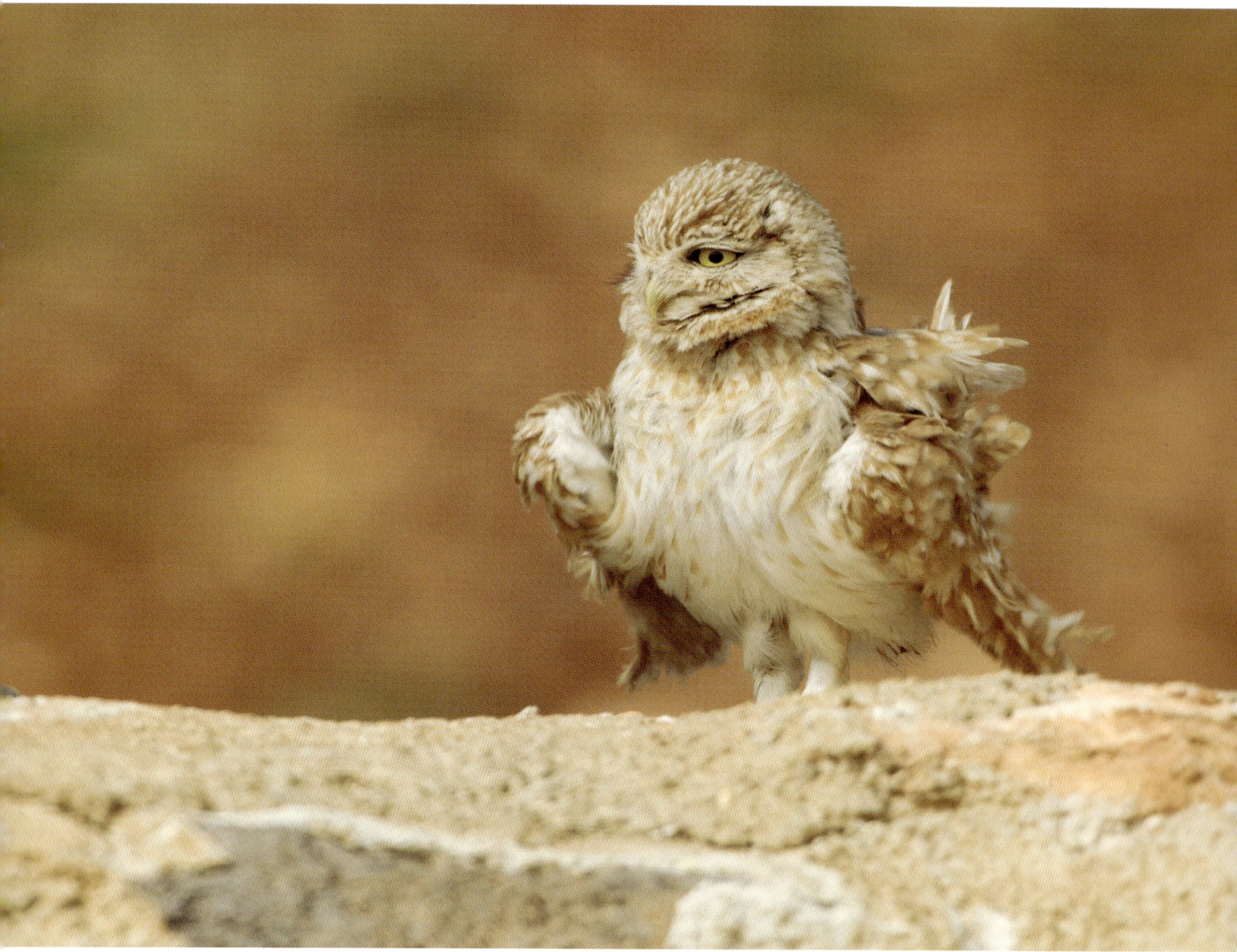

▲ 3-12

Little owl (Lilith) | Turkey | I was able to shoot the rare little owl (Lilith) in Turkey after I had convinced the guide and driver of my car to stop. | 500mm, aperture 6.3, 1/1600 s, ISO 1000

   CHAPTER 3

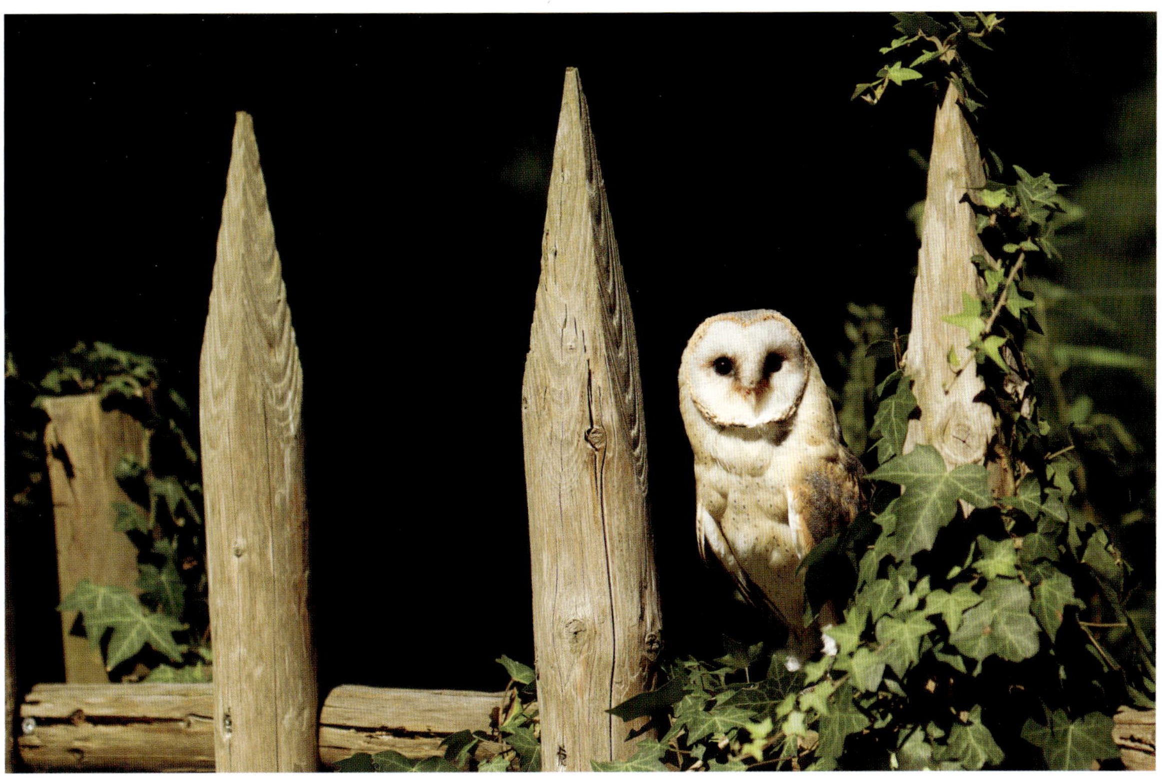

Barn owl | German Raptor Research Center at Guttenberg Castle, Germany | This picture was taken during one of my workshops on "Owl and Bird of Prey Photography." | 158mm, aperture 5.0, 1/4000 s, ISO 640, -1 1/3 exposure compensation

I have taken many trips abroad and, after some research, have always found an experienced local guide who could take me around for a few days to find particular bird species. But even then, the guide must understand and accommodate the needs of a photographer. I've had a guide drive me past countless little owls, saying, "We're going to see lots more of those!" I simply couldn't make him understand that I would like to grab every opportunity to photograph a little owl. It took some considerable effort to get him to pretty please stop at the next little owl, come what may….

It's best to check online for what's being offered. You'll find workshops with many different focuses.

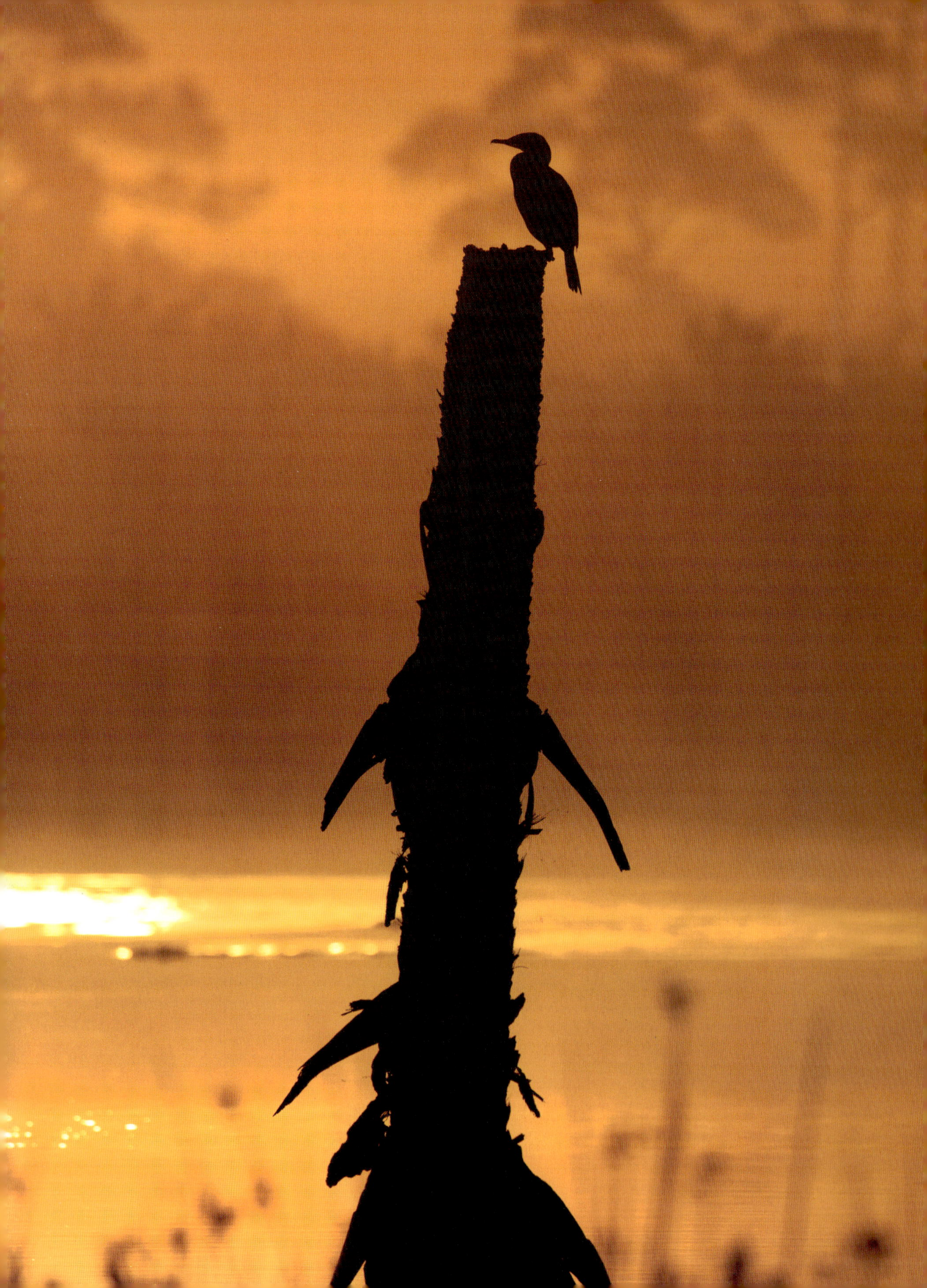

4 SHOOTING TECHNIQUES AND COMPOSITION TIPS

On the following pages, I want to share tips and explanations that will help you create eye-catching bird photos. The individual sections can be read in order or you can pick out the ones that are most relevant to you.

◄

Double-crested cormorant | Florida | Sunsets are always magical— and when I manage to include a bird in the picture as well, the results are often stunning. | 500mm, aperture 5.6, 1/6400 s, ISO 125, -2 exposure compensation

4.1 Image Composition, Framing, and Leading the Eye

Put Yourself at Eye Level

If you want to take effective wildlife photos, one of the most important rules is: "Put yourself at eye level with the animal." A majestic eagle photographed from above is simply not captivating, and neither does it do the animal justice. It also means that there's no eye contact between the bird and the viewer with the result that there's little intrigue in the photo.

We're used to birds soaring above us so the view from below is more acceptable and even the norm in bird-in-flight photos. But if a bird is on the ground or close to the ground, the photographer should also go low if possible. Even just five or six inches up or down can make a huge difference in the effect that a photo has! This is particularly important with waterfowl. Never photograph them from a standing position just because it's more convenient. Go to the bird's eye level. That's the only way to achieve an impactful image.

I have taken many pictures while lying flat on the ground and holding or resting the camera as low as possible. This is when a bean bag is very helpful. If you photograph in a lot of situations like this, for example on the beach, it may be worth investing in a special ground tripod.

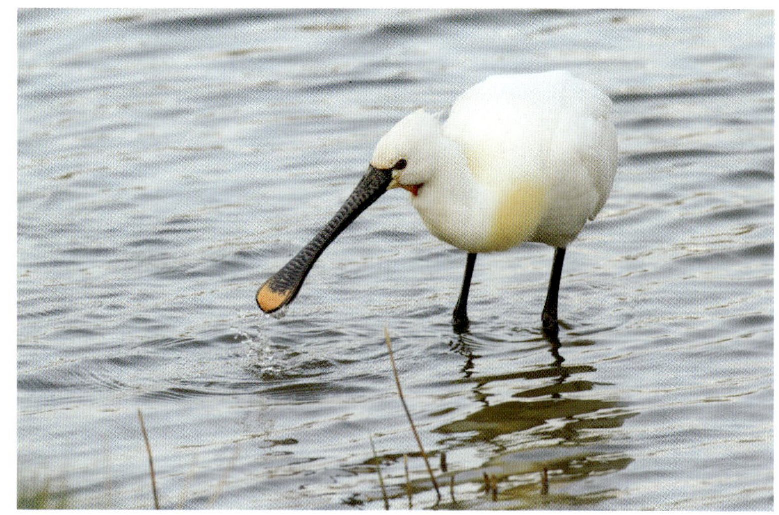

CHAPTER 4

Eurasian spoonbill | Serbia | Here I was able to photograph from a tree stand, which put me at eye level with the birds. Accordingly, the angle is much better and the viewer can really connect with the bird. | 300mm, aperture 3.2, 1/2000 s, ISO 1000

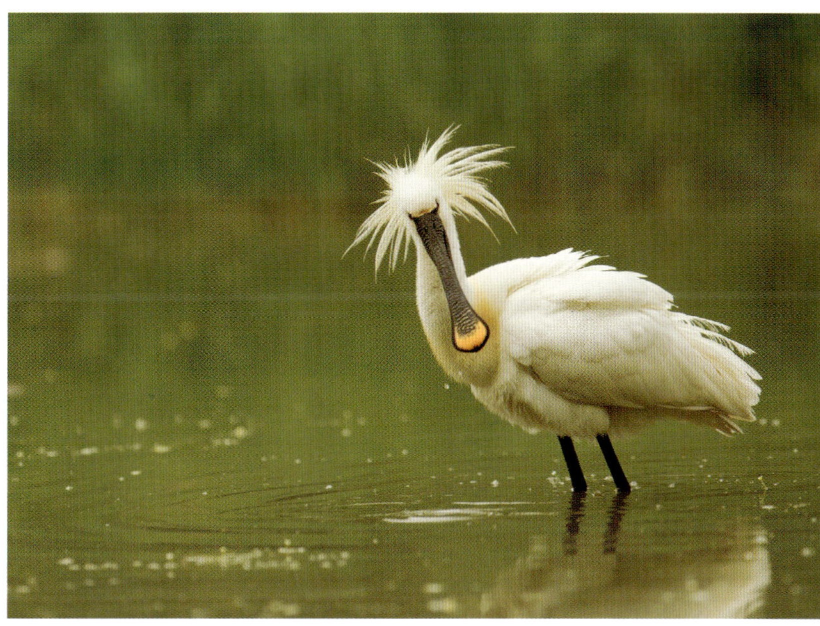

House martin | Germany | To get to this house martin's eye level, I had to lower myself all the way to the ground and rest the camera and lens on a bean bag. | 840mm (600mm + 1.4x converter), aperture 7.1, 1/800 s, ISO 640

Things get tricky if you photograph from a car and the bird is on the ground. In a case like this, you should lower the window completely and rest the camera on something as thin as possible. Sometimes, you can also very carefully leave the car and go to the eye level of the bird, while hiding behind the door. Of course, this only works if it doesn't get spooked and fly away….

Pay Attention to the Background

It's a very common beginner's mistake not to pay sufficient attention to the background. But the background crucially affects images and their message: If it's uncluttered and soft, the viewer's gaze lands more directly on the actual subject rather than getting distracted. You can achieve a soft focus by using a fast telephoto lens and a wide-open aperture. It's also important that there's as much distance as possible between the subject and the background. If the bird is too close to the background, inevitably the latter won't be as blurred even if you shoot with an open aperture.

Generally, it's distracting if the background is unintentionally divided into two halves. This can very easily happen when the background is sky and forest or sky and meadow. If the horizon line sits right behind the subject, the picture will be inharmonious. In the worst case, the horizon line also runs through the center of the picture! Usually, this is easily resolved by crouching down a bit so that the horizon line ends up being above the bird.

You should also get into the habit of checking the entire perimeter of the image before releasing the shutter: Is anything protruding into the background that could be a distraction? Are there any bright spots that can be particularly discordant when located at the boundary? The perimeter of the image needs to be clear to keep the viewer's gaze focused.

4-4 ▼

Barn owl | German Raptor Research Center at Guttenberg Castle, Germany | In principle, this could have been a good photo if the background wasn't split into sky and forest. Shot before a uniform background of either sky or forest, the image would have been much calmer and the owl would have stood out much more clearly. | 300mm, aperture 6.3, 1/4000 s, ISO 1000

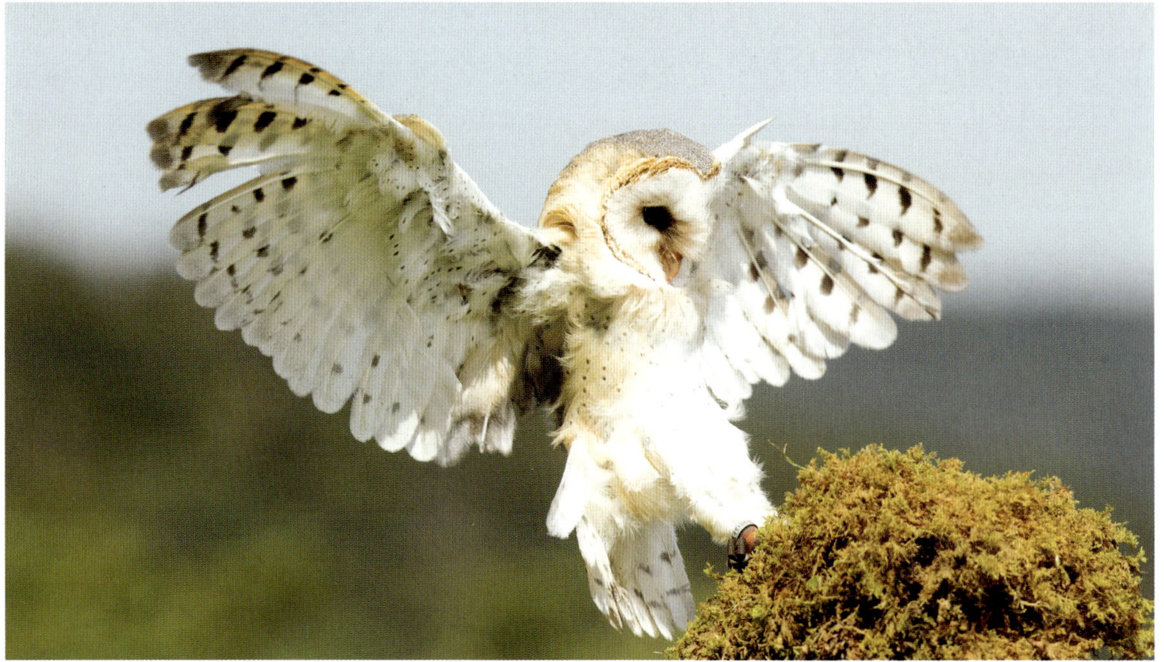

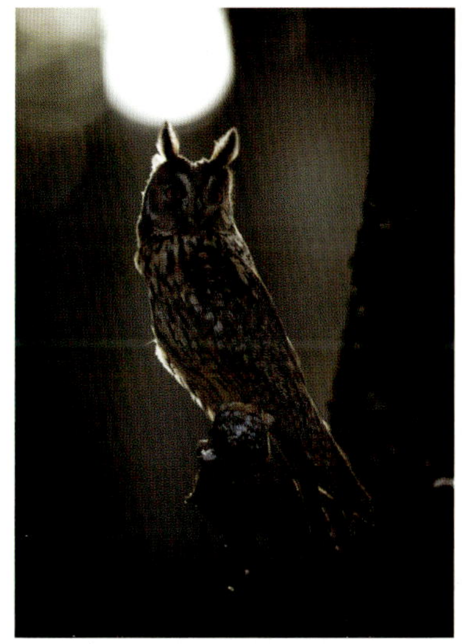

Long-eared owl | Germany | This would be a good picture if it weren't for the bright and rather dominant spots in the background. As is, it's unusable! | 300mm, aperture 2.8, 1/2000 s, ISO 800, -1 1/3 exposure compensation

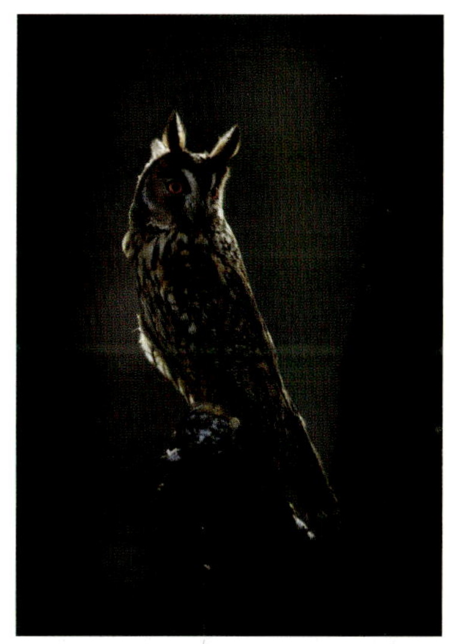

On top of that, you'll also need to develop an eye for any lines that run through the image. Most of the time, they'll be the trunks or branches of trees in the background. It's unattractive to have lines like this right behind the bird, i.e., if a tree "grows" out of its head. Tree trunks can, however, make for a good and beautiful background, especially if they frame the bird.

Sometimes, the background enriches the picture. This can happen when the background matches the color of the bird, or it provides pretty color accents, for example, through autumn foliage or flowers. But even then, it's usually more effective if these splashes of color are blurry—otherwise, they might again distract too much from the main character, the bird.

▲ 4-6

I had to move only a tiny bit to get a uniformly dark background! | 300mm, aperture 2.8, 1/1250 s, ISO 800, -1 1/3 exposure compensation

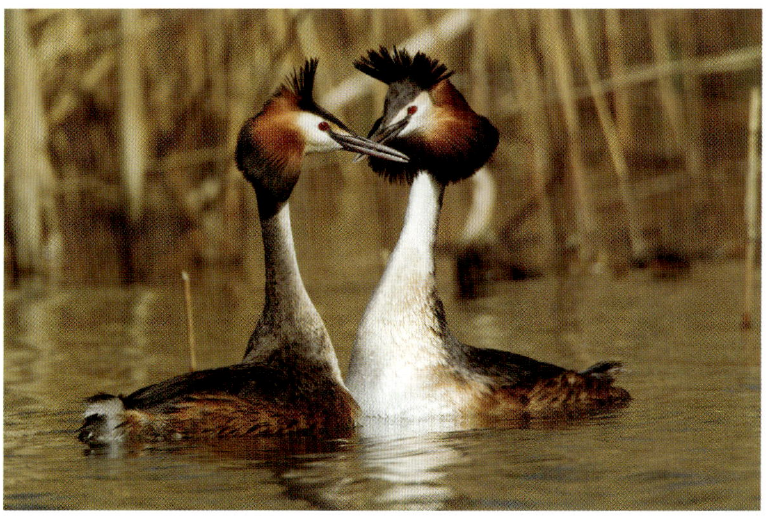

◀ 4-7

Great crested grebe | The Netherlands | Although the motif is interesting, the cluttered background is very distracting, and the courtship display of the great crested grebe loses some of its effect. | 700mm (500mm + 1.4x converter), aperture 8.0, 1/1600 s, ISO 400

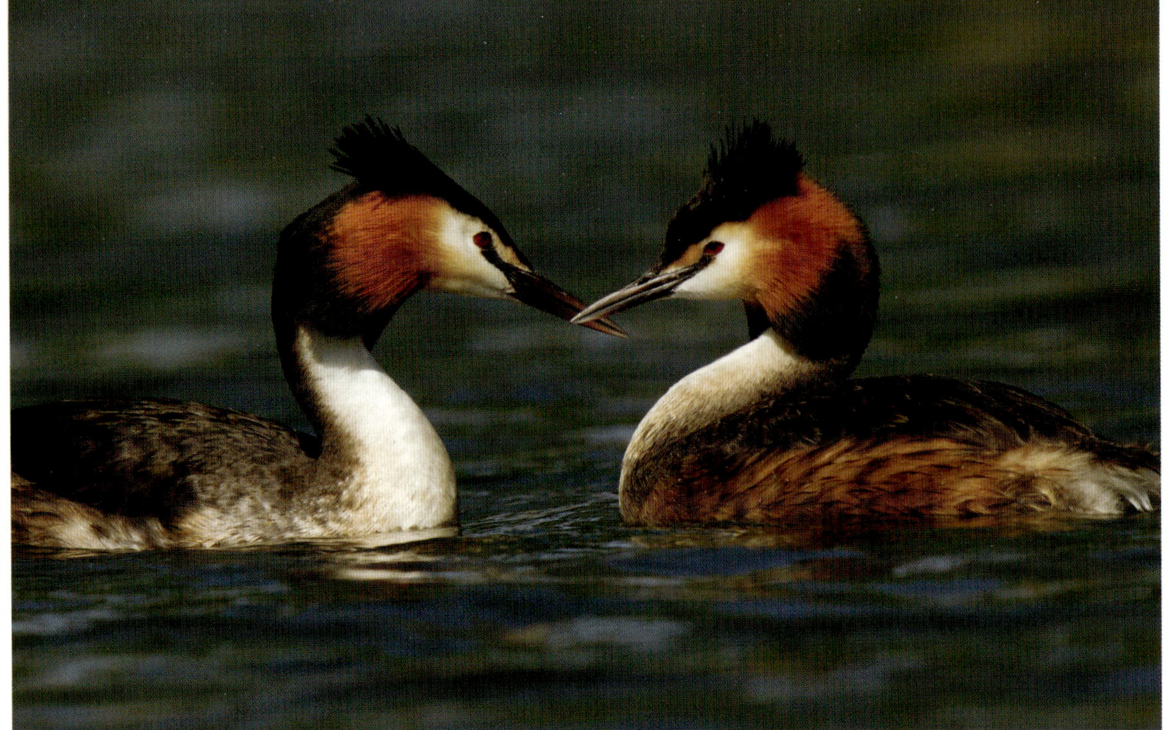

Great crested grebe | The Netherlands | Less is more. The message of this photo is focused on the courting pair of great crested grebes. The background doesn't distract but enhances the birds' colors. | 840mm (600mm + 1.4x converter), f/8.0, 1/2000 s, ISO 500, -2/3 exposure compensation

4-9 ▶

Northern hawk owl | Norway | It's a nice photo of a young northern hawk owl, but unfortunately the background is quite cluttered. | 600mm, aperture 5.6, 1/800 s, ISO 800, +1/3 exposure compensation

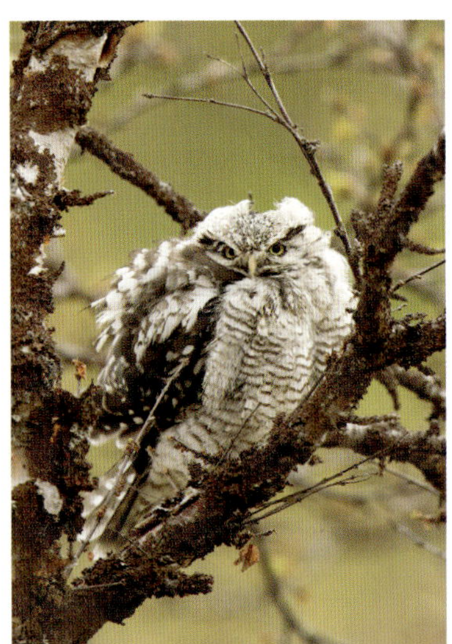

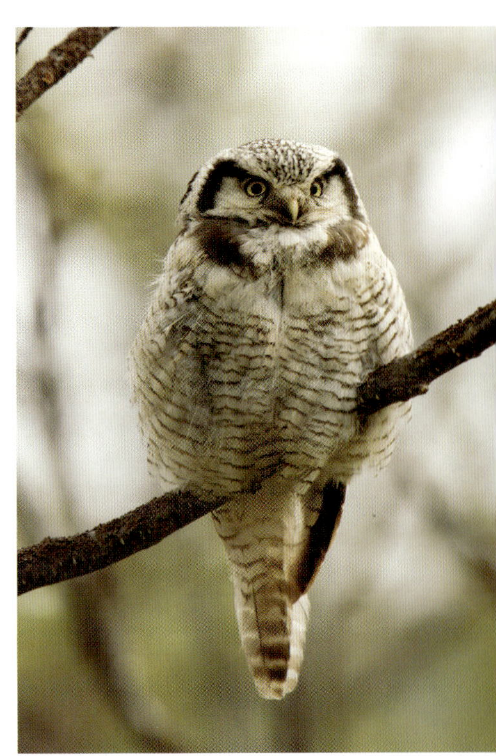

4-10 ▶

In this shot, the background is much less cluttered and the owl stands out better. | 600mm + 1.4x converter, aperture 7.1, 1/800 s, ISO 800, +1 exposure compensation

Shaping the Foreground

It's not just the background that plays a big role in determining how effective a photo is. The foreground does too. Often, there won't be a foreground in the photo because the bird is above us. But if it's possible to include a foreground, doing so can be very worthwhile. Leaves, blossoms, grasses, or flowers are particularly suitable. Snow, too, can be a nice foreground.

Depending on the aperture setting and on whether the bird is close to the foreground or farther away, the latter can be in or out of focus. The wider you open the aperture and the farther away the bird is, the blurrier the foreground becomes. Ideally, the foreground should harmonize with the background; for example, the same flowers can be in front of and behind the animal.

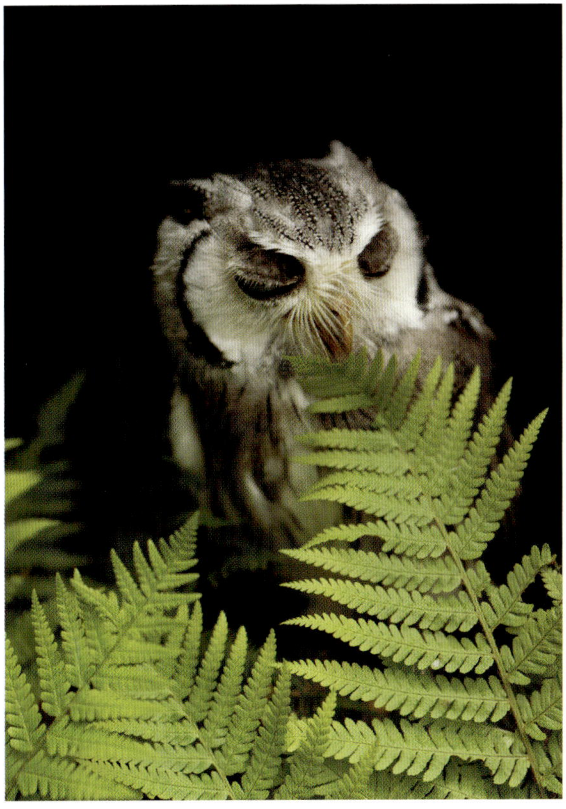

▲ 4-11

White-faced owl | Germany | If the foreground is close to the subject, it will be sharp even if the aperture is open and it'll become part of the story that the image tells. | 135mm, aperture 3.2, 1/1600 s, ISO 640

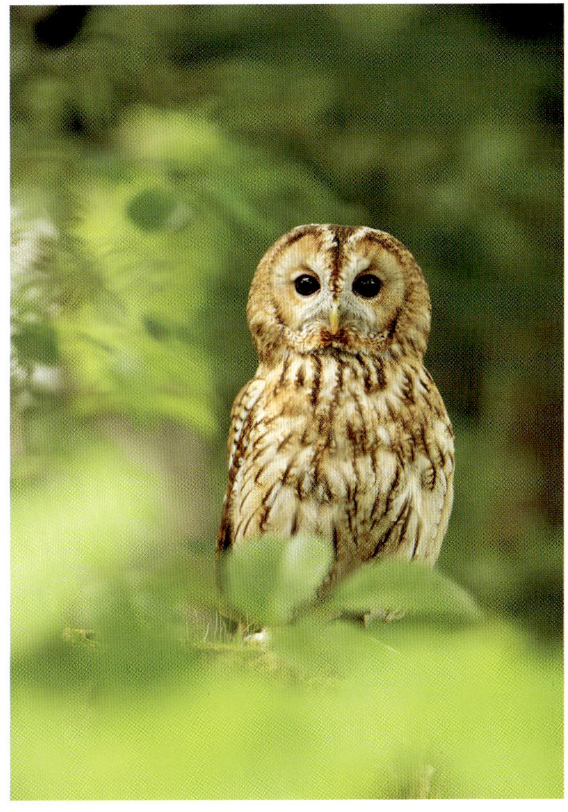

▲ 4-12

Tawny owl | Germany | If the foreground is a bit farther away from the subject, it can be blurred. Here, the foreground and background frame the attentive tawny owl. | 135mm, aperture 2.8, 1/250 s, ISO 500, +1/3 exposure compensation

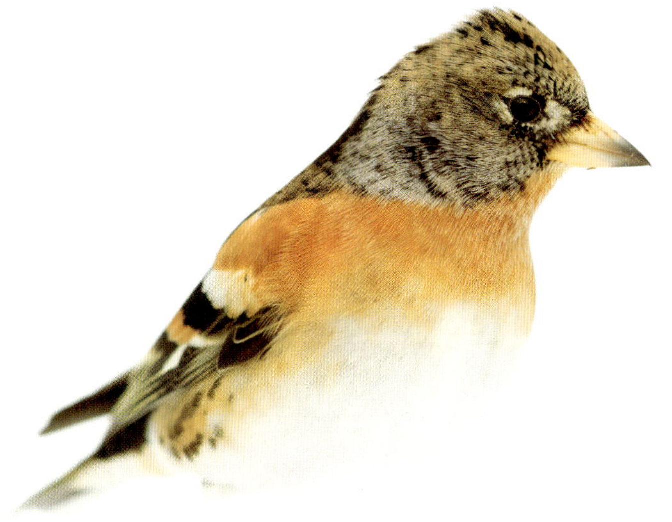

Brambling | Germany | The snowy foreground blends beautifully with the background and you see nothing but snow except for the pretty brambling. | 600mm, aperture 10, 1/2000 s, ISO 1000

Blending the Foreground and Background

Sometimes, you can blend the foreground with the background, putting the focus exclusively on the bird. This works especially well when the foreground and background are uniformly uncluttered and similar in color. It's also a great method for shots in the snow!

For such an image, the bird must be on the ground and the photographer at eye level with it. And you'll need a fast telephoto lens, preferably with the aperture wide open, so that the image doesn't have too much depth of field.

Eurasian dotterel | Norway | Having the tripod at ground level gave me a low angle and allowed me to gently blend the foreground and background. | 840mm (600mm + 1.4x converter), aperture 5.6, 1/2000 s, ISO 800

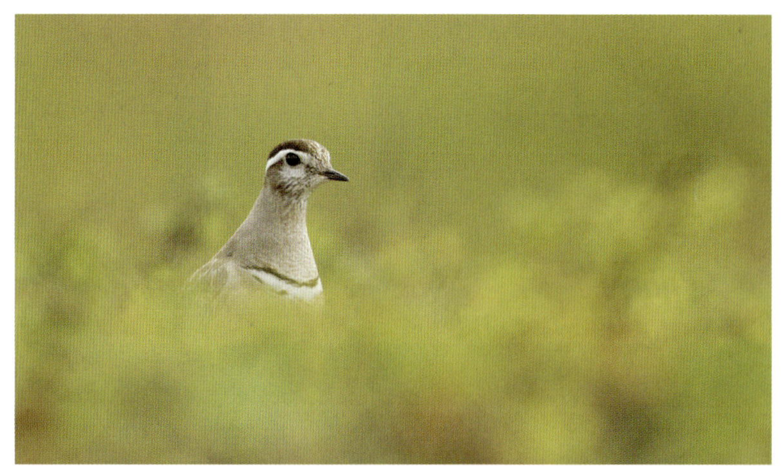

Avoid Distracting Elements

Anything that doesn't contribute to the image is superfluous and distracts the viewer. It's one of the great challenges of photography to clear unnecessary and distracting elements from the picture. The longer the focal length of your lens, the easier this becomes because as the focal length increases, the field of view shrinks, even if the size of the bird in the picture remains unchanged. If you're using a zoom lens, try taking a few steps back and using the longest focal length to eliminate distracting elements at the periphery of the image. Get into the habit of carefully examining the photo you plan to take before you release the shutter to eliminate distractions. Often, you only need to move a little bit to the right or left to change the background. If that's not enough, give it a moment—the bird might change position, allowing you to compose a better picture.

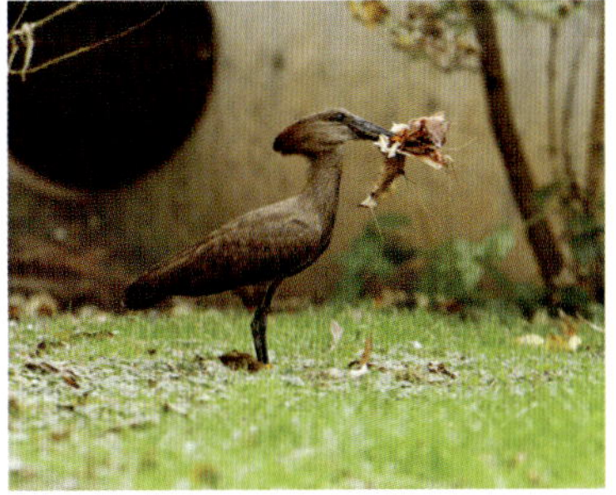

▲ 4-15

Hamerkop | Wilhelma Stuttgart, Germany | The bird is collecting nesting material—an interesting behavior. But the concrete wall in the background is a major distraction. | 300mm, aperture 4.5, 1/200 s, ISO 1600, -1/3 exposure compensation

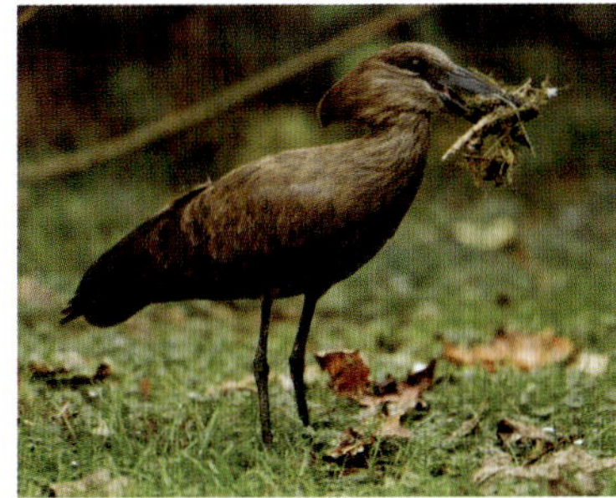

▲ 4-16

A better background, but the diagonal branch still distracts from the main subject. | 500mm, aperture 4.5, 1/320 s, ISO 1600, -2/3 exposure compensation

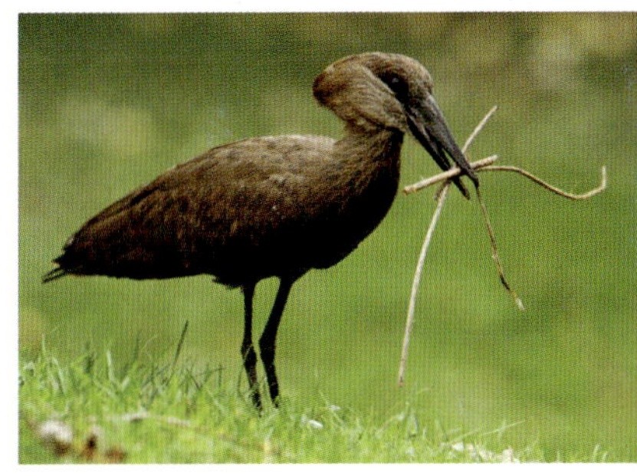

▲ 4-17

In this composition, everything is focused on the hamerkop and its behavior. | 300mm, aperture 4.5, 1/320 s, ISO 1600, -1/3 exposure compensation

In zoos, common distractions are fences, trash cans, food bowls, or other visitors that show up in the background. You should exclude these elements from your photo unless they contribute to its message. You also need to pay a lot of attention when photographing in nature. I've gotten into the habit of checking the entire periphery of an image before taking the shot. Are there branches protruding into the picture that I can eliminate by changing position? Are there spots that distract? Bright spots in a picture in particular attract the eye and our attention. Dark spots are less of a concern as we don't notice them as much.

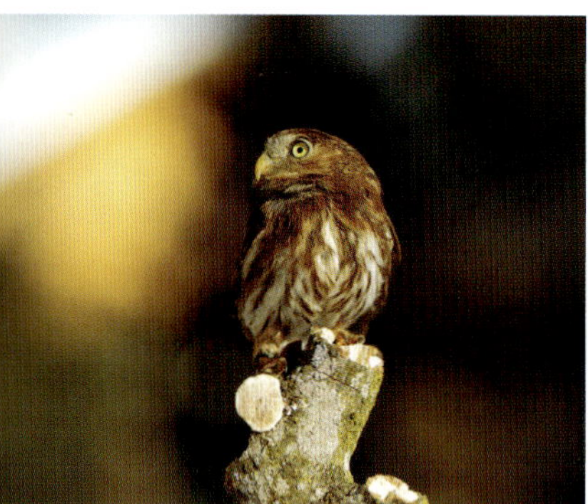

▲ 4-18

Ferruginous pygmy owl | Germany | The white in the upper-left corner dominates in this picture and greatly disturbs the overall effect. | 135mm, aperture 3.2, 1/2000 s, ISO 800

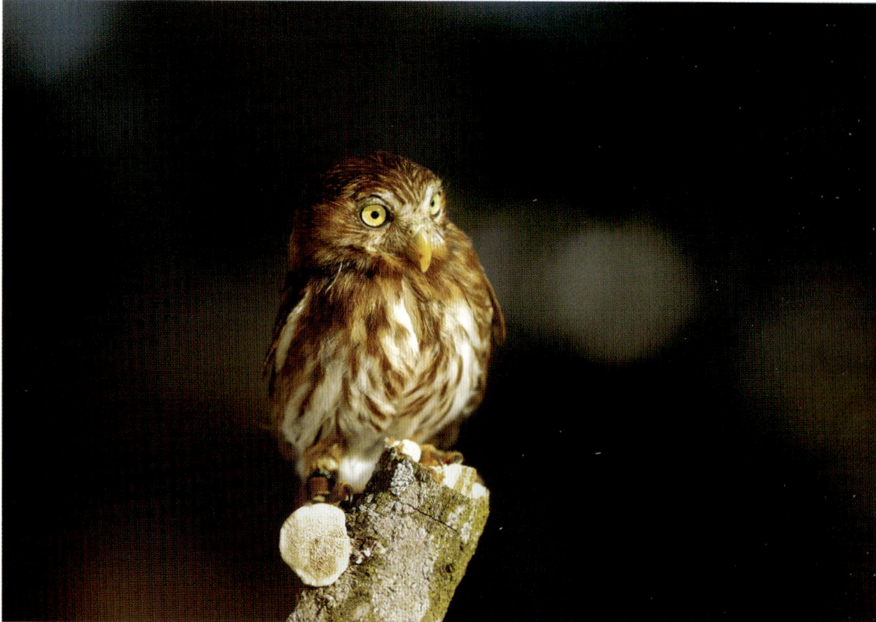

▲ 4-19

Taking just one step to the left eliminated the white corner and made the composition much more harmonious. | 135mm, aperture 3.2, 1/3200 s, ISO 800

Motifs for Horizontal Images

Novice photographers tend to take all their images horizontally. This is the normal way to hold the camera as it makes the shutter release easy to reach. But not all motifs have a horizontal orientation, and it's useful to learn to discern which subjects are better in which format. To start with, it's important how large the bird will be in the picture. Often, the smaller it is, the better suited it is for a horizontal image, especially if you want to include some of the surroundings, the bird's habitat.

Things get more complicated when the bird fills the frame. Some birds, for example, most songbirds, ducks, or geese, are shaped wide rather than tall. For birds like these, the horizontal format is a very good fit, especially if you photograph them in profile. It's stable, and the photo is grounded.

Portraits, too, are mostly well suited for the horizontal formal if taken in profile.

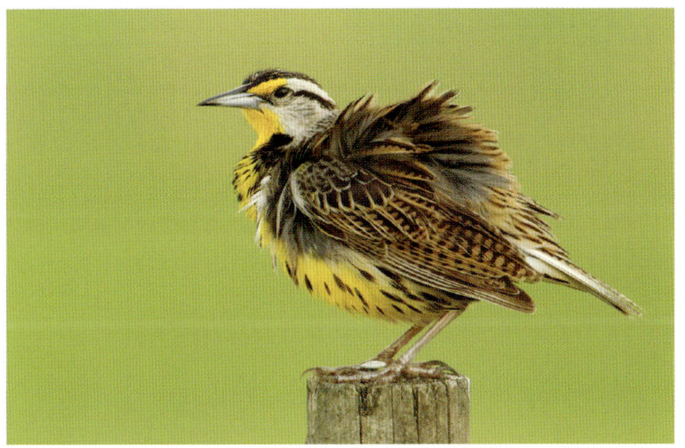

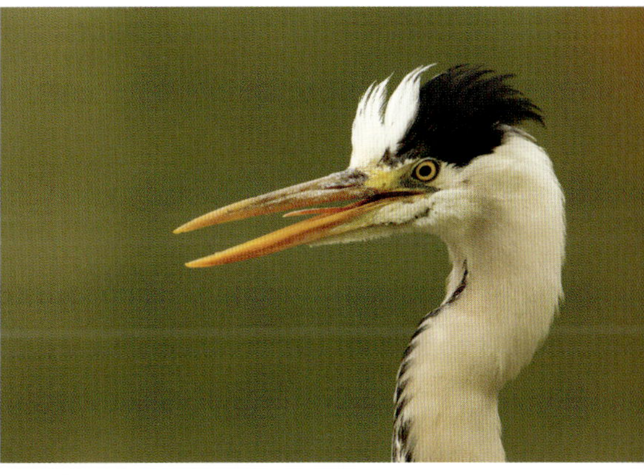

▲ 4-20
Eastern meadowlark | Florida | A classic motif for the horizontal format | 500mm, aperture 5.6, 1/500 s, ISO 1250

▲ 4-21
Gray heron | Serbia | A horizontal composition works well for most portrait shots, too. | 300mm, aperture 3.2, 1/800 s, ISO 800

Motifs for Vertical Images

As you become more experienced, you'll discover more and more motifs that work best vertically. They might be images that show how high up some birds have built their nest and are raising their young. Height works much better in vertical rather than horizontal images.

Some birds have long legs or tall, slender bodies, such as waders, storks, and herons. Some have a lifestyle that is destined to be photographed in a vertical format, like woodpeckers. Or, they have a very upright posture, as do many owls. If you take frame-filling photos of birds like these in a horizontal format, you are often cramped for space at the top and bottom, while having too much negative space on the right and left of the image.

Vertical also works well for taking front-facing portraits of birds; ditto for portraits of long-necked birds, like herons.

It almost always matters which format you pick for a picture. Sometimes, I take photos both horizontally and vertically so that they can be used in many different ways. Calendars and photos in magazines, for instance, often require both formats.

To take pictures in the vertical format, it is helpful to have a camera equipped with a vertical shutter release. Some can also be retrofitted with a special battery grip with a vertical shutter release. That way you don't have to awkwardly bend your arms when tilting the camera into vertical mode.

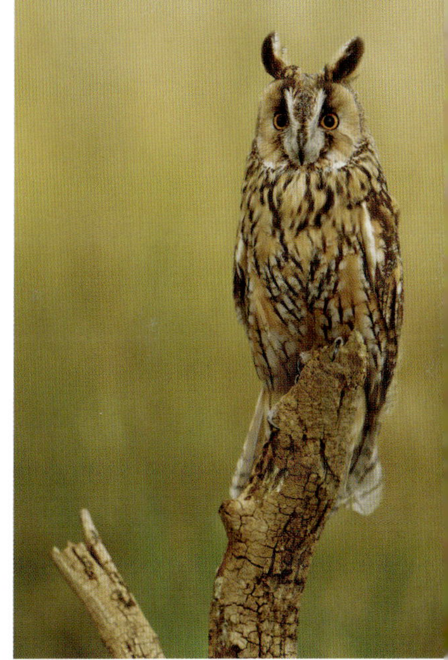

▲ 4-22
Long-eared owl | Wales | Owls are among the birds that usually adopt a rather upright posture, so vertical images work well for them. | 300mm, aperture 3.2, 1/640 s, ISO 500

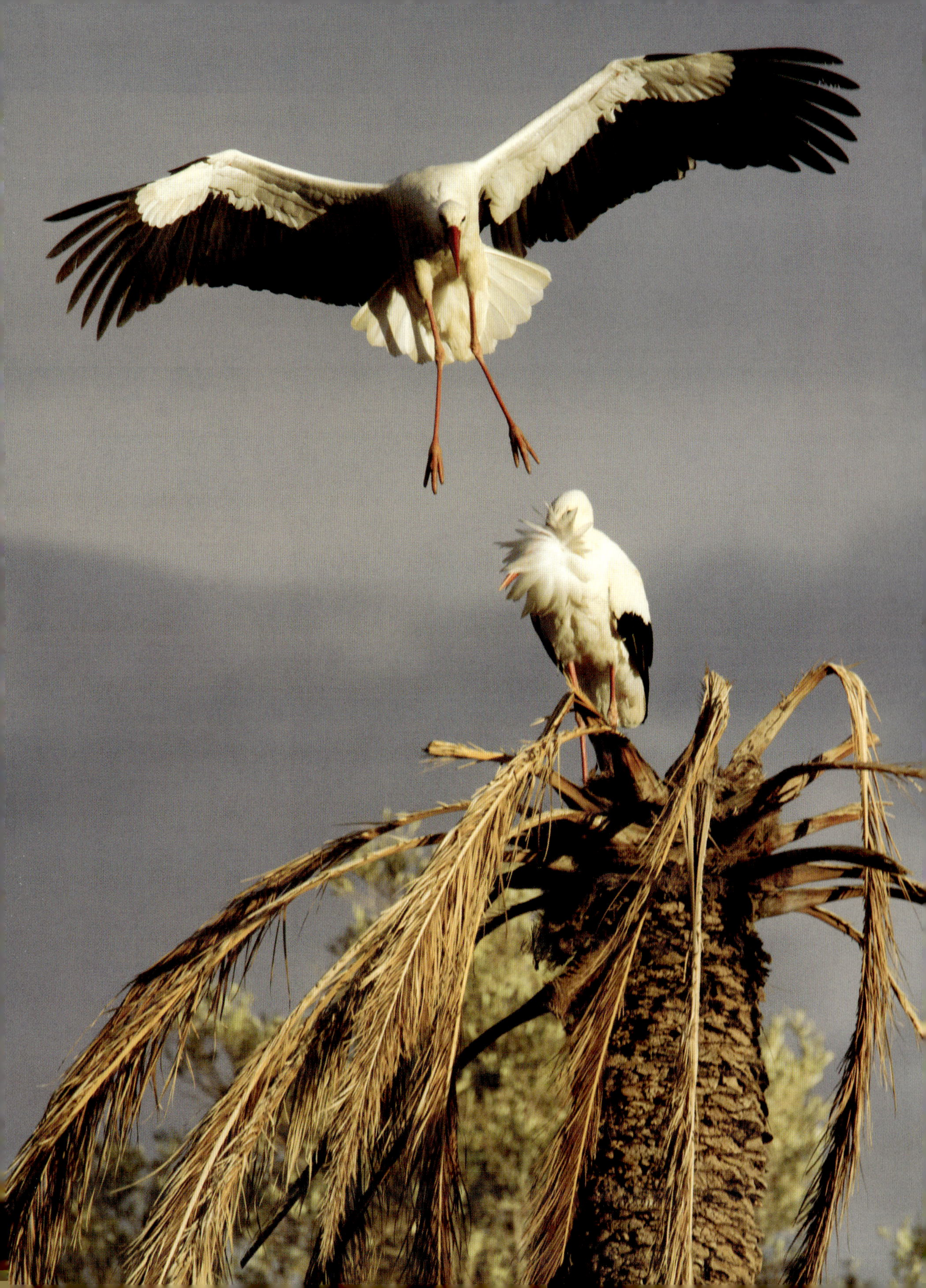

White storks | Turkey | The slender, tall palm tree with the two storks is a motif that is predestined to be photographed vertically. | 700mm (500mm + 1.4x converter), f/11, 1/1250 s, ISO 800

Motifs for Square Images

You rarely find a subject that works best in a square format. Usually, square photographs of a bird will be too constrictive or leave too much negative space. But sometimes it's possible to make an image square during editing. The square form condenses images a lot, and I often use it for detail shots.

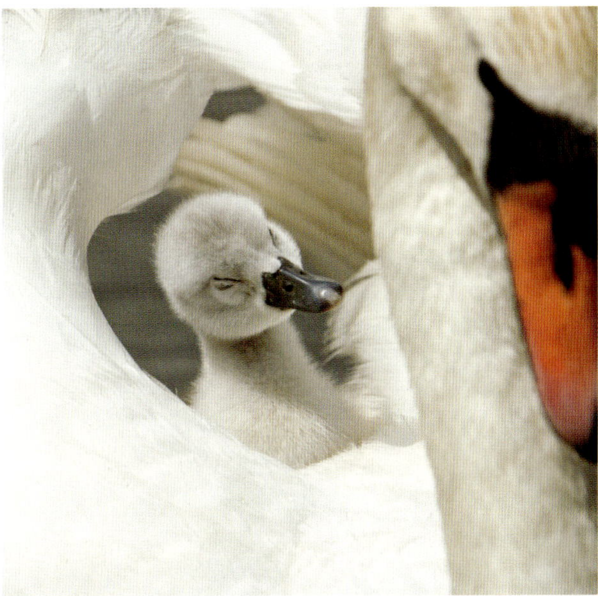

▲ 4-24

Mute swans | Wales | The square format puts the focus on the chick, framed by its parents. | 320mm, aperture 8.0, 1/5000 s, ISO 800

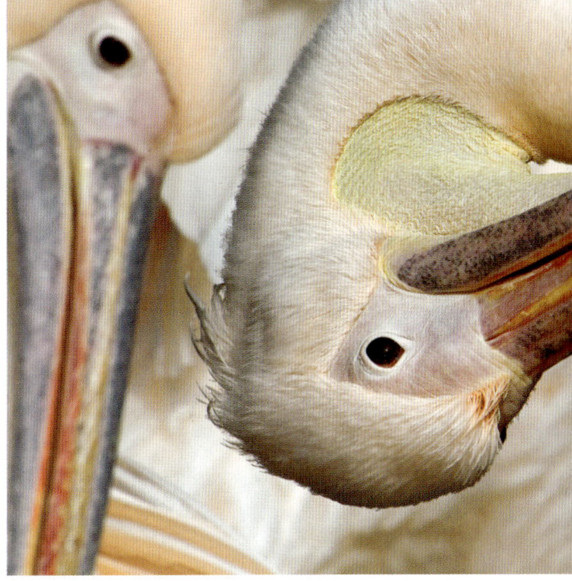

▲ 4-25

Great white pelican | Karlsruhe Zoo, Germany | The square format eliminates anything that doesn't contribute to the image. | 400mm, aperture 9.0, 1/400 s, ISO 250

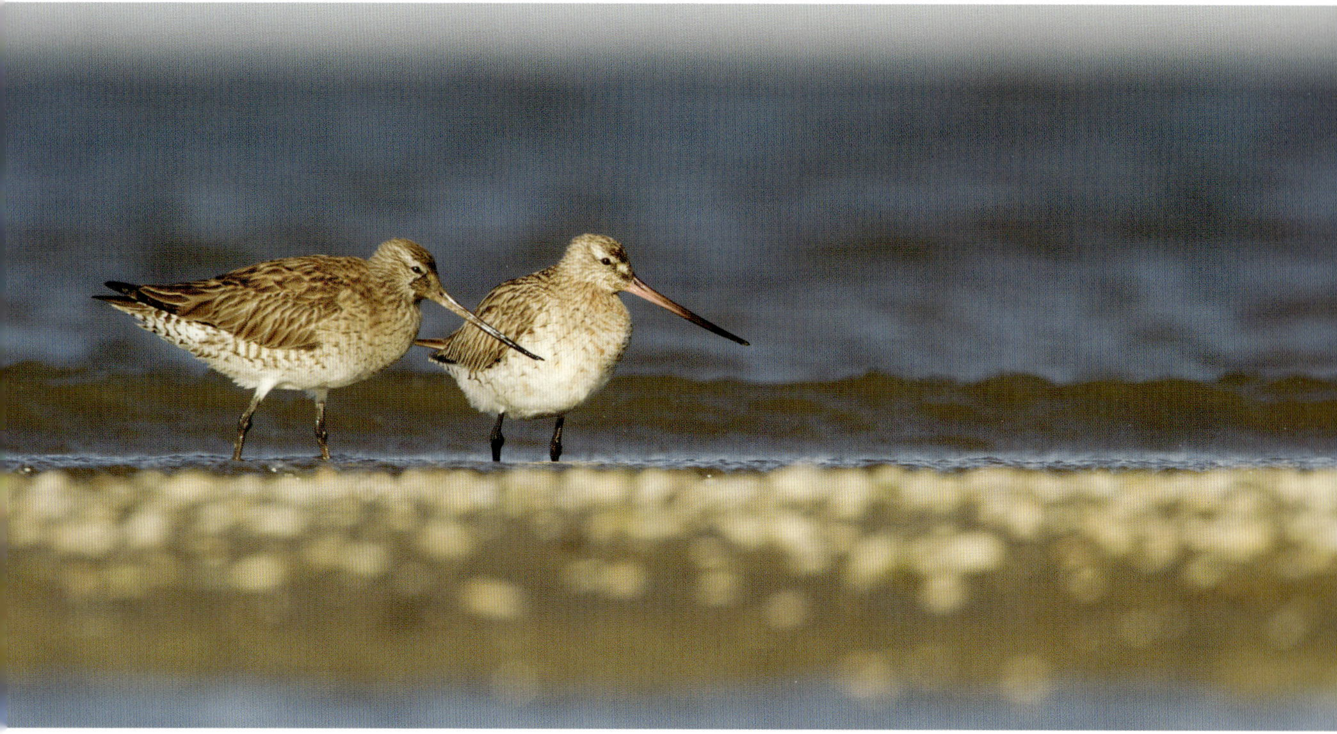

Bar-tailed godwits | Texel, The Netherlands | The original had too much sky, which did not contribute to the picture's message. So I cropped it to a wide format. Having the line between the sea and the beach in the lower third creates harmony. | 700mm (500mm + 1.4x converter), aperture 9.0, 1/1250 s, ISO 400, -1/3 exposure compensation

Panoramic Photos

There is one more format that I use from time to time in photos: the panoramic shot. It usually looks harmonious when cropped to a ratio of 1:2, so that the image is twice as wide as it is high.

This kind of format works well, for example, if you want to show a large flock of waterfowl at the shore. A normal horizontal photo often leaves too much negative space at the top and bottom in images like this, and the flock of birds does not come into its own. The format also works well for aerial shots or when you want to convey the vastness of a landscape.

Go Off-Center!

It's one of the most important rules in photo composition: "Move the subject off-center!" A subject that is placed right in the center often looks boring and leaves too much negative space behind the bird. You can use the so-called rule of thirds as a rough guideline. According to this rule, the important compositional elements of the photo should be placed at approximately the intersection of lines that divide the photo into thirds vertically and horizontally. If a bird is shown before a relatively large background, it's easy to follow this rule and end up with a harmonious and well-balanced picture.

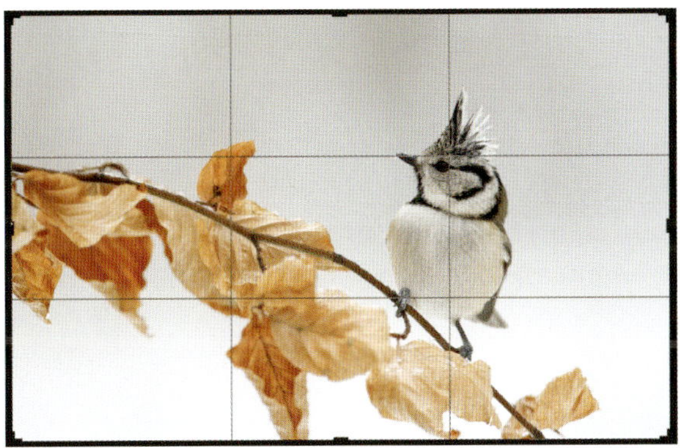

Crested tit | Germany | A very harmonious composition, which adheres to the rule of thirds in a good way. | 500mm, aperture 5.6, 1/500 s, ISO 1250, +2/3 exposure compensation

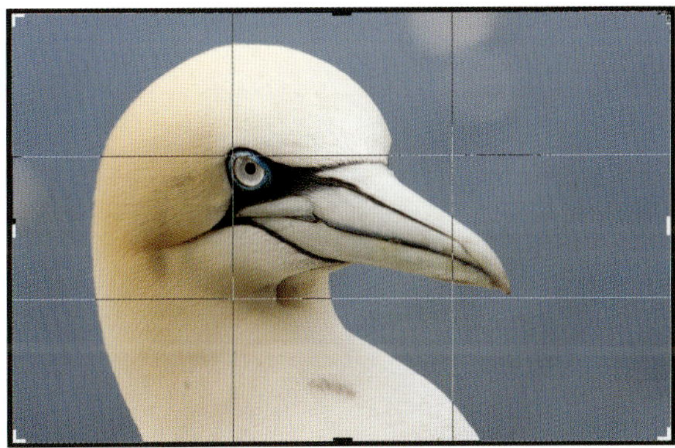

Northern gannet | Bass Rock, Scotland | In this portrait, the eye sits exactly at an intersection of the rule of thirds grid. | 250mm, aperture 9.0, 1/800 s, ISO 320

Things become a bit more difficult when you take a frame-filling shot of a bird in profile. Here, you should try to place the eye at approximately the intersection of the lines that divide the image into thirds without cropping the image too tightly in front of the head (from the bird's point of view). This is fairly easy to do for bird species with a short tail. But for birds with a long tail obeying the rule of thirds can be tricky. However, you shouldn't take this rule too literally anyway. The important thing is: "Go off-center!"

You should also follow this rule when shooting vertically and place the bird slightly off to the side. For full-frame portraits, you can try placing the eye at roughly one of the grid intersections. Depending on the proportions of the head and the length of the beak, this will sometimes work well, other times less so. But generally speaking, the rule offers a good basic guideline.

Of course, there are exceptions to every rule—and situations when it's appropriate to break the rule of thirds in photography. This is especially true for full-frontal images when both sides of the body are symmetrical.

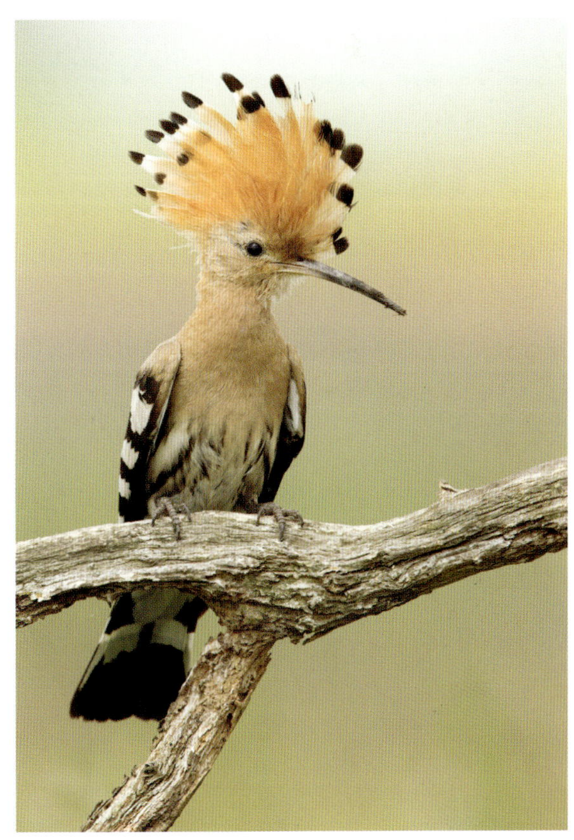

Hoopoe | Serbia | The rule even applies to vertical shots: Go off-center! | 600mm, aperture 6.3, 1/2000 s, ISO 500

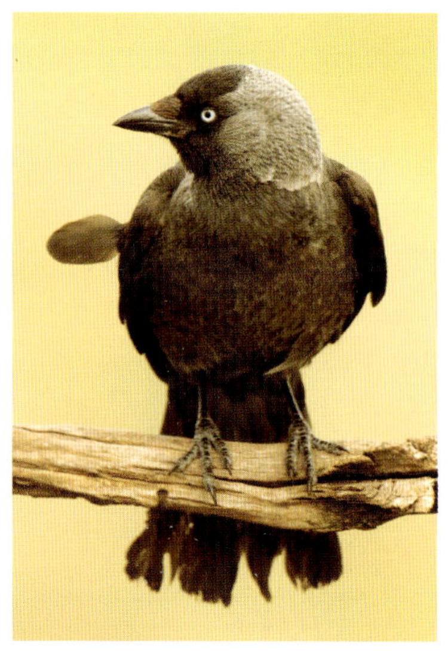

Western jackdaw | Serbia | I was actually taking pictures of some smaller European rollers when this jackdaw suddenly landed in front of me. I immediately photographed it, but it's obvious that I was too close. The jackdaw has an almost cramped-in look. | 700mm (500mm + 1.4x converter), aperture 6.3, 1/320 s, ISO 1000

Negative Space

Usually, a picture has a subject surrounded by an area that is not directly relevant to the image's message. This space is also called negative space. Negative space is very important because it prevents the subject from being cramped into the image. If the image zooms in too much, it will look as though the bird is sitting in a cage and has no room to breathe. You should avoid that if you want a harmonious composition.

But it does matter how the negative space is distributed in the image. You only need to have a little bit of negative space behind the bird, but there should be quite a bit more in front of it. If we want to make a rule, we could say that the space in front of the bird should be about twice as large as the space behind it. This allows the viewer to feel that the bird could move into this space and have enough room to do so. But you should take the eye gaze direction into account, as we will see in the next chapter. This rule is especially important for shots that show a bird in motion—if you disregard it, it'll look as if the bird is flying against a wall.

The space behind the bird is a dead space. It neither contributes to the image nor interests us. We only want to know what's in front of the bird. This is especially true for portraits: If there's too much negative space behind the head, the picture can easily look boring and static. It helps to observe the rule of thirds here and place the eye at roughly a grid intersection, as described above.

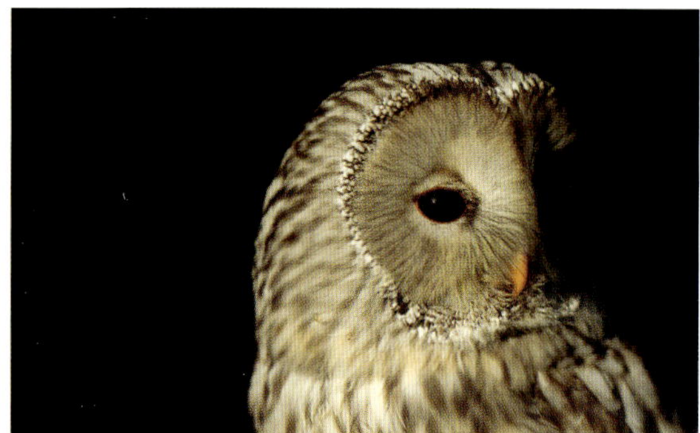

Ural owl | Germany | This picture leaves far too little space on the right and has far too much negative space on the left. It looks as if the bird is staring at a wall. | 135mm, aperture 2.8, 1/8000 s, ISO 320, -1 exposure compensation

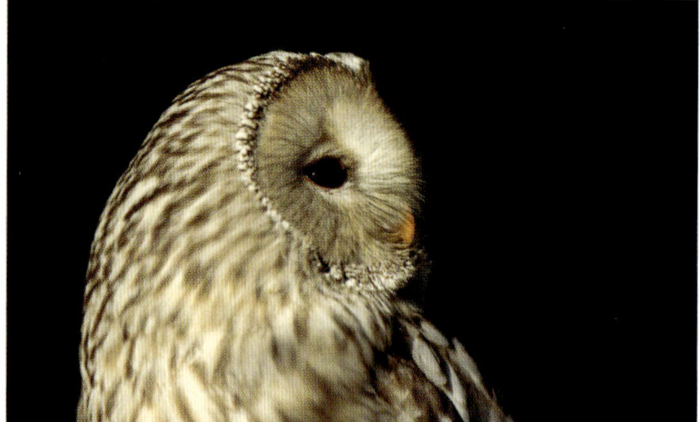

Things are much better balanced in this shot. There is more space in the direction of the bird's gaze to the right and the (boring) negative space on the left is much smaller. | 135mm, aperture 2.8, 1/8000 s, ISO 400, -1 exposure compensation

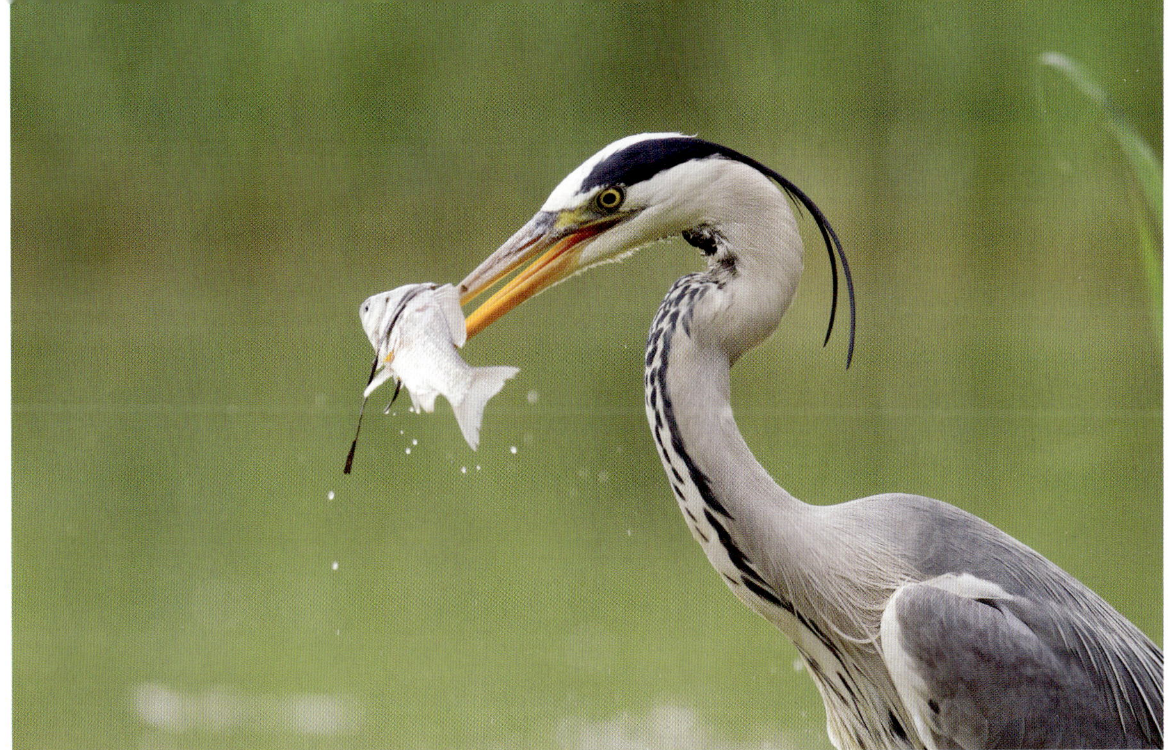

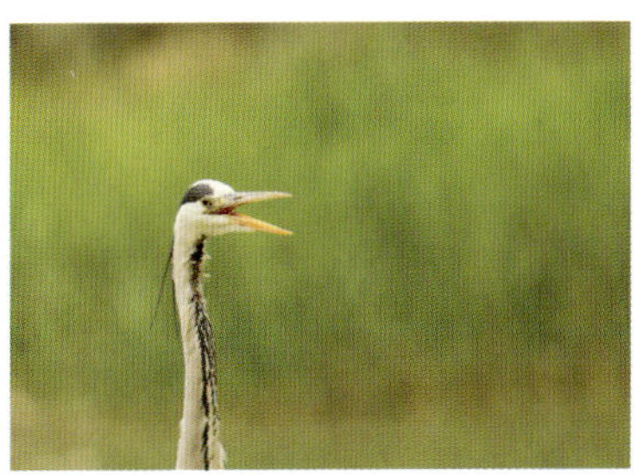

Gray heron | Serbia | A fun picture for sure, but the crop is unbalanced. The slender neck looks a bit unstable and the image has too much negative space overall. | 300mm, aperture 4.0, 1/640 s, ISO 1250

A better crop: Including part of the shoulder and chest area anchors the photo. | 300mm, aperture 3.5, 1/500 s, ISO 1250

Getting the Crop Right

You don't always have to show a bird in full in the photo. Especially if it's a large bird and you photographed it from up-close, you sometimes can—or want to—show only part of it. But if you crop the wrong parts, the composition quickly ends up looking inharmonious. In portraits, it's rarely pleasing to see just the head and neck of a bird. Photos like this often seem to lack an anchor and the head looks unbalanced. Instead, it's better to either crop tighter and make it a head-only portrait or go wider and leave in part of the chest as well. The image will be more balanced and have a more pleasing composition. On the other hand, if you cut off some of the bird's body, make sure that you crop just behind and not in front of the legs. Without the legs, the image will look unbalanced and like it's tilting.

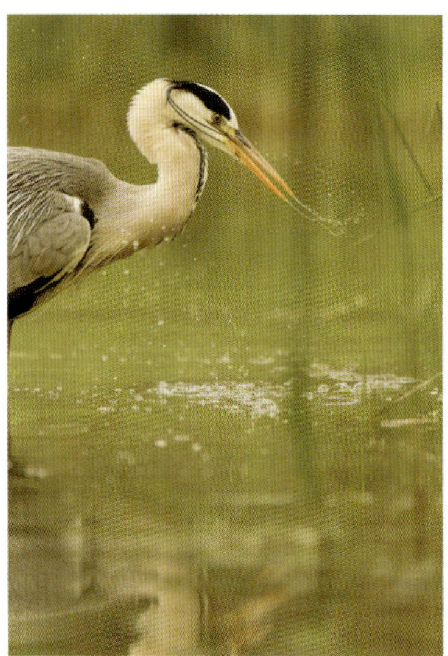

Gray heron | Serbia | A very careless crop: The body was cropped just before the legs and lacks support. | 300mm, aperture 2.8, 1/2500 s, ISO 1000

Here's how to crop if you need to: The legs are still part of the picture and the body is cropped at the rear third. | 300mm, aperture 4.0, 1/1600 s, ISO 1000

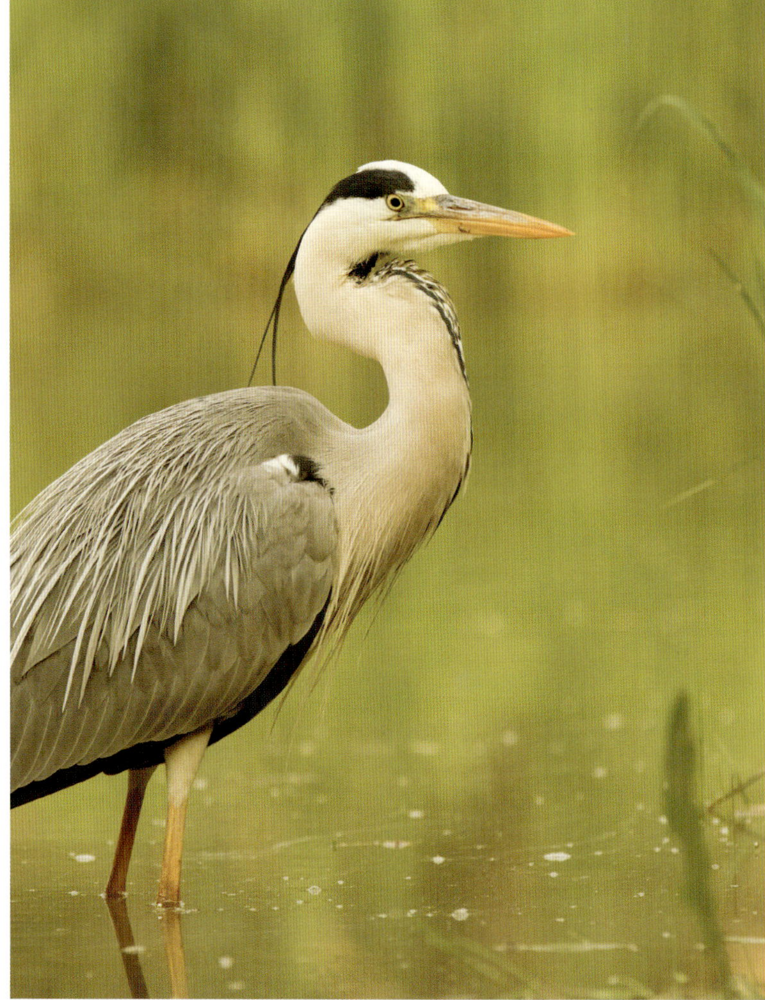

You also need to be careful when cropping at the lower edge of a photo. If you cut off the legs above their midway point, things will look unbalanced. As a rule, it is better to crop only the lower third of the legs, especially if the bird is standing in water or snow.

If you want to draw attention to a specific detail, say, the eye, it makes sense to crop really tightly and cut off everything in the image that distracts from it. It works especially well if there is nothing but the eye and feathers left in the photo and no other background clutters the image's message.

Check the edges of your photo carefully even before you take the shot. It would be a shame to photograph a beautiful motif only to later realize that you cut off the feet, the tip of the tail, or the wings. Particularly in shots that show a bird flying or taking off, you need to consider the enormous wingspan that some species have and leave room in the frame accordingly before you press the release button.

Rule of the Gaze

For a harmonious image composition, the bird must have enough space in front of it so it doesn't look boxed in. But note that "in front of the bird" is always determined by the direction of its gaze. If the image shows the bird with its body pointing left but its head turned and looking right, it needs space on the right side of the picture. Otherwise, it would seem too close to the edge of the image.

It's incredibly important that the bird should look at the viewer. A photo can only captivate if the bird's gaze is directed at the lens. That's why I always wait until the bird's head is turned at least slightly toward me before I release the shutter. The one (rare) exception is pictures in which the bird is looking at something that the viewers themselves can see or at least imagine, like the expanse of the horizon at sunset or the view of the sea from a cliff.

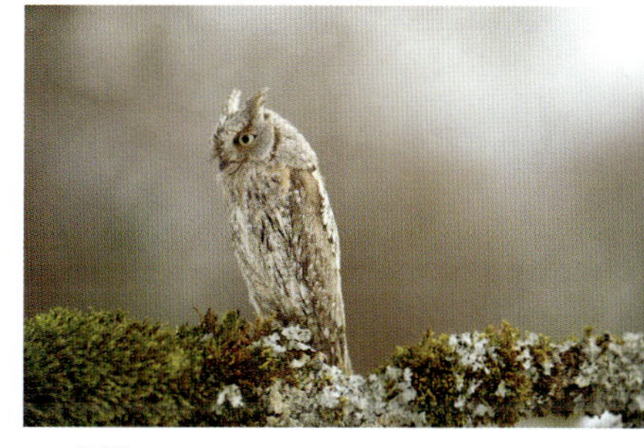

▲ 4-37

Scops owl | Germany | A very bad composition: The bird is looking straight at the edge of the picture. And because its head isn't turned toward the viewers, they can't connect with it. | 135mm, aperture 2.5, 1/6400 s, ISO 1000

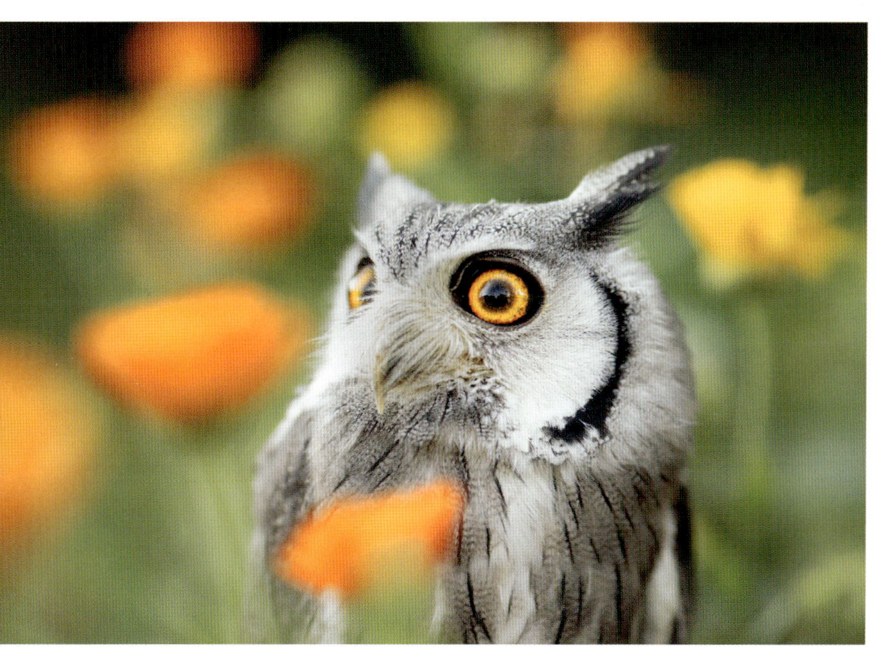

▲ 4-38

White-faced owl | Germany | Here, the bird is located on the right but gazing toward the left. This means that it needs space on the left. | 135mm, aperture 2.5, 1/1000 s, ISO 1000

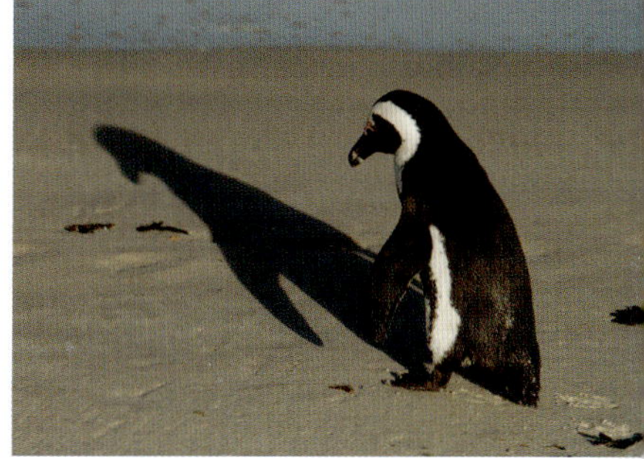

▲ 4-39

African penguin | South Africa | This picture works even though there's no eye contact between the penguin and the viewer. The bird seems to be looking at its shadow—that's the little story the image tells. | 235mm, aperture 6.3, 1/1250 s, ISO 200, -2/3 exposure compensation

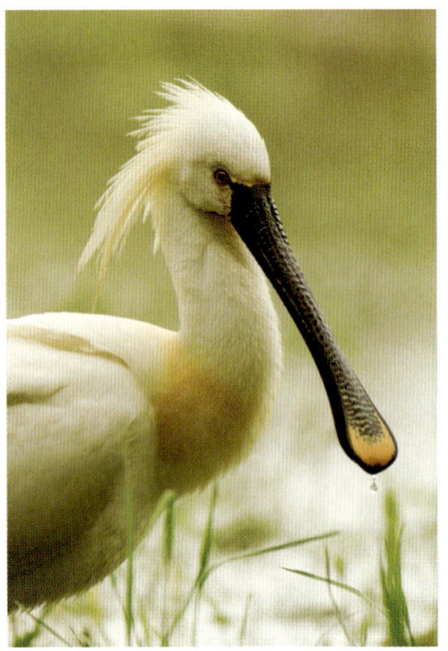

Spoonbill | Serbia | The gaze of the viewer wanders from the bird's eye to the beak and the drop of water at its tip. | 300mm, aperture 4.0, 1/1000 s, ISO 1000

Left and Right

In bird photographs, our gaze usually moves from left to right and stops at the bird's eye. That's because in Europe we tend to look at pictures the same way that we read and that is from left to right. In cultures where people read in a different direction, they also look at pictures differently. Once our gaze reaches the eye of the bird, it lingers for a moment before moving farther to the right. Since our brain is lazy, it's very rare that our gaze returns and moves back toward the left half of the picture.

We also usually move our gaze from the top to the bottom. As an aside, this is why the logo of a company is usually displayed in the lower right corner of a print advertisement. That's where our gaze lands and if the logo is eye-catching, it lingers for a moment and imprints the logo in our memory.

What does this mean for bird photography? Let's take a closer look at these two photos of a Eurasian spoonbill: In the first version, our gaze starts at the eye, quickly moves along the beak, then lingers at the drop of water at the tip. Compare that to the mirrored version: The gaze moves immediately to the eye and lingers there. The viewer may not even notice the drop of water on the beak. It's unlikely that the viewer's gaze will leave the eye and move backward, meaning left, toward the beak. It depends on how interested the viewer is in the image. Therefore, both photos tell a very different story even though they're identical, just mirrored. Some photographers use this knowledge and mirror images if that works better for the message they want to convey. This is particularly common in advertising.

In this mirrored version, our gaze is drawn directly to the eye and the viewer may not even notice the drop of water on the beak. | 300mm, aperture 4.0, 1/1000 s, ISO 1000

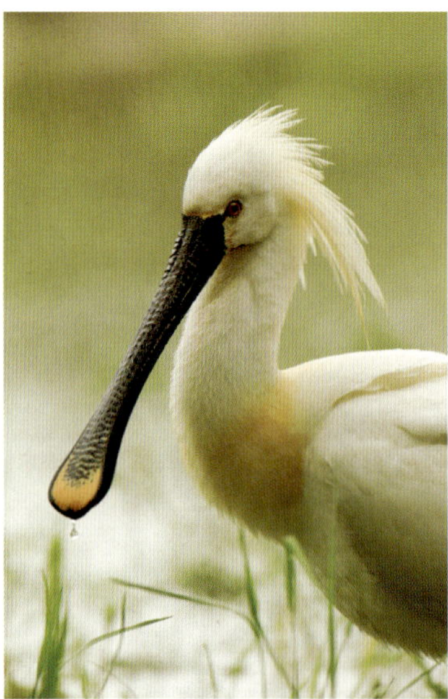

The way we read and see influences yet another dimension of how we perceive photos. Because we usually move our gaze from left to right, we tend to interpret the right side of an image as the future and the left more as the past. According to this automatic interpretation, a bird looking from left to right is looking toward the future, and in the mirrored version it is oriented more toward the past. The first image tends to make us feel more optimistic than the second—another psychological effect that advertisers exploit.

CHAPTER 4

Catchlight

If we want viewers to connect with the bird, the animal must appear alive. To achieve this, the eye must be clearly visible and, in the best case, we should be able to see some catchlight in it. If both eyes are visible, there should be catchlight in both.

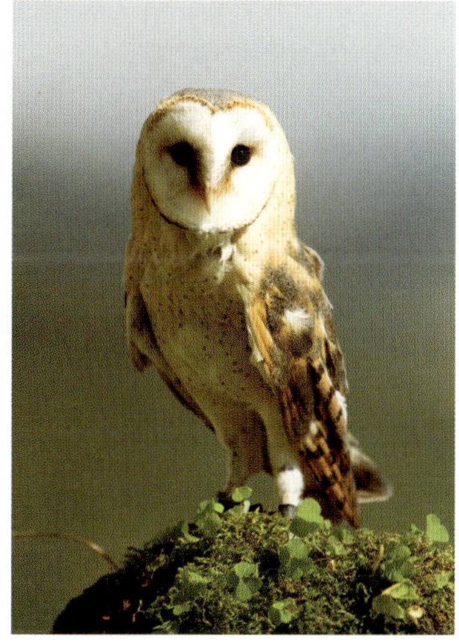

▲ 4-42

Barn owl | German Raptor Research Center at Guttenberg Castle, Germany | With half of the face in the shade, there's no catchlight in the eye, making it look lifeless. It's something I would avoid. | 300mm, aperture 4.0, 1/4000 s, ISO 400

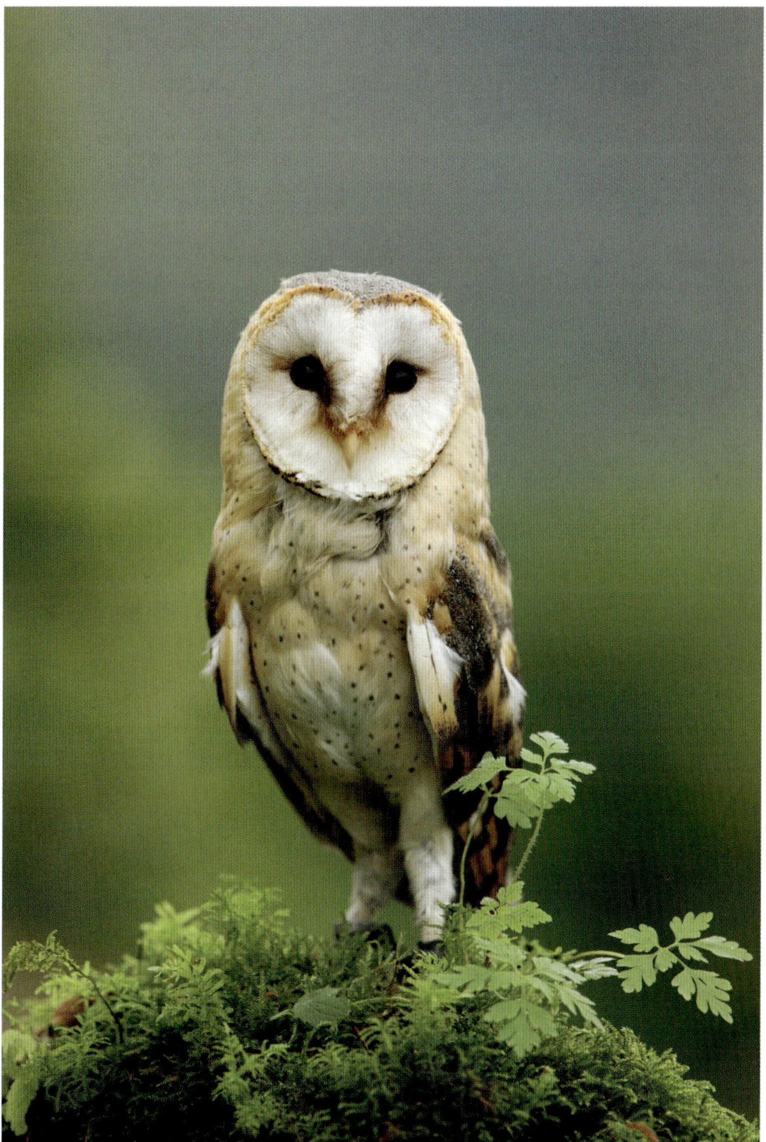

◀ 4-43

The same situation, but now under an overcast sky. The plumage is evenly illuminated and there is catchlight in both eyes. | 300mm, aperture 4.5, 1/1250 s, ISO 1000

So, what should you do if one eye is in the shade? The best approach is to wait until the bird turns its head slightly so the eye catches the light. Sometimes, it will need to turn its head so far that only half of its face is still visible but is then also illuminated by the sun. This is much less of a problem under overcast skies, since then both sides of the face tend to be illuminated evenly.

Having catchlights in the eyes is particularly important when photographing birds with large, dark eyes since they will tend to look dead and lifeless otherwise. Nocturnal owls such as the tawny owl or barn owl are good examples.

Getting the Proportions Right

The following is particularly relevant when taking photographs at a feeding station. In that situation, you can choose the branches that the birds will use as perches and can match them to the animals. Whereas in the wild, you have to take things as they come and can't easily influence where a bird perches.

Personally, I feel that it's very important that the bird and its perch are in proportion. A small tit will be overwhelmed by a thick branch and will look much better sitting on a slender one. Of course, the branch must offer enough stability to hold the bird's weight. But for the small tit, even a pretty thin one will do. The bigger and bulkier the bird, the more stable and substantial its base can be.

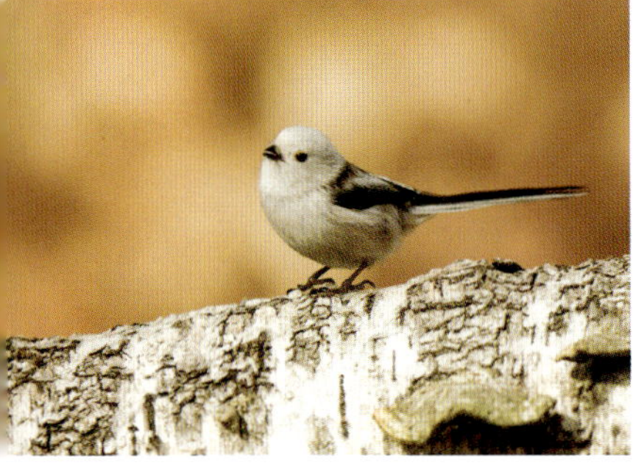

4-44 ▲

Long-tailed tit | Germany | The pretty, long-tailed tit is balancing on the thick trunk of a tree. I don't particularly like the proportions in this image. | 600mm, aperture 5.6, 1/4000 s, ISO 1000

4-45 ▶

Here the proportions are much better: The slender branch of a beech works well with the delicate bird. | 600mm, aperture 5.6, 1/4000 s, ISO 800

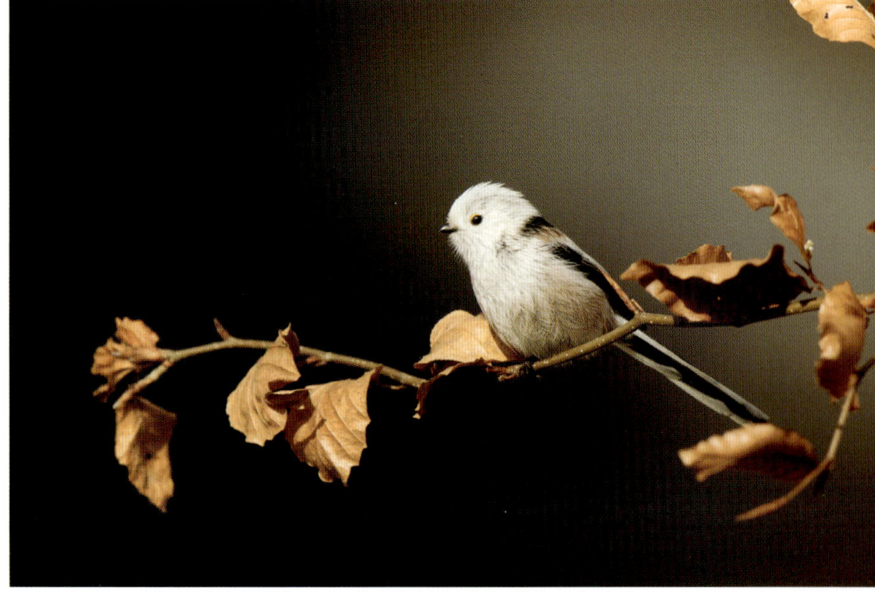

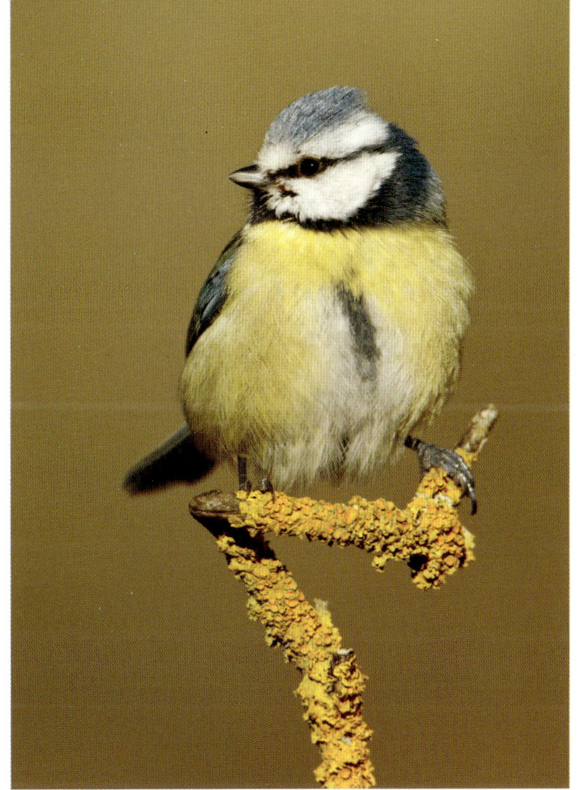

▲ 4-46

Blue tit | Germany | At your own feeding station, you can vary the perches according to your preferences, creating many variations of your motifs. | 600mm, aperture 7.1, 1/800 s, ISO 640

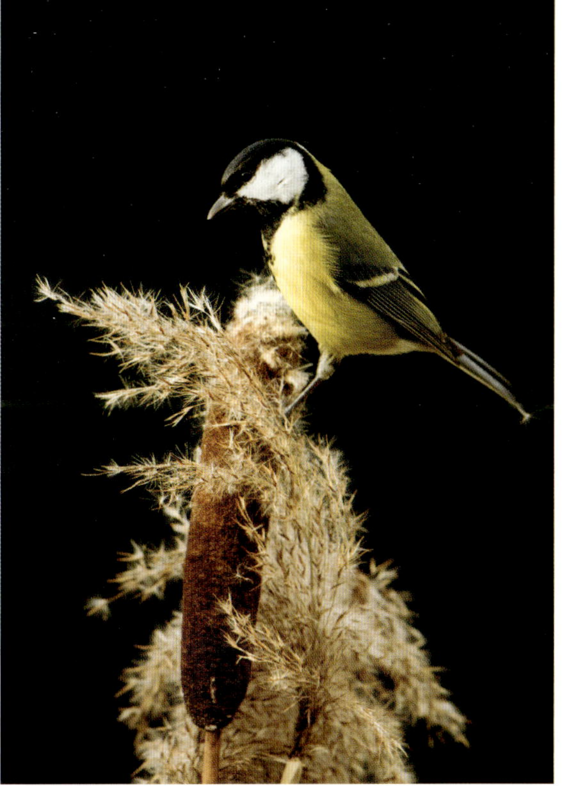

▲ 4-47

Great tit | Germany | Another photo taken at the feeding station. The background is already in the shade, but the sun still illuminates the subject wonderfully. | 600mm, aperture 5.0, 1/800 s, ISO 1250, -1 1/3 exposure compensation

Creating Variety

If you have the good fortune to have your own feeding station where you can take photographs, it's worthwhile to be a bit creative when setting up the branches and twigs that will serve as perches for the birds. Of course, this can take a bit of time, but the effort really pays off! Branches with berries, cones, or dried fruit stalks work well as do branches that are covered with moss or lichen or that have an interesting shape. You can choose reeds, seed heads, evergreen twigs, or branches with fungi.

It's a good idea to put the branches in place the day before a photo shoot so that the birds have time to get used to them before you show up with your camera. This way you can create ever-new photo ideas even at the same feeding station.

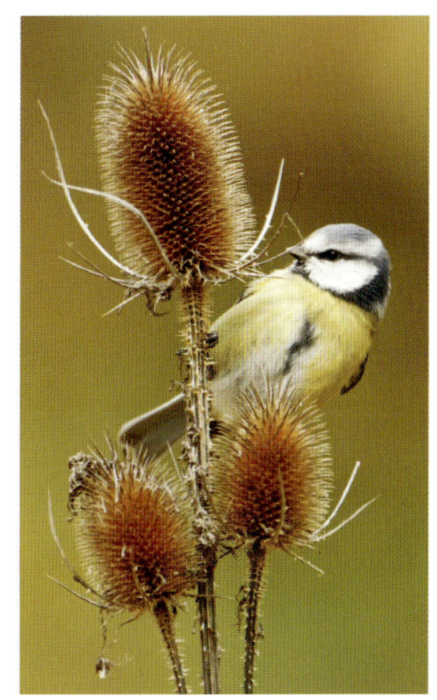

4-48 ▶

Blue tit | Germany | A blue tit is looking for food on a dry seed head. | 500mm, aperture 5.6, 1/400 s, ISO 1600

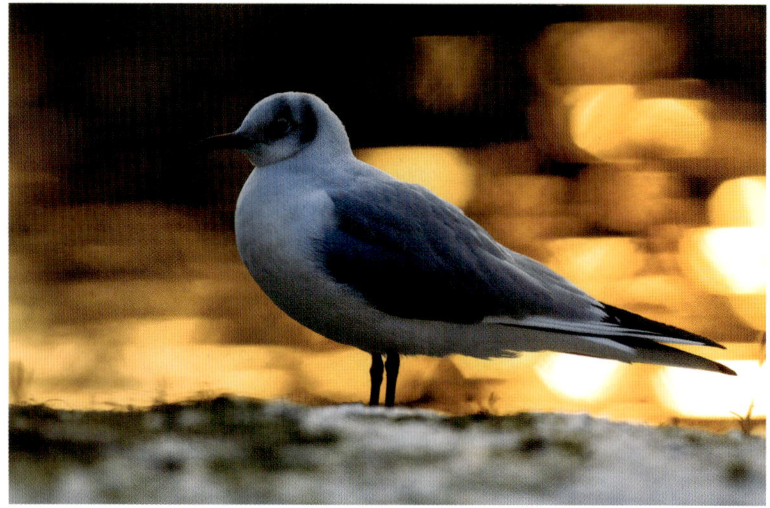

Black-headed gull | Germany | The reflected, golden backlight makes for pretty bokeh. | 500mm, aperture 5.6, 1/1000 s, ISO 1250

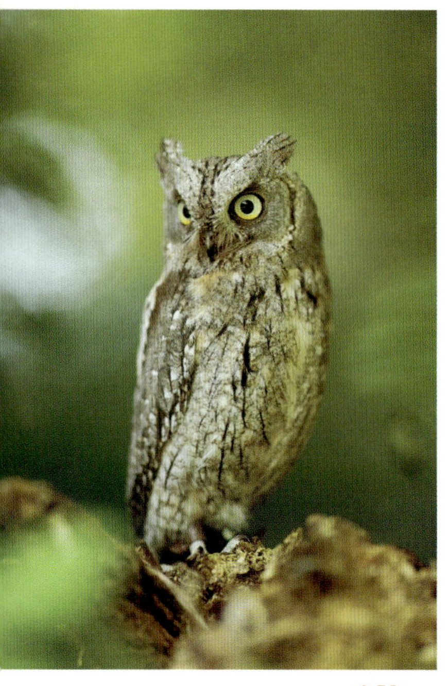

4-50 ▲

Scops owl | Germany | The background blurs beautifully into a soft-focus bokeh. | 135mm, aperture 2.0, 1/1600 s, ISO 1000

4-51 ▶▶

White-faced owl | Germany | Colorful bokeh, created by the blooming Himalayan balsam in the background. | 135mm, aperture 2.8, 1/2000 s, ISO 1000, -1 exposure compensation

Beautiful Bokeh

The word "bokeh" comes from Japanese and means "blur." In photography, it is used to describe the out-of-focus area surrounding the main subject in an image. For "beautiful" bokeh, this area can either be in soft focus or have smooth circles of light.

Beautiful bokeh requires several things. First, you need a fast lens and a relatively wide-open aperture. Secondly, a lot depends on how far the subject is removed from the background. If it's too close, you won't manage to get a nice blur because the background will still be sharp.

For bokeh with circles of lights, it is, of course, necessary to have small lights in the image in the first place. It's impossible to have circles of light with a monochrome background. The light can come from artificial light sources such as streetlamps or the headlights of cars, or you can use natural lights, which is easily done when the sun flashes between trees.

Long fixed focal lengths are particularly good at creating a harmonious background blur and thus an attractive bokeh. When using a zoom lens, it's best to go to the end of the zoom range, even if that means you'll have to take a few steps back.

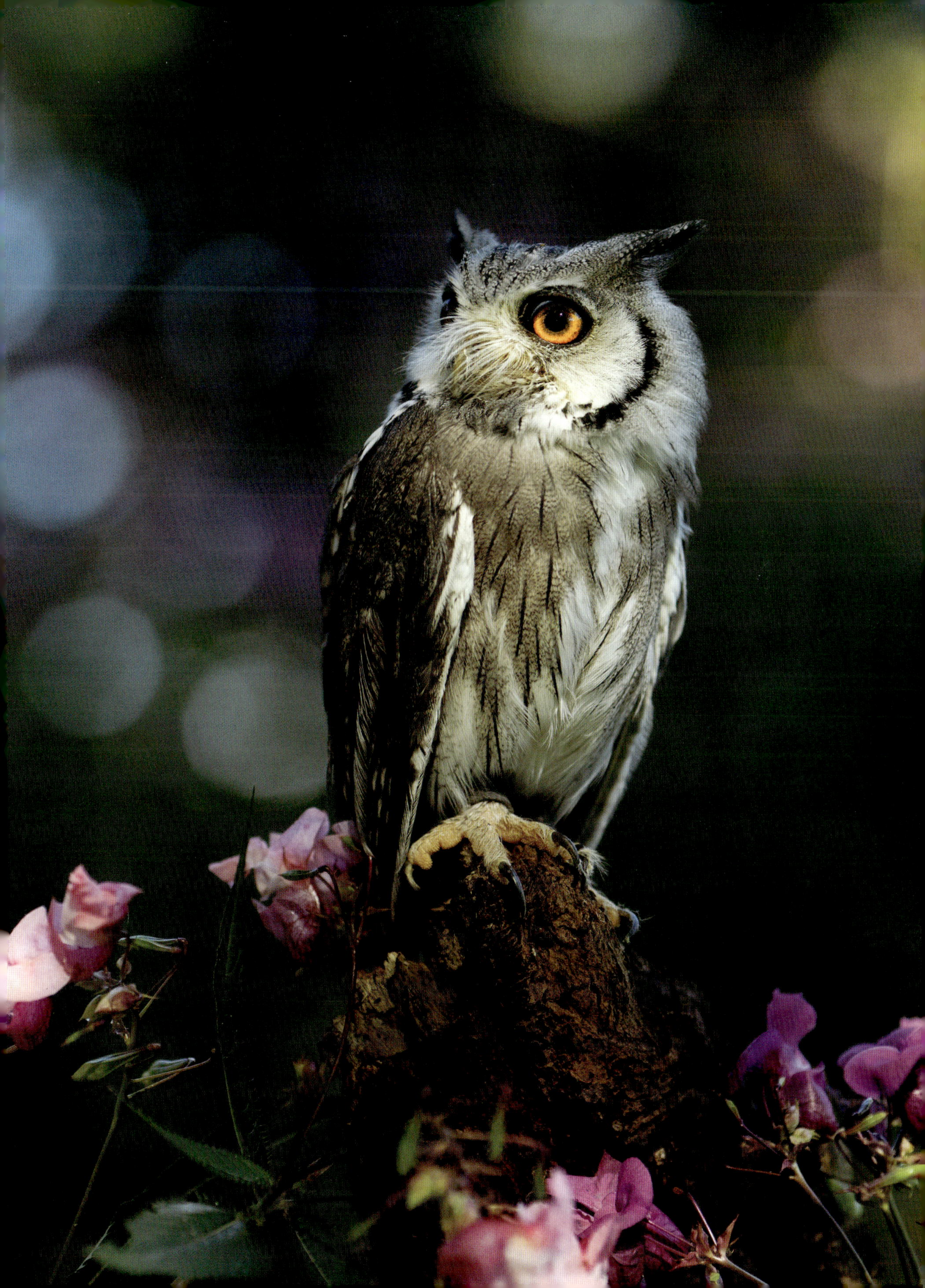

The bokeh is not just about the background, by the way. A blurred foreground can also contribute to the composition and help guide the viewer's gaze to the actual subject. In bird photography, grasses, flowers, leaves, or even snow are particularly good for creating a foreground. It's best to use the lowest possible viewpoint to achieve a nice blur gradient from foreground to background.

Framing

Framing here doesn't mean what you do with a photo once it's been printed but rather how we frame the main subject in the image. A tree cave can work as a frame, for example, or the plants around the bird. It's also possible to photograph through plants in the foreground to create a blurred frame around your subject. Framing creates stability and calm and draws the gaze clearly to the subject.

You can also create a kind of frame when you blend the foreground with the background by blurring them together as described in the previous section.

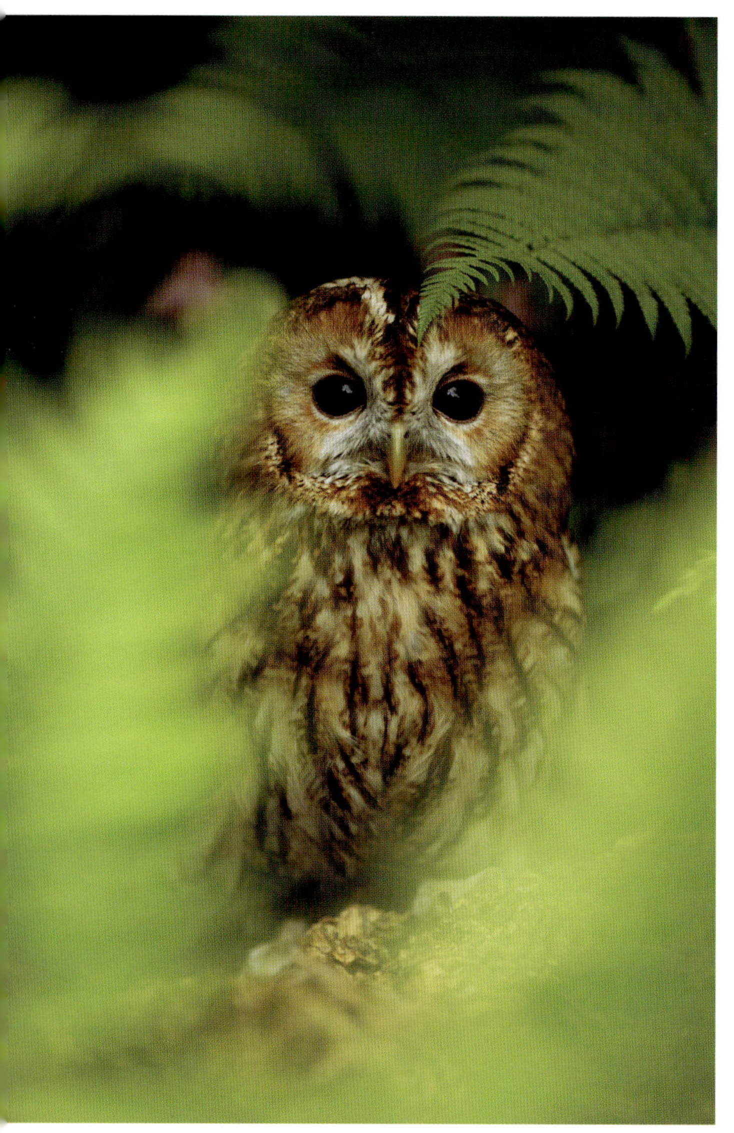

◀ 4-52

Tawny owl | Germany | The fern nicely frames the subject. | 135mm, aperture 2.0, 1/2000 s, ISO 1000, -2/3 exposure compensation

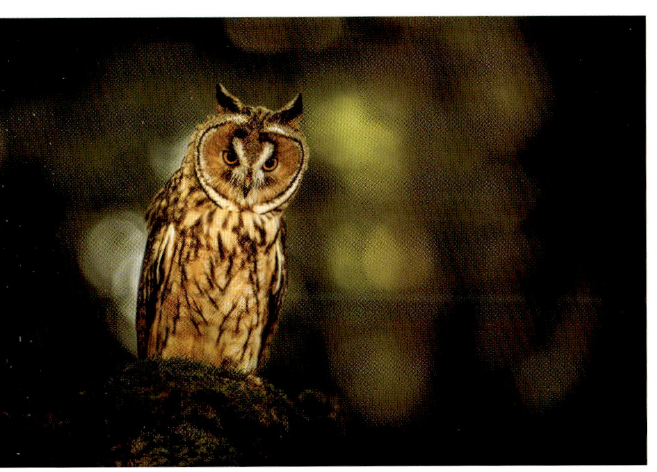

▲ 4-53

Long-eared owl | Germany | Different levels of brightness can work as a frame, too. Here, the dark trees frame the long-eared owl. | 135mm, aperture 2.0, 1/1000 s, ISO 1000

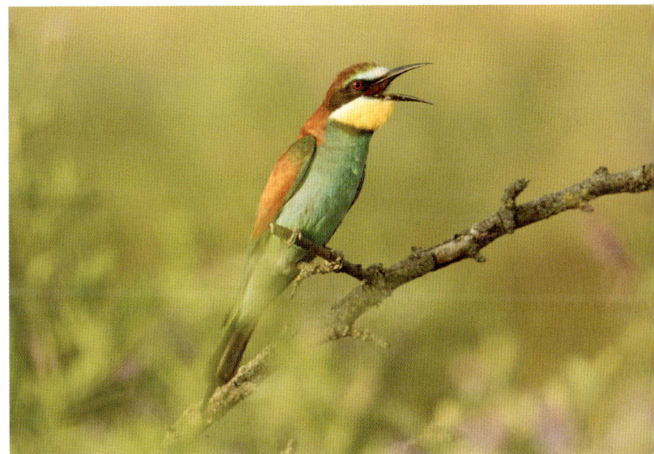

▲ 4-54

Bee-eater | Serbia | The blurred plants in the foreground merge with those in the background, framing the bird. | 600mm, aperture 5.6, 1/1600 s, ISO 800

Pay Attention to the Lines

Some images work particularly well because they contain lines that guide our eyes. They can be blades of grass, branches, clouds in the sky, waves, or colors. But lines can also be created by the bird itself. It may have particularly distinctive coloration, such as the gannet. Or the bird's shape or posture creates a strong line.

If two or more birds are in the picture, they can form a line as well, either through an imaginary connection between them or as a real line in the image.

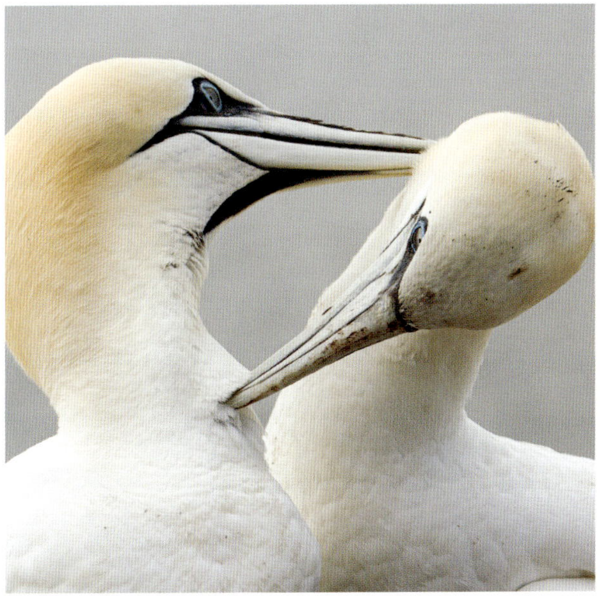

4-55 ▶

Gannet | Bass Rock, Scotland | Some images work primarily through their strong lines. Here, the beak of the left bird draws the eye from the top left to the bird on the right, and then from the bird on the right back again via the beak to the bird on the left. The resulting, almost circular motion creates a good dynamic in the composition. | 80mm, aperture 8.0, 1/1600 s, ISO 400

Desert cardinal | Texas | The lines going diagonal from the bottom left to the top right convey aspiration and optimism. | 840mm (600mm + 1.4x converter), aperture 5.6, 1/1000 s, ISO 1000, +1/3 exposure compensation

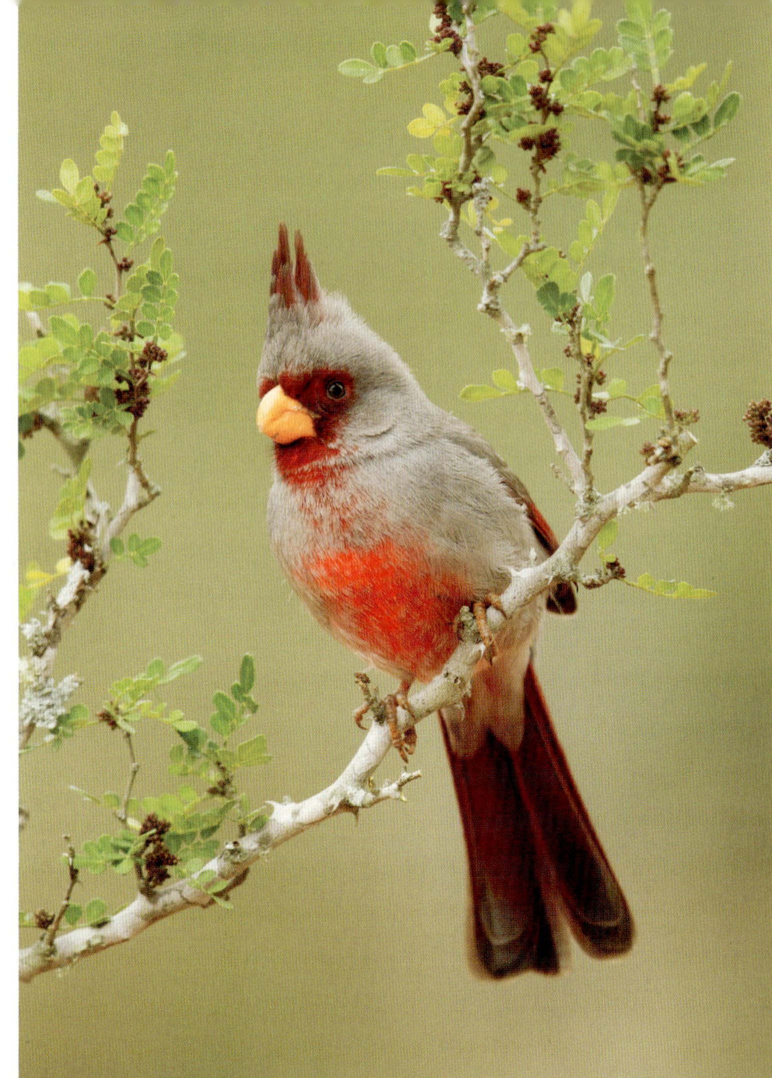

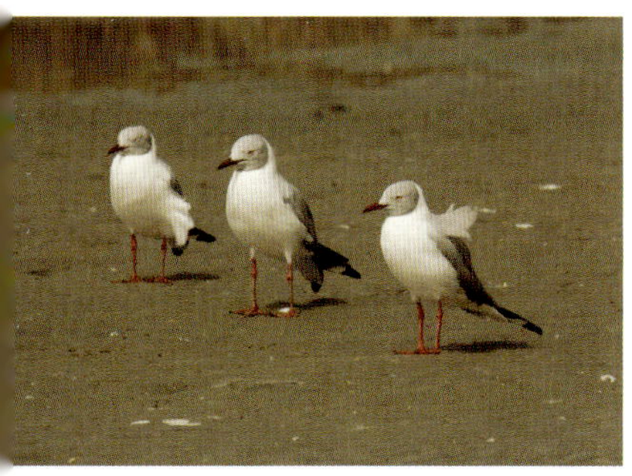

Gray-headed gulls | Gambia | Having several animals in an image can also create a diagonal line. | 840mm (600mm + 1.4x converter), aperture 13, 1/1250 s, ISO 800

Diagonal Lines

Diagonal lines in particular make an image dynamic, especially when they go from the bottom left to the top right. Lines like this give the viewer the impression of "going upward," both in the actual and figurative sense.

It's better if these diagonals don't start and end right at the corners, if possible. Having them emerge a tad above the corner and vanish a little bit or well below the other corner is more harmonious.

Crested tit | Germany | The pretty crested tit perches on a horizontal branch which looks a bit static and boring. | 500mm, aperture 5.6, 1/1000 s, ISO 1250, +2/3 exposure compensation

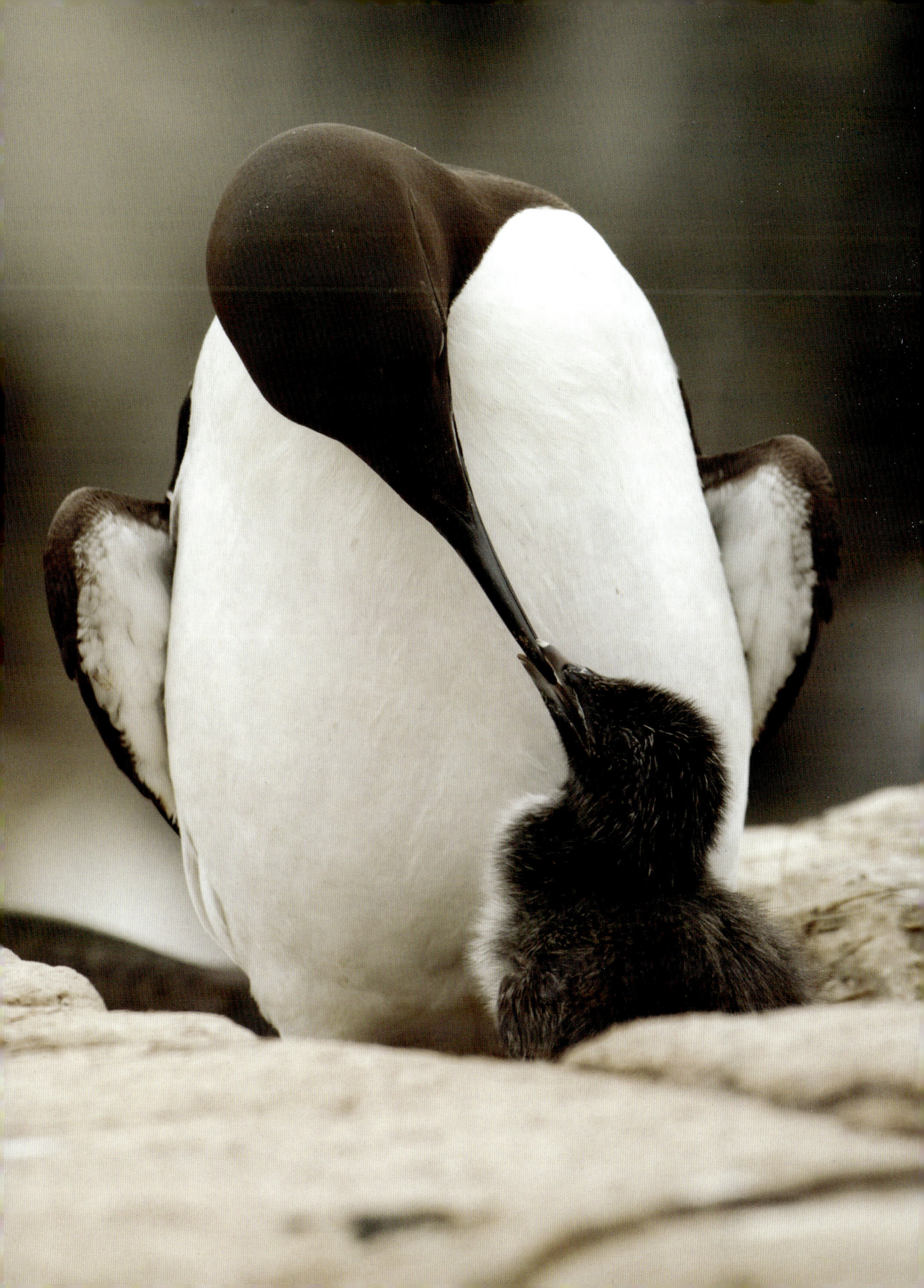

Horizontal Lines

Horizontal lines anchor an image but can also act as a barrier, especially if they run through the center. Pictures with a horizontal perching branch can easily look boring.

If the horizontal line is the horizon, you should avoid having it run through the center. It's better to place it in either the bottom or top third. A horizon in the center tends to look static and divides the image into two halves. Once again, using the rule of thirds creates a more dynamic image.

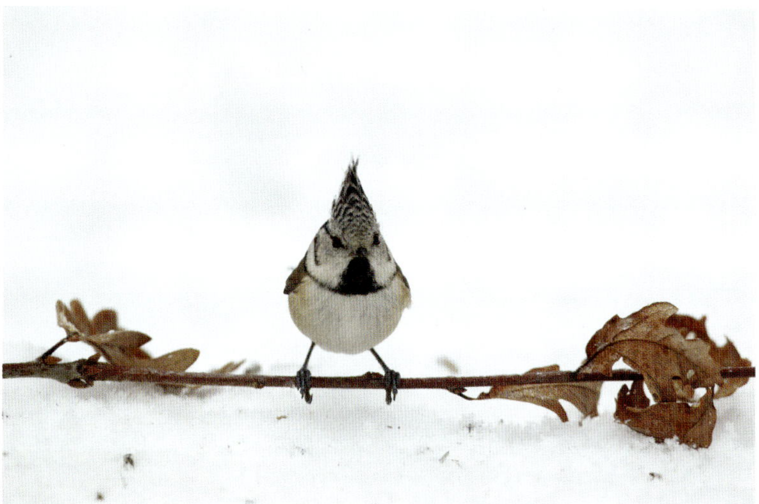

◀ **4-59**

Crested tit | Germany | The pretty crested tit perches on a horizontal branch, which looks a bit static and boring. | 500mm, aperture 5.6, 1/1000 s, ISO 1250, +2/3 exposure compensation

4-60 ▶

Pheasant | The Netherlands | Horizontal lines look harmonious in an image if they are placed in the bottom or top third; the composition quickly becomes boring if they run through the center. | 700mm (500mm + 1.4x converter), aperture 10, 1/640 s, ISO 1000

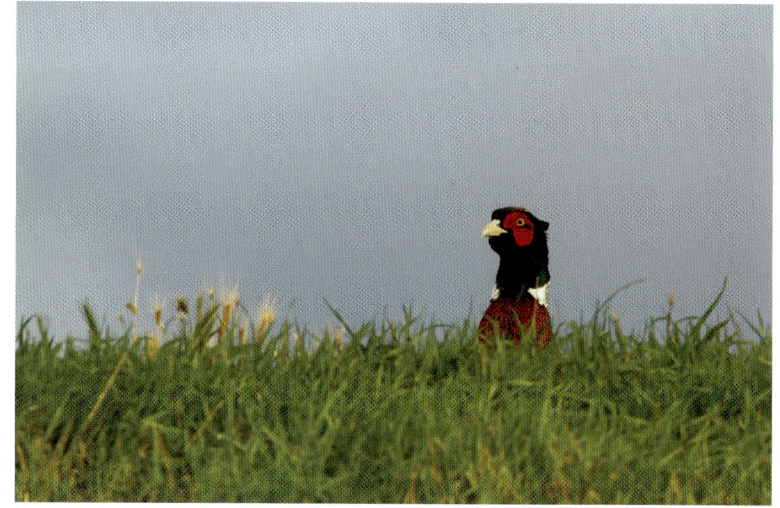

CHAPTER 4

Vertical Lines

Vertical lines that are more on the thin side convey a feeling of height, maybe even lightness. Vertical lines can quickly look a bit unstable. On the other hand, they can also become quite dominant, especially in horizontal photos.

A bird itself can create vertical lines, as can trees, posts, or similar. These can often frame the motif and enhance the image's message.

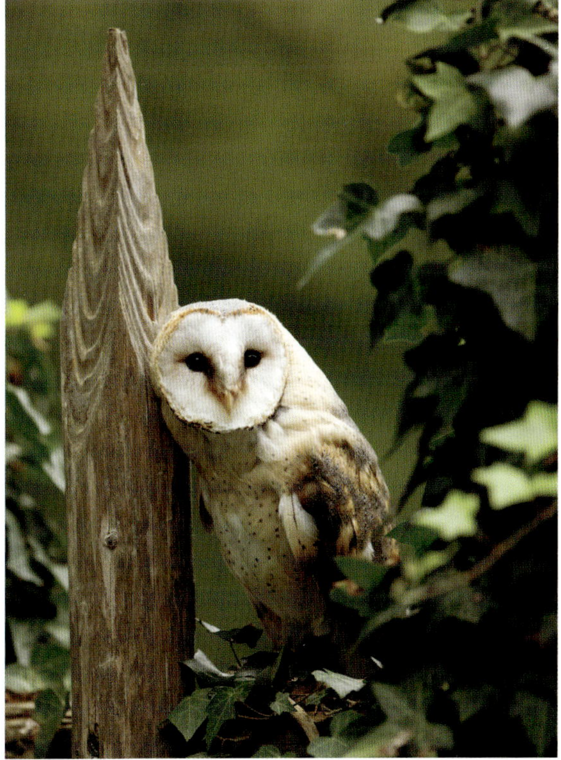

4-61 ▶

Great egret | Florida | The great egret creates a vertical line that looks fragile and a bit unstable. | 500mm, aperture 5.6, 1/8000 s, ISO 500, -2/3 exposure compensation

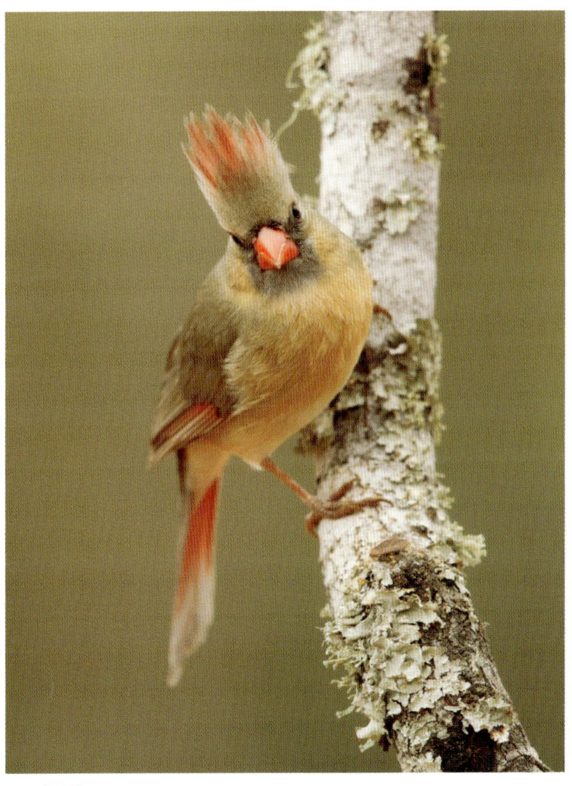

▲ 4-62

Northern cardinal | Texas | This strong-looking branch, on the other hand, is quite dominant. | 840mm (600mm + 1.4x converter), aperture 5.6, 1/1250 s, ISO 1000, +1/3 exposure compensation

▲ 4-63

Barn owl | German Raptor Research Center at Guttenberg Castle, Germany | The two vertical lines formed by the ivy on the right and the post on the left nicely frame this shot. | 300mm, aperture 3.2, 1/1000 s, ISO 1000, -2/3 exposure compensation

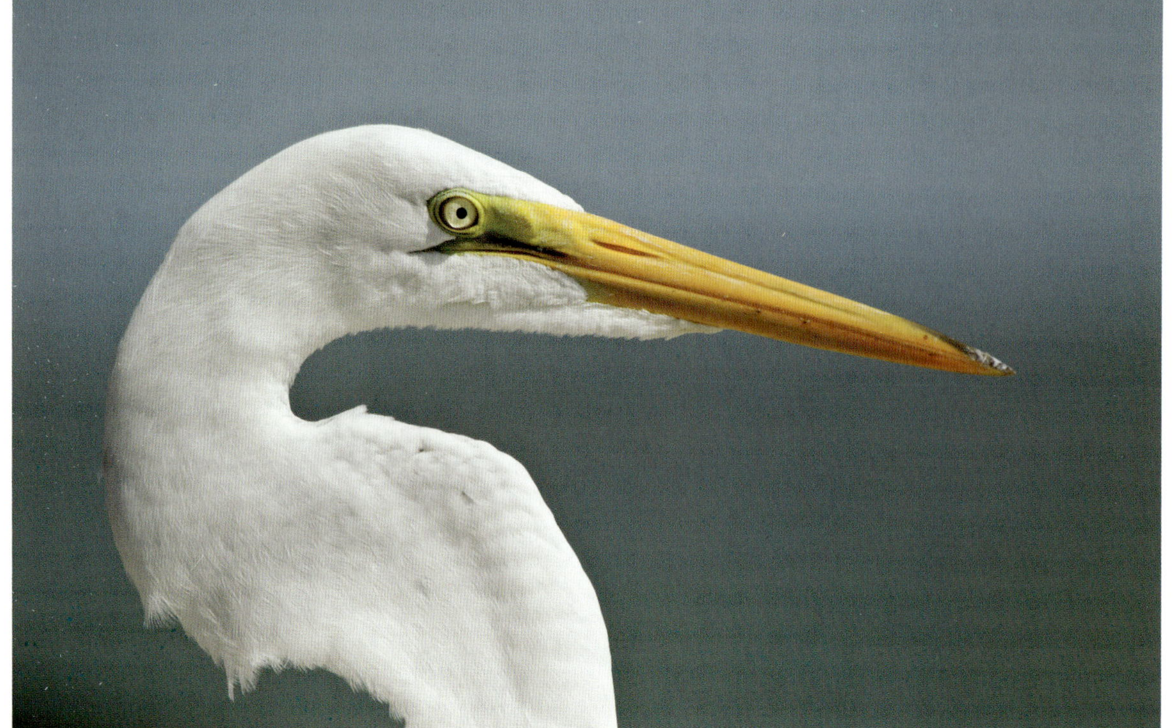

Curved Lines

Lines that curve are particularly interesting, and S-curves especially make us curious. Our gaze follows the line and the "S" conveys tension. We've all seen pictures in which a path winds its way from the front to the back, following the shape of an "S," and we wonder where it goes and what lies behind the next curve.

Of course, in bird photography, it's rather tricky to use this element of composition. But when you succeed, your image will have a very specific effect and you should be aware of it.

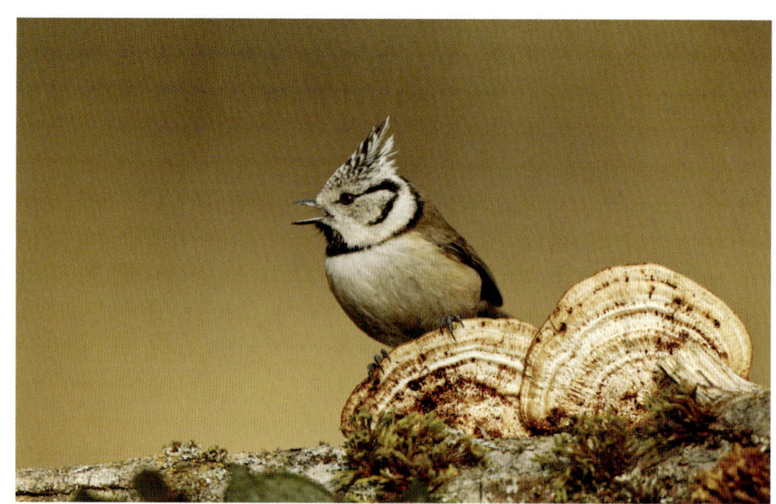

CHAPTER 4

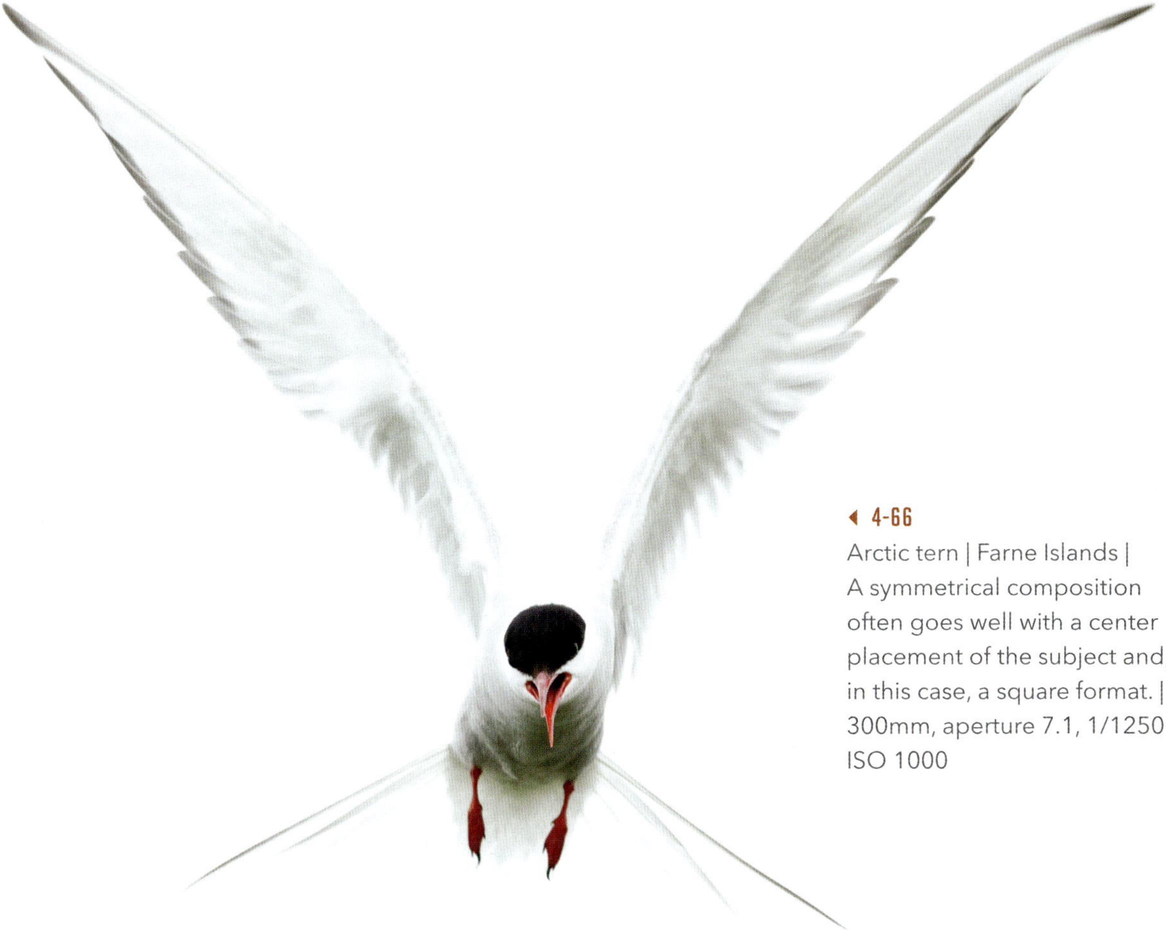

Arctic tern | Farne Islands |
A symmetrical composition
often goes well with a center
placement of the subject and,
in this case, a square format. |
300mm, aperture 7.1, 1/1250 s,
ISO 1000

Symmetry and Asymmetry

Some images achieve their effect mostly through their symmetry. For example, an image of a bird that stretches out both wings at the same angle. In this case, you can even place the subject in the center of the photo and it will work well since it further enhances the symmetry.

Or, maybe there are two or more birds that have almost the same posture. Then you need to put some thought into the depth of field: Do you want all the birds to be in focus or just the one closest to the camera? Shoot with the aperture wide open if you want the birds in the background to blur and close the aperture if you want to get as much depth of field as possible.

Instead of deliberately aiming for symmetry, intentionally asymmetrical images also work well. This option is particularly interesting for photos that show a flock of birds.

Tordalk | Farne Islands |
The slant of the head and the
many diagonals create an
asymmetrical image and give it
more tension than if the head
had been straight. | 500mm,
aperture 9.0, 1/2000 s, ISO 800

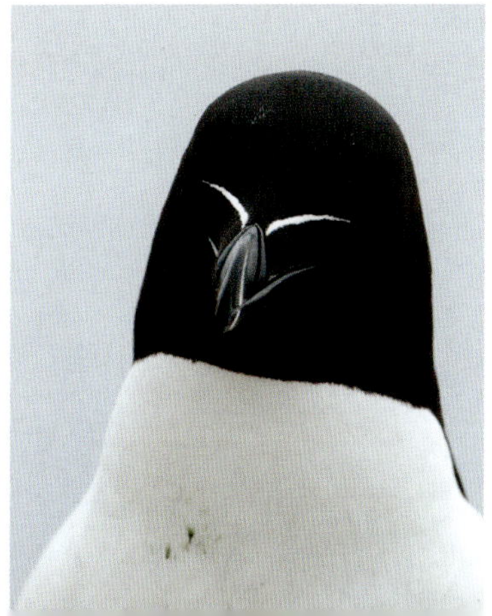

Reflections

I love reflections and whenever I shoot next to water I try to capture some in the photos. But pictures with reflections only work under certain conditions. First, the water must be as calm as possible. Even just a tiny bit of wind and ripples can disturb a reflection.

To capture a reflection, you'll need to break the rule to always go as low as possible when photographing waterfowl. Reflections require a slightly elevated position. But even then, I only go up as much as necessary while still following the "go to the eye level" rule to the extent possible.

Pied avocet | Texel, The Netherlands | Because the water was quite calm, there is a clear reflection of this pretty bird. | 700mm (500mm + 1.4x converter), aperture 8.0, 1/1600 s, ISO 640

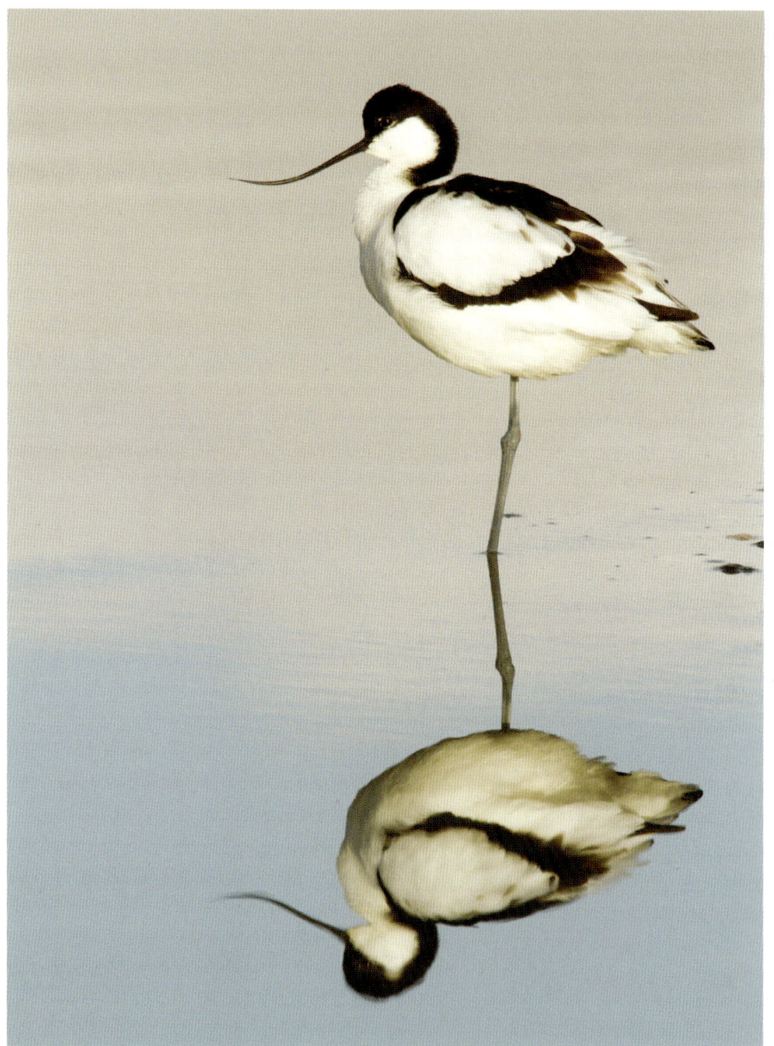

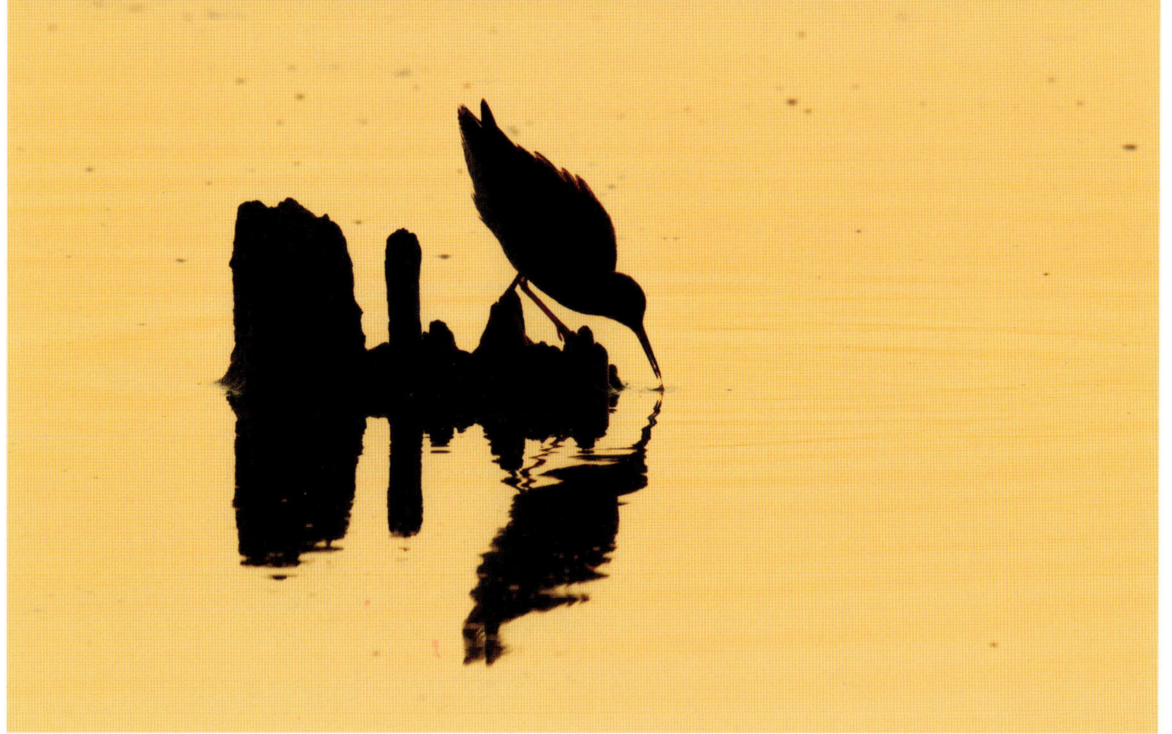

Redshank | Texel, The Netherlands | Reflections are also appealing as silhouettes. And the addition of rocks or something similar often makes for a charming composition. | 840mm (600mm + 1.4x converter), aperture 9.0, 1/1000 s, ISO 1000, +1 exposure compensation

Since reflections create highly symmetrical images, it's often appropriate to deviate from the rule of thirds and place the line dividing the subject and its reflection roughly in the center. Reflections can be particularly attractive if there's more than one bird in the picture or if there are rocks or something similar that also get reflected.

Some places have observation towers that you can access near sites where birds bathe. They often offer the opportunity to photograph beautiful reflections!

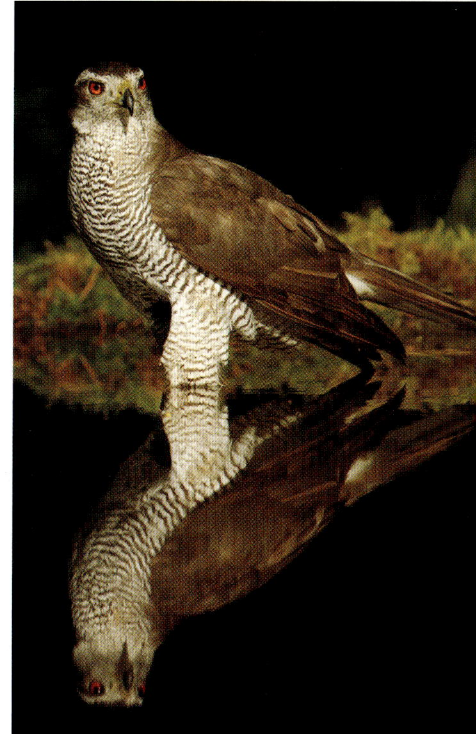

Northern goshawk | Serbia | Observation stands allow you to photograph even shy birds such as the goshawk and its mesmerizing reflection. | 150mm, aperture 4.0, 1/2000 s, ISO 1250, -1 exposure compensation

Two Birds in One Picture

While it's reasonably easy to follow the rules of composition if there's just one bird in your viewfinder, things become much more challenging as soon as there are two or more birds.

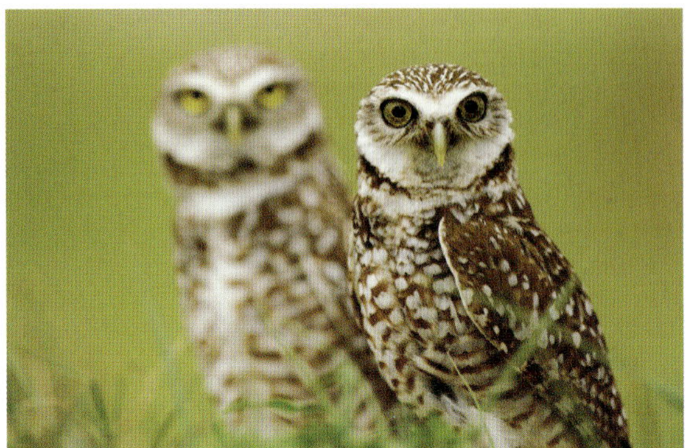

▲ 4-71

Burrowing owls | Florida | Because the aperture was open, there wasn't enough depth of field to get both birds sharp. The autofocus point was set manually on the owl closer to the camera. | 500mm, aperture 5.0, 1/2500 s, ISO 640

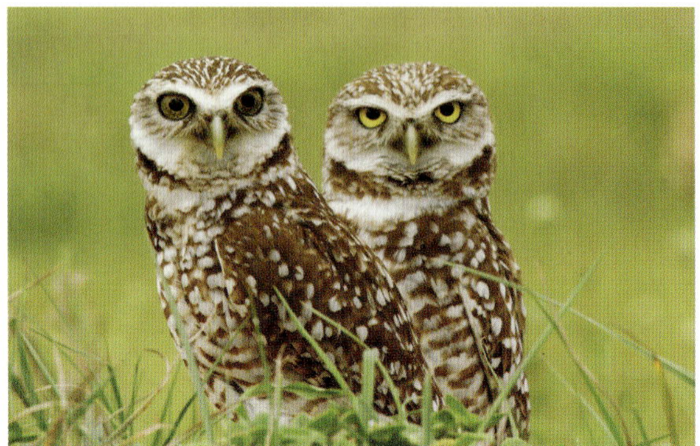

▲ 4-72

Stopping down to f/25 gave the image a tremendous depth of field, but it still wasn't enough to show both birds in equal focus. | 500mm, aperture 25, 1/100 s, ISO 800

Let's first consider the technical aspects: the camera settings you'll need. You might get lucky and both birds are exactly equidistant to the camera. In that case, you can just start shooting without having to pay any particular attention to the settings. But usually, one bird will be closer to the camera than the other. In that scenario, you need to consider the depth of field. The depth of field will be determined by the aperture you choose. It can be as little as a few millimeters with an open aperture, depending on the lens and the distance to the subject. To get both birds sharp, you'll need to close the aperture significantly and decrease it by a few stops. Aperture values of 11 to 16 can be absolutely appropriate.

However, even with aperture values like these, you won't always manage to get both birds equally sharp when using a large telephoto lens and focal lengths of 500mm or 600mm. And sometimes I don't even want to as I might actually prefer to have just one bird in focus. If the birds are interacting, it's usually better to have both sharp. But if they are just sitting and dozing side by side, ideally in a parallel line, it won't detract from the image's message if only one of them is in focus.

CHAPTER 4

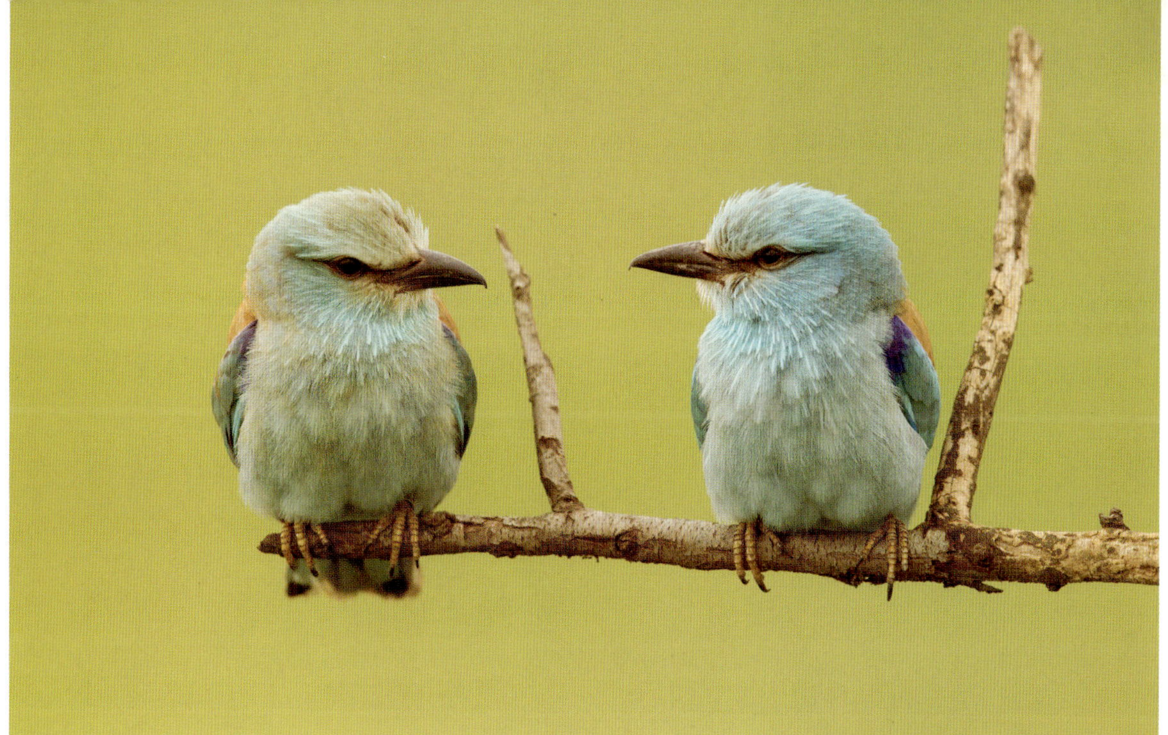

▲ 4-73

European roller | Serbia | If the two birds are just about equidistant to the camera, it's possible to get both sharp even with the aperture wide open. Pictures of two birds are particularly effective when the birds interact. | 600mm, aperture 5.6, 1/125 s, ISO 1600

It matters which bird it is—normally, it should be the one closest to the viewer. That's the best match for how we usually see things and won't confuse our eyes or brain.

It's particularly nice if you manage to capture specific bird behaviors in the photo such as courtship, mating, preening, or even squabbles.

Most of the time, one bird will be on the right and the other on the left side of the image. You will need to move the focus point off-center and place it on the one closer to the camera. This usually leads to a harmonious composition. If the birds are not next to each other but one is behind the other, you should remember to leave enough space in front of the head of the bird closest to the camera to avoid a boxed-in look.

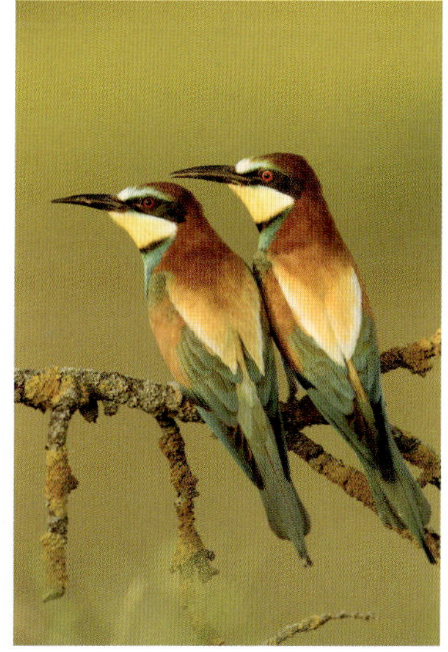

▲ 4-74

Bee-eaters | Serbia | Pairs of birds often synchronize their movements. This can make for interesting photos. | 600mm, aperture 7.1, 1/640 s, ISO 800

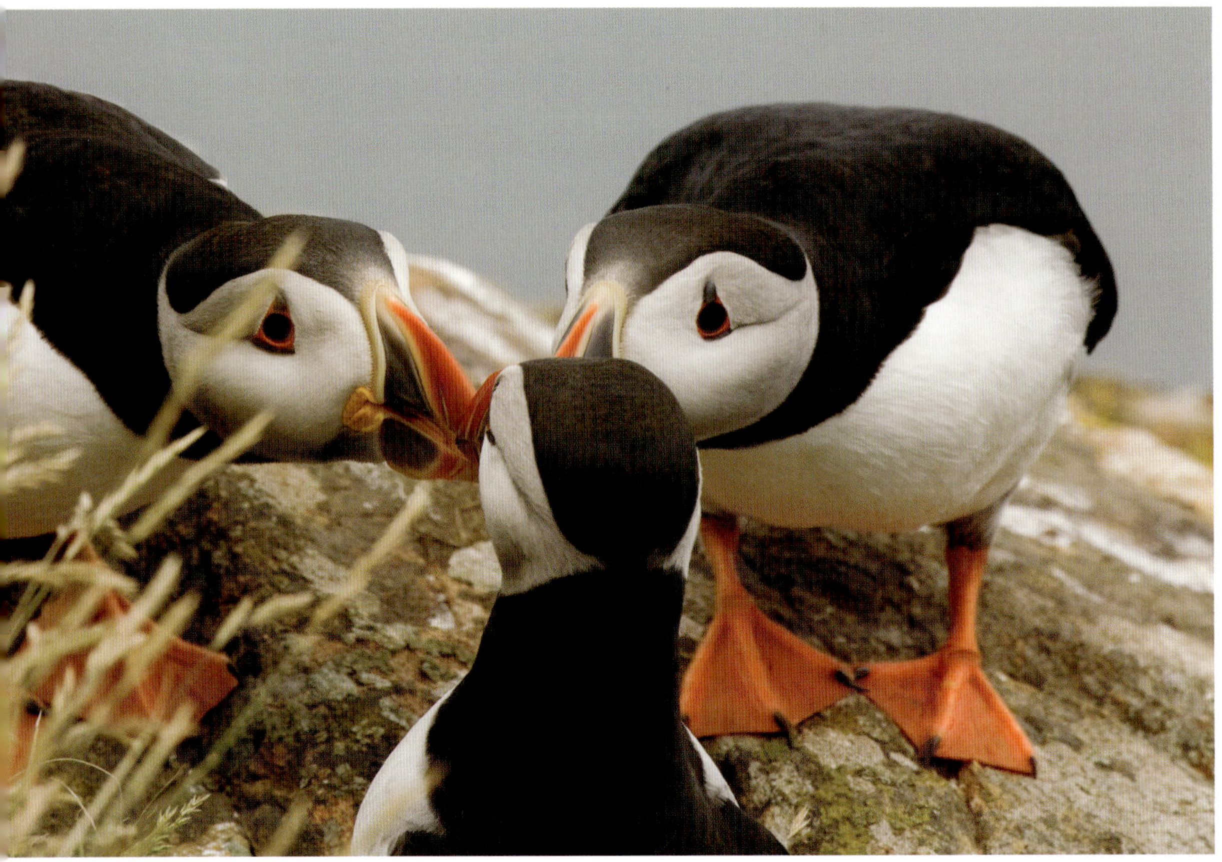

Three Birds

Don't worry, we won't continue to "four birds," "five birds," etc. But it can be a bit of a challenge to successfully bring three birds into a picture and therefore warrants its own section.

The most important thing is that the three birds must interact in some way. If they only happen to be near each other in the photo, it'll look as coincidental as it was and the image won't have much of a message.

Ideally, all three birds are interacting and touching each other. Or maybe two of the birds are interacting and the third one watches. What matters is that there's a connection between them that the viewer can perceive. Similar to what was said in the section on two birds, it's also important that you deliberately pick a depth of field. Do you want all three birds to be in focus? If they are equidistant to the camera, this is easily achieved and you can leave the aperture open. This will also do a great job of separating the birds from the background. On the other hand, if the distance to them varies, you'll

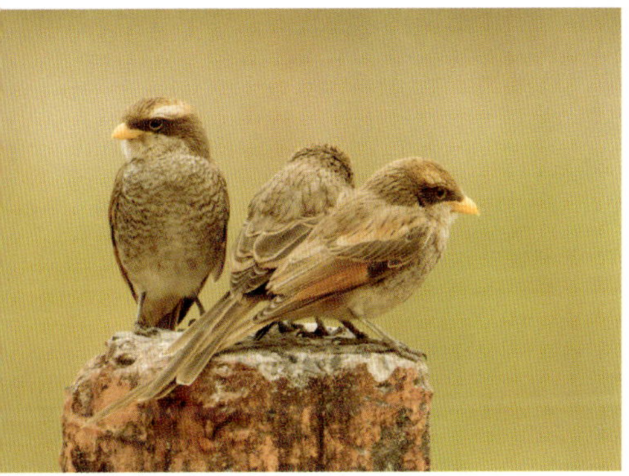

▲ 4-76

Yellow-billed shrike | Gambia | The viewer can't connect to any of these three birds, which makes the image not very attractive. | 840mm (600mm + 1.4x converter), aperture 7.1, 1/1250 s, ISO 1000

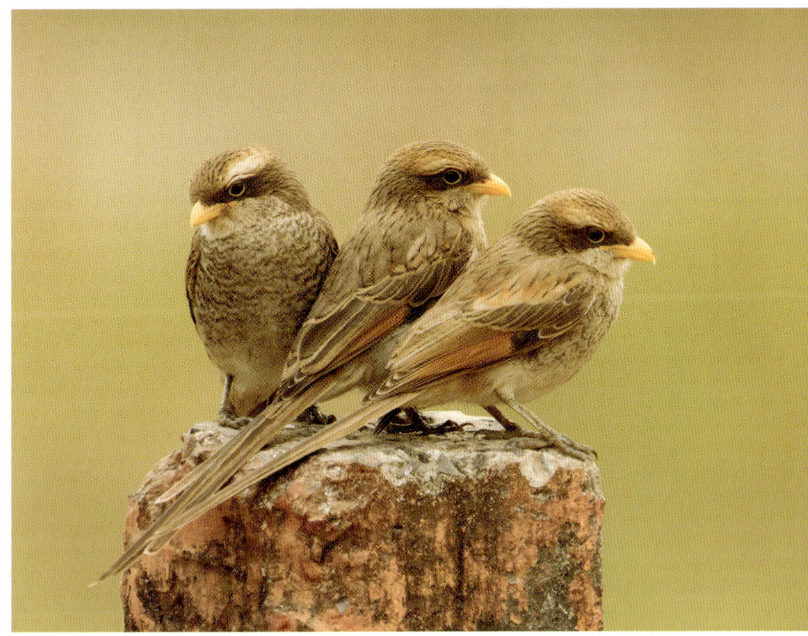

▲ 4-77

A much better picture! All three birds are alert and you can look each in the eye. | 840mm (600mm + 1.4x converter), aperture 7.1, 1/1000 s, ISO 1000

have to close the aperture to get a greater depth of field. Even then it may not be possible to get all three birds in focus if you're using a focal length of 500mm or more and are relatively close to the birds. In that case, you should focus on the bird closest to the camera or on the one that is most important for the image's message.

Groups of Birds

It's more challenging to create a harmonious photograph of a group of four or more birds. If possible, you should avoid cutting off any bird in such a way that only a body without the head stays in the picture. Especially if it's the rear half of a bird's body, it doesn't look very attractive. If you have to cut off part of a bird, cutting the rear and keeping the front is better.

In the fortunate situation that you get to observe a whole group of birds, try to get an overview first. Are they standing in a chaotic jumble? Is there a smaller party that might be a bit apart? Most of the time it's better to focus on a smaller cluster than to haphazardly photograph the whole group. Observe the assembled birds carefully and take your time photographing them.

Audouin's gulls | Morocco |
A very unstructured shot of
this group of Audoin's gulls.
No birds were cropped, but
you also can't make eye contact with the gulls and their
arrangement is boring. | 840mm
(600mm + 1.4x converter),
aperture 7.1, 1/2500 s, ISO 640,
+2/3 exposure compensation

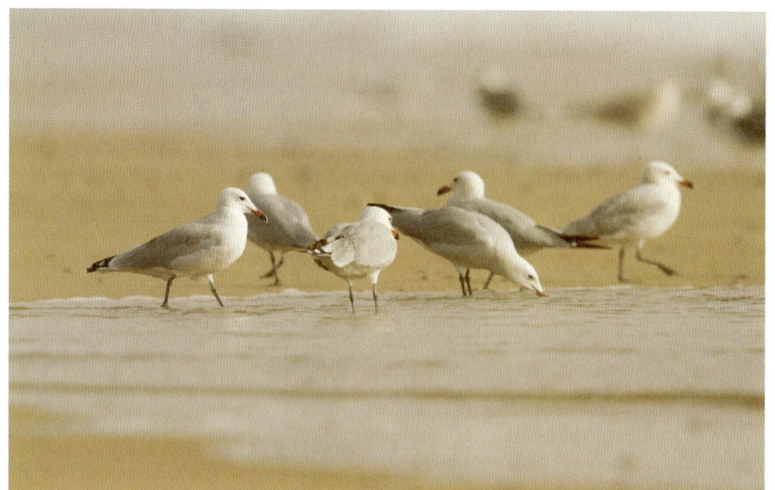

Here, the birds are positioned
much better. The gaze of the
viewer travels along the diagonal
line and lingers on the bird
closest to the camera. It's the
only bird that is in focus, the
others are blurred. | 840mm
(600mm + 1.4x converter),
aperture 6.3, 1/3200 s, ISO 640,
+1/3 exposure compensation

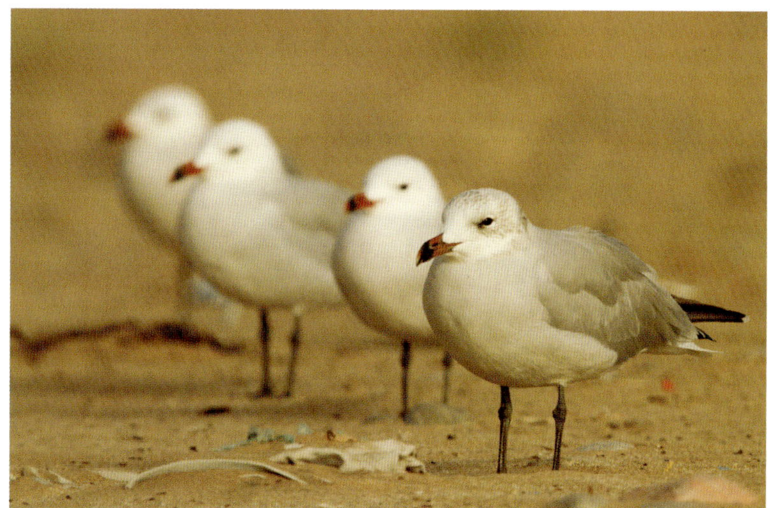

Sometimes, having an abundance of birds in front of your lens is actually hard! Think carefully about the depth of field you want to achieve.
Do you want all the birds to be in focus as much as possible, or do you
want one bird to be sharp while the others are blurred? Depending on
what you decide, close the aperture or open it as wide as possible.

Also, when photographing a group, make sure that the first bird
in the frame has enough space in front of its head and that the whole
group has some space in the frame in the direction of their gaze.

If you have a choice, pick an odd number of birds to include in
the picture. Odd numbers create more tension in a photo than even
numbers.

CHAPTER 4

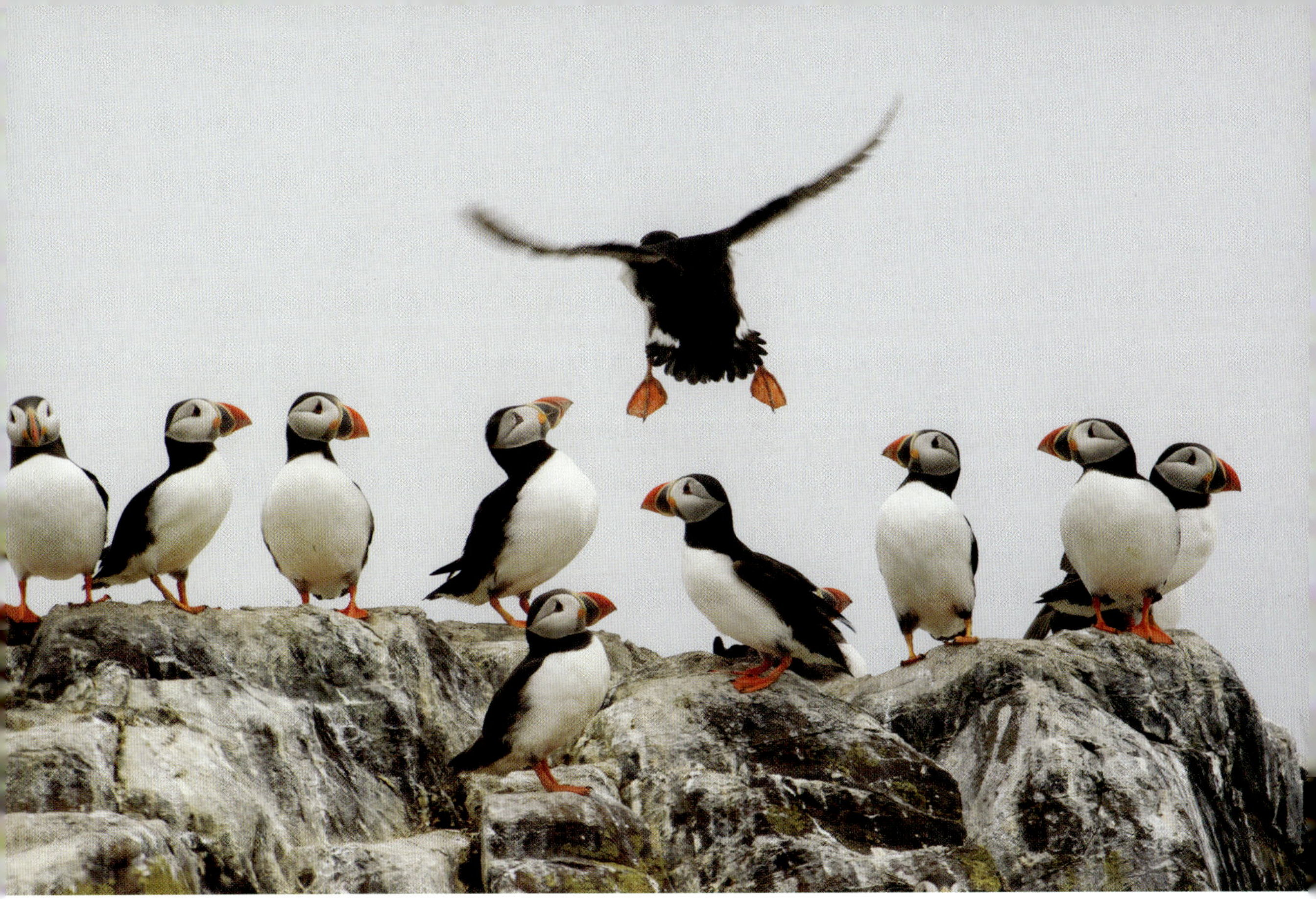

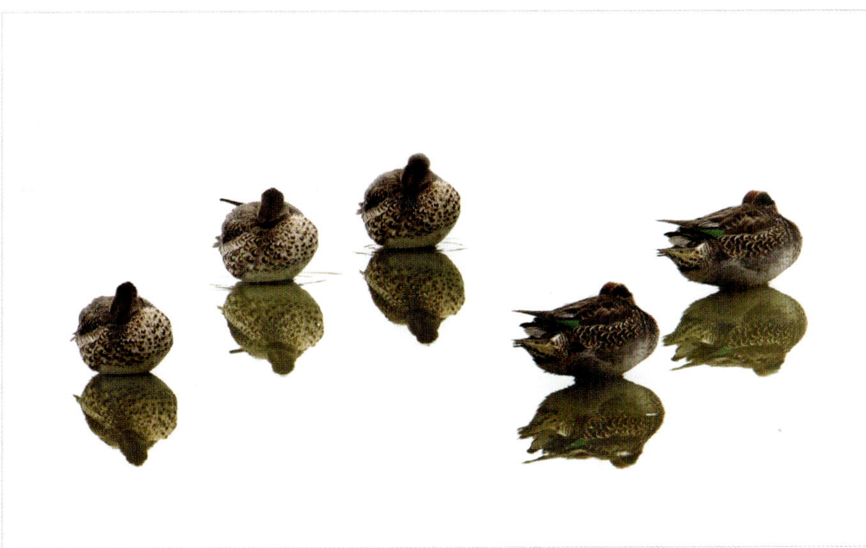

Puffin | Farne Islands | The birds are watching the approach of a puffin that is looking for a free landing spot. One bird at the far left has been cropped but it's hardly noticeable. All are pretty equidistant from the camera, bringing them largely into focus at f/10. | 500mm, aperture 10, 1/400 s, ISO 1000, +1 exposure compensation

◀ 4-81

Eurasian teals | Iceland | The fact that it's an odd number of birds, the way they're arranged, and the reflection are the main reasons that this photo works. | 700mm (500mm + 1.4x converter), aperture 8.0, 1/640 s, ISO 1000, +1 1/3 exposure compensation

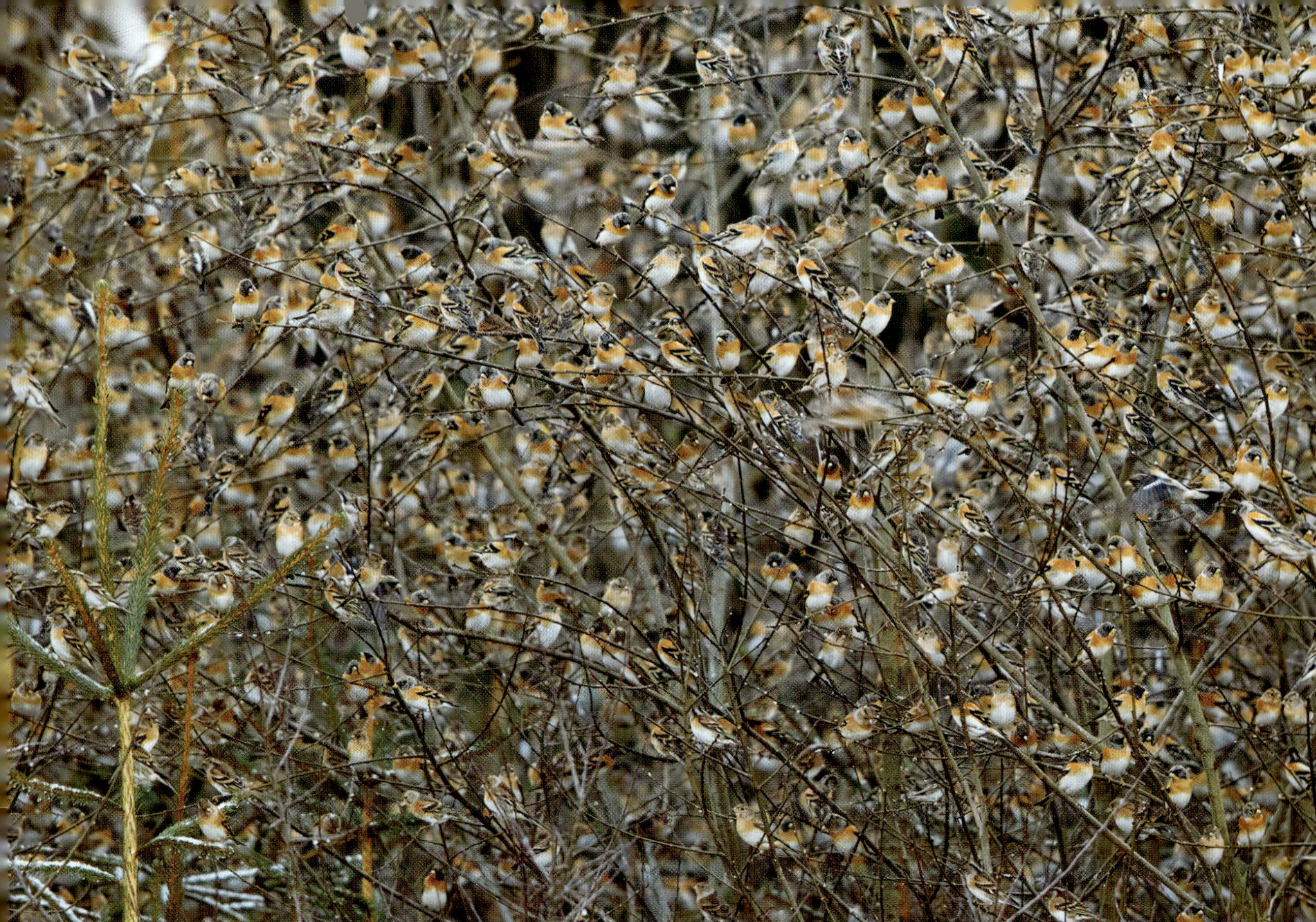

Brambling | Germany | Every few years, there's an invasion of bramblings and several thousands of these birds gather at their roosting sites at dusk. The photo shows a tree that has been completely taken over by roosting bramblings. It was late in the day and the light was low, so I couldn't close the aperture any further. | 600mm, aperture 5.0, 1/200 s, ISO 1600

A Whole Flock

What is the difference between a group and a flock? By a whole flock, I mean a really large group that easily fills the entire frame. One example are starlings, which tend to gather in large flocks at known roosting sites in the fall. Or cranes that arrive by the hundreds at their roosting places.

In a case like this don't even try to avoid cropping birds—it's impossible. With this kind of picture, my only goal is to show off the sheer number of birds. I try to fill the entire image with birds because that's what usually works best for large groups. And I aim to get as many of the birds as sharp as possible, which means I'm definitely stopping down, preferably to f/11 or even f/16 if there's enough light.

Most of the time when you see a large flock of birds they will be in flight. I will talk more about taking aerial shots in section 4.5, "Achieving Success with Bird-in-Flight Photography," starting on page 115.

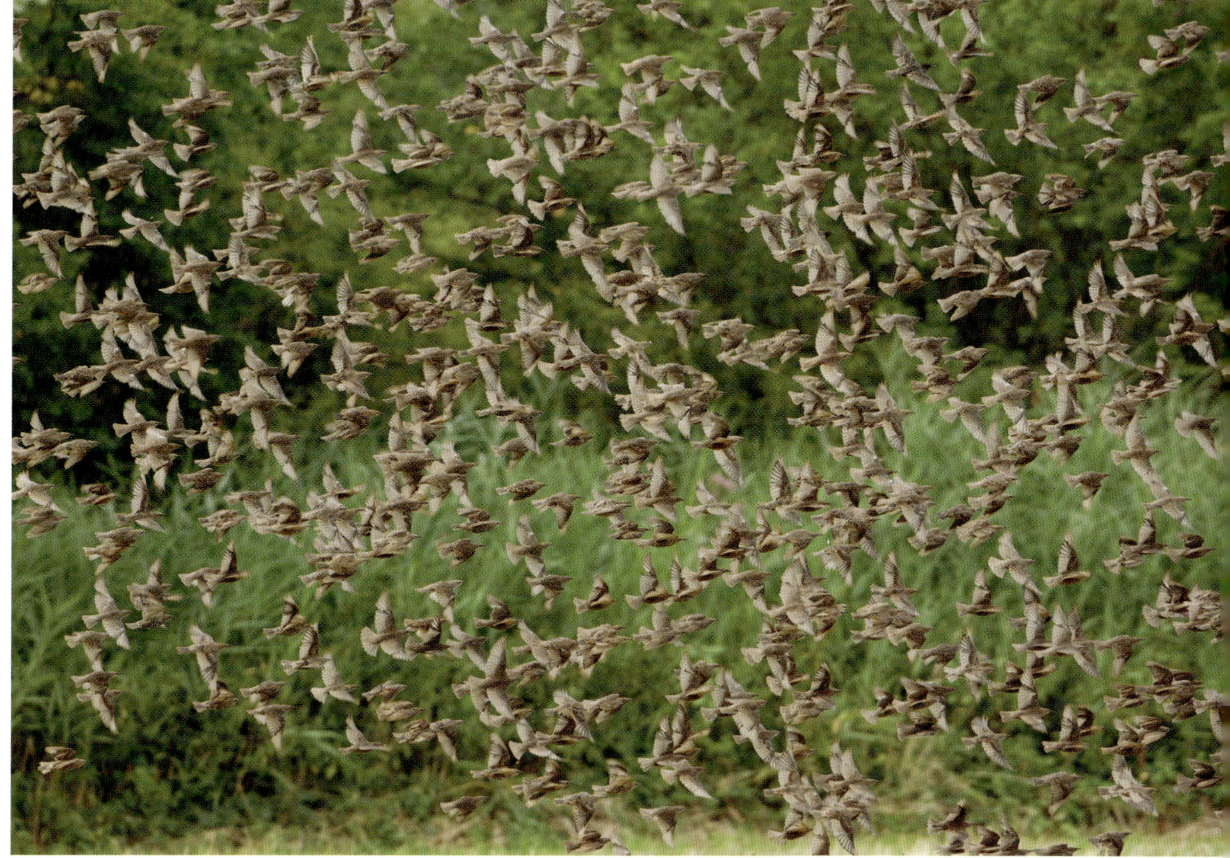

4.2 Sharp and Blurry Images

Sharp Images

The most beautiful composition is wasted if the subject isn't sharp. When taking pictures of animals or people, it's the eyes that must be sharp. Whether the tip of the beak also has to be sharp depends on the taste of the viewer, but blurry eyes are completely unacceptable.

Unfortunately, in order to make sure that the eyes are really in focus, we must interfere a bit with the camera's autofocus system. As a rule, the camera doesn't "know" which part of the image you want to be in focus. At least, not unless you have a camera with an automatic eye detection feature. Usually, the camera focuses on an area with strong contrasts. In a portrait, that might be the eyes, but it can just as easily be the beak. This means that you must manually set the point on which the camera should focus, the autofocus point. It isn't rocket science, and every manual will tell you how to do it. It's the only way to ensure that the focus is exactly where you want it to be! Setting the autofocus area must become second nature to any bird photographer, and the more you shoot this way, the easier it will be for you to change the autofocus area as quickly as the bird turns its head, for example.

▲ 4-83

Starlings | Germany | You can observe and photograph flocks of starlings arriving at their communal roosts in the evenings. It's an impressive spectacle…. | 500mm, aperture 5.6, 1/640 s, ISO 640, -1/3 exposure compensation

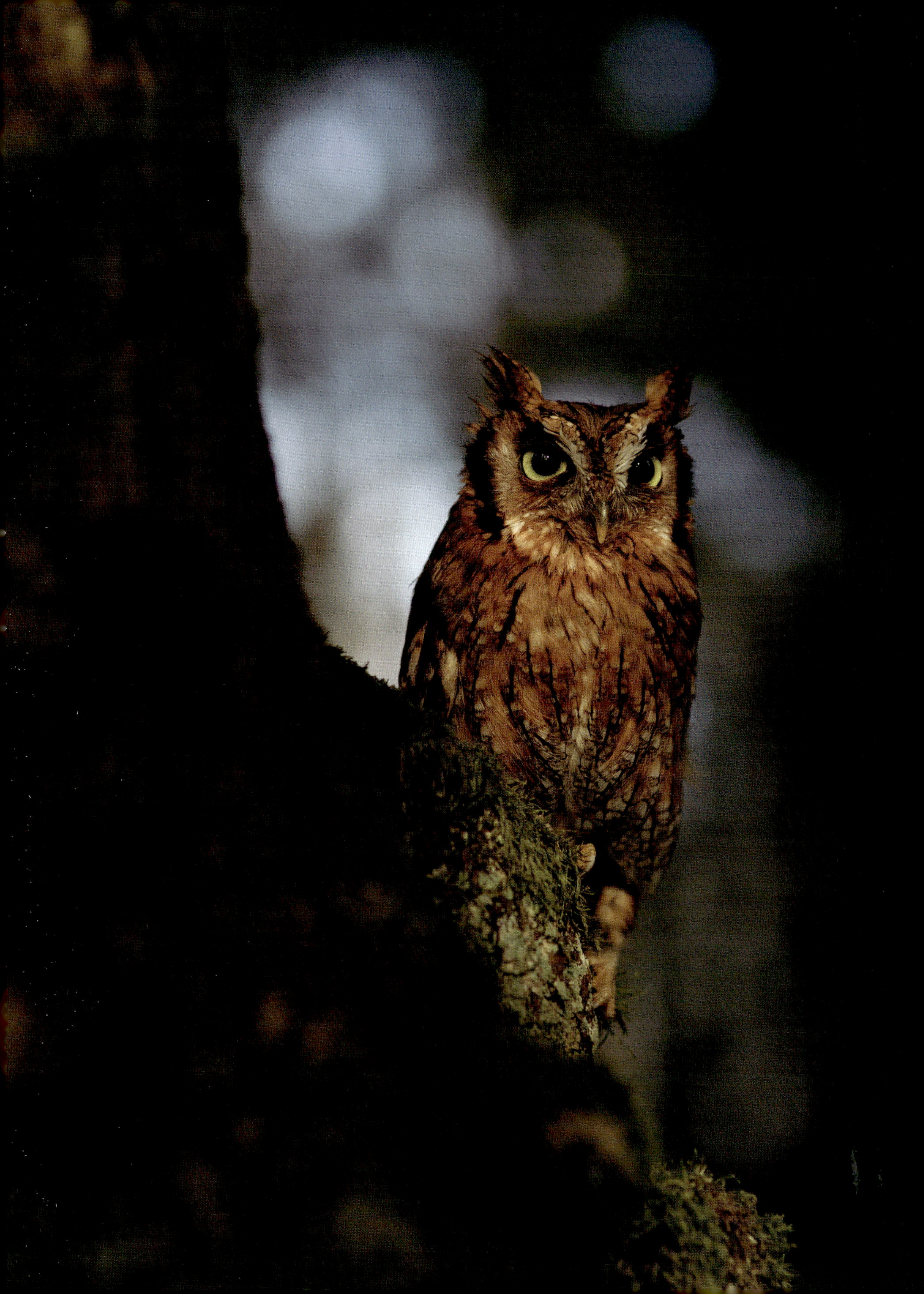

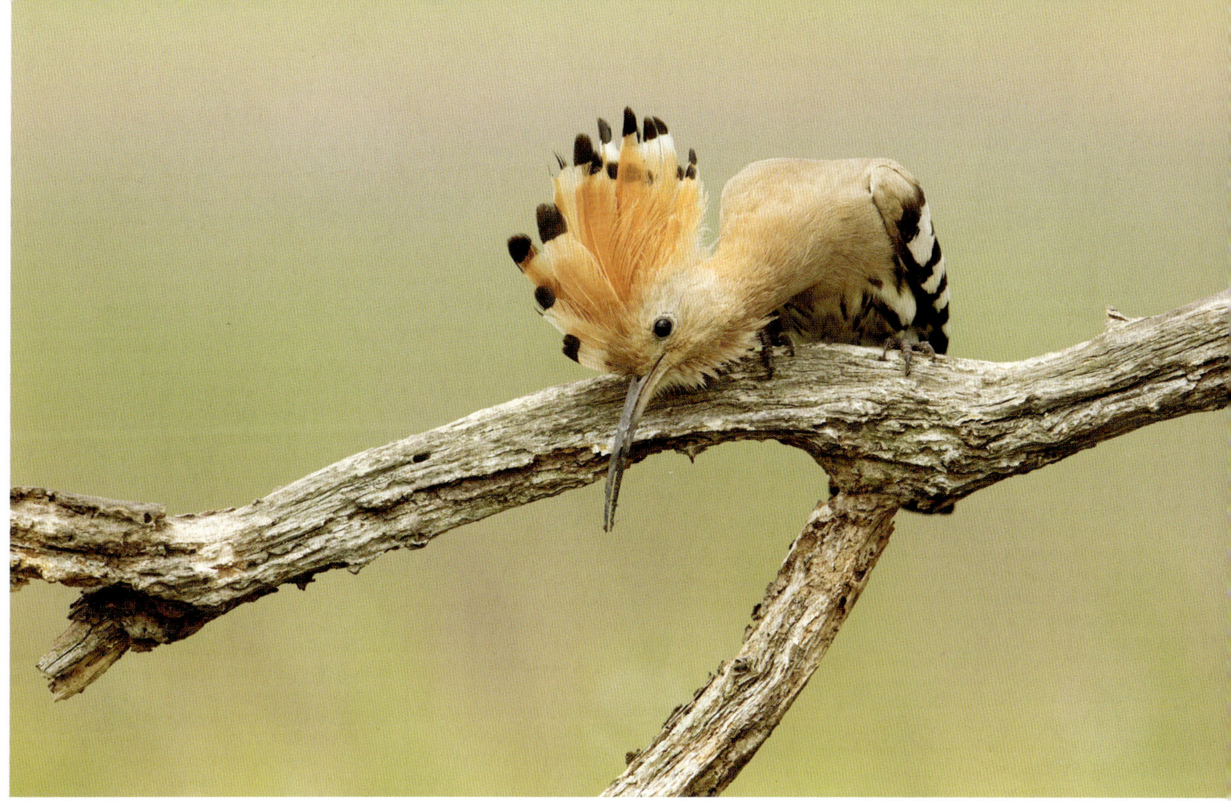

The next important camera setting that you'll need to activate is focus tracking. Focus tracking means that the camera will keep the focus on a certain point once it's been set, even if the bird should move. Many beginners shoot portraits without focus tracking and only use it to photograph birds in flight. But don't forget that birds are always in motion, even while you are doing portraits, and just an inch back and forth will cause blurring if the camera doesn't constantly adjust the focus to account for this movement! I'd keep this setting activated at all times when photographing animals and your manual will tell you how to do that.

Hoopoe | Serbia | The eye is perfectly in focus. It means that the viewer can have direct and intense eye contact with the subject. | 600mm, aperture 6.3, 1/1600mm, ISO 500, -1/3 exposure compensation

◄ 4-85

Tropical screech owl | Germany | In animal portraits, the eyes must be sharp. The foreground and background can be blurry. | 85mm, aperture 2.2, 1/1600 s, ISO 400

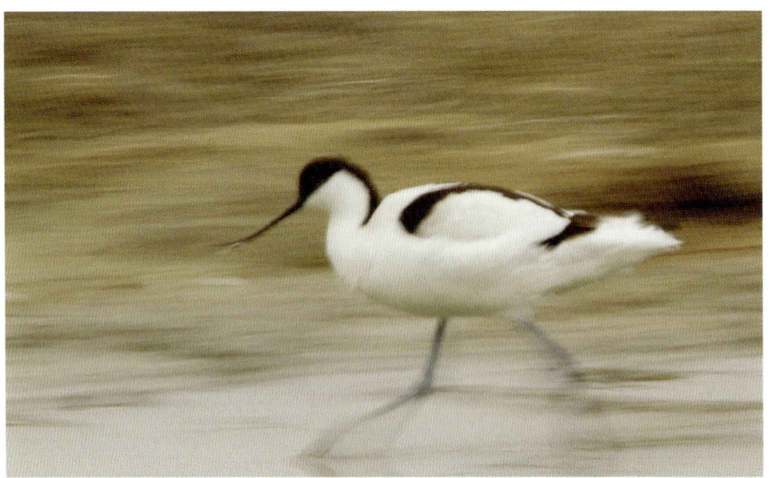

Exposure Time

If the shutter speed is too slow, two things can cause an image to be blurry: camera shake or motion blur. It's easy to spot the difference: If an image is blurry because the photographer failed to keep the camera steady, the entire picture is out of focus. A camera shake can happen very easily when you shoot with a handheld camera and a large telephoto lens. But even smaller, lighter lenses require adjustments in the shutter speed. Of course, photographers differ in how much exposure time they can manage without blurring, but there's a golden rule which is based on the focal length of the lens. Generally speaking, the average photographer can hold a lens with a focal length of 200mm still for a shutter speed of 1/200 s or less, but can only manage a much shorter 1/500 s for a 500mm lens. Of course, there are exceptions to every rule. If your equipment has image stabilization, the shutter speed can be a lot slower and not cause blurring. With a tripod, blurring is almost impossible, at least unless you do long exposure photography.

The other possible cause of blurring is motion blur. This, too, is caused by a too-slow shutter speed but in this case, it's not the photographer who blurs the image but the subject, by moving too fast for the selected exposure time. You can tell because the subject is out of focus but the background or any other static area in the image stays sharp. This is particularly an issue with in-flight photography but can also happen in portraits if the exposure time is too long, of course.

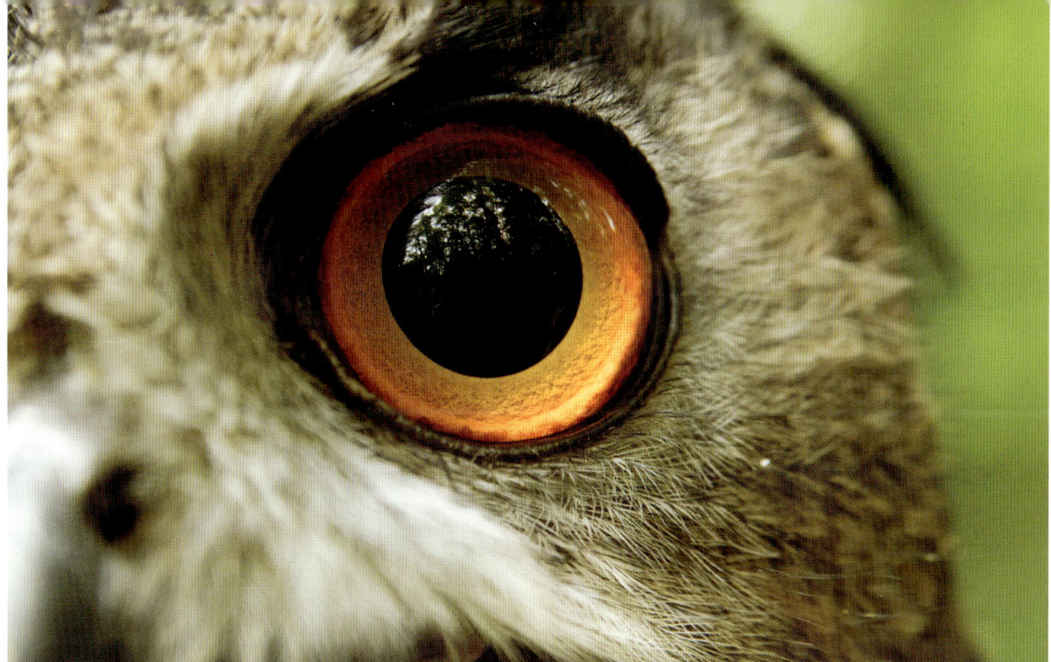

It's possible to select the exposure time manually by setting the camera to shutter priority mode. Enter the ISO value and the shutter time and the camera automatically selects the aperture that will give you the correct exposure (i.e., brightness of the image). But personally, I take a different approach: I set the aperture manually and then adjust the ISO until I get the right shutter time. Why? The aperture determines the depth of field. I prefer a shallow depth of field because I like the background and foreground to be blurry. Only the subject should be sharp. This requires a wide-open aperture, which I deliberately select and set. Then I set the ISO value and increase it until I get the shutter speed I need. For portraits, I usually choose a shutter speed of at least 1/400 s although it's generally not a problem to go down to 1/200 s in low light. I've even successfully taken pictures at 1/30 s. But in that case, you should take several photos and later choose the one that is as sharp as you want it because many will show signs of camera shake or motion blur. We'll discuss the shutter speed needed for in-flight shots in section 4.5, "Achieving Success with Bird-in-Flight Photography," starting on page 115.

Personally, I feel fine going up to ISO values of 1000 or 1600 on my equipment, since modern cameras still produce excellent image quality in this range. If you're using an older camera, you might have to experiment to see how far you can go before you get unwanted noise in your photos.

▲ **4-87**

Eagle owl | German Raptor Research Center at Guttenberg Castle, Germany | This picture was taken in a dense forest. Despite an ISO value of 2500, 1/50 s was the fastest shutter speed I could get with f/5.6. But the sharpness is good and the picture isn't blurry. However, other images from that series were blurred. | 75mm, aperture 5.6, 1/50 s, ISO 2500, -1/3 exposure compensation

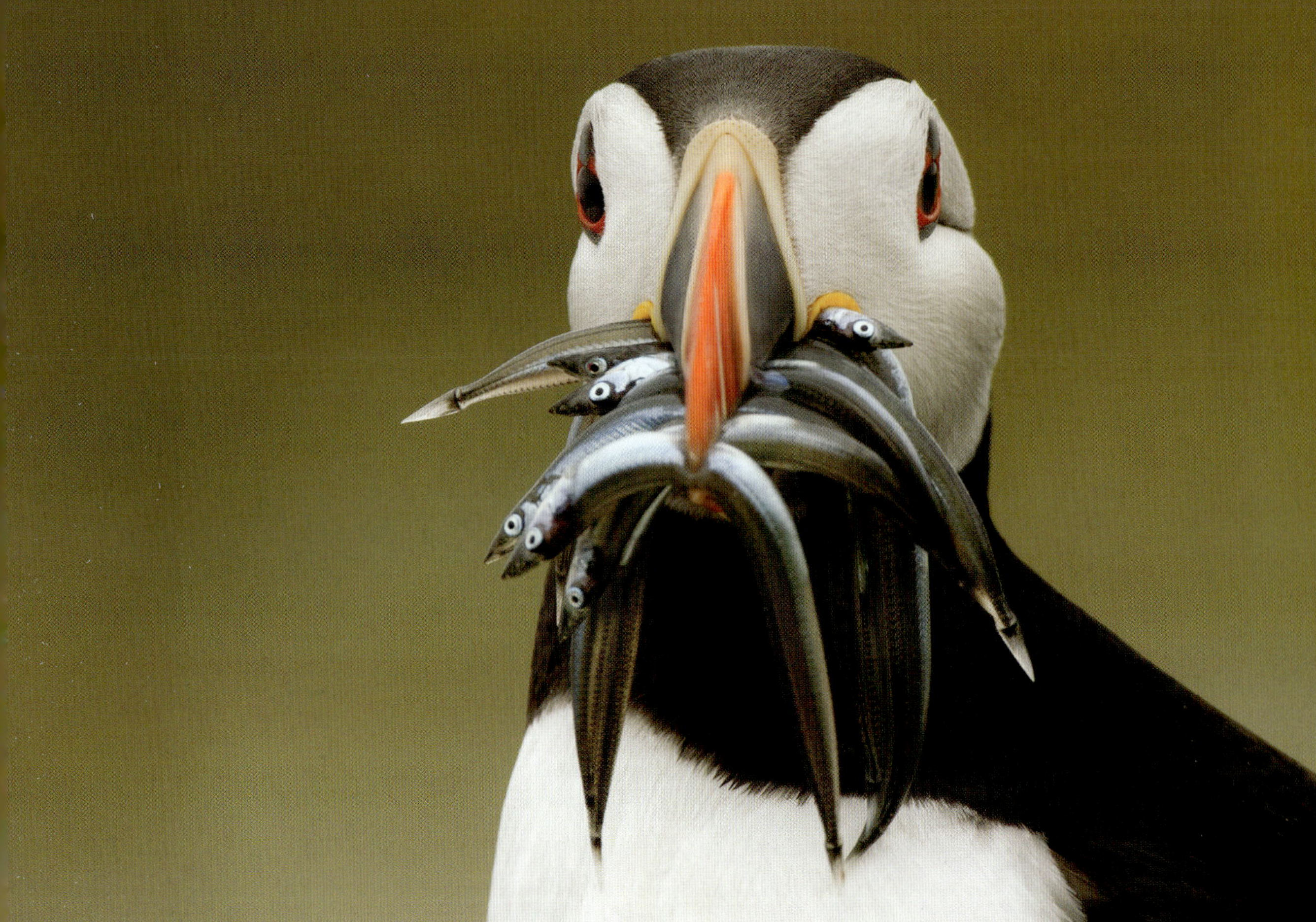

Puffin | Farne Islands | Although I closed the aperture to 7.1, the tip of the beak and the frontmost fish were no longer in the depth of field and are slightly out of focus. | 500mm, aperture 7.1, 1/400 s, ISO 500, -1/3 exposure compensation

The Aperture

Your choice of aperture determines the depth of field in the image. I set the autofocus point on the eye and my chosen aperture will dictate how much of an area behind and in front of the eye will be in focus. With a 500mm telephoto lens and a wide-open aperture, it may be little more than a quarter-inch at close range. If the subject is farther away or the lens has a shorter focal length, the depth of field range will be bigger. To estimate the depth of field, you'll need to become very familiar with your equipment and play around with different apertures.

If the eye of the bird is sharp in one of your pictures but not the tip of its beak, it's because the aperture was open too wide and the depth of field too shallow. This is when stopping down, i.e., decreasing the diameter of the aperture, comes in handy. As a rule of thumb for portraits with a telephoto lens, for example, I recommend setting the aperture to f/8, then checking to see if the image is sharp enough. If it's not, you can switch to f/11. But keep in mind that the background will be much more in focus and can start to look cluttered at times.

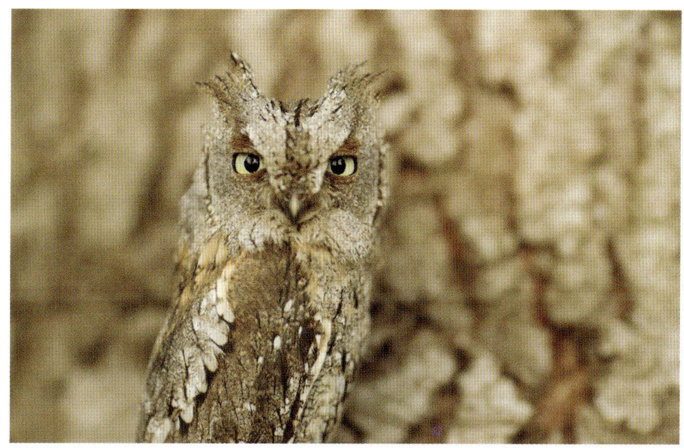

Scops owl | Germany | With an f/2.5 aperture, only the eyes of the small owl are sharp. Its beak and the bark of the tree are out of focus and the bird is separated well from the background. | 135mm, aperture 2.5, 1/3200 s, ISO 1000

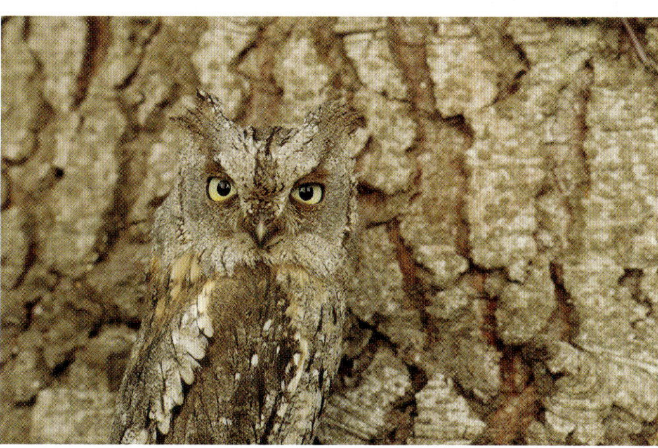

In this case, I didn't want to separate the owl from the background but emphasize its camouflage. To achieve this, I closed to an f/11 aperture. Not only is the whole bird in focus now but the tree trunk is sharper, too, and the similarly patterned plumage blends in better. | 135mm, aperture 11, 1/200 s, ISO 1000

Personally, I don't feel that strongly that everything up to and including the tip of the beak needs to be sharp in a portrait. I'm happy if the eyes are in focus.

Intentional Blurring

There are several ways in which blurring can improve an image: Motion blur, for example, can emphasize the movement of a bird in the image. But even then, the head of the bird, or at least its eye, should be fairly sharp. Motion blur can also accentuate snow or rainfall. In rare cases, it can even be acceptable if the head is out of focus—for example, if the bird is shaking itself—but otherwise, blurring can quickly appear unintentional.

Blurry shots of birds in flight can get very creative. Tastes differ, of course, but it's a lot of fun to experiment with slow shutter speeds when photographing a flock of birds in flight! Although you will, without a doubt, waste a lot of shots to create one or two successful pictures.

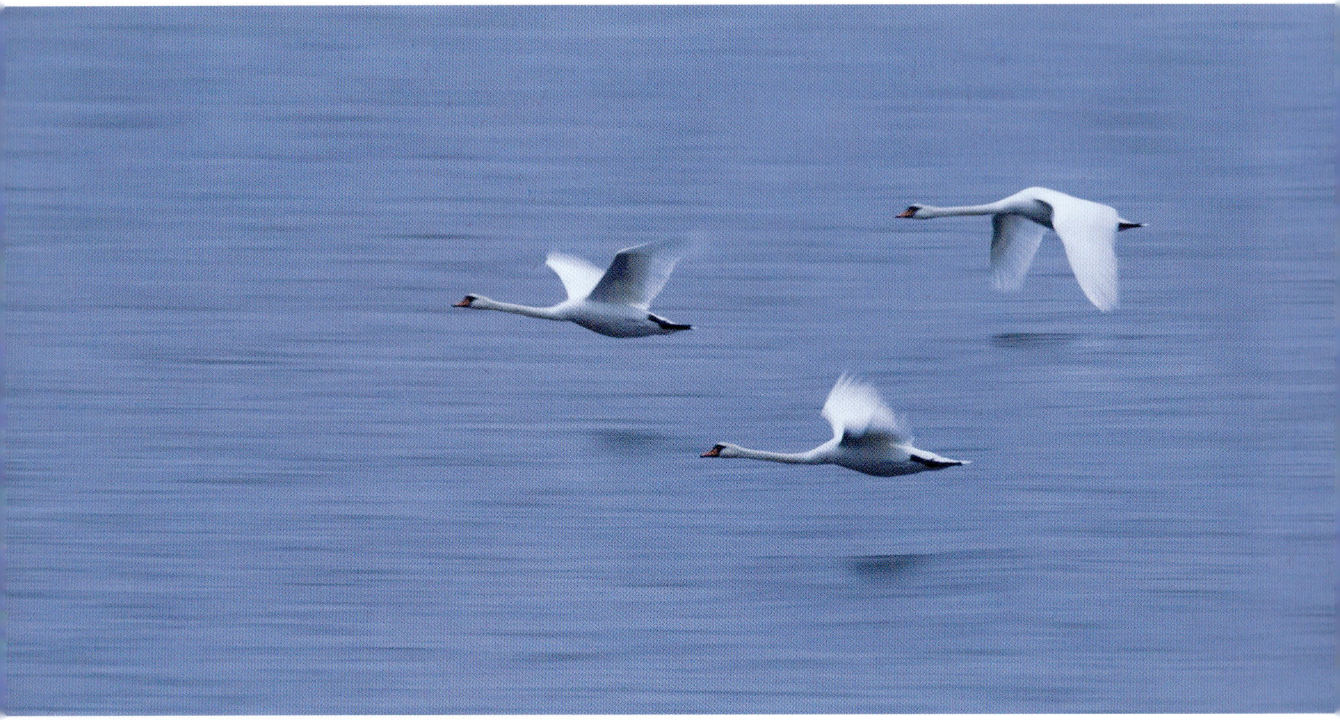

Mute swans | Wales | When using the technique of "panning," you follow birds with the camera so that they'll stay somewhat sharp while the background is blurry. | 500mm, aperture 5.0, 1/30 s, ISO 1250

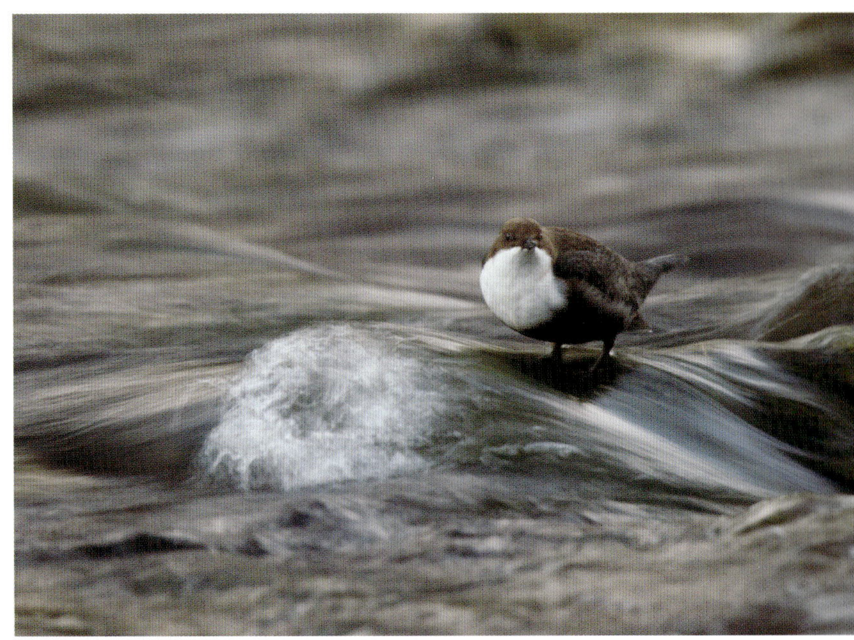

4-92 ▶

White-throated dipper | Germany | Due to an extremely slow shutter speed of 1/8 s, the water became very blurry, while the dipper is still sufficiently sharp since it barely moved. | 840mm (600mm + 1.4x converter), aperture 5.6, 1/8 s, ISO 200

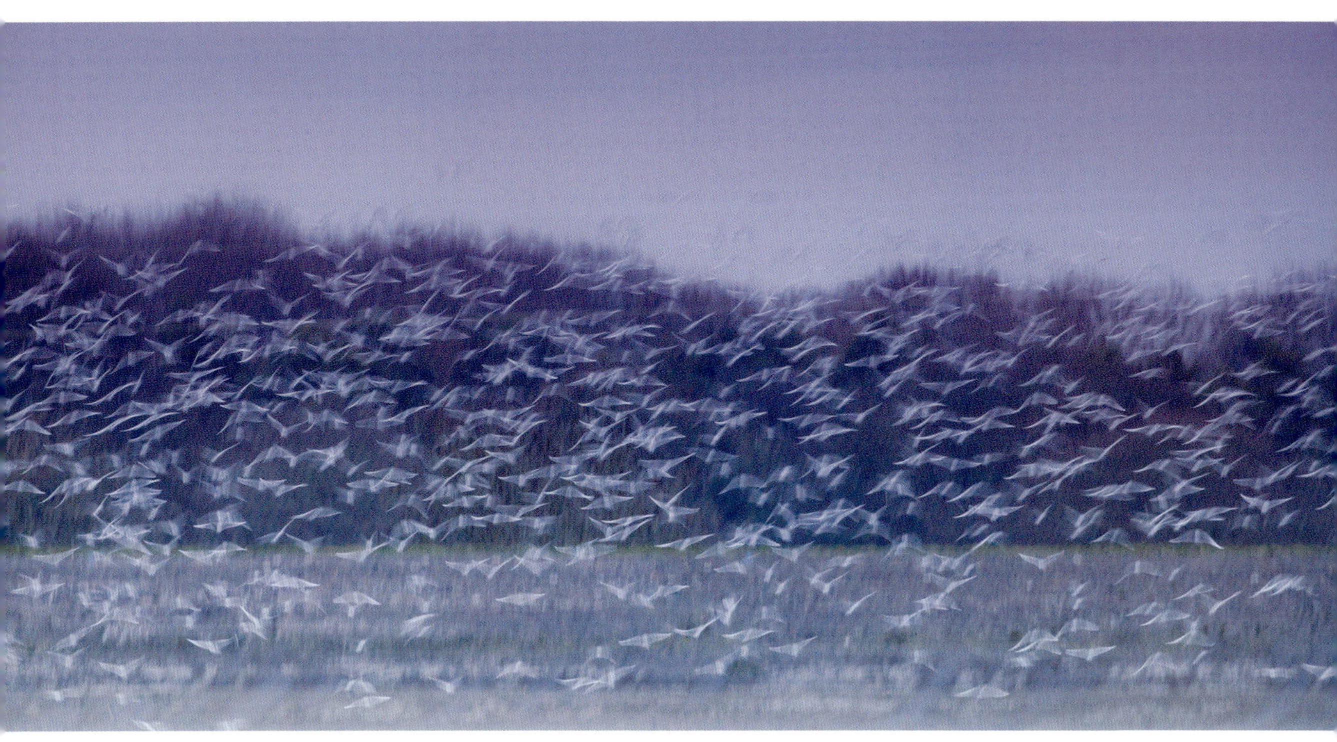

Black-headed gulls | Wales | The soaring colony of black-headed gulls has a pronounced motion blur; coupled with the blue hour mood it makes the image quite poetic. | 500mm, aperture 5.0, 1/25 s, ISO 1250

A second way to intentionally bring blur into a picture is called panning. You do this to keep the bird sharp while blurring the background. This is achieved by using a relatively slow shutter speed and following the flying bird with the camera. Again, you'll produce a lot of pictures that are only worth deleting. But if just one turns out really well, it'll enrich your portfolio!

Intentional blurring also affects the background and foreground of a photo, of course. It's a matter of taste how much blur a viewer enjoys. Especially if there's more than one bird in the picture, it can bother some people if not all are in focus. Personally, I like playing around with sharpness and blur.

4.3 Light and Exposure

Correct Exposure

Here is some good news: Under normal conditions, a modern camera will have no problem correctly exposing a typical image. Cameras offer several metering modes for exposure, all of which are useful in different situations.

I usually shoot with either matrix metering (also called multi-segment metering) or center-weighted metering. Matrix metering takes a light reading across your entire scene, i.e., subject, foreground, and background. Center-weighted metering prioritizes a light reading in a large area in the middle of the frame.

Some photographers swear by spot metering, where the camera sets the exposure according to the light in a small area. I find the risk too high that this spot might fluctuate between being bright or dark, especially when there's movement. This would result in completely differently exposed images.

4-94 ▼

Oystercatcher | Iceland | Your camera's auto mode will ensure a correct exposure for most motifs in nature. | 500mm, aperture 5.0, 1/2000 s, ISO 800

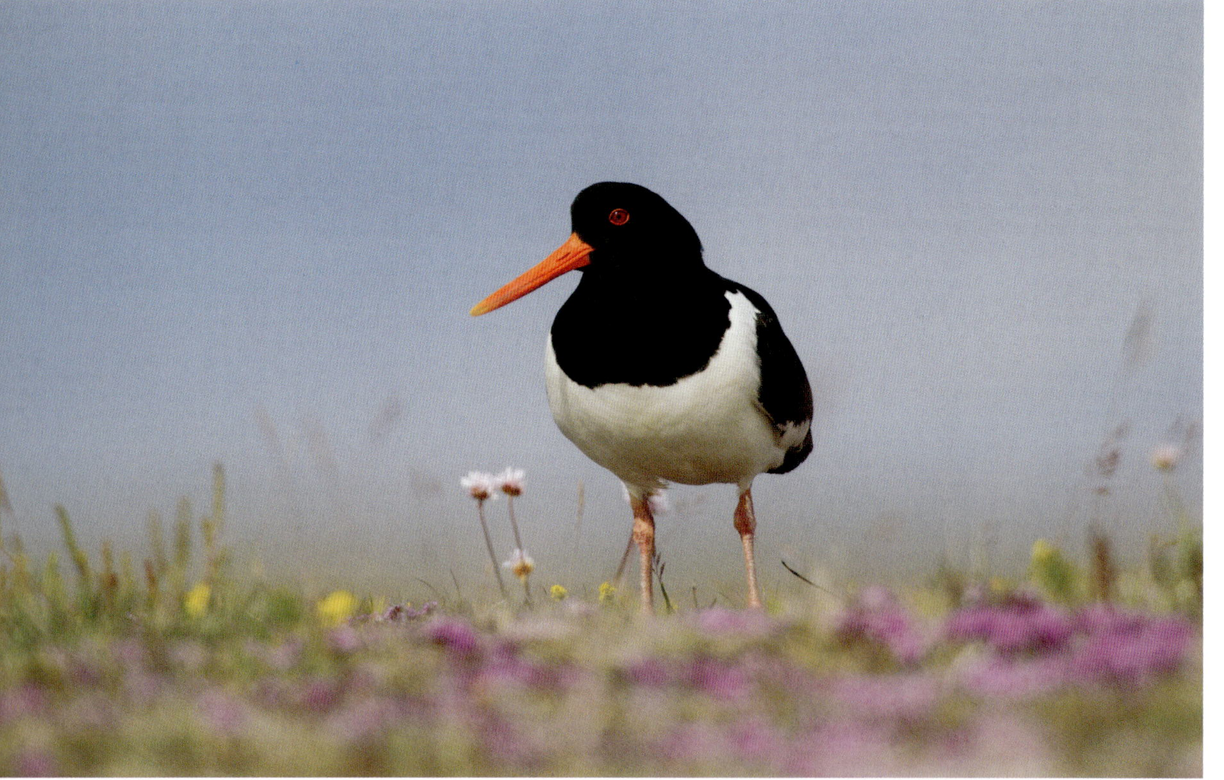

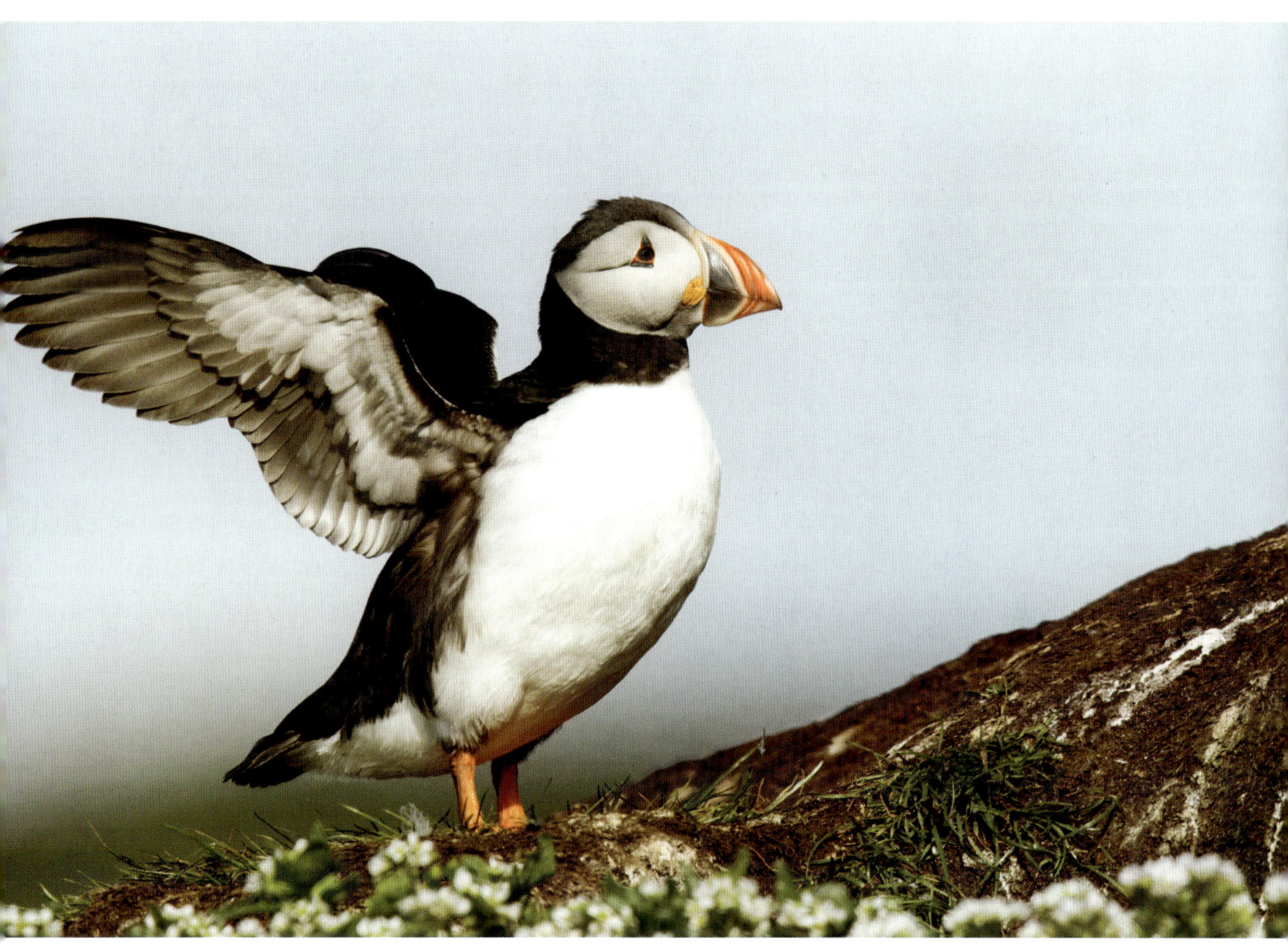

In general, the camera's automatic exposure always assumes that you want to photograph a subject with an average level of brightness. This works well for most subjects and in these cases, we can happily delegate the exposure to the camera. But for some shots, we need to understand how exposure metering works and override the automatic system to get the results we want. This will be discussed in the following sections.

▲ **4-95**

Puffin | Iceland | A tough case for spot metering: If the bird moves, the spot might land on either a white or black part of the plumage, resulting in a wildly different exposure. | 840mm (600mm + 1.4x converter), aperture 8.0, 1/1600 s, ISO 640, +1 exposure compensation

Mute swan | Wales | For this detail shot, I corrected the auto exposure by dialing in two stops of positive exposure compensation. | 500mm, aperture 10, 1/1600 s, ISO 1000, +2 exposure compensation

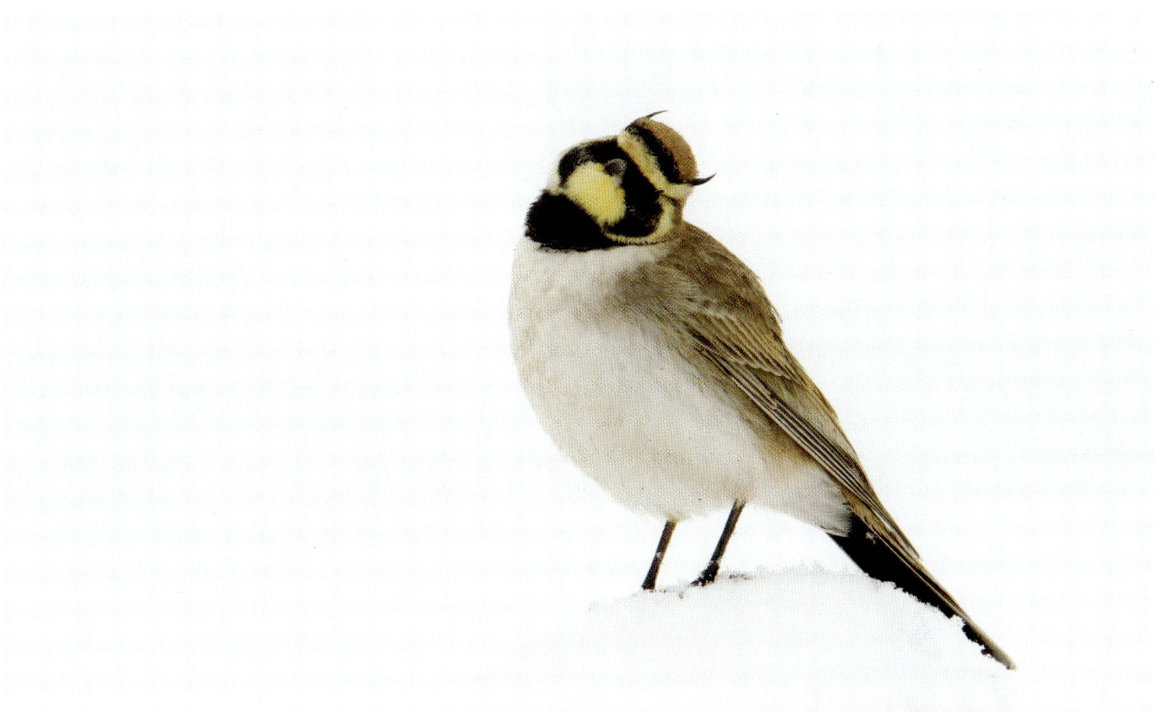

Brighter Than Average Images

Automatic exposure metering becomes a problem when a subject is much brighter or darker than the average picture. This can happen when photographing something in the snow, for example, or before the background of a dark forest.

Let's consider the first case: You want to photograph a white bird in the snow or against a bright sky. The auto exposure system "thinks": "This can't be, nobody photographs anything this white." Accordingly, it will expose the image in such a way that you get a picture of average brightness—and that means gray. So all that beautiful white snow turns to a murky gray.

You can solve this by outsmarting the camera and overriding its automatic system. This feature is called "exposure compensation," and it allows you to correct the exposure up to two or three stops—depending on the camera type—in 1/3-stop increments. In our example, you must tell the camera to please go brighter than gray. This means dialing a positive number. With some experience, you'll learn how much you have to correct the auto exposure. The more white there is in the picture, and the brighter the image is overall, the more stops of positive exposure compensation you have to dial.

▲ 4-97

Horned lark | Morocco | Photos with a lot of snow are much brighter than the average image. Here I corrected by 1 1/3 exposure stops. | 700mm (500mm + 1.4x converter), aperture 13, 1/2000 s, ISO 1250, +1 1/3 exposure correction

Darker Than Average Images

Just as with overly bright images you will also need to correct the auto exposure if an image is dark and "tell" the camera to make it darker than average gray. This can happen, for example, if you want to photograph a raven against a dark background. If you rely on the auto exposure, you'll end up with a gray image that doesn't show the scene as it was!

Depending on how dark the image is, you'll need to dial only a few 1/3-stops or several full stops of negative exposure compensation.

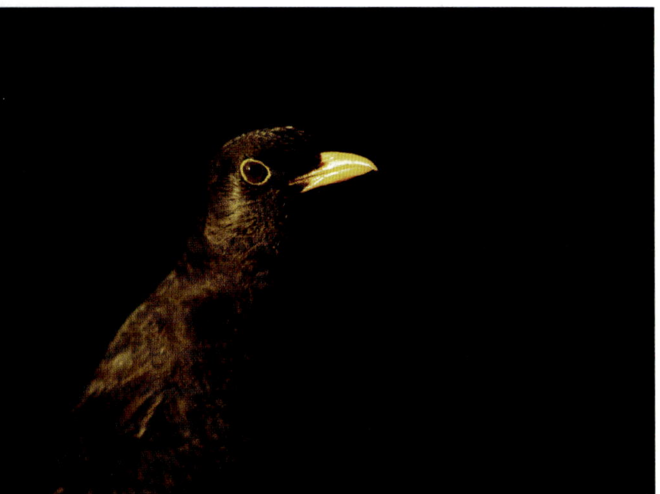

▲ **4-98**

Blackbird | Germany | For this shot of a dark blackbird against a shady background, I corrected with two full negative exposure stops. | 600mm, aperture 5.6, 1/800 s, ISO 1250, -2 exposure compensation

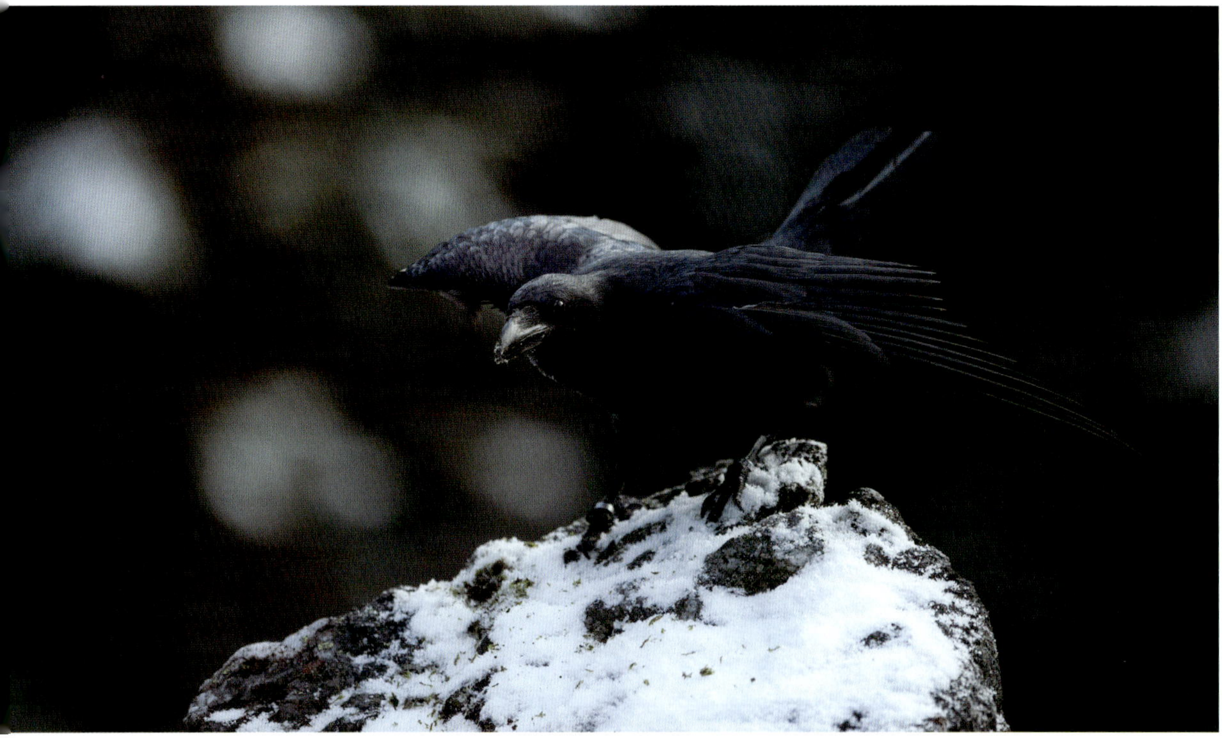

▲ **4-99**

Common raven | Germany | This photo of a raven against a dark forest also required a correction of the auto exposure system. | 300mm, aperture 2.8, 1/1600 s, ISO 1000, -1 1/3 exposure compensation

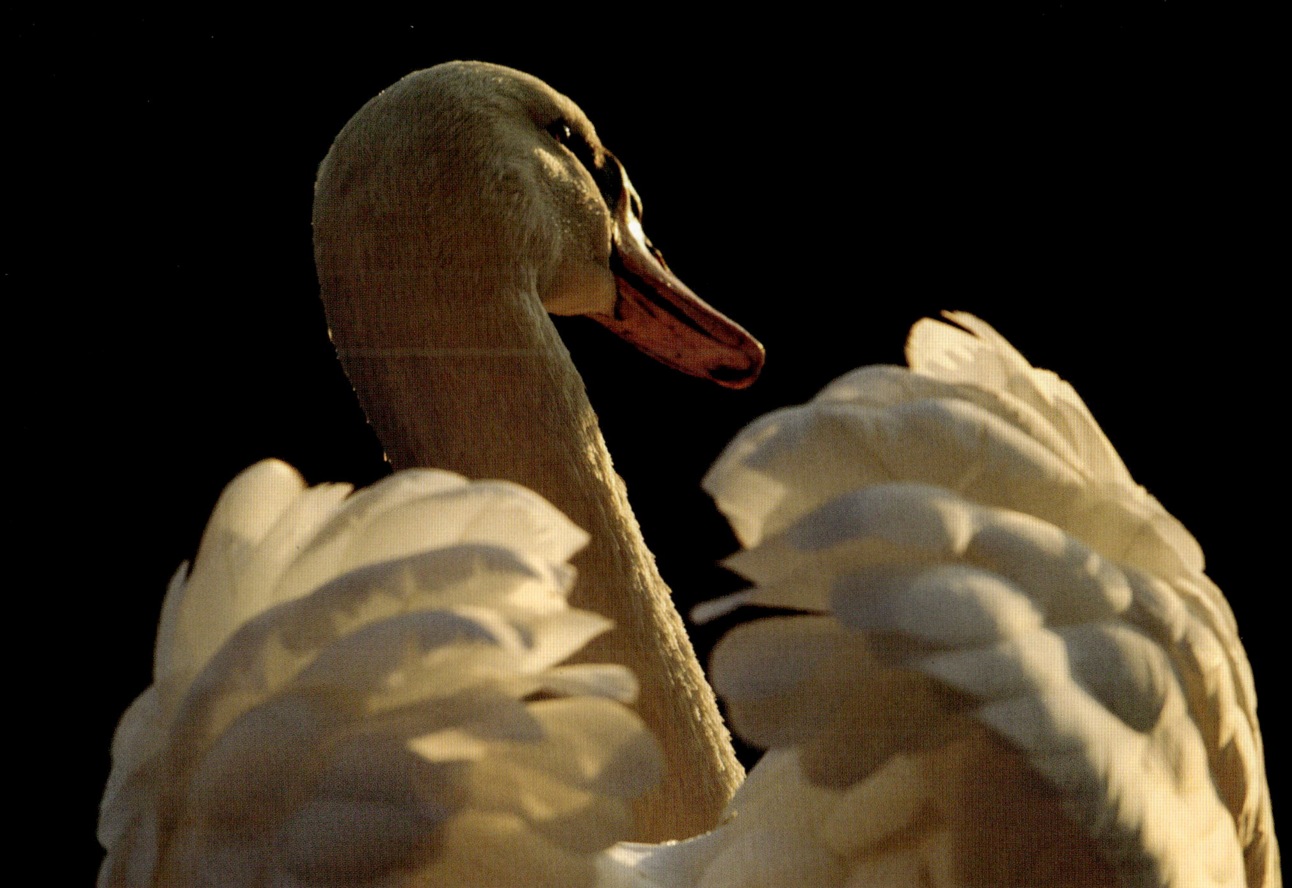

Tricky Motifs

Exposure becomes tricky when there are extremes of light and dark—or black and white—in the same picture. In that case, you have to try to guess the ratio of both. If the image is about half white and half black, the camera (if set to matrix metering) will probably expose it correctly. If the dark parts dominate, you have to dial a negative exposure compensation; if the white part predominates, you have to dial a positive compensation. It's important to check the result on the display, preferably with the help of a histogram.

Another tricky exposure situation is backlit photos, which we'll discuss in the section "Backlight" starting on page 95.

Of course, other metering modes can also be used to get the results you want. Many photographers swear by manual metering as an alternative to exposure compensation. I find that the approach described above works best and I have taught it successfully to many participants in my workshops.

Mute swan | Germany |
The backlit mute swan against a dark background required dialing a negative exposure compensation. | 600mm, aperture 5.6, 1/2000 s, ISO 1250, -1 1/3 exposure compensation

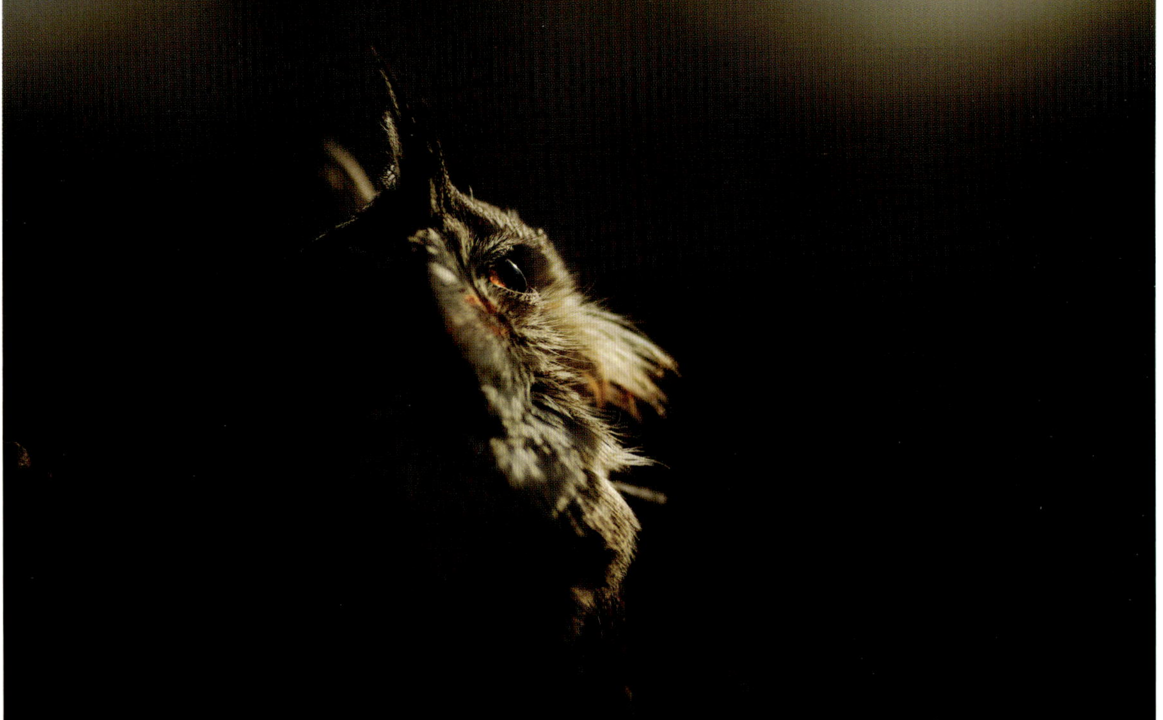

Front Light

Working with front light is usually recommended. What this means is that the sun is behind the photographer and the bird is illuminated by the sun. Beginners in particular tend to think that strong frontal sunlight is best for successful photos. Unfortunately, this isn't always true, since these pictures can often look flat and have strong drop shadows, for example under the beak, especially under a high midday sun. You often hardly notice these drop shadows when you take the picture, but they can turn out to be very distracting when you look at images.

That's why most nature photographers only go out in the early morning hours and again in the afternoon when the sun is already lower on the horizon. During the middle of the day, you can take a leisurely nap or review the pictures you took during the morning.

Nevertheless, the standard front light situation usually does work well unless the sun is shining right above the subject.

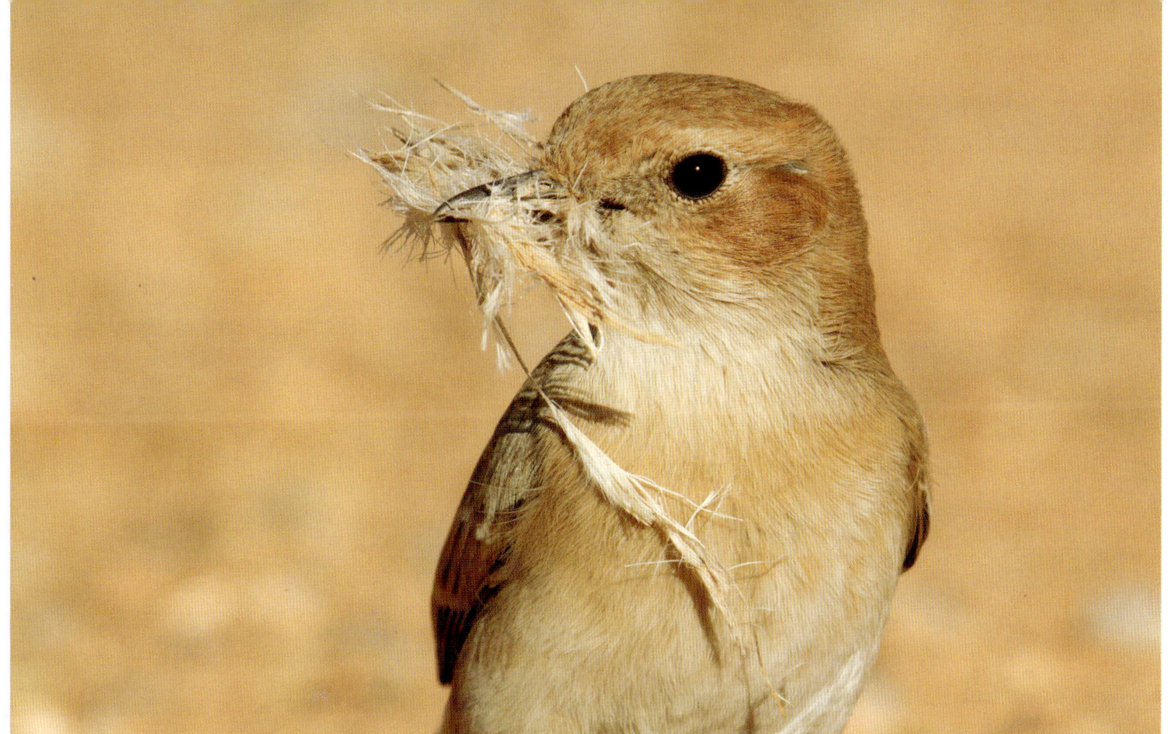

Red-rumped wheatear | Morocco | With front light, I often wait until the bird turns its head to avoid drop shadows. | 840mm (600mm + 1.4x converter), aperture 9.0, 1/1600 s, ISO 500

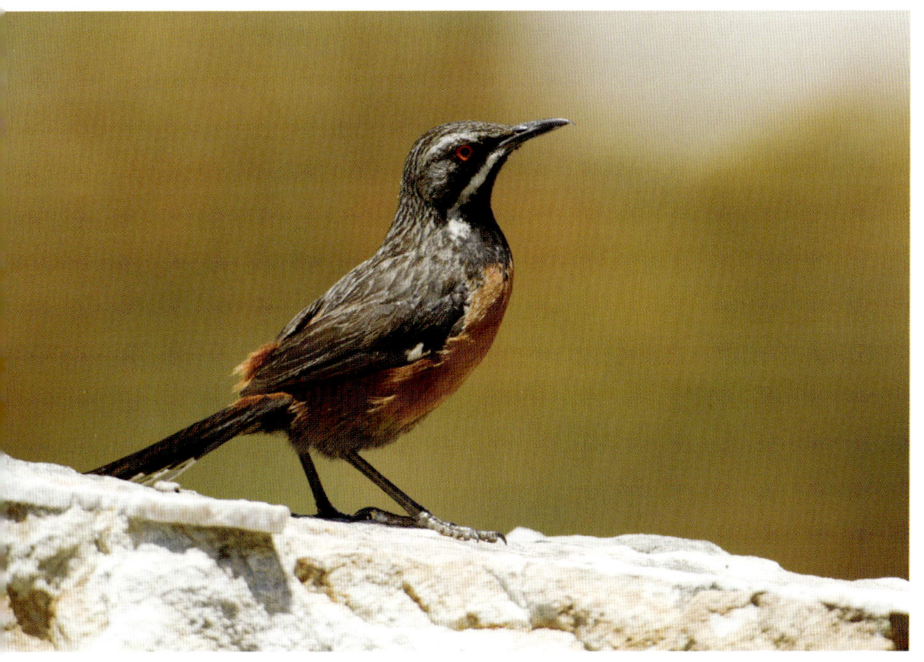

4-103
Rockjumper | South Africa | The harsh midday sunlight hits the bird straight from above. There's an unattractive shadow under the chin, and the colors look dull, while the light-colored background shines too brightly. | 500mm, aperture 4.0, 1/1600 s, ISO 500, -1/3 exposure compensation

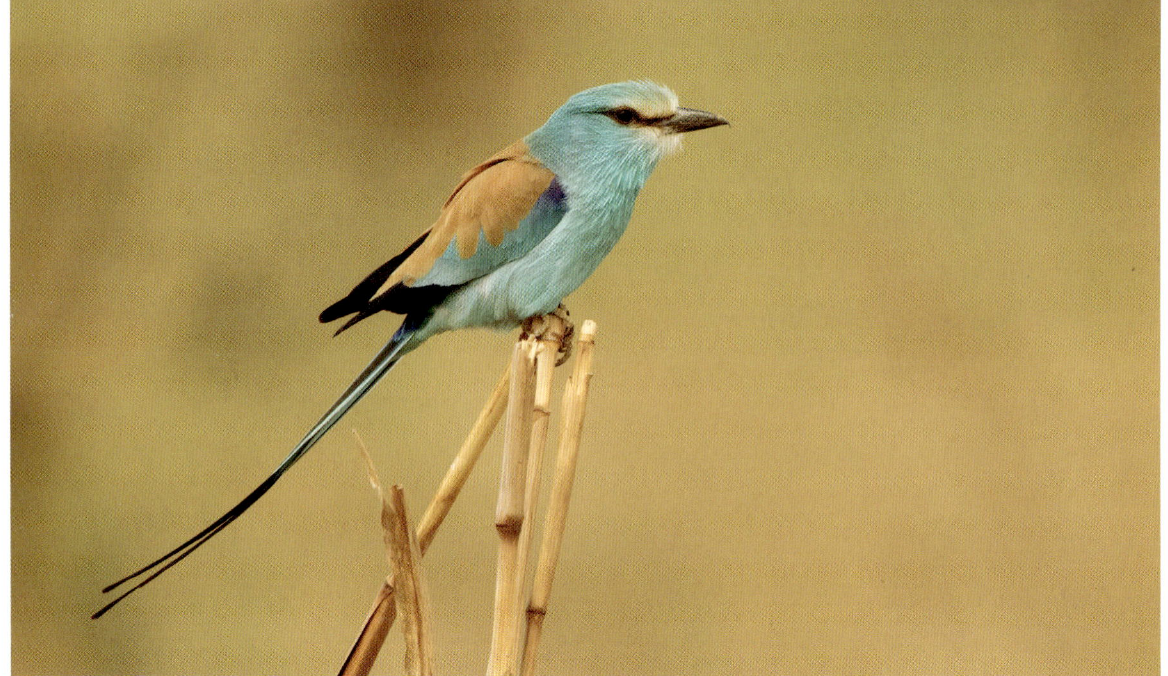

Abyssinian roller | Gambia | With an overcast sky it's even possible to take photographs in the middle of the day. This picture was taken shortly after noon. | 840mm (600mm + 1.4x converter), aperture 7.1, 1/1250 s, ISO 800, +1/3 exposure compensation

Cloudy Skies

I'm usually delighted to see a bit of cloud cover when I want to take photos. It means that the bird will be bathed in beautifully soft light and its colors and markings will often be displayed much better.

With a few clouds in the sky, you don't need to worry about drop shadows and the bird's face is usually well lit no matter how it turns its head. Under an overcast sky, you can even take pictures during the noon hours, although many birds, especially in warmer climates, rest during the middle part of the day.

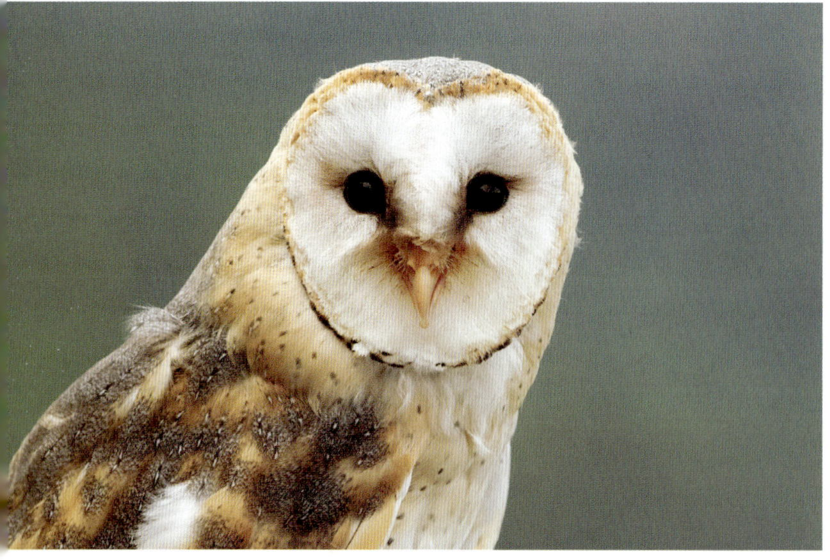

◀ 4-105

Barn owl | German Raptor Research Center at Guttenberg Castle, Germany | The various shades of cream in the barn owl's plumage really came into their own under an overcast sky. And there are no shadows on its face. | 400mm, aperture 8.0, 1/2000 s, ISO 2000

CHAPTER 4

Side Light

Side light is great for bringing out textures and shapes. Pictures taken with side light are often quite atmospheric, especially in the early morning or low afternoon sun. You will need to check the auto exposure, since it may expose images a little too brightly with the result that details on the sun-facing side might get lost. You may have to correct the automatic mode and dial a negative exposure compensation.

▼ 4-106

Scops owl | Germany | Side light works especially well against a dark background. | 135mm, aperture 2.5, 1/2500 s, ISO 400, -1 exposure compensation

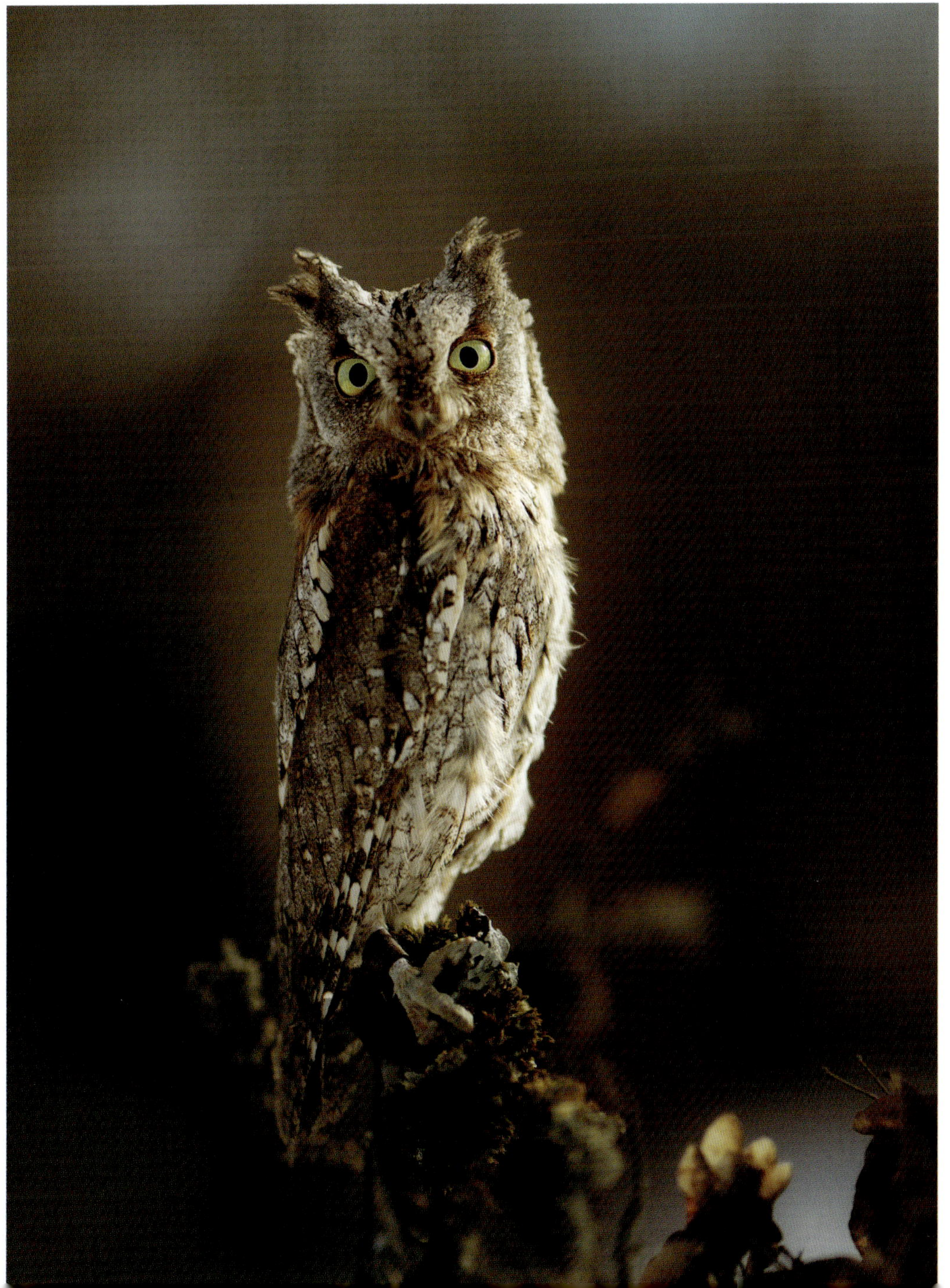

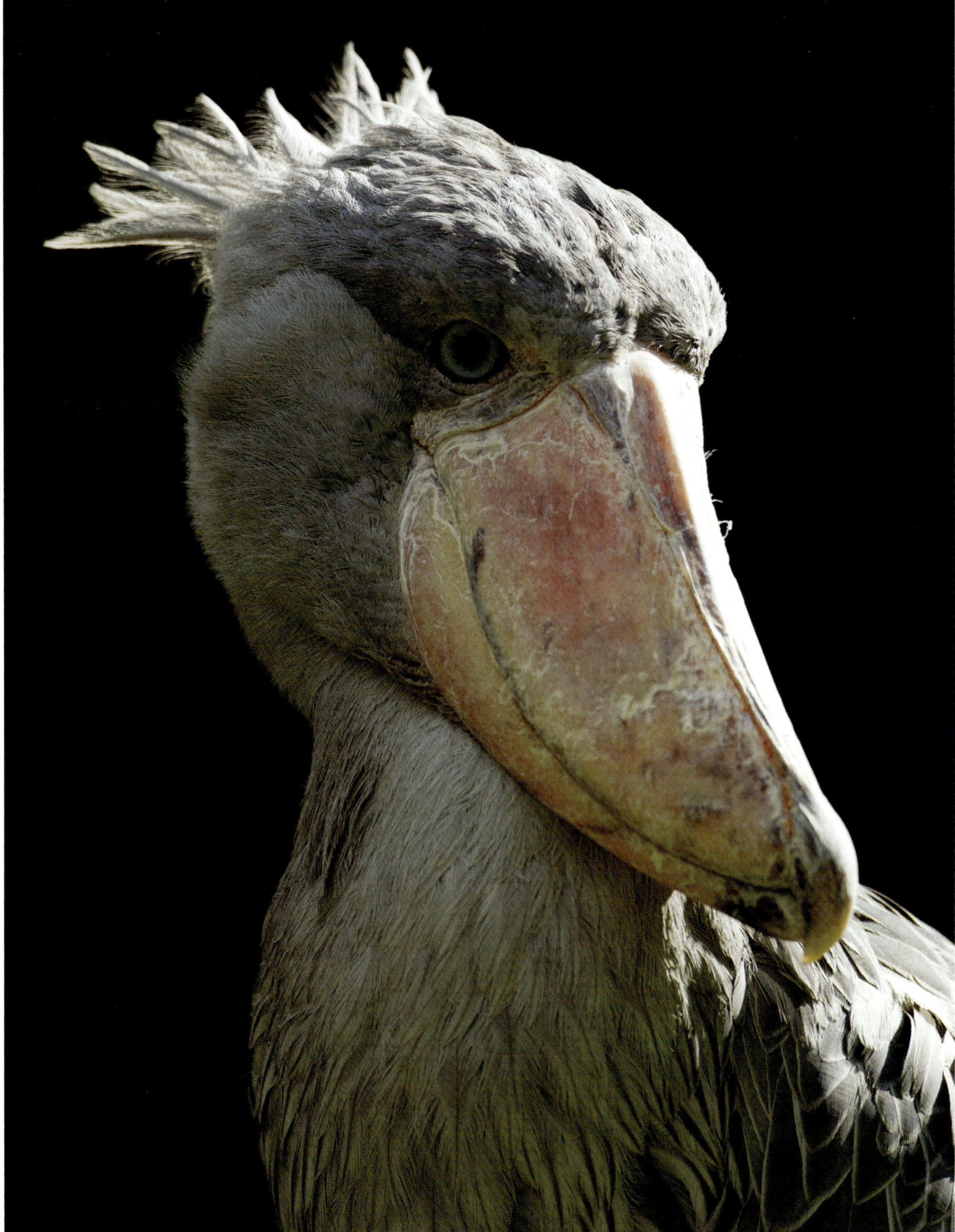

Shoebill | Weltvogelpark Walsrode (Walsrode Bird Park), Germany | The side light accentuates the shoe-bill's outline, while the side facing the viewer is shaded. The exposure needed to be corrected by one stop to ensure that the bright edges showed up correctly. | 500mm, aperture 5.0, 1/1600 s, ISO 500, -1 exposure compensation

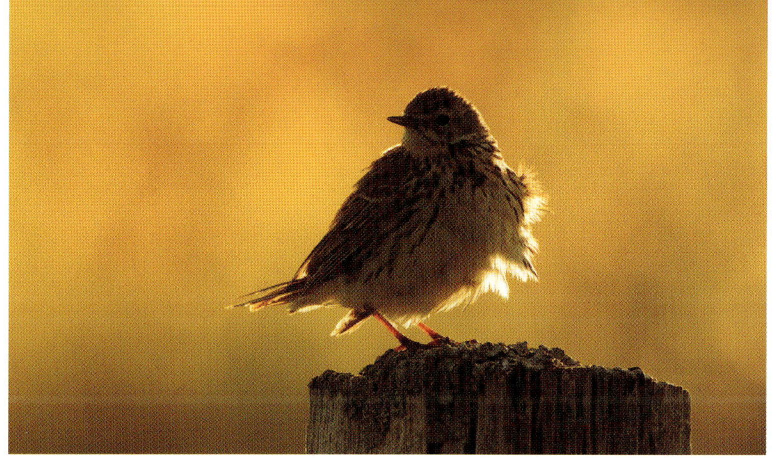

Meadow pipit | Texel, The Netherlands | The backlight creates a so-called rim light around the outline of the bird. The effect is particularly beautiful on the protruding breast feathers. | 500mm, aperture 5.6, 1/640 s, ISO 1600, -2/3 exposure compensation

Backlight

When it comes to photographing with backlight, I want to consider two scenarios. One is backlight at sunset and the other backlight during the day. I'll discuss backlight at sunset in the "Capturing Silhouettes" section of the book.

But backlight during the day is a different situation. Generally speaking, backlight is great for creating a so-called rim light, meaning a glow around the outline of a subject. Rim light develops when the source of light is either located right or even obliquely behind the subject. But it requires a dark background, otherwise, it's impossible to see.

For such a picture to work, you must correct the auto exposure. Otherwise, it'll expose the subject correctly by making the image too bright. Accordingly, you'll need to dial a negative exposure compensation.

You'll achieve the best effects with birds that have a distinctive outline, such as a head with ear tufts, like some owls. Birds with a crown of feathers like the hoopoe or crested lark also look great.

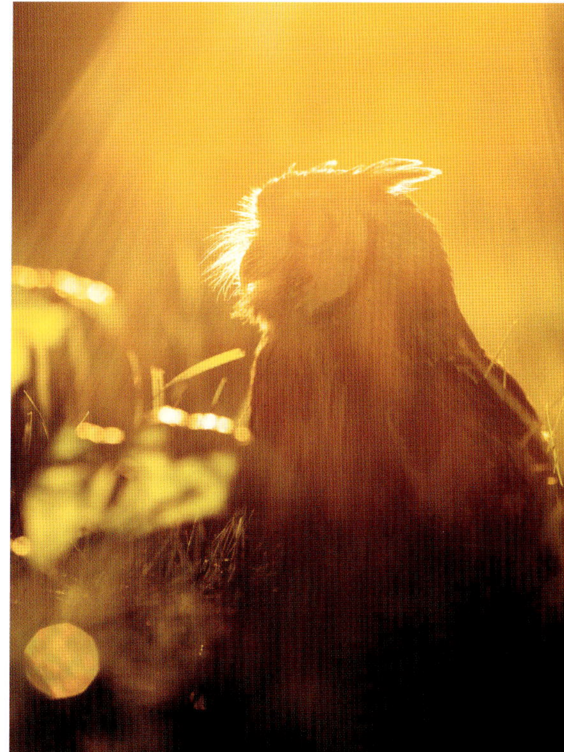

White-faced owl | Germany | Photographing directly against the sun can lead to interesting light effects, as in this image, which had to be darkened some more during editing as two stops of negative exposure compensation had not been enough. | 135mm, aperture 3.2, 1/3200 s, ISO 1000, -2 exposure compensation

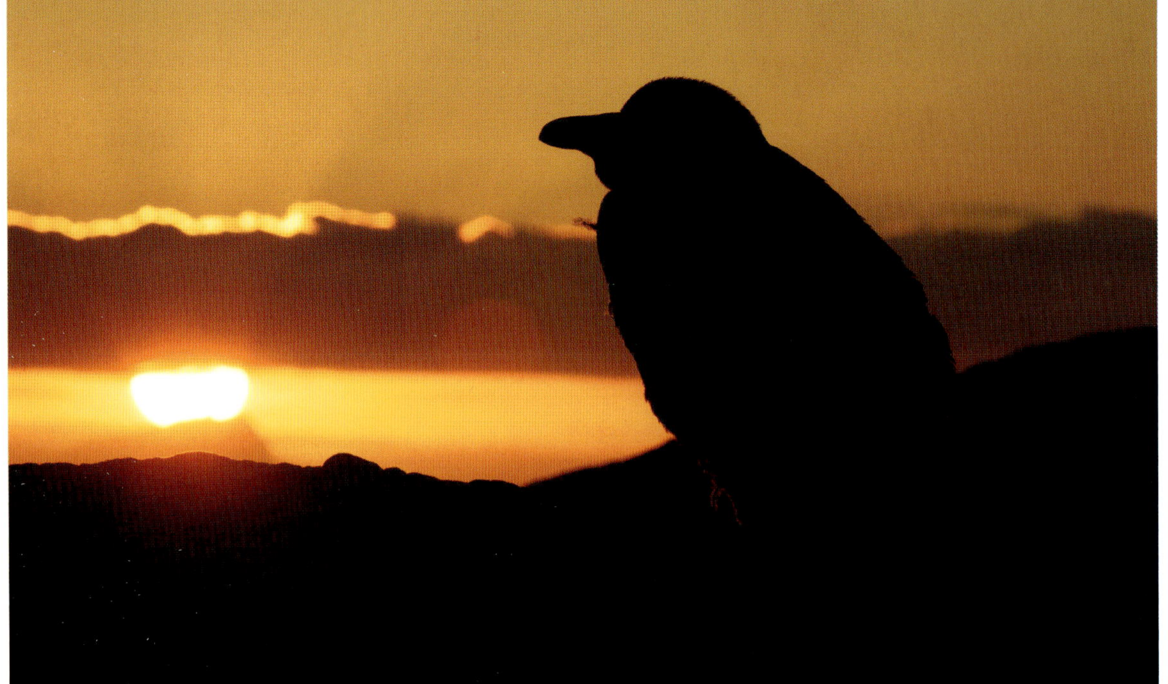

African penguin | South Africa |
The silhouette of an African
penguin captured at sunrise. |
180mm, aperture 14, 1/250 s,
ISO 800, -1 exposure
compensation

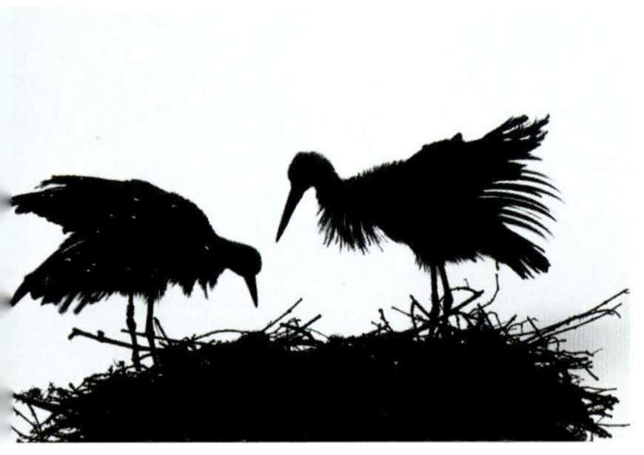

White storks | Germany |
Even without a sunrise or sunset
it's possible to capture attractive
silhouettes. | 700mm (500mm
+ 1.4x converter), aperture 7.1,
1/320 s, ISO 1250

Capturing Silhouettes

The easiest way to photograph attractive silhouettes is to shoot against the sun at sunset. You'll get particularly beautiful images, if the sky has an appealing red tint, possibly even with some dramatic clouds thrown in. Again, photos like this are especially effective if the bird has a distinctive silhouette, with a crown or tufted ears.

If the sun is still up in the sky you usually have to correct the auto exposure. At least, that has been my experience. The automatic system would overexpose the images, by exposing the bird correctly while turning the sun into a white dot in the sky. A light situation like this requires dialing a negative exposure compensation. (With matrix metering, mind you!) If the sun is still fairly bright, you might even have to dial three full stops of negative exposure compensation. The more the sunlight fades, the less correction is required. If the sun has already set, you can usually get good results with regular auto exposure.

Sometimes, it can be difficult to focus using the autofocus. That's because the autofocus has trouble finding the contrasts it needs when pointed at a completely black area. In that case, you must either place the autofocus point on the edge of the bird's body, i.e., the outline of the silhouette, or turn the autofocus off and focus manually.

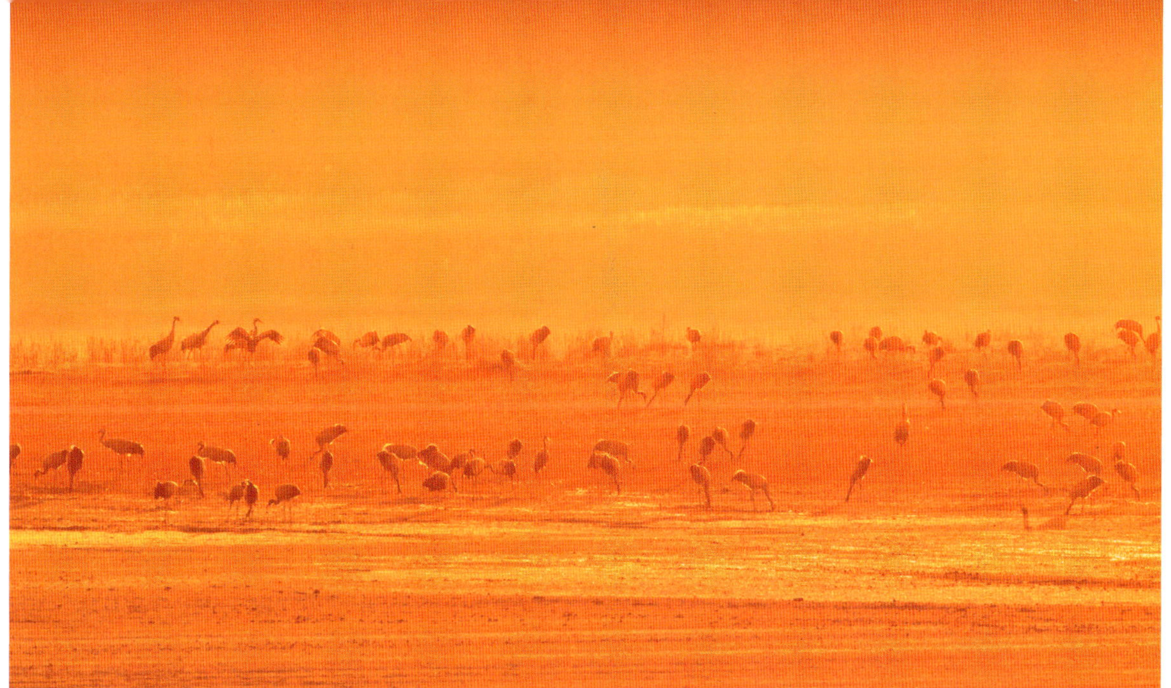

Morning Light

When doing nature photography, it's always a good idea to get up early and this also applies to photographing birds. Especially if the first rays of sunlight are accompanied by some early morning fog, this can result in beautiful images. The mood is soft and dreamy, and depending on the setting, you're rewarded with gorgeous colors.

The orange-red light that sometimes dominates in the morning can confuse the camera's automatic white balance and might not show up correctly in the photos. In that case, it's highly recommended to use RAW image files so you can adjust the white balance later without losing quality.

In matrix mode, the auto exposure usually does a good job getting the exposure right without needing correcting. So the main difficulty is getting up at the crack of dawn….

▲ **4-112**

Cranes | France | The morning light conjures a unique mood in this image of cranes. | 1000mm (500mm + 2x converter), aperture 13, 1/640 s, ISO 1250, +2 1/3 exposure compensation

White Balance

Different light sources have different color temperatures. We talk of warm light when it's more in the orange spectrum, and of cold light when subjects appear bluish. Sunsets have a warm, i.e., orange-red mood, while blue light dominates on a shady winter day. Our brains can adjust for this so that a white sheet of paper always looks white to us regardless of the color temperature that prevails at the moment: The auto-white balance mode of the camera tries to do the same and filter out any color cast that is present in the image.

But that might be something that you don't want for a particular picture. Maybe you'd prefer to keep the warm or cool colors. If that's the case, check the white balance that is set on your camera and correct it. If the color casts are particularly strong, it's a good idea to fine-tune the white balance later during image editing to make sure the photo reflects what you saw in real life.

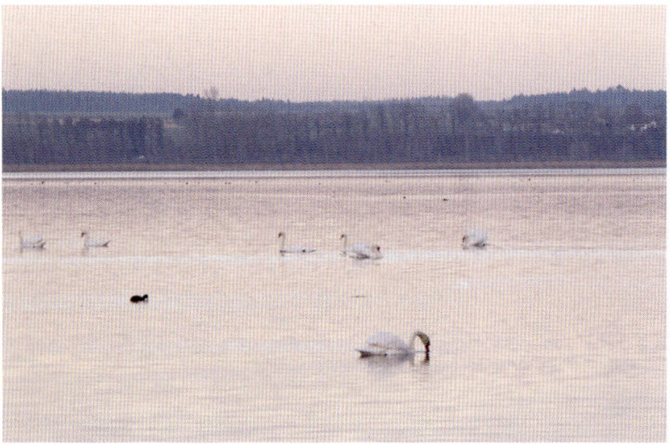

▲ 4-113

Mute swans | Germany | This photograph of swans shows the light as it was in real life. | 200mm, aperture 8.0, 1/320 s, ISO 1250

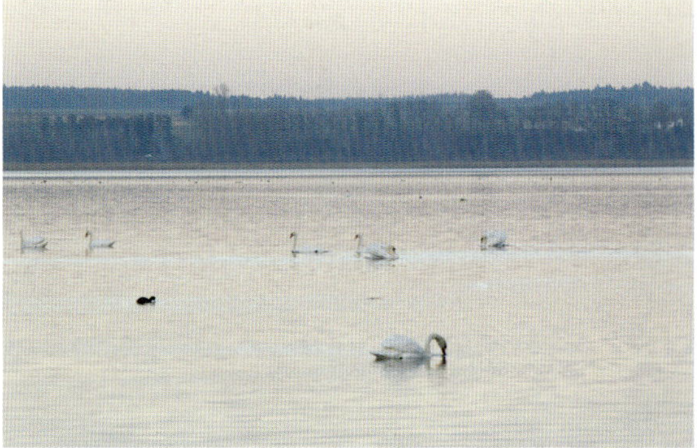

▲ 4-114

This is what the camera might have done if I had shot the photo using JPEG with auto-white balance. | 200mm, aperture 8.0, 1/320 s, ISO 1250

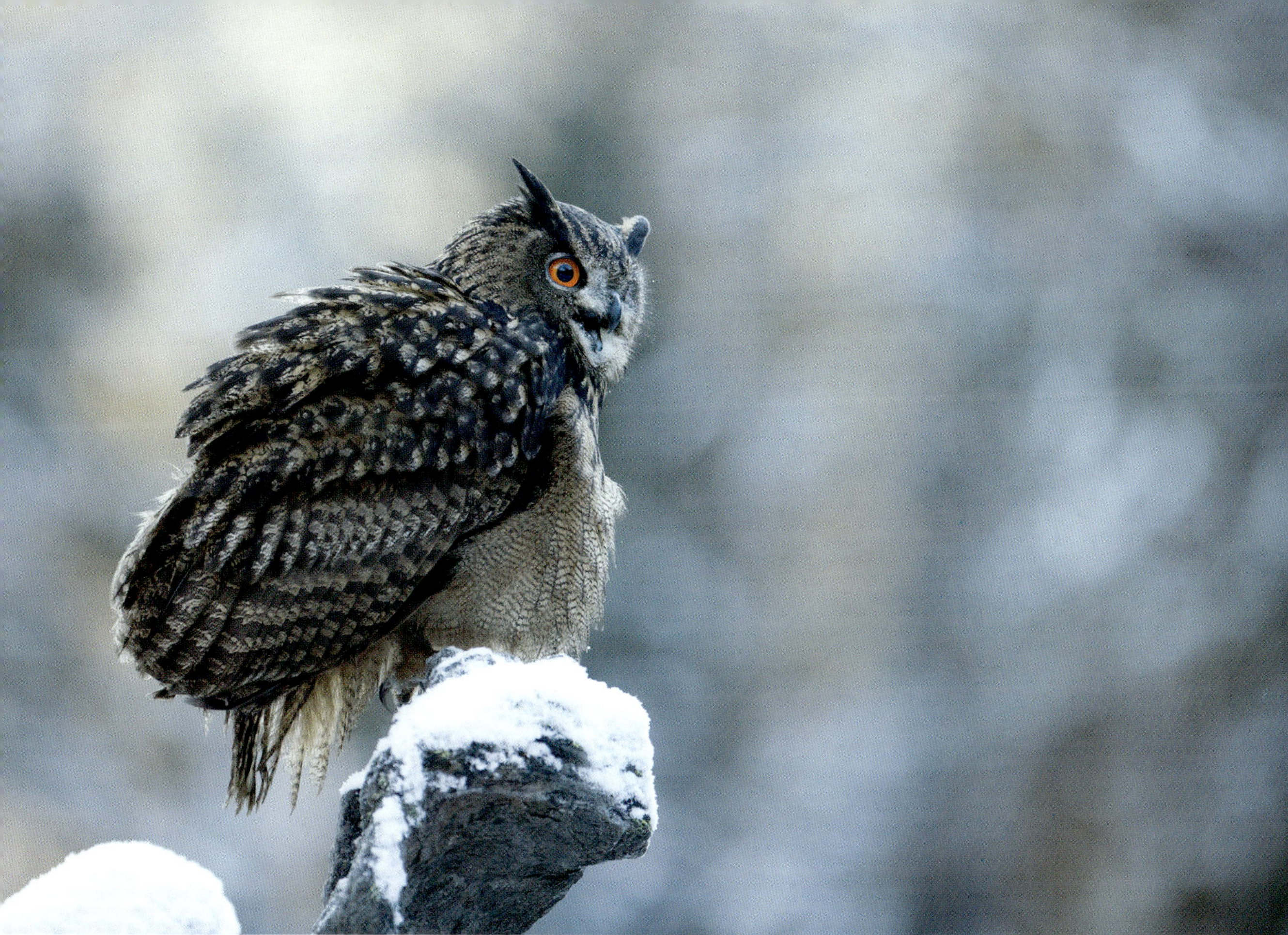

▲ 4-115

Eagle owl | Germany | This picture was taken on a frosty morning, and the cool blue emphasizes the winter-day vibe. | 300mm, aperture 2.8, 1/500 s, ISO 1250, +1/3 exposure compensation

Not Enough Light

If you photograph from a tree stand in the forest, you're often confronted with the problem that there might not be enough light for a fast shutter speed on a cloudy day. You might encounter the same issue as the sun sets at the end of the day. This leaves me with several options:

- I can pack my bags and go home. But if I had planned to spend the day in the tree stand, this is the worst of all possible choices.

- I can also try setting the ISO as high as possible while keeping the aperture wide open. Normally, modern cameras can handle an ISO of 1600 just fine and, if needed, I'll even go as high as 2000-3200. Usually, that'll get me shutter times that are fast enough for most subjects.

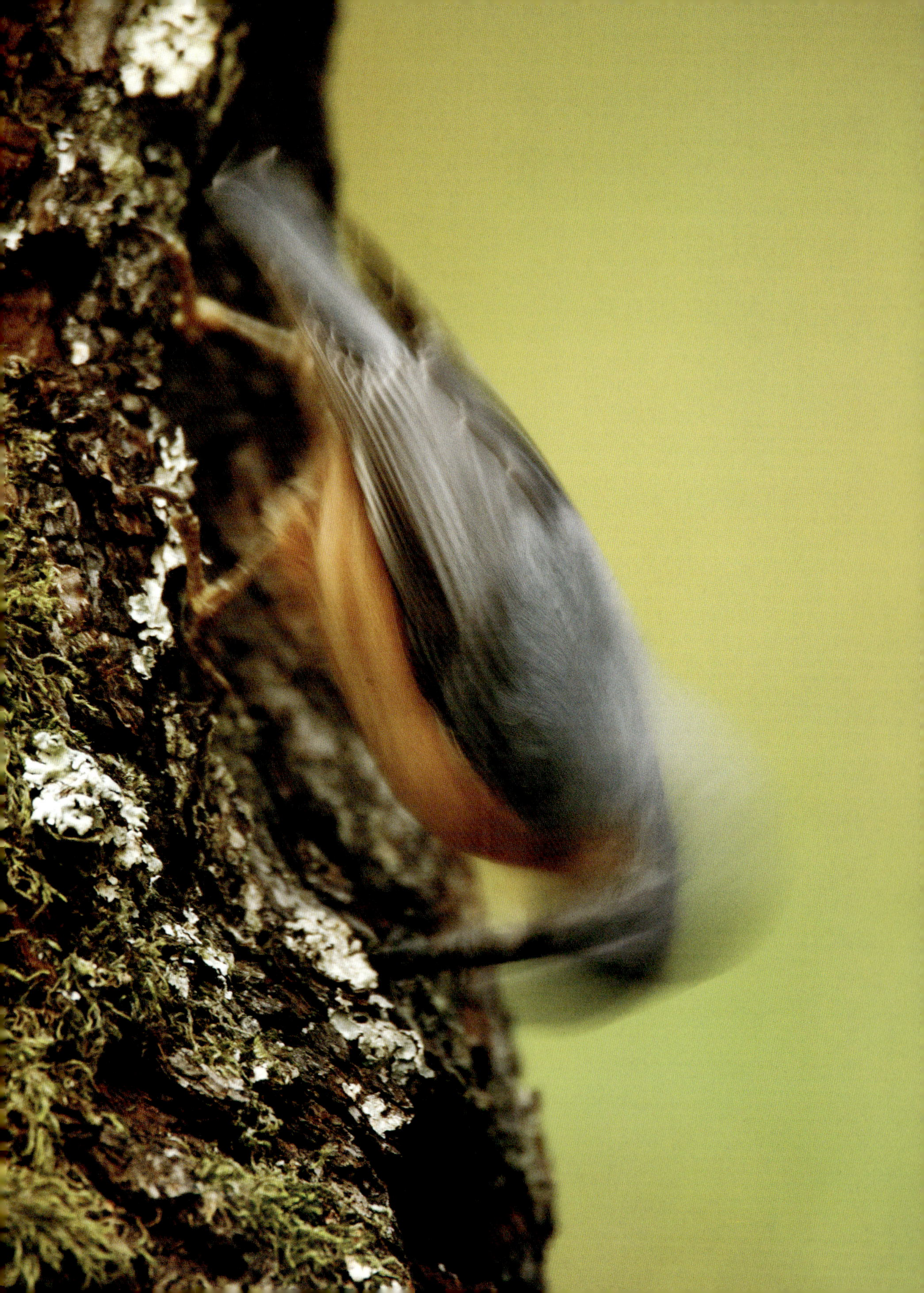

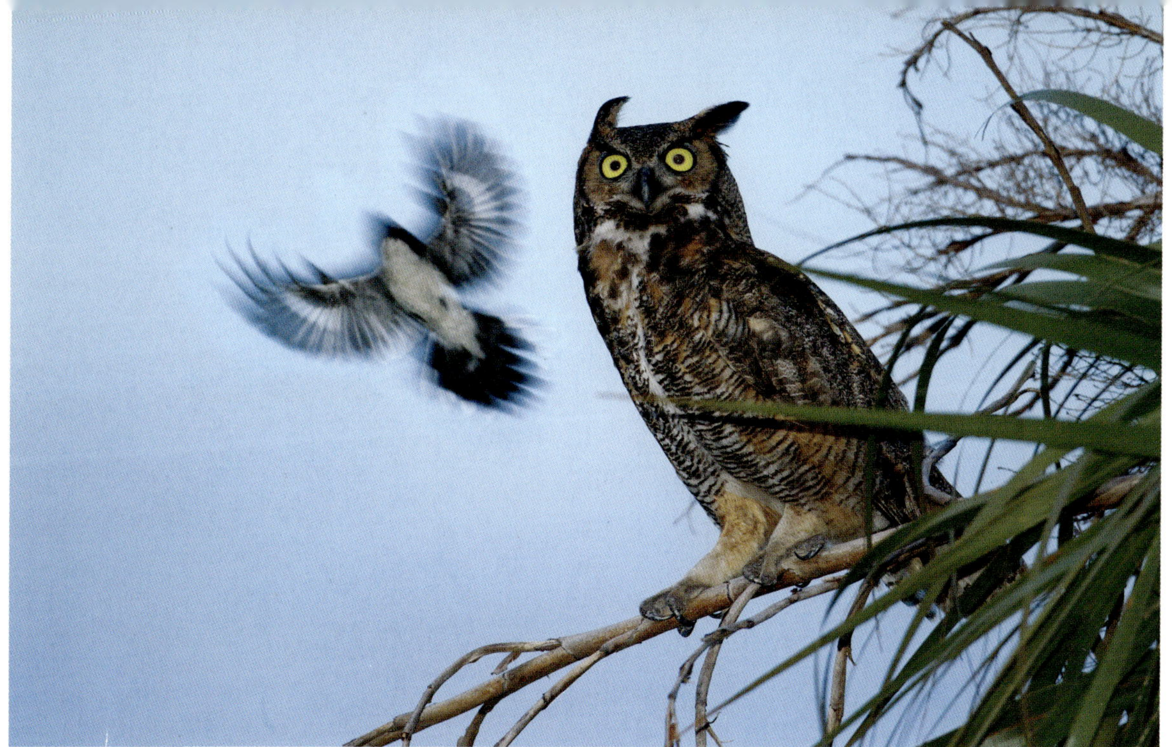

- If that doesn't do the trick, I often experiment with slower shutter times and creatively blurred images. Of course, it doesn't work all that often, but occasionally it produces interesting results.

- In a pinch and only when it's a subject that I might not encounter again, I'll resort to using the flash. It doesn't really bother the birds, and to the best of our knowledge, the flash also doesn't harm them, so you don't need to worry about that. But using the flash often produces unnatural-looking pictures with an unattractive light reflection in the birds' eyes. How to use the flash successfully is a science in itself and beyond the scope of this book.

◄ 4-117

Great horned owl | Florida | I rarely use the flash and only if I feel that I might not get another chance to photograph the bird in question, like this great horned owl being attacked by songbirds. | 500mm, aperture 4.5, 1/200 s, ISO 1600, +1 1/3 exposure compensation, flash

Rainy Day Pictures

Pictures taken on a rainy day can be very atmospheric, and they are special because not many photographers venture out in that kind of weather. Certainly, this has a lot to do with worries about the camera. But buying protective gear for your equipment isn't very expensive and you should definitely consider going on a photo shoot on a drizzly day. However, even I would avoid lashing rain unless it's possible to shelter from it. In a tree stand, rain is no problem and has never stopped me from spending the day! A heavy cloud cover and low light can be more of an issue. You'll need to keep an eye on your shutter speed to avoid undesirable blurring due to camera shake or motion blur. Open the aperture as wide as you can and adjust the ISO to get an exposure time that's short enough.

Rainy day pictures look best when the shutter speed is long enough to show the raindrops as blurry lines. Play around with settings between 1/125 s and 1/250 s. If the shutter speed is too slow, the rain will just be a gray veil in the image. If it's too fast, on the other hand, you'll only see individual dots and lose some of the effects.

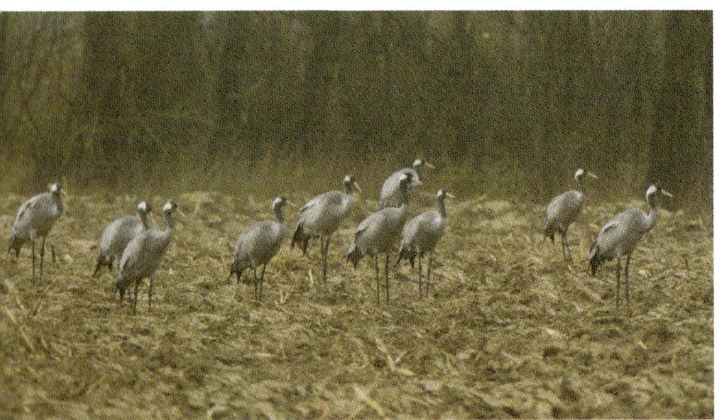

▲ 4-118

Cranes | Germany | This image was taken on a rainy, gloomy day and captures the dreary mood well. A long exposure time of 1/80 s turns the raindrops into blurry lines. | 500mm, aperture 5.6, 1/80 s, ISO 1600

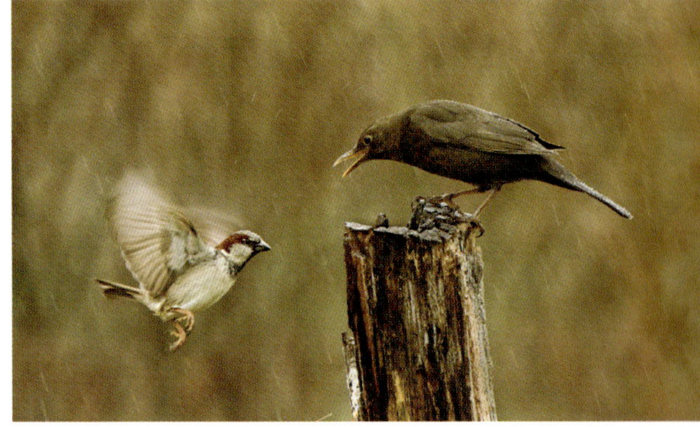

▲ 4-119

Blackbird and house sparrow | Germany | Another slow shutter speed transforms the drops into blurry lines although it actually rained less in this photo than in the one with the cranes. | 500mm, aperture 5.6, 1/200 s, ISO 1600

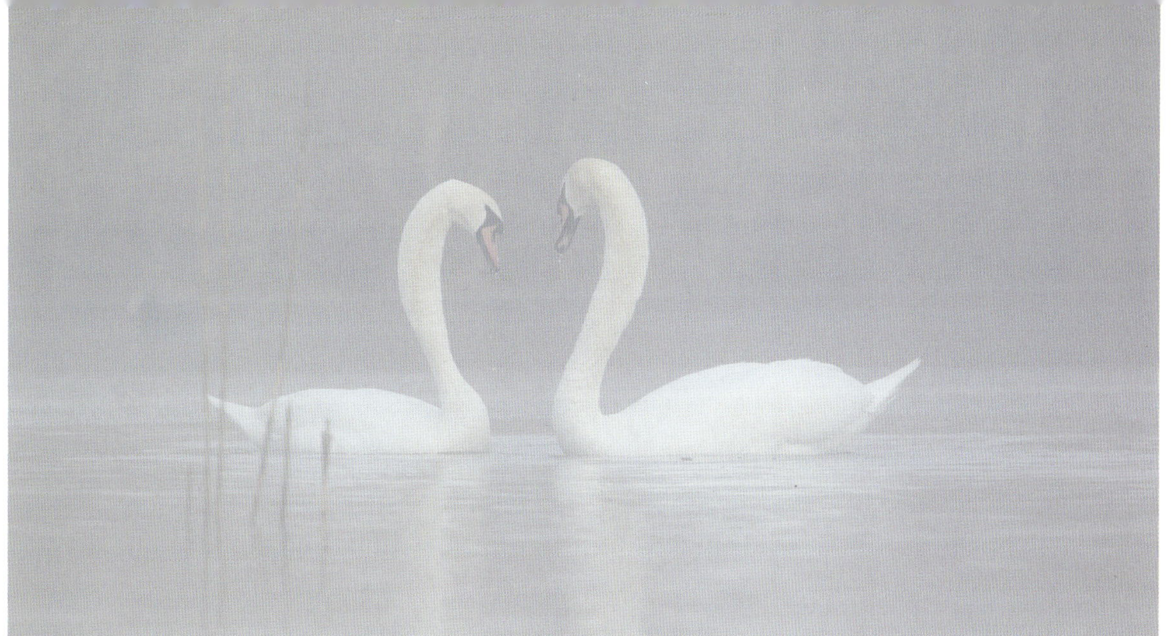

Foggy Day

You wake up and it's foggy and dim outside? No reason to leave the camera at home! With a bit of luck, you might capture some wonderful shots in the fog! Particularly, early morning fog hovering over a lake can add a wonderfully tender mood to a photo. But again, you will need to consider the exposure time when setting up your camera. As a rule, photographs taken in the fog will be brighter than average gray. This means that you'll have to correct the auto exposure once again and dial a positive exposure compensation. How many stops are needed depends on the overall level of brightness you want to achieve. The more you practice the more you'll develop a feeling for this and adjust the exposure compensation intuitively.

A second issue when photographing in the fog is that the auto-focus might fail to find enough contrast in the image to work. If this happens, you'll need to turn it off and focus manually.

▲ 4-120

Mute swans | Germany | The fog adds a tender mood that accentuates the courtship of the two swans. | 700mm (500mm + 1.4x converter), aperture 7.1, 1/800 s, ISO 1250, +1 exposure compensation

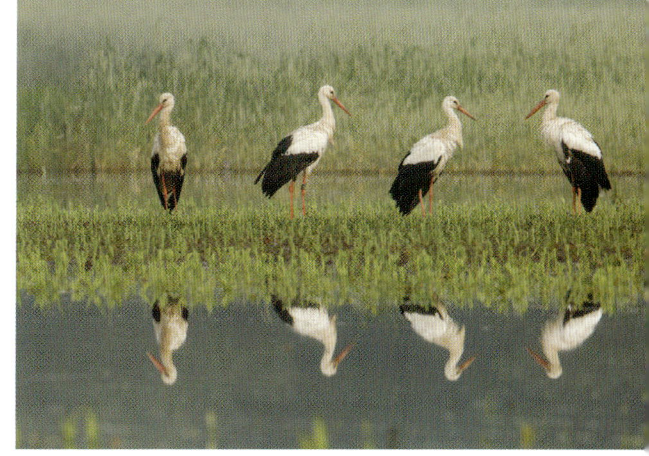

4-121 ▶

White storks | Germany | It was still early that morning and the day had started with some fog, which is still visible as a thin veil in the image. But I am very happy I took pictures that day. | 700mm (500mm + 1.7x converter), aperture 8.0, 1/800 s, ISO 800, +1/3 exposure compensation

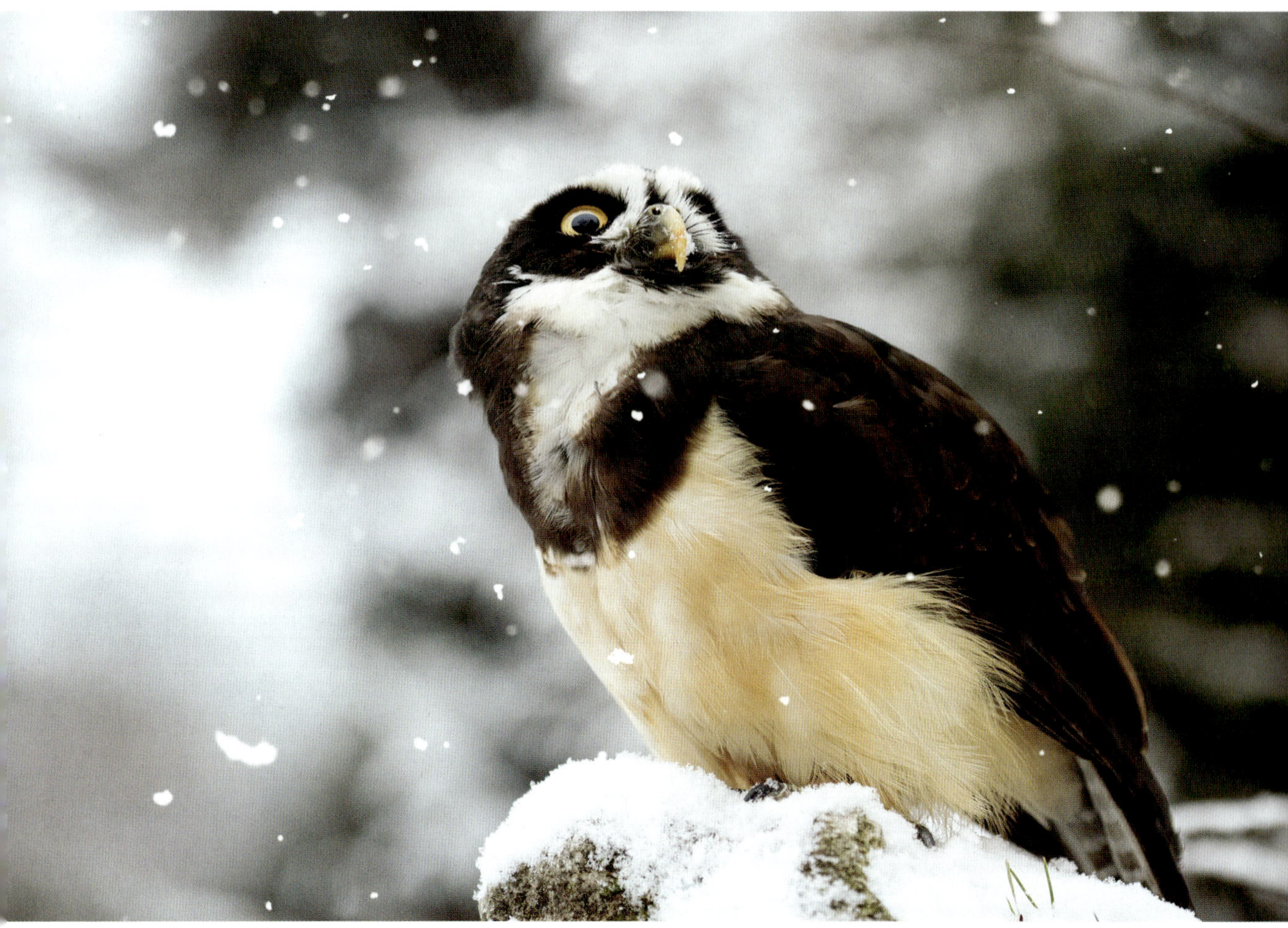

Spectacled owl | Germany | Winter's magic captured in a photo. | 135mm, aperture 2.8, 1/320 s, ISO 1600, +1/3 exposure compensation

Photographing in the Snow

Even if you'll shiver a bit, photographing in the snow is a whole lot of fun! You might have your own feeding station in the backyard or maybe you'll head out and visit a lake or even just a nearby zoo. But you'll most definitely come back with some very special pictures.

Bring a rain cover for your camera and lens, if you expect heavier snow showers, and remember to wear warm but thin winter gloves. There are wonderful photographer's gloves available with flap-back finger caps. Pack plenty of batteries as they drain faster in the cold than on warm days. If possible, carry your spare batteries in pockets close to your body instead of in your photo backpack so they don't get too cold.

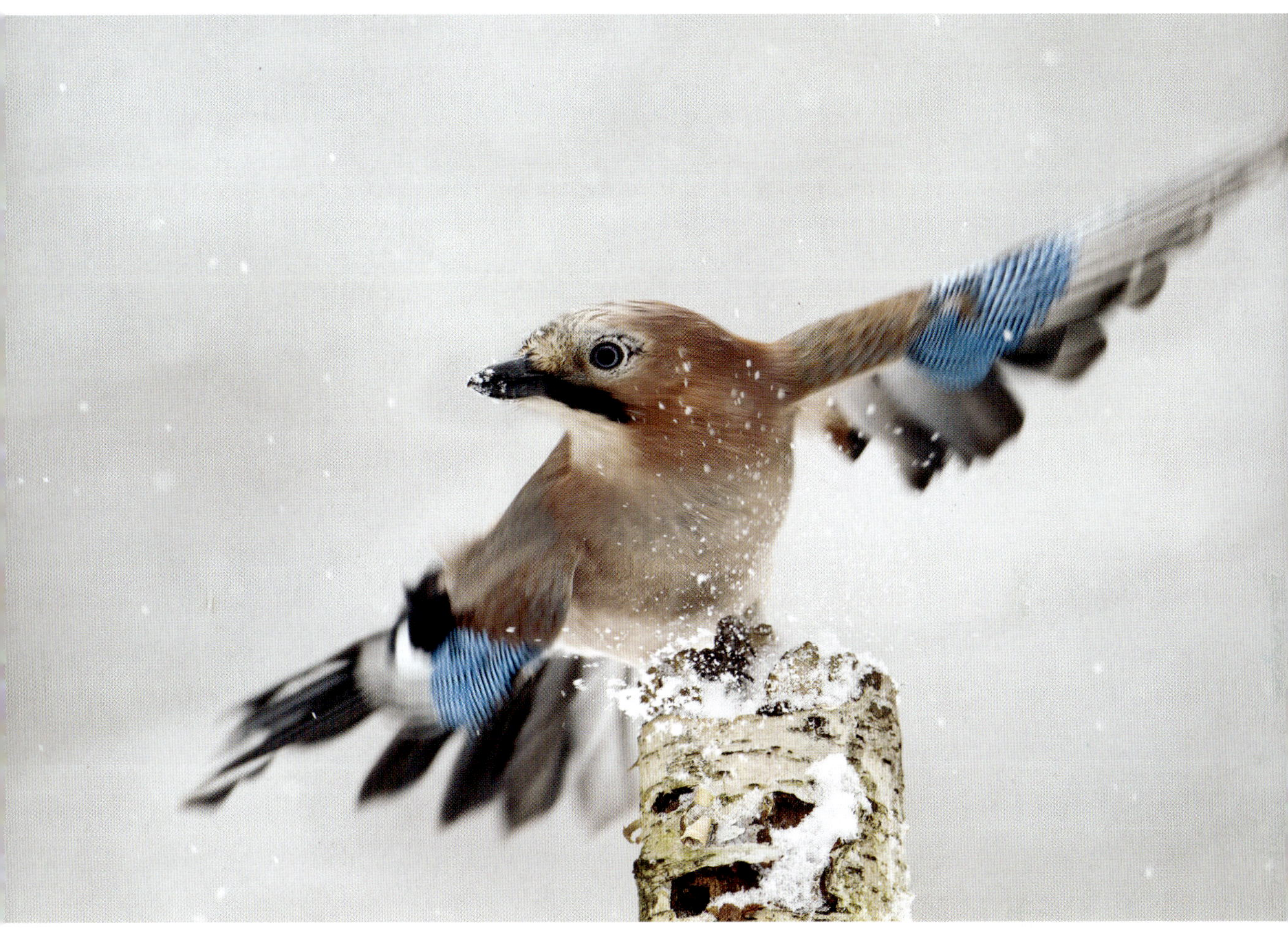

Snowflakes look best in photos when they are slightly blurred; shutter speeds can easily be around 1/250 s. And remember: If there's a lot of snow in the picture, you'll have to trick the auto exposure and work with exposure compensation. The more white there is in the picture, the more stops of positive exposure compensation you have to dial. And your pictures will be especially beautiful if you photograph at eye level—even if you have to kneel or sit in the snow to achieve this.

Don't rub at snowflakes that might cling to your camera, since you might rub moisture into the housing. Just blow them off or gently dab at the camera and leave it to dry. After you're done photographing, don't put the camera into a very warm room right away; give it some time first to "acclimate" to higher temperatures again.

▲ 4-123

Jay | Germany | Remember to use exposure compensation when photographing in the snow! | 500mm, aperture 5.0, 1/500 s, ISO 1250, +1 exposure compensation

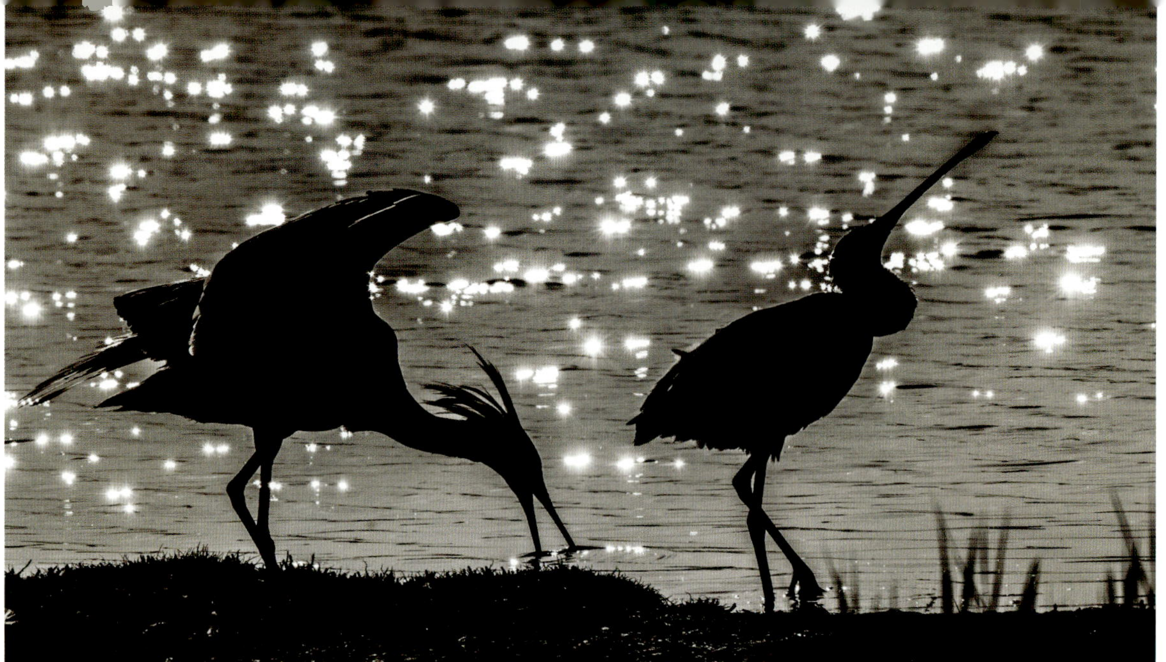

Starburst Effect

In certain situations, it's possible to create a so-called starburst effect by using some tricks. One method is to shoot against the sun at sunset, with the sun partially blocked by something—ideally our subject, the bird. To do this successfully you'll need to get the placement just right and start photographing once you've found the right spot. The sun should only peek out slightly from behind the subject. Any bigger and it'll become just a bright white spot in the photo. You'll recognize the right moment by looking through the viewfinder. But you must keep the aperture closed to get the effect. In my experience, an aperture of about f/16 is ideal. I don't want to get too technical here, but it has to do with the number of blades and the shape of the lens. Unfortunately, this also means that not every lens will allow you to create starburst effects. This is another case where only trial and error will tell!

A second scenario in which starburst effects become possible are pictures of choppy water with backlight. Again, close the aperture to about f/16.

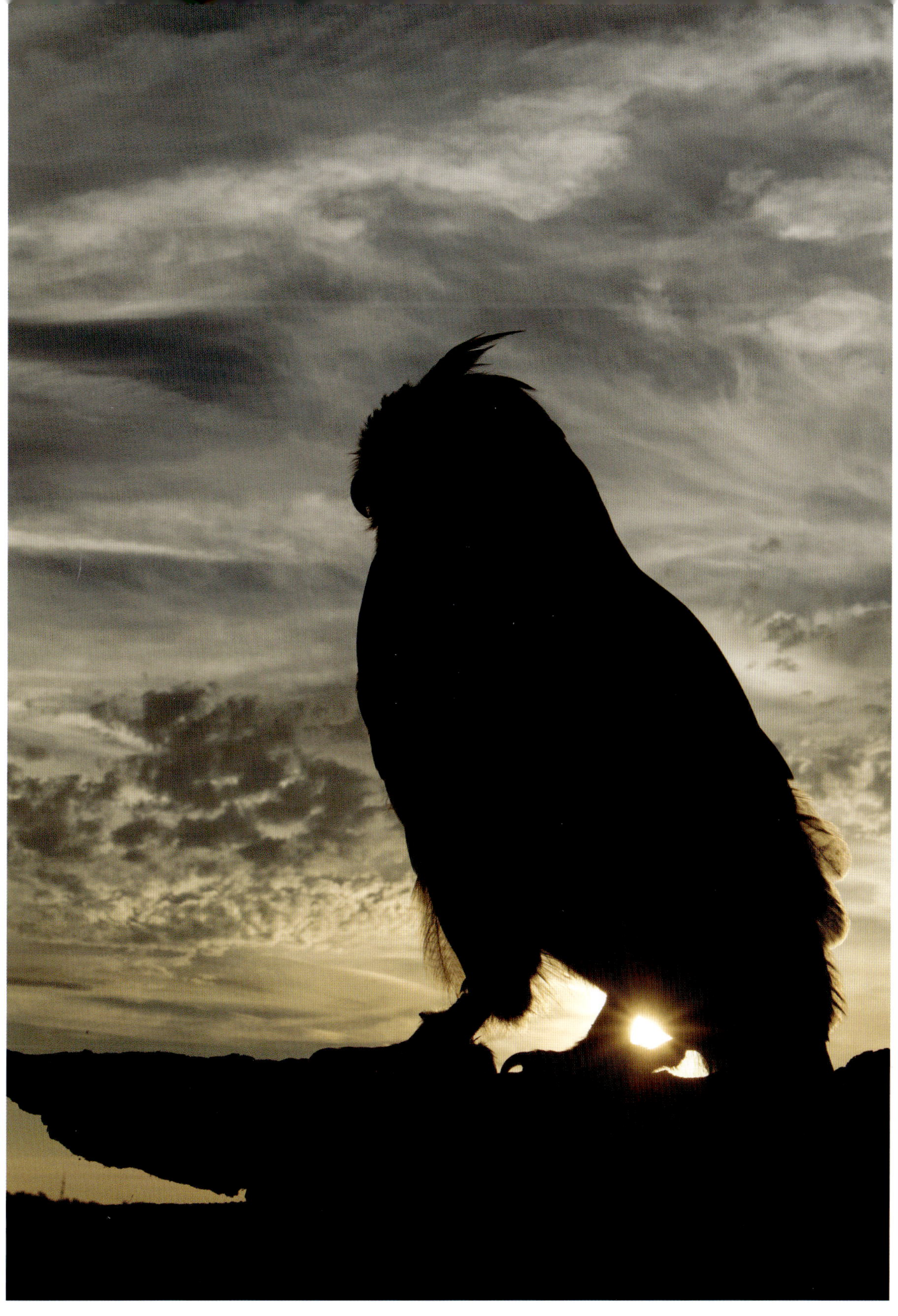

4.4 Colors in Images

Photographing in Black and White

In my opinion, very few motifs in bird photography work well in black and white.

The idea behind black-and-white photography is that everything is reduced to its essence, and the eye doesn't get distracted by colors. I've experimented now and then with conversions to black and white but have rarely liked the results. To get an attractive image there needs to be very little that detracts from the main subject. In other words: There needs to be clear structures and an uncluttered background. It's best to do the conversion on the computer during editing and you can use any standard editing software. This also allows you to compare which version of the photo looks better: color or black and white.

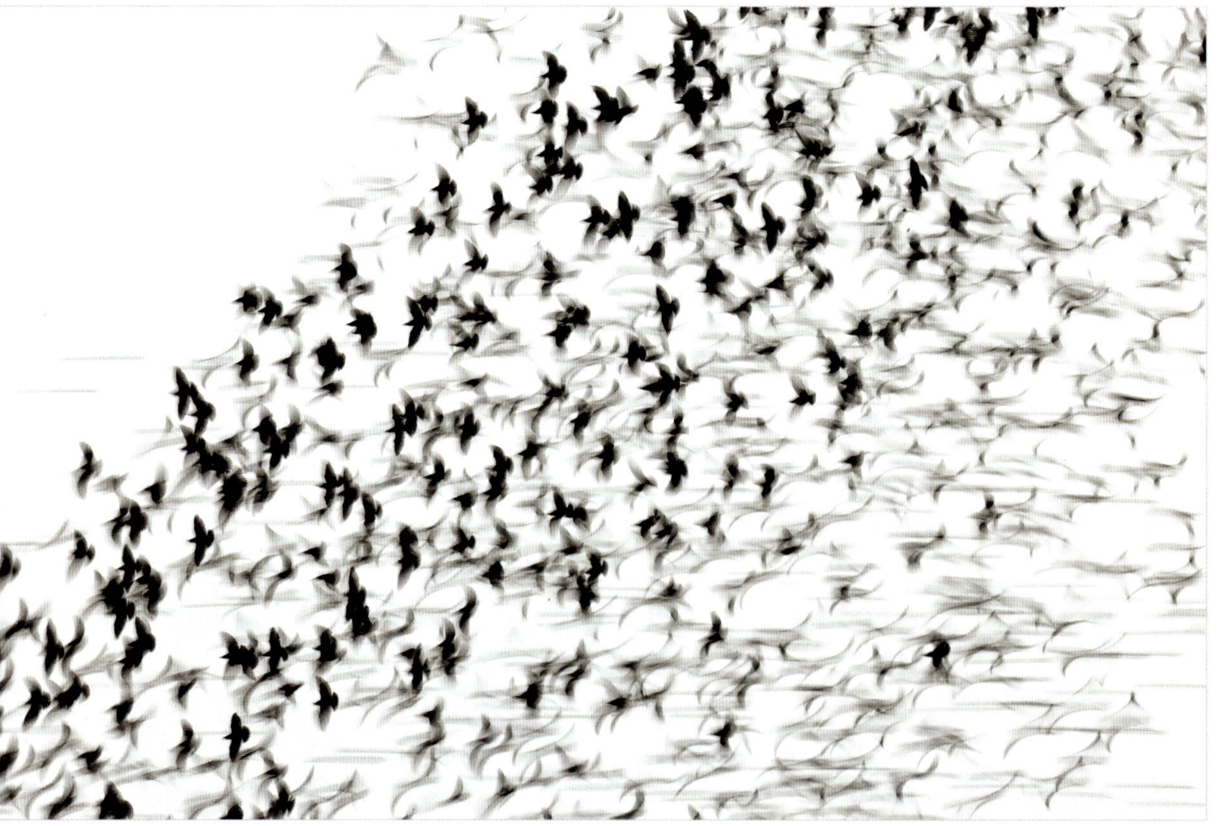

▲ 4-126

Starlings | Germany | Even in the original, this image of starlings was mostly composed of just blacks and whites. By converting it to black and white, the image's message is reduced to its essence. | 200mm, aperture 25, 1/25 s, ISO 1000, +1 1/3 exposure compensation

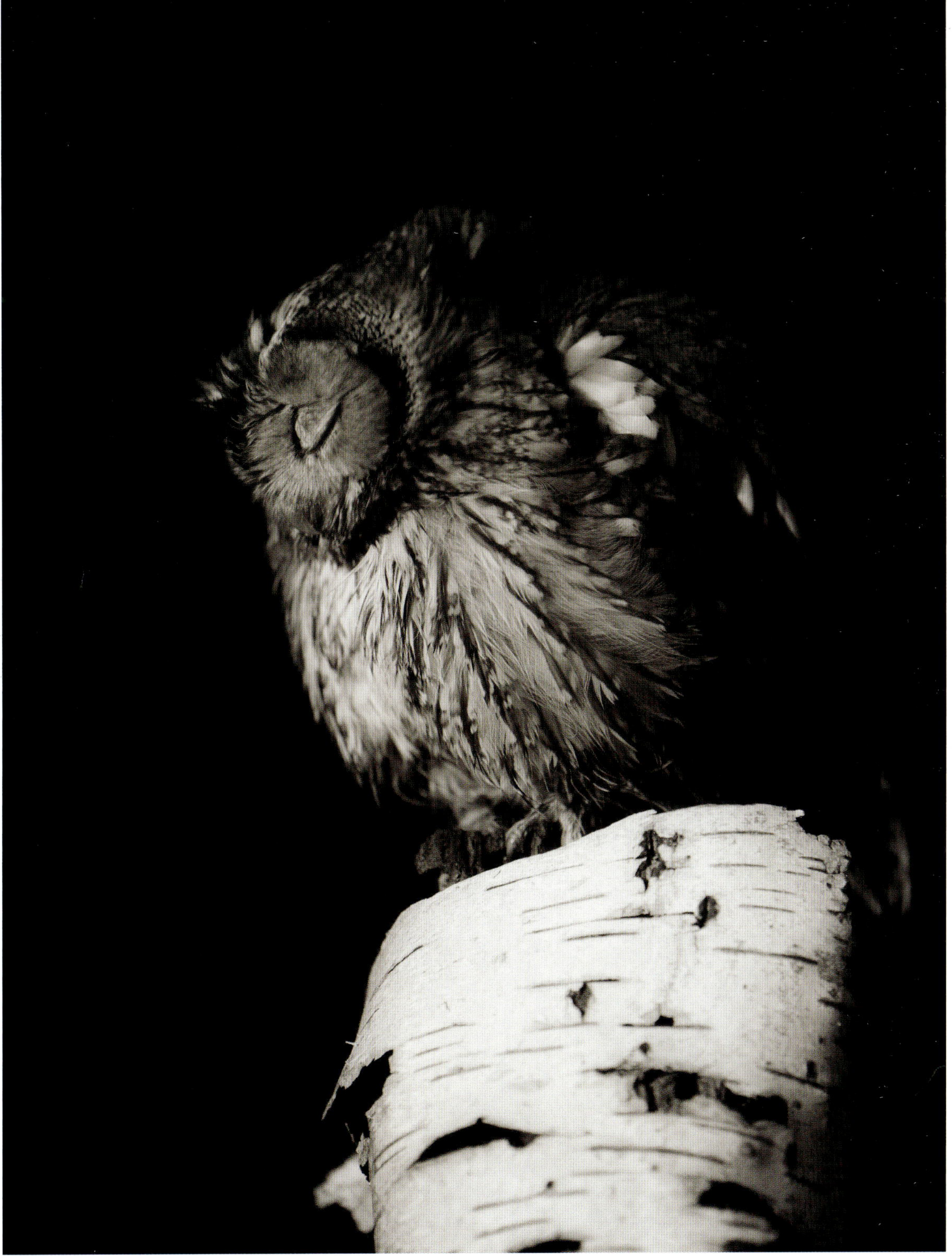

Tawny owl | Germany | The black and white highlights the nocturnal nature of the owl's activity as well as the texture of its plumage. | 135mm, aperture 2.2, 1/8000 s, ISO 500, -1 1/3, exposure compensation

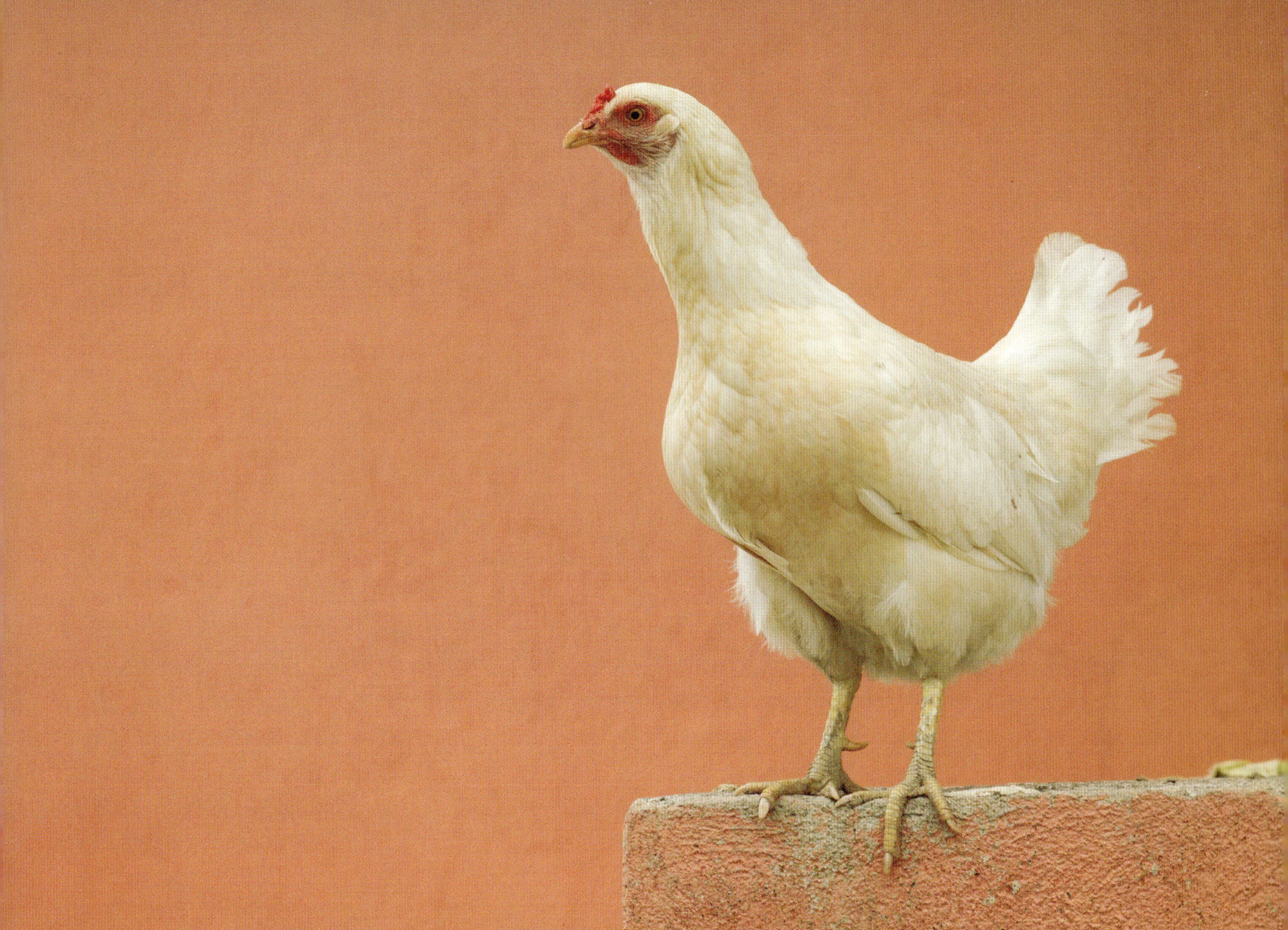

Capturing Colors

I like tone-on-tone pictures but photos in which the colors stand out can also be very charming. On photo tours, I make it a habit to look for opportunities to include color accents in pictures. Zoos or bird parks offer good opportunities for this. Berries, blooming plants, colorful flower beds, or containers can be attractive backgrounds or even foregrounds.

Color may even become the main motif, as in the picture of a chicken that I photographed in Turkey against the background of a salmon-hued wall. On its own, the chicken would have probably been rather boring, but combined with the paint of the wall it becomes interesting.

Of course, it's especially nice when the colors are taken up again in the bird's plumage. But that might really be asking too much….

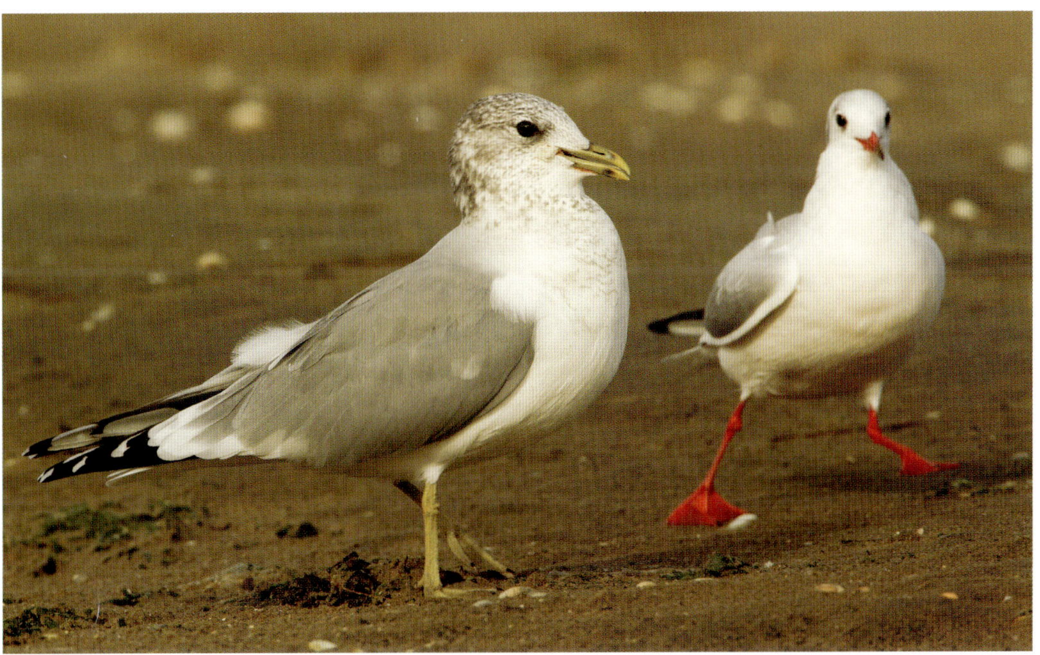

▲ 4-129

Common and black-headed gull | Texel, The Netherlands | This photo, too, only works because of the red of the black-headed gull's feet. | 700mm (500mm + 1.4x converter), aperture 10, 1/1250 s, ISO 640

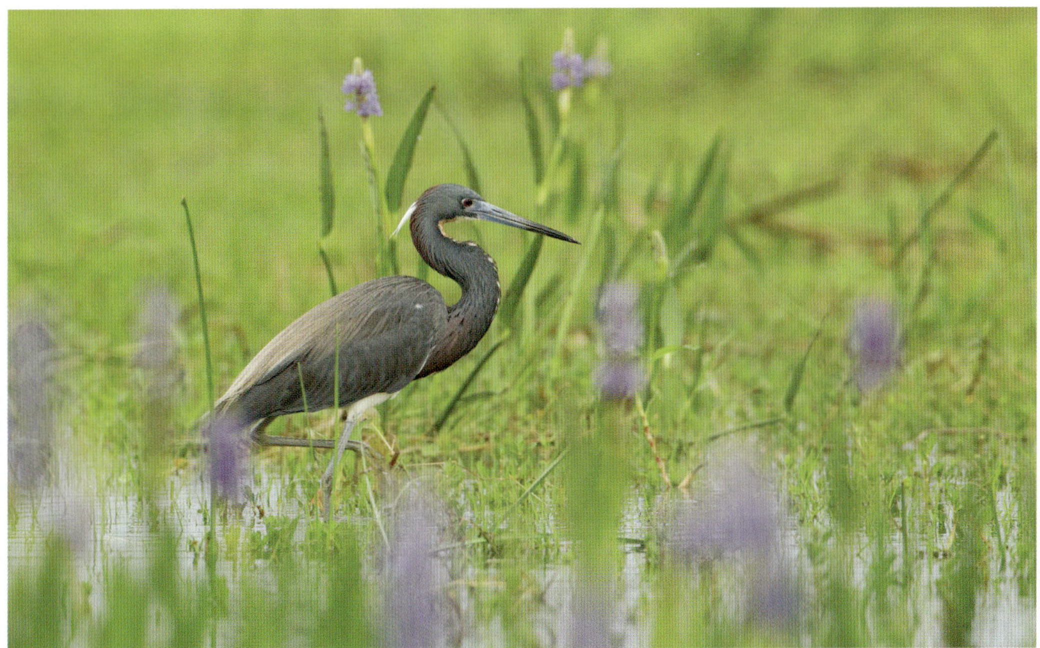

▲ 4-130

Great blue heron | Florida | The purple of the flowers in the foreground and background appear again in the feathers of the great blue heron. | 500mm, aperture 5.6, 1/200 s, ISO 1600

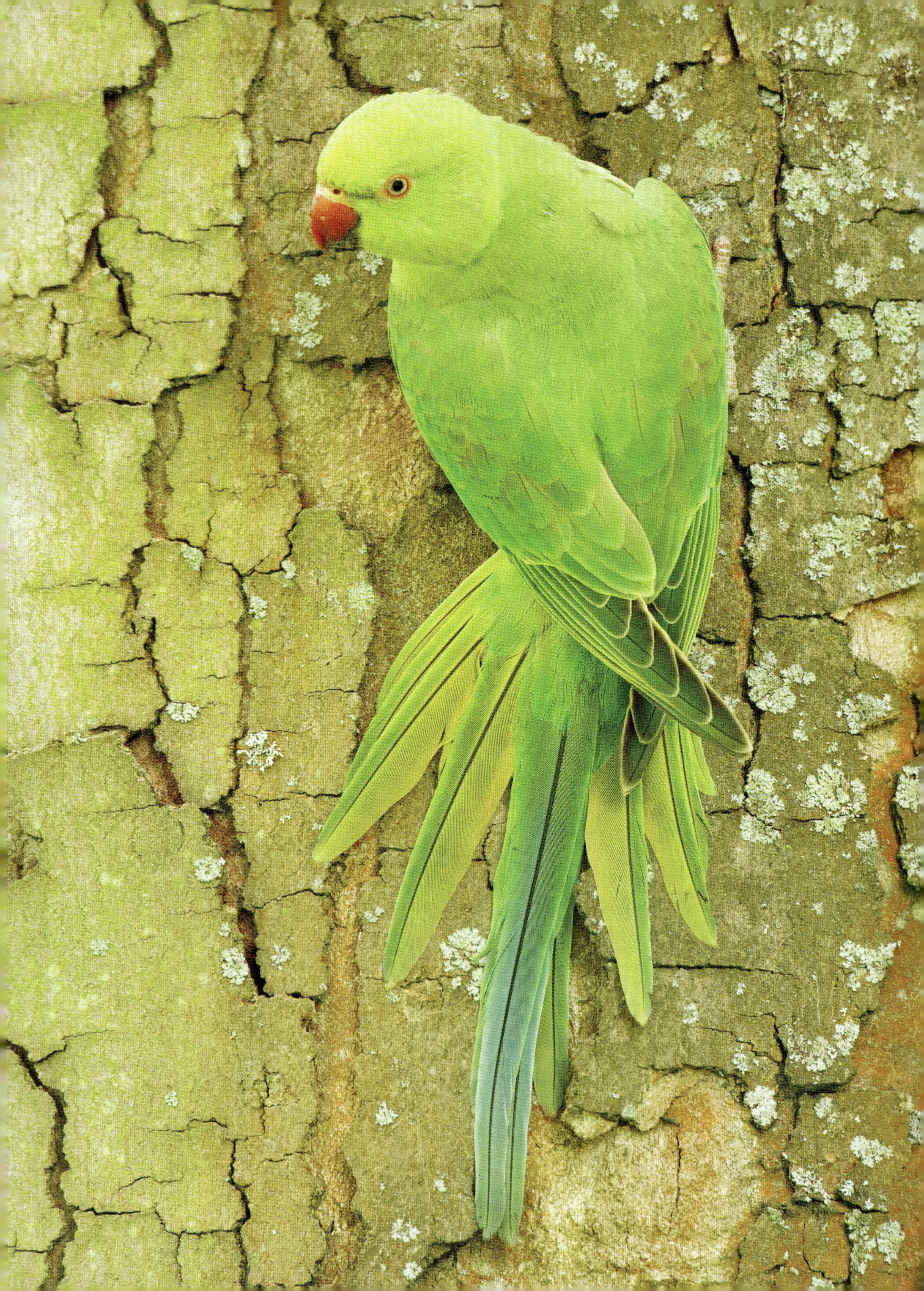

Rose-ringed parakeet | Germany | This image of the colorful bird is a symphony in green. | 500mm, aperture 5.6, 1/80 s, ISO 1000

Tone on Tone

I often try to capture what's essential or use a "less is more" approach. For that reason, I tend to like pictures in which the same color shows up again and again and nothing distracts from the main subject, the bird. Of course, it's often pure luck if that happens. But you can increase the chances by your choice of location and composition.

Try taking a step or two to the right or left while photographing. A different angle creates a different background—and often different colors. I know it's quite common to find a good spot and keep photographing but I always encourage the participants of my workshops to keep looking for new viewpoints!

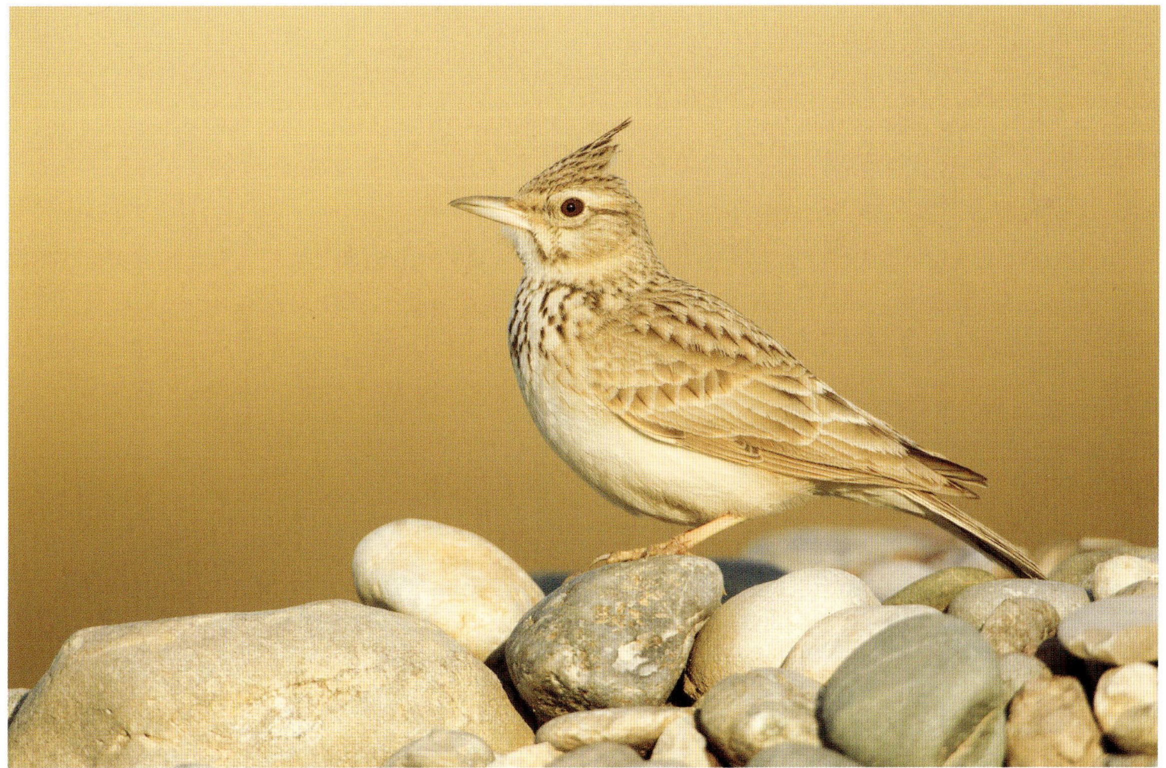

▲ 4-132

Crested lark | Morocco | This image is a palette of beiges. The result is a very warm, harmonious photograph. | 500mm, aperture 5.0, 1/2000 s, ISO 1250

Background Colors

Sometimes, the photo is less about the bird itself and more about the exciting background colors. Especially when photographing waterfowl, including the often splendid reflections of their surroundings in the water can be a good way to include some color in the photo. In zoos particularly, trees or colorful buildings are often reflected in the water.

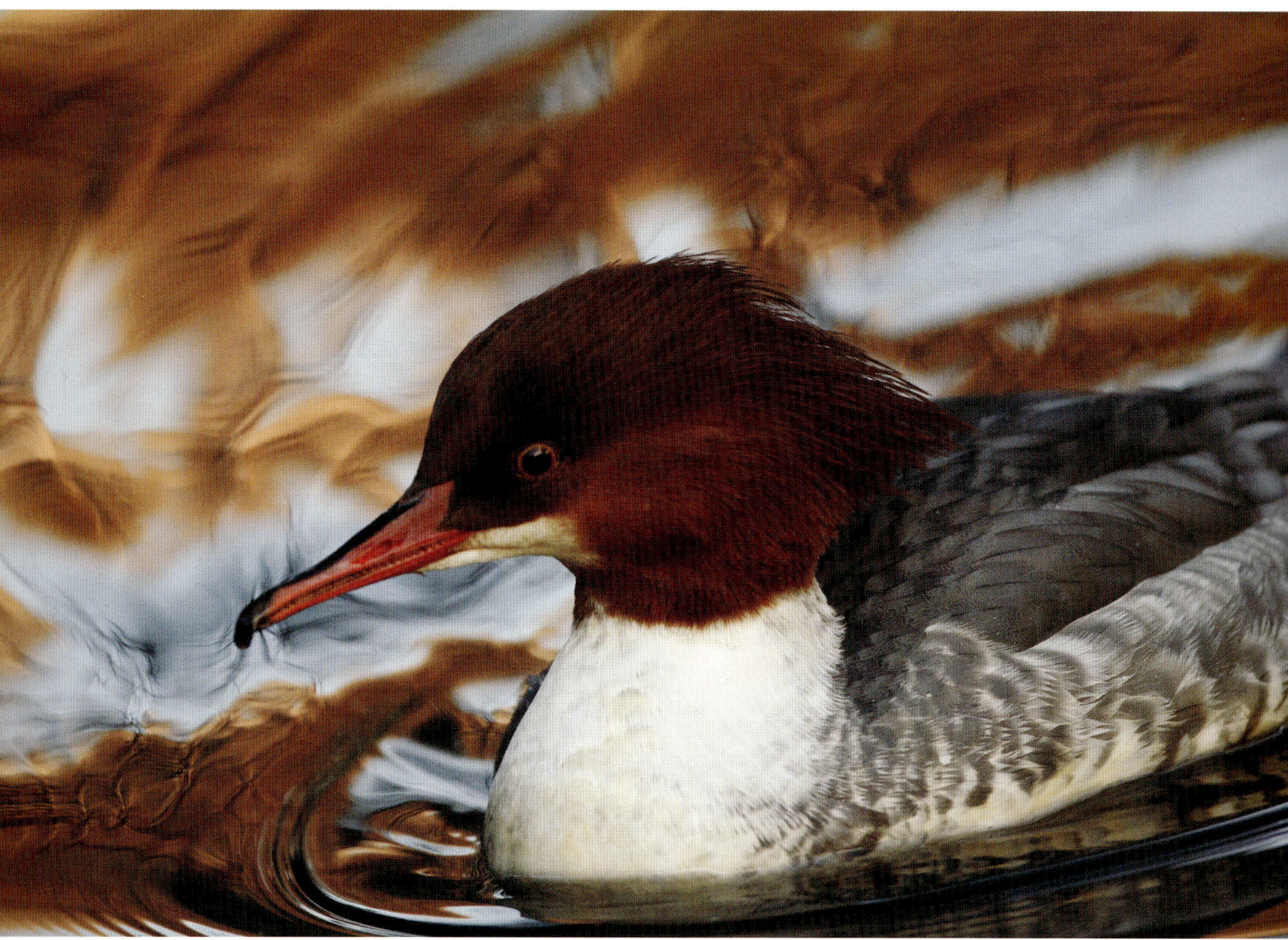

▲ 4-133

Common merganser | Cologne Zoo, Germany | The reflected fall foliage of some trees adds some magnificent color accents. | 500mm, aperture 4.0, 1/320 s, ISO 1000, -2/3 exposure compensation

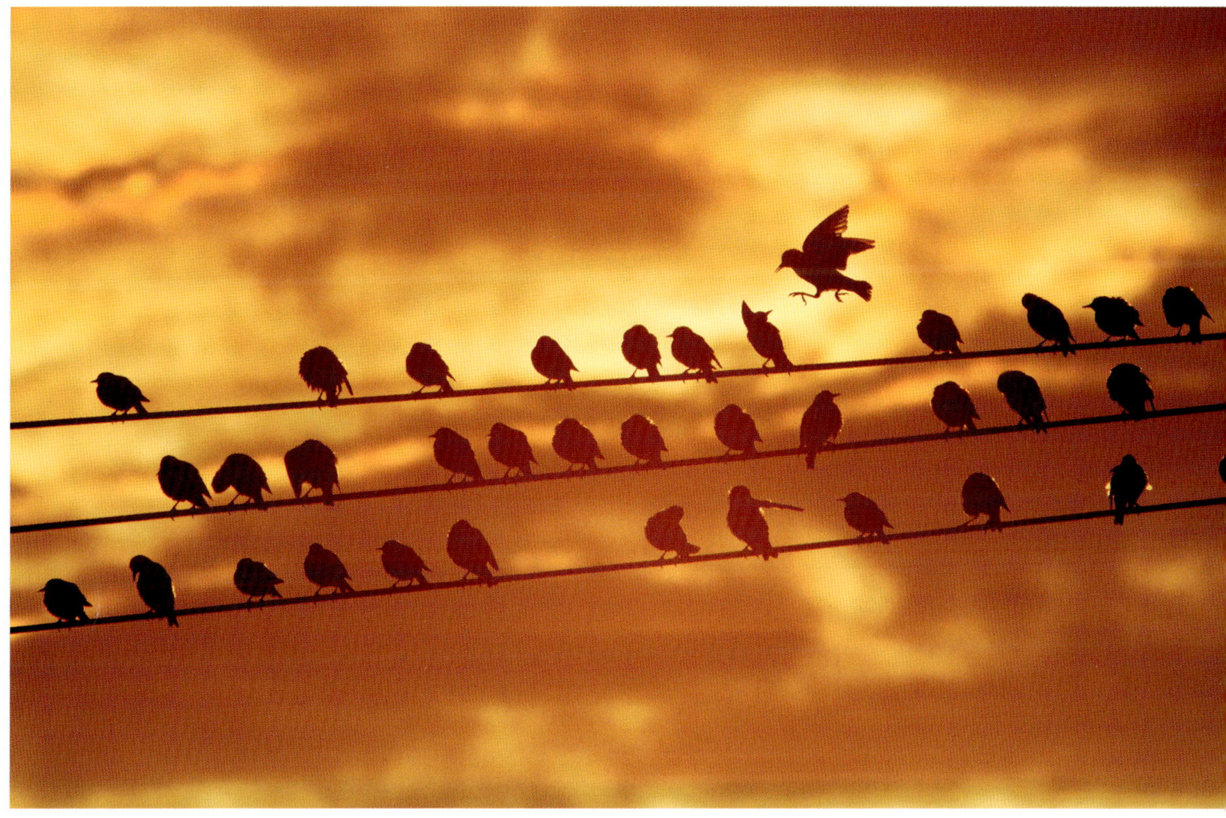

▲ 4-134

Starlings | Germany | It's the strong orange of the sunset and the silhouette of the lone starling in motion that makes this image effective. | 700mm (500mm + 1.4x converter), aperture 16, 1/5000 s, ISO 500

4.5 Achieving Success with Bird-in-Flight Photography

Perfect Focus

If you're into bird photography, then you also want to take impressive bird-in-flight shots. After all, it's one of the fascinating characteristics of most birds that they can move effortlessly through the air.

Getting them sharp is the most important criterion for successful in-flight shots. You'll need to decide from the get-go if you want to freeze the motion or include motion blur. Depending on the size of the bird this means adjusting the shutter speed. In addition to the size of the bird, it's also important in which direction it's flying and how far away it is. A small house martin prowling for insects will beat its wings fast and fly in a barely predictable zigzag pattern, while a large white

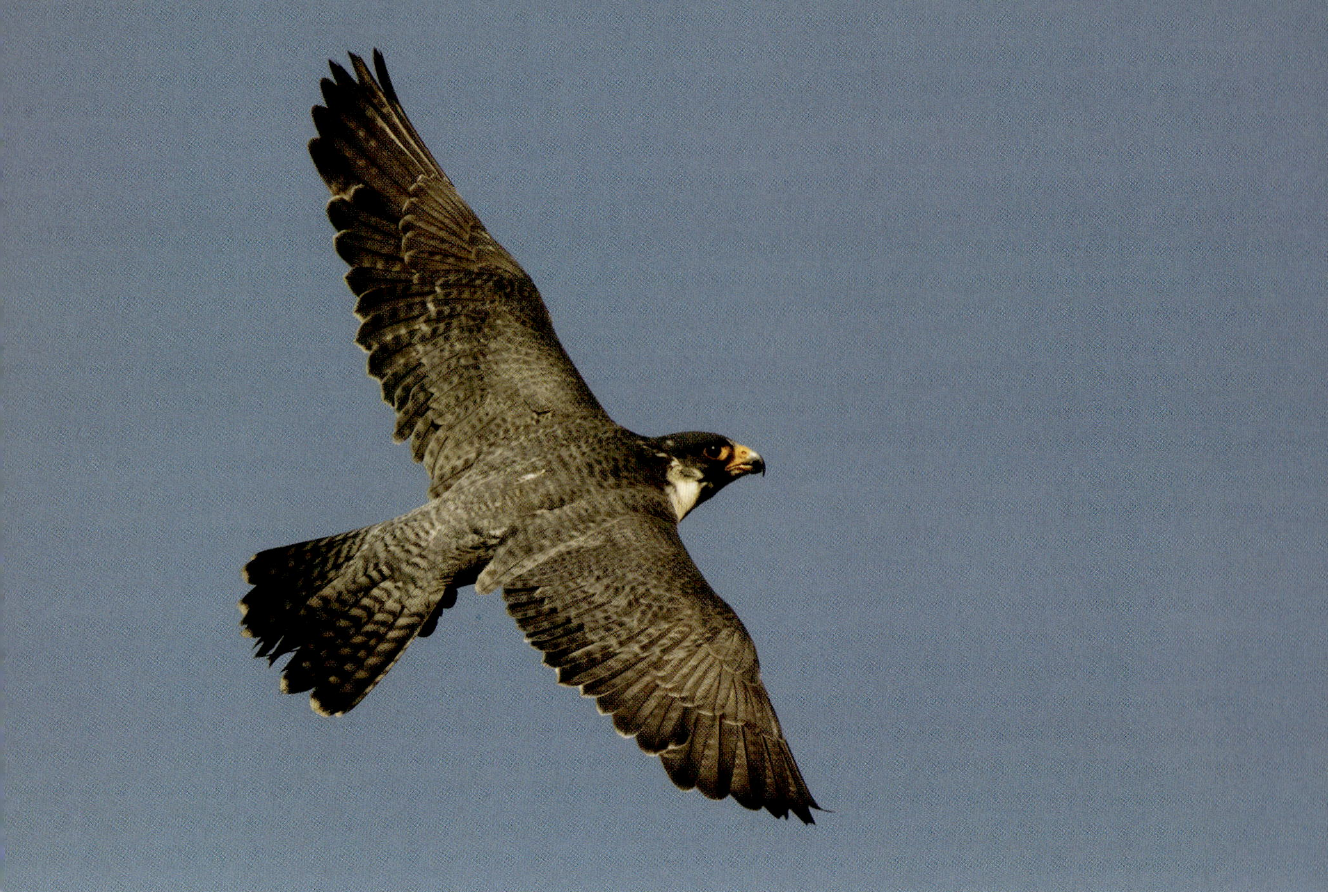

Peregrine falcon | German Raptor Research Center at Guttenberg Castle, Germany | The peregrine falcon is the fastest bird in the world, and to capture it in-flight, you need a fast shutter speed. | 400mm, aperture 5.6, 1/8000 s, ISO 800

stork will usually travel in a straight line with slowly beating wings. Furthermore, it makes a difference whether the bird is flying parallel to the camera or toward it. For a large bird traveling parallel, a shutter speed of 1/500 s is often fine, while for small songbirds at the feeder, times of 1/2000 s can still be too slow to get the wingtips perfectly sharp.

There are several ways to achieve the appropriate fast shutter speed. You can either measure the correct exposure and set all the values manually—this can be a good option if the light doesn't change, for example, because you're only photographing in one direction and there is steady sunlight. It's also a useful method if you photograph an unchanging subject against a changing background. It allows you to ensure that the main subject, the bird, is always evenly exposed, regardless of whether the background is light or dark.

If the background is stable, it's a good idea to pick an exposure time and set the ISO to a value that will make the camera choose an

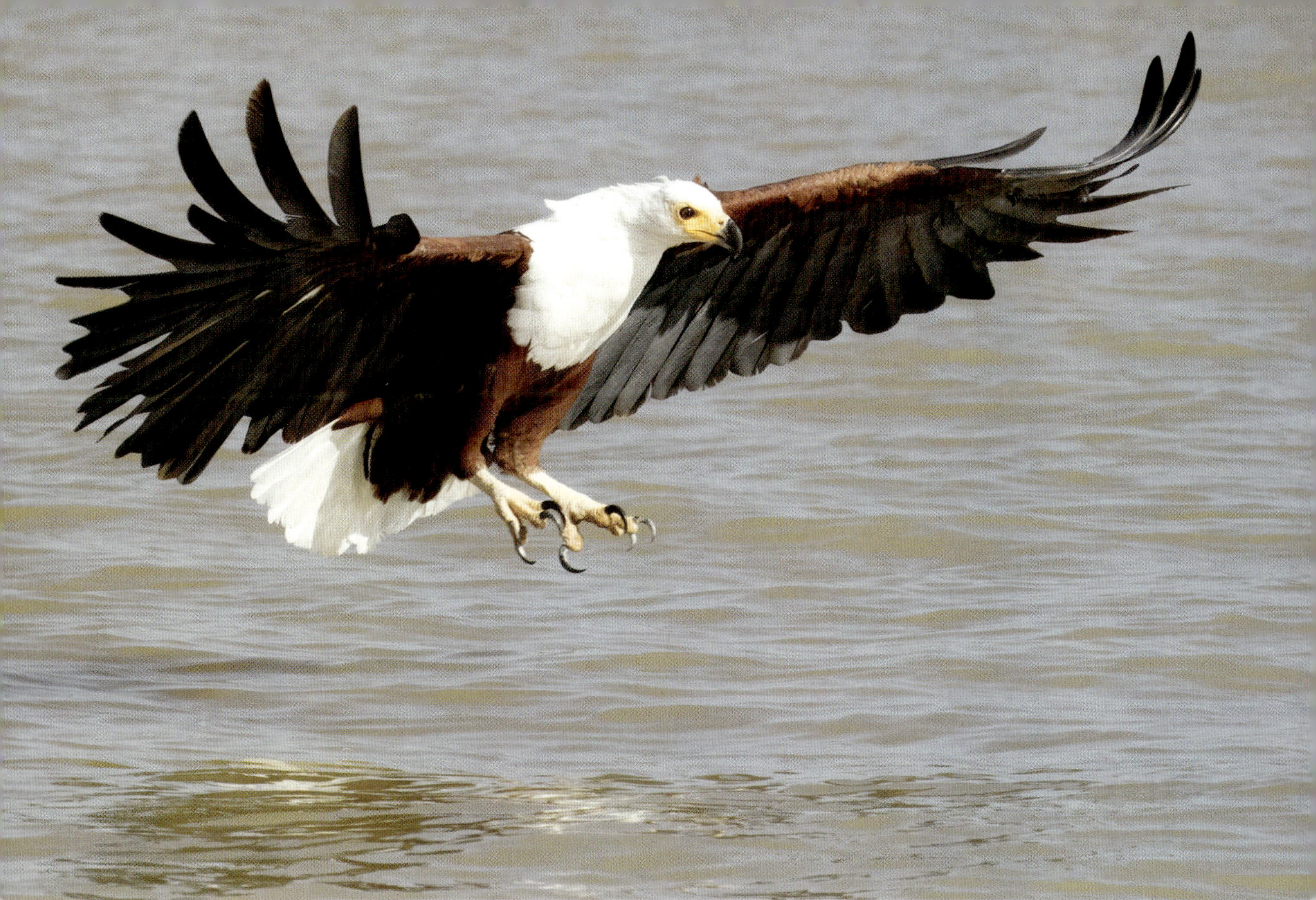

African fish eagle | Kenya | One moment later, the African fish eagle pulled a fish from the water. A situation that calls for continuous shooting! | 200mm, aperture 13, 1/1600 s, ISO 1250

aperture that will expose the image correctly. For example, you can pick a shutter speed of 1/2000 s and an ISO of 800, and the camera will calculate the appropriate aperture.

But for myself, I again prefer to pick the aperture, then set the ISO to ensure a fast, i.e., short, exposure time. I usually open the aperture fully or stop down one or two stops and increase the ISO until I get the desired shutter speed of, say, 1/2000 s. However, my method means I must always keep an eye on the exposure times that the camera picks, especially if the light changes, for example, because clouds are moving in.

It's purely a matter of personal preference and routine what kind of exposure metering you choose. Every photographer swears by his or her method.

But there can't be any debate about what autofocus settings you'll need. It's crucially important that it's set to focus tracking. This means that the camera continuously adjusts the focus when the

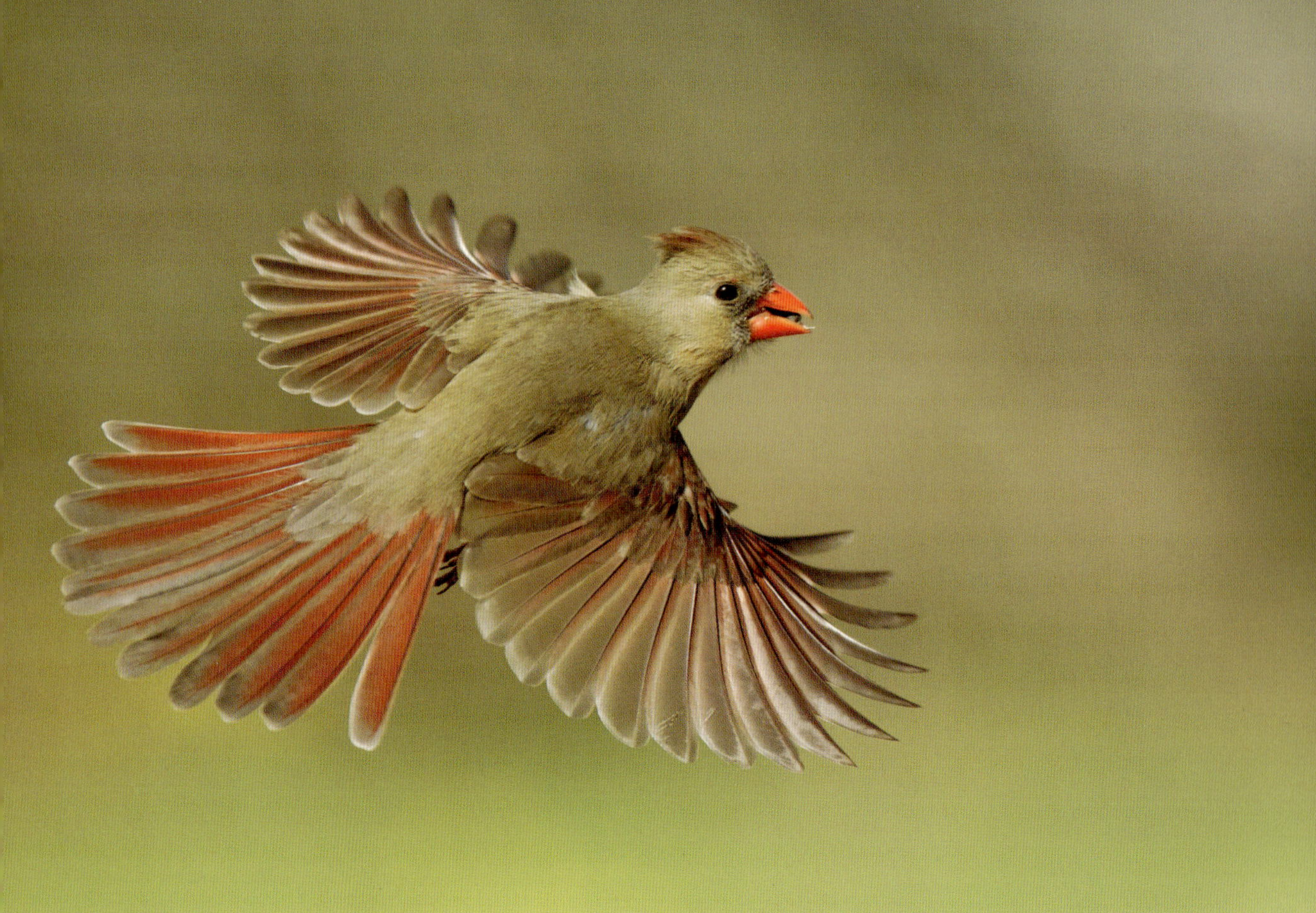

Northern cardinal | Texas | Bird-in-flight shots of small songbirds are particularly challenging. Their flight paths are often unpredictable. But you'll still have a good chance at the feeding station if you can guess their landing spot. | 300mm, aperture 4.0, 1/6400 s, ISO 800

shutter-release button is half-depressed or even when you release the shutter and take a series of pictures. This is the opposite of the so-called one-shot mode, in which the autofocus "locks in" when the shutter button is half-depressed, then stops focusing when the subject moves. So make sure you activate focus tracking.

On top of that, I recommend activating the continuous shooting mode so you can take a whole series of bird-in-flight shots. Not every phase of bird flight is equally attractive. The most beautiful moments are when the wings are in their highest position.

You'll also have to put some thought into the autofocus area. You can activate all areas and let the camera decide where it puts the focus—this works quite well with most cameras, especially if the sky is uniformly blue. But for a bit more control you can set the focus area yourself. I recommend that you select the center focus area since it's the one that works most precisely. Usually, when taking aerial shots,

CHAPTER 4

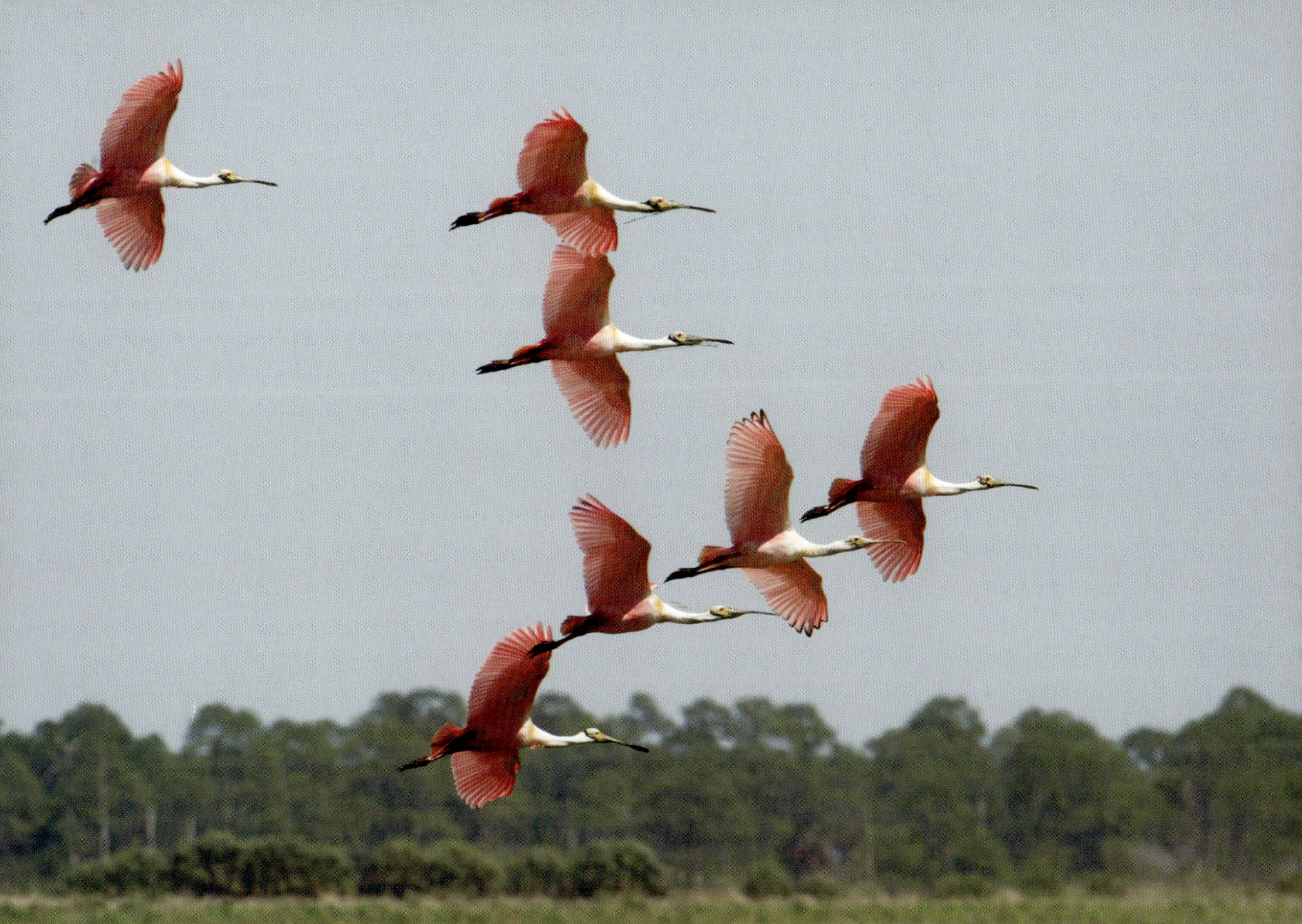

▲ 4-138

Roseate spoonbill | Florida | In this photo, the flight formation as well as all of the birds' wing positions work. | 500mm, aperture 13, 1/1250 s, ISO 640

the bird will be far enough away that there is enough depth of field to keep the eye in focus, even if the autofocus targets the bird's breast, for example.

Finally, there's the issue of finding and keeping the bird in the viewfinder at all. Especially with long focal lengths, this is easier said than done. Try locating the bird with your naked eye first, then pointing the camera exactly in your line of sight. This works much better than starting with the viewfinder and trying to locate the bird through it.

The most important thing for successful bird-in-flight shots is practice and lots of it. Setting up a routine will make them much easier!

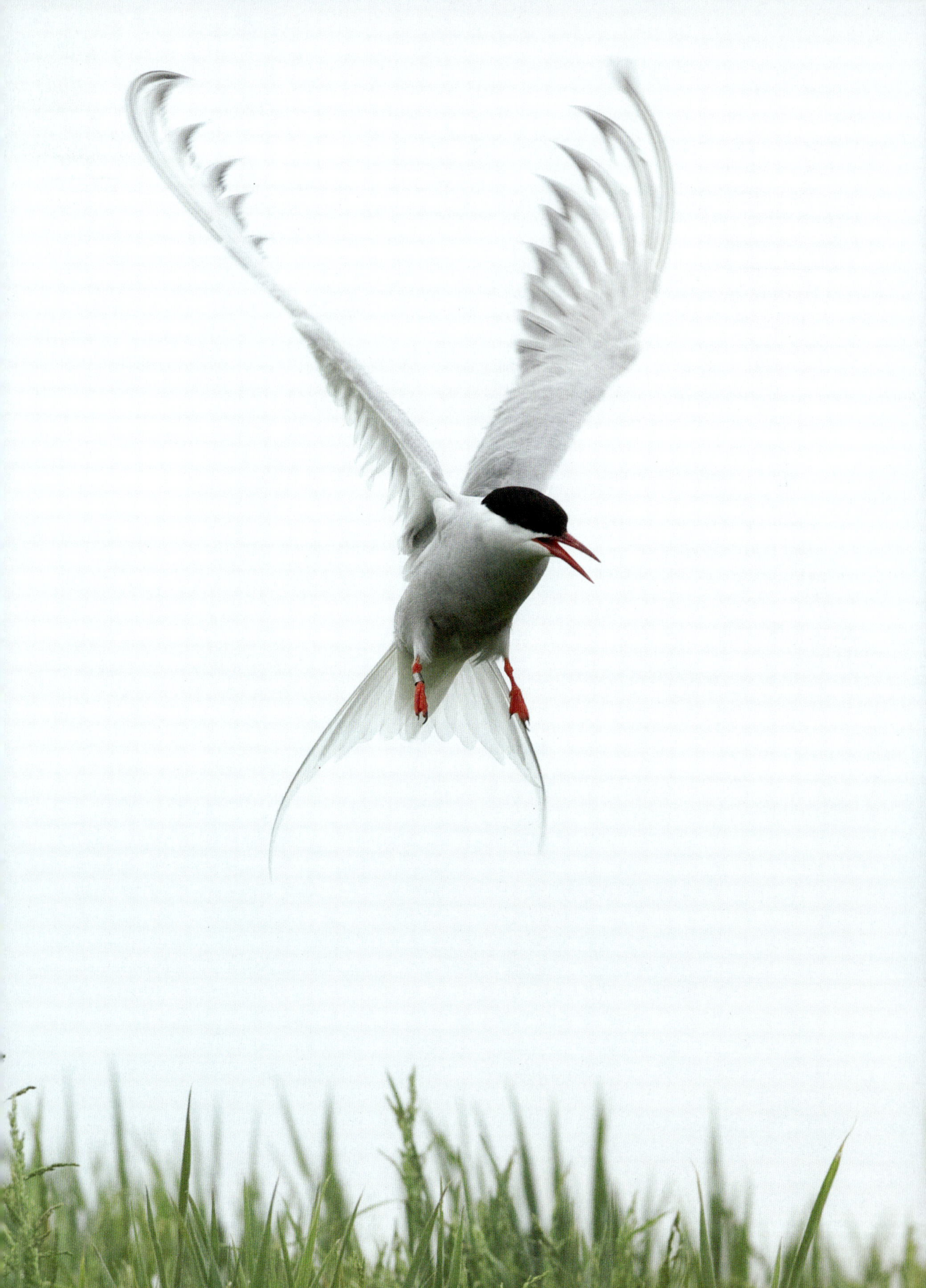

The Sky in Bird-in-Flight Shots

Most bird photographers dream of bird-in-flight shots under blue skies. The exposure is straightforward and the autofocus will have little trouble finding the subject. If the sky is blue, you don't have to consider anything beyond what was described in the previous section on "Perfect Focus." Unfortunately, the weather isn't always that glorious, and we're often dealing with an overcast and thus almost white sky. This means that if you don't correct the exposure, you'll be disappointed in your pictures: The sky will look gray and the bird will be only a black silhouette.

So you'll have to continuously adjust the exposure and either expose completely manually or, as I usually do, dial a positive exposure compensation. This is especially important when photographing white birds against a white sky. Of course, the opposite is true for bird-in-flight shots against a dark forest background. In that case, you must dial a negative number to correct the exposure.

◀ **4-139**

Arctic tern | Farne Island | White bird against a white sky—this calls for exposure compensation! The 1 1/3 exposure stops I chose were not quite enough and I had to increase the level of brightness some more during editing. | 300mm, aperture 7.1, 1/1000 s, ISO 1600, +1 1/3 exposure compensation

Birds During Landing

One of my favorite subjects is birds during landing. It's a situation that is relatively easy to control, and the images tend to show the bird with their wings magnificently displayed, fully fanned out and raised to decelerate before landing.

There are two ways to capture this in a photo: You can either start tracking the bird in the viewfinder while it's still far away and release the shutter as it comes in. Or you focus on the landing site and release the shutter when the bird enters that view.

With the first option, you mustn't release the shutter too early. Otherwise, the autofocus will lose track of the subject just as it's about to land. Only release the shutter once the bird is almost at its landing site.

Eagle owl | Wales | Just before landing, the eagle owl spread its wings to decelerate. | 110mm, aperture 5.6, 1/640 s, ISO 1250

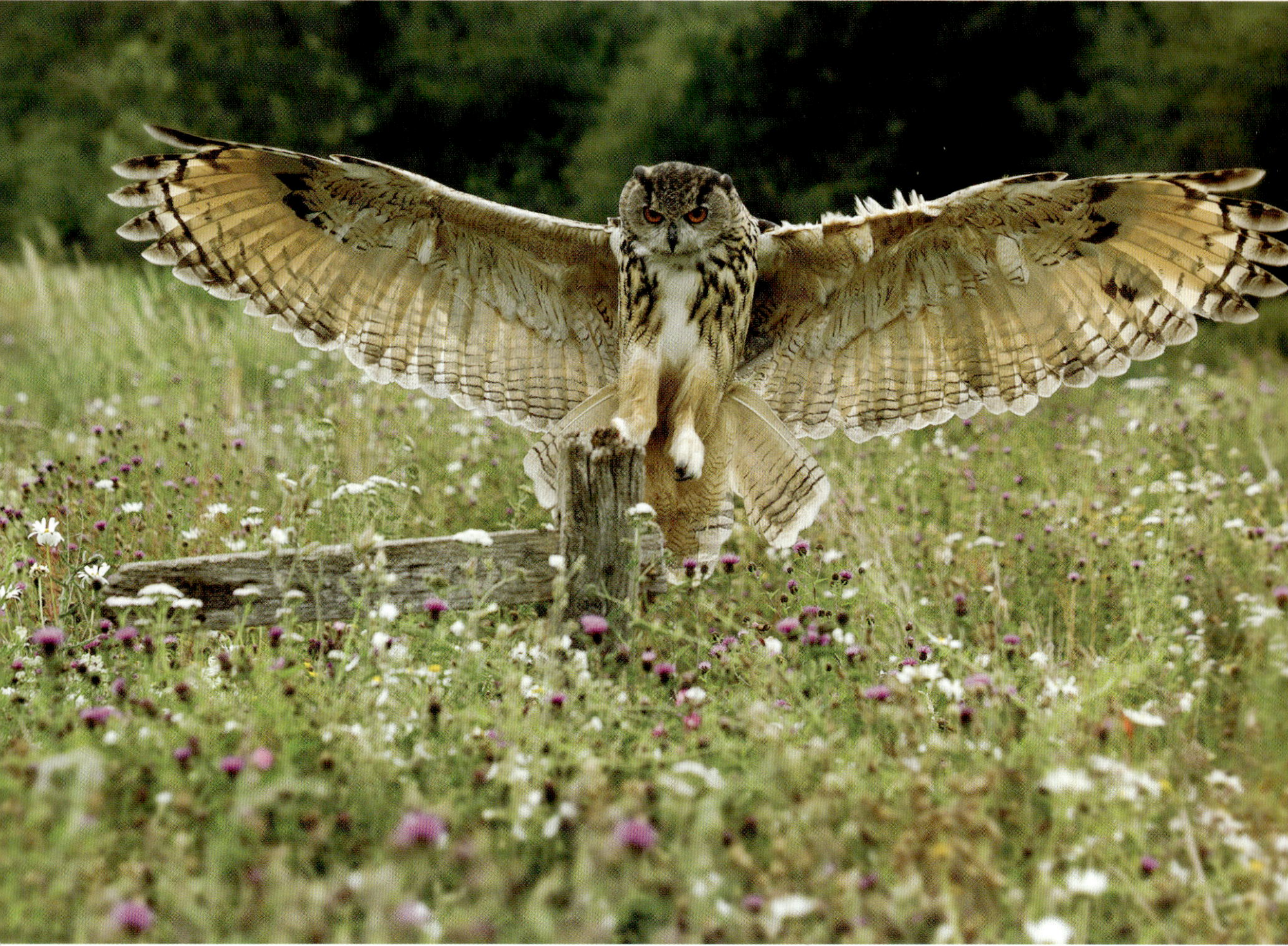

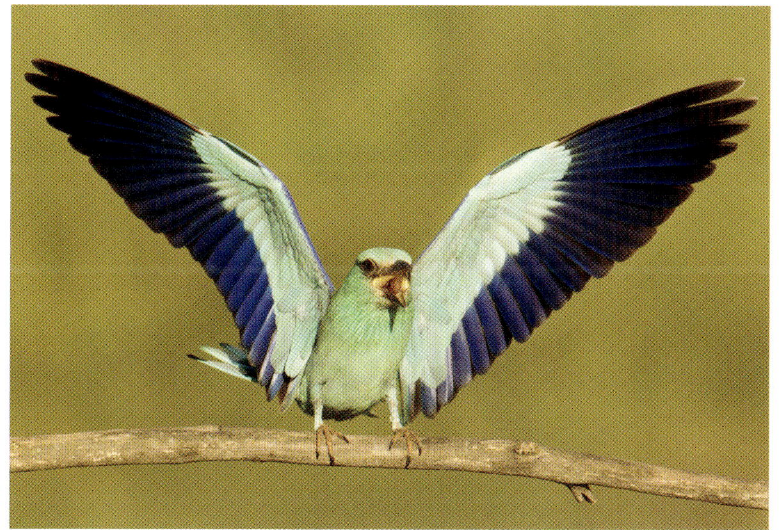

European roller | Serbia | During landing, the European roller displays the beautifully colored undersides of its wings. | 300mm, aperture 5.0, 1/800 s, ISO 320

For the second option, it's best to work with a tripod and turn off the autofocus completely. I place the camera on the tripod and manually focus on the perch or a bit behind it. With the autofocus off, the focus stays on the perch and I release the shutter as the bird comes into view. To have some flexibility with the depth of field, I usually stop down a bit, to f/8 for example, as long as the background is relatively uncluttered. This method is especially successful with a wired or radio-controlled release. That way, you don't have to keep your eye glued to the viewfinder while waiting for the bird to approach, but can watch it at leisure and press the remote release once it has gotten close.

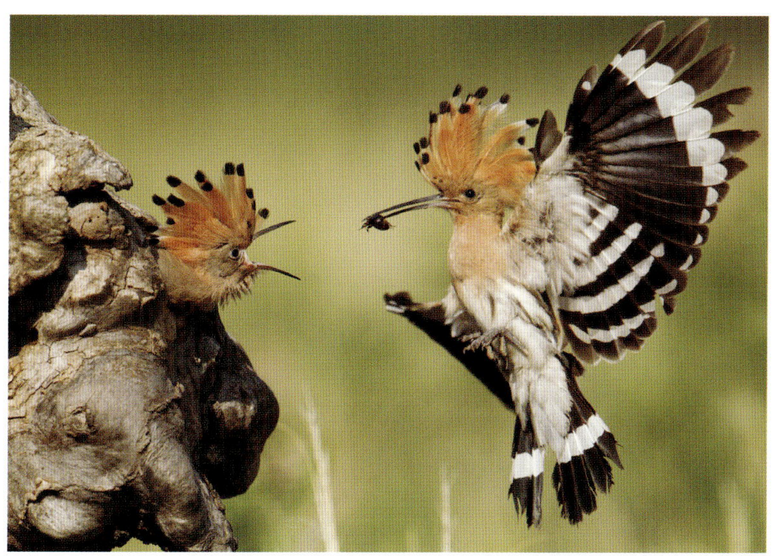

Hoopoe | Serbia | This shot was taken from a camouflage tent; the camera was mounted on the tripod and manually prefocused on the begging fledgling. I took the picture with a wired release. | 600mm, aperture 6.3, 1/4000 s, ISO 800

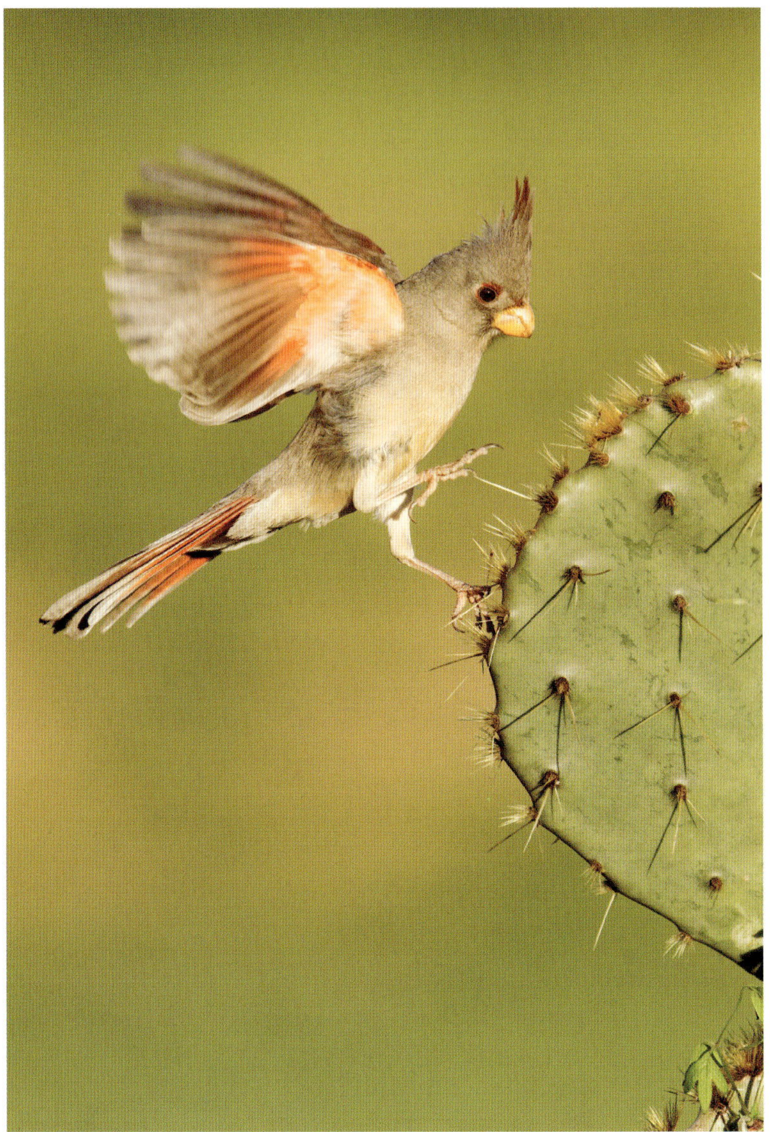

4-143 ▶

Desert cardinal | Texas | Having to land on a cactus looks a bit uncomfortable–but the bird didn't have any problems with it! | 420mm (300mm + 1.4x converter), aperture 5.6, 1/1600 s, ISO 800

Also, make sure you don't frame it too tightly. After all, you usually don't know exactly where the bird will land, down to the last inch. Give it a bit more space in the picture than it needs. It's easy enough to crop the image afterward. But you can't add wings back in that have been cut off! Don't fret if you waste a lot of shots—if you achieve just one or two perfect pictures after a day of shooting, it was well worth the effort! Plus, taking these kinds of pictures is a lot of fun!

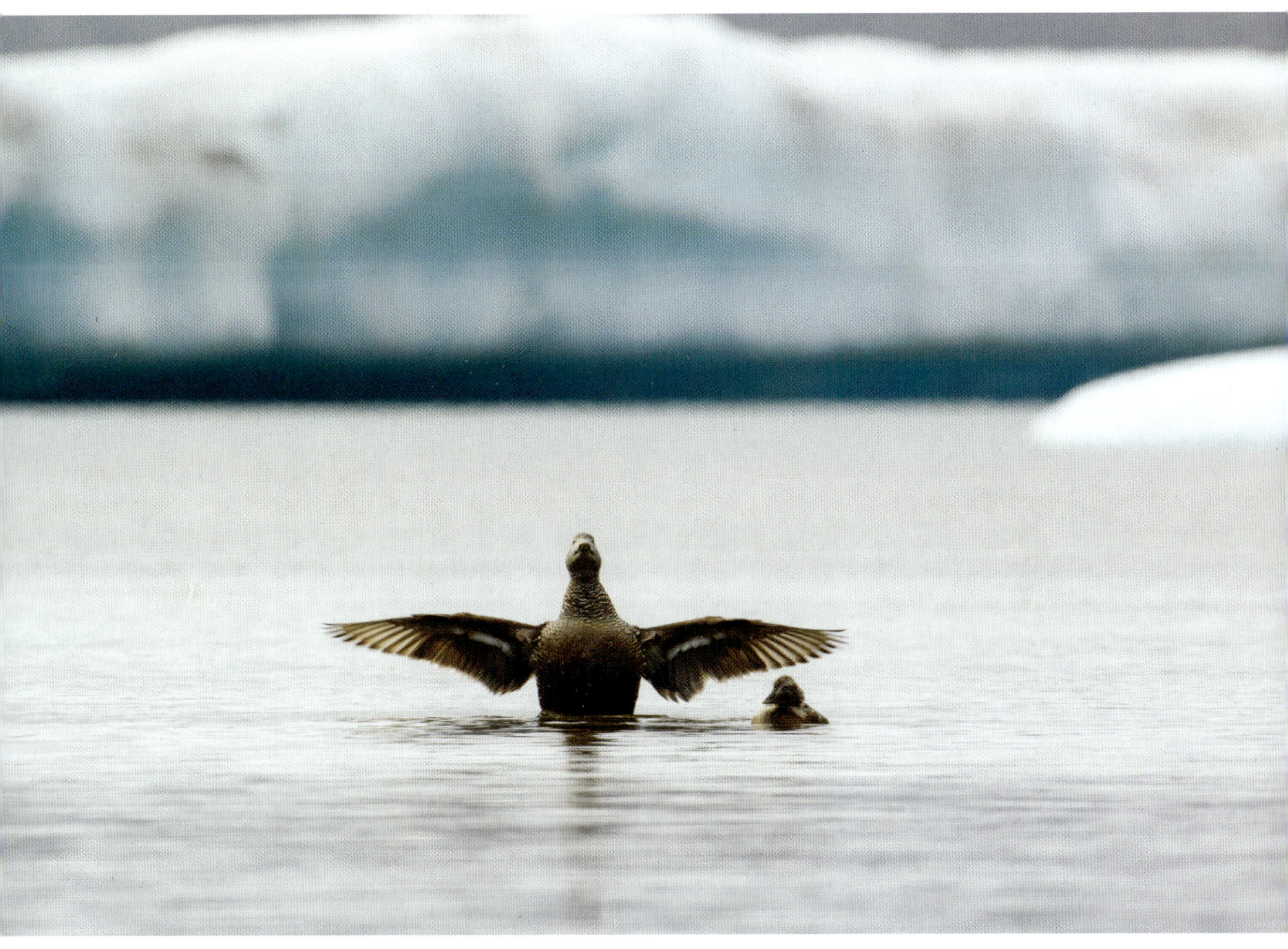

4.6 Birds in Their Habitat

Capturing a bird in its natural habitat is a completely different kind of photography, one that deliberately includes the bird's surroundings in the picture. Images like this are particularly exciting if the habitat is a bit unusual.

If you want to include the bird's habitat, lenses with a shorter focal length are a good option, or maybe a light wide-angle lens. But even a telephoto lens can work for shots like this. Decrease the aperture if you want the surroundings to be in focus and keep it relatively open if you prefer to put the focus mainly on the bird.

In practice, I often start with shots like this when I'm still some distance away from the bird anyway. Once I've been able to slowly get closer, the bird takes up more and more of the frame until I might end up with frame-filling images.

▲ 4-144
Common eider | Iceland | Including the eider ducks' habitat in the image makes this photo effective. As the ducks approached, they filled the frame more and more until I took frame-filling pictures. | 500mm, aperture 9.0, 1/250 s, ISO 1000, +1 exposure compensation

Approaching the Subject

Unless you're in a stand, you'll often find yourself faced with the situation that you need to get closer to your subject, the bird, to get frame-filling shots. When doing so, the most important thing is not to alarm the bird since it may just fly away. I often approach very slowly and almost as if by chance, as unobtrusively as possible. On the beach, for example, it's best to act like a normal beach walker. I pause now and then to look at the sea or lake and watch the birds out of the corner of my eye. Many birds are alarmed when you look at them directly, so I try to do it very covertly. But you should keep an eye on them because there are signs that show that they might be about to depart: They raise their heads and freeze while watching the photographer. In that case, don't go any closer. Once they lower their heads again and go back to their business, you can cautiously continue your approach. It's often useful to take a slight zigzag course. Don't make a beeline for the birds, but head toward a point somewhat next to them.

◄◄ 4-145

Glaucous gull | Iceland | Sometimes, the surroundings of a bird may even become the main subject, as in this photo of a glaucous gull at Iceland's Jökulsárlón glacier lagoon. | 500mm, aperture 9.0, 1/400 s, ISO 1000, +2/3 exposure compensation

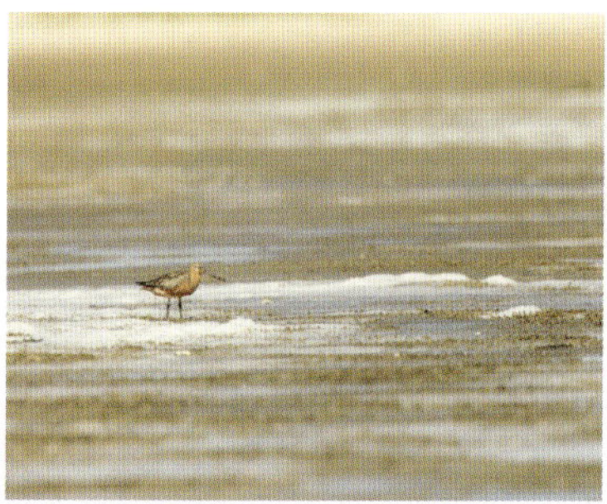

▲ 4-146

Bar-tailed godwit | Texel, The Netherlands | I started taking pictures early in my approach, showing the bird in its habitat. | 700mm (500mm + 1.4x converter), aperture 9.0, 1/2500 s, ISO 800

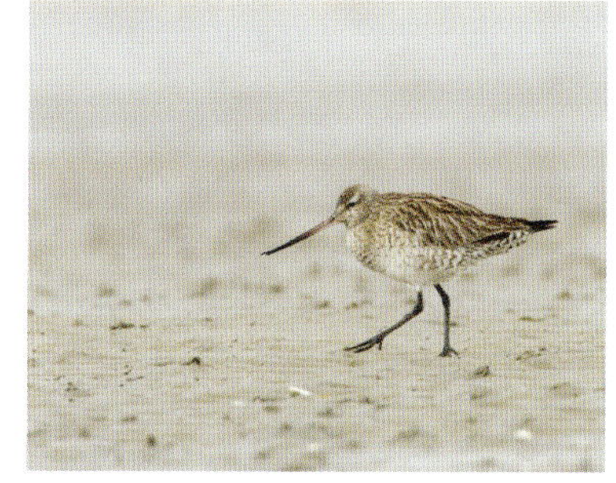

▲ 4-147

Slowly getting closer. | 700mm (500mm + 1.4x converter), aperture 9.0, 1/500 s, ISO 500, +2/3 exposure compensation

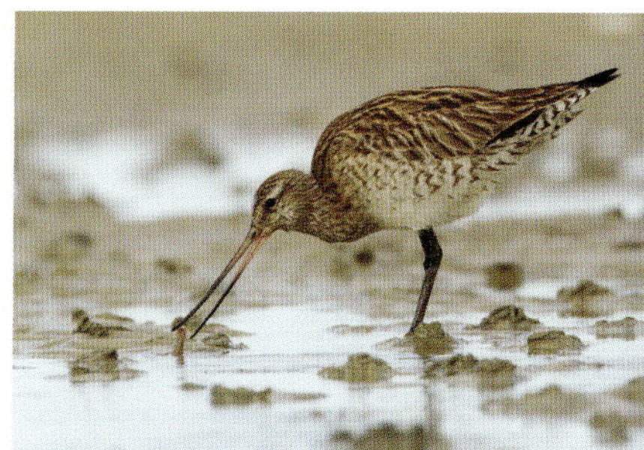

▲ 4-148

Once the birds have gotten used to the presence of the photographer, you can take frame-filling shots, showing their natural behavior. | 700mm (500mm + 1.4x converter), aperture 9.0, 1/640 s, ISO 500, +2/3 exposure compensation

Once I've gotten close enough to shoot the first pictures showing the bird in its surroundings, I crouch down or (in the case of birds on the beach) lie down flat on the ground and start photographing. It gives the bird the chance to get used to my presence, and I already have the first photos on my memory card. The next thing that's important is not to stand back up. I move in a squat or crawl on the ground to get closer to the bird. Or I might wait to see if the bird happens to move in my direction. Eventually, we'll get close to each other and if all goes well I get frame-filling shots of the bird showing a natural behavior. The same principles of approach apply to birds in all settings, not just waterfowl on the beach, of course.

Portraits

When I say portrait, I don't necessarily mean just detailed shots of the head but also photographs in which the bird fills the entire frame, more or less. For a classic headshot of a bird, you need to be either very close or use a large telephoto lens with a lot of focal length, maybe combined with a converter. Any portrait must show the bird's eye very sharp. And normally the bird should not turn its head away from the viewer but instead slightly toward the photographer. Of course, you can also take frontal pictures. Depending on the shape of the head

4-149 ▼
Bearded vulture | German Raptor Research Center at Guttenberg Castle, Germany | With a focal length of 300mm and at a close distance, an aperture of 5.6 was not enough to get the tip of the beak sharp while focusing on the eyes. | 300mm, aperture 5.6, 1/1000 s, ISO 1000, +2/3 exposure compensation

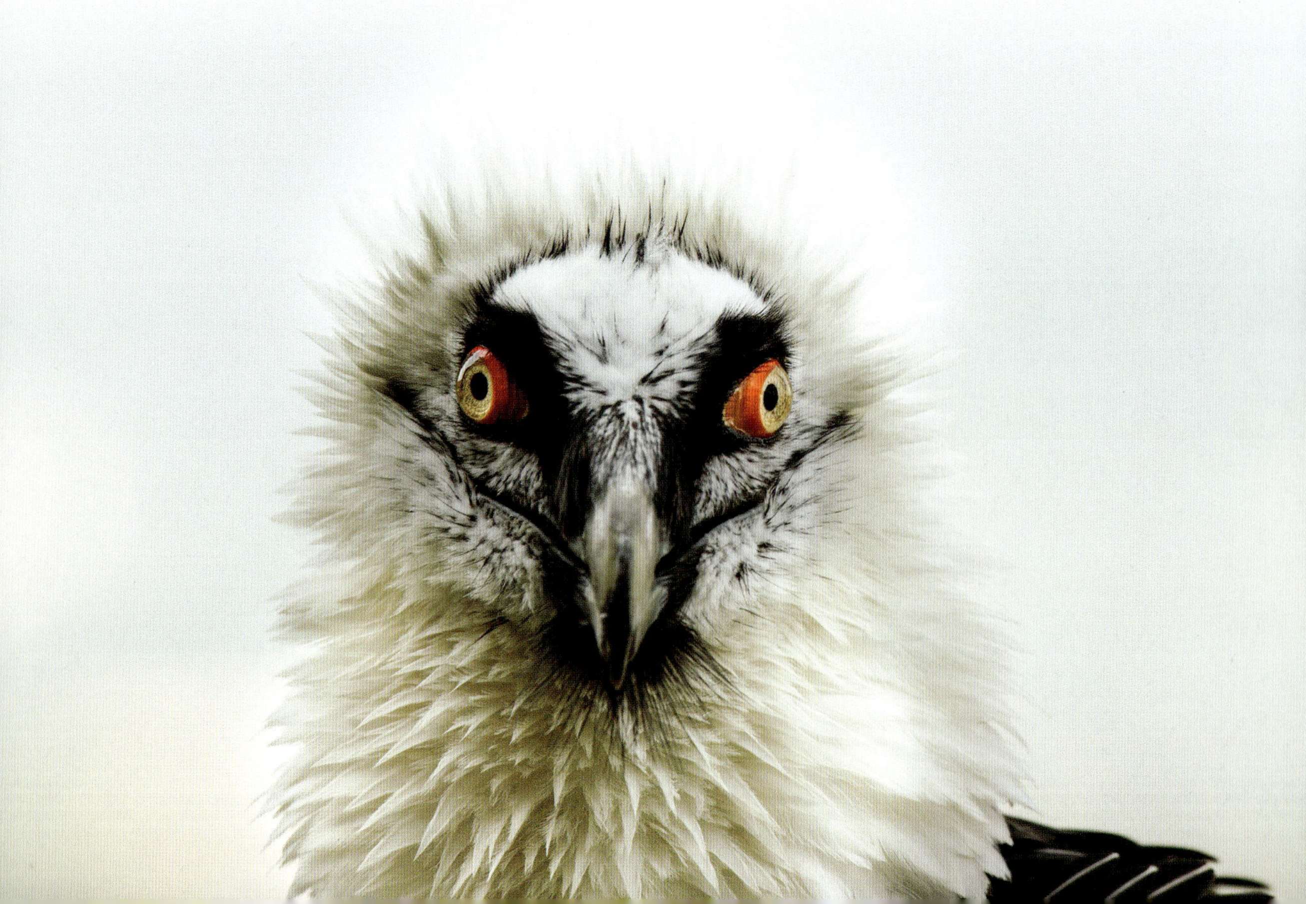

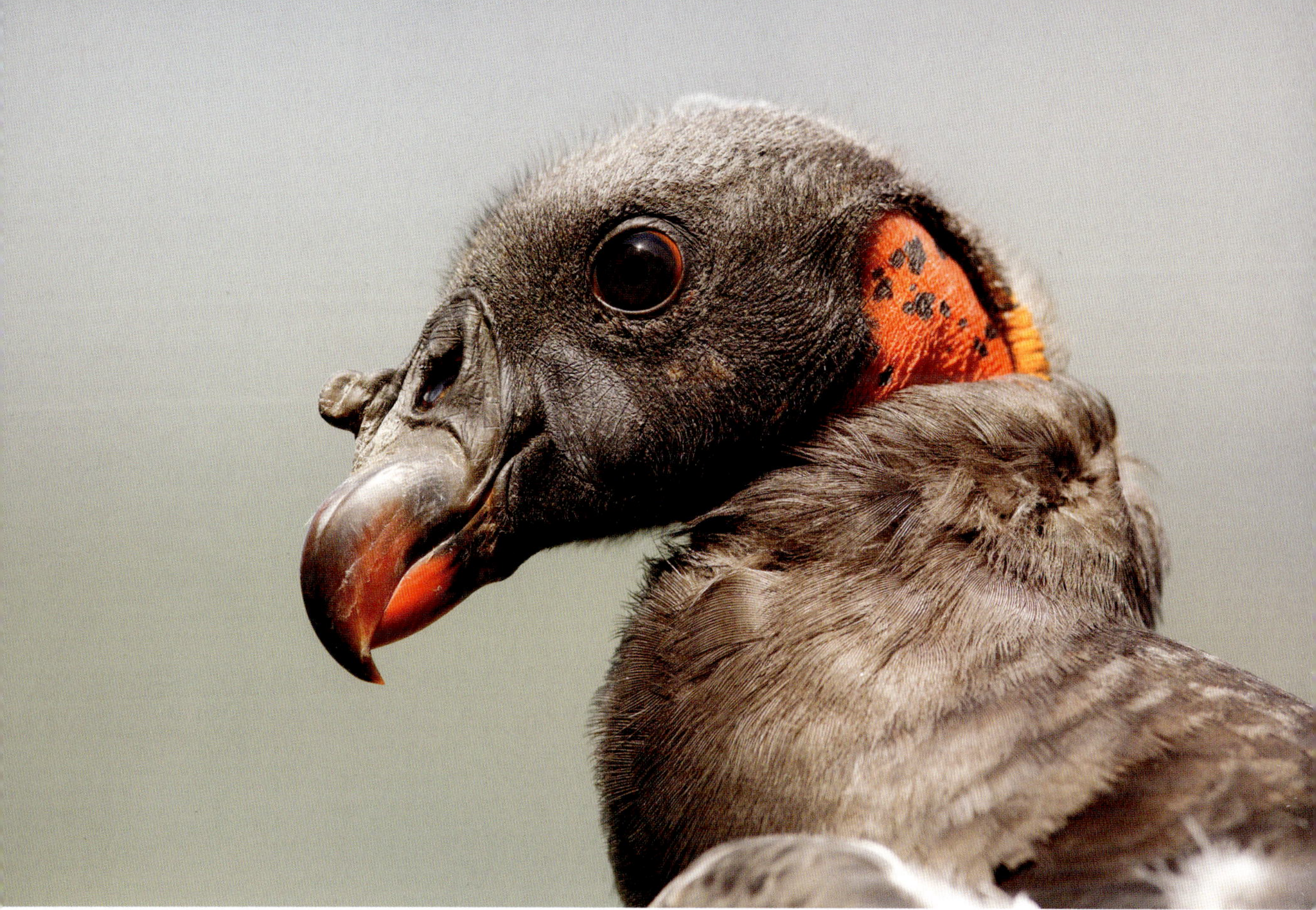

King vulture | German Raptor Research Center at Guttenberg Castle, Germany | Photographing the head of a bird in full profile means you don't have to close the aperture as much to obtain all-over sharpness. | 300mm, aperture 4.5, 1/1600 s, ISO 500

and beak, it may be difficult to get both the eyes and the beak in focus with the aperture open. If that's your goal, you'll need to decrease the aperture by a few stops, but keep in mind that doing so will also make the background sharper and therefore more cluttered.

Personally, I don't mind at all if the tip of the beak isn't sharp, but that's a matter of taste. What's important is that by choosing the settings on your camera you can decide what effect you want to achieve.

Detail Shots

If you get very close to a bird, which mostly happens in captive settings, it can be worthwhile to experiment with detail shots. They might reveal the magnificent iridescence of the plumage, for example. Or maybe you want to try to showcase the eye of the bird.

Images like this work especially well when they are utterly sharp all over, from top to bottom and right to left, and when there is nothing but the subject in the frame. Therefore, I recommend closing the aperture a bit for detail shots.

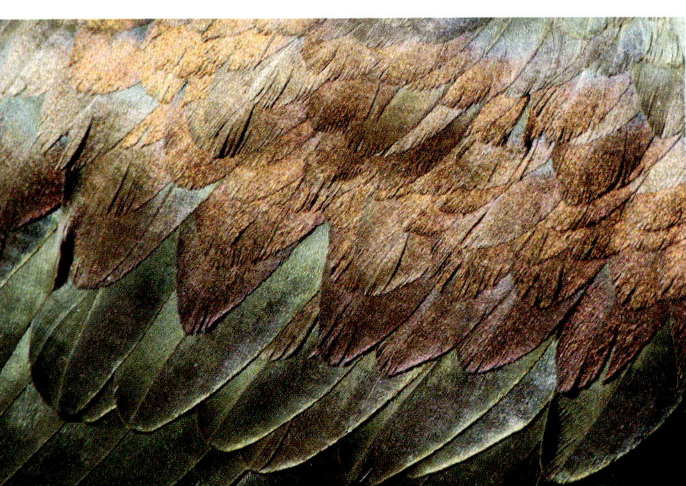

◀ 4-151

Northern bald ibis | Alpine Zoo, Innsbruck | Photographed in great detail, the feathers of the bald ibis shimmer brightly. | 500mm, aperture 6.3, 1/640 s, ISO 1600, -2/3 exposure compensation

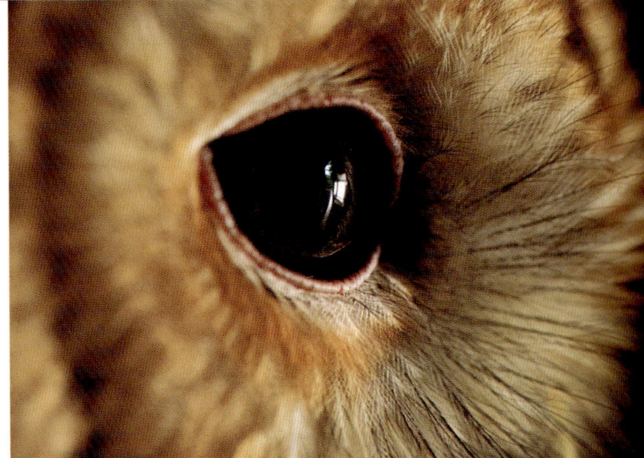

4-152 ▶

Tawny owl | Germany | This macro shot puts a clear focus on the eye; at f/5, the depth of field is insufficient to bring the entire subject into sharp focus. | 105mm, aperture 5.0, 1/200 s, ISO 5000, -1 1/3 exposure compensation

4-153 ▶

Southern cassowary | Weltvogelpark Walsrode (Walsrode Bird Park) | Bird parks and zoos are great places to explore and photograph interesting details. | 500mm, aperture 7.1, 1/2500 s, ISO 1250, -1 1/3 exposure compensation

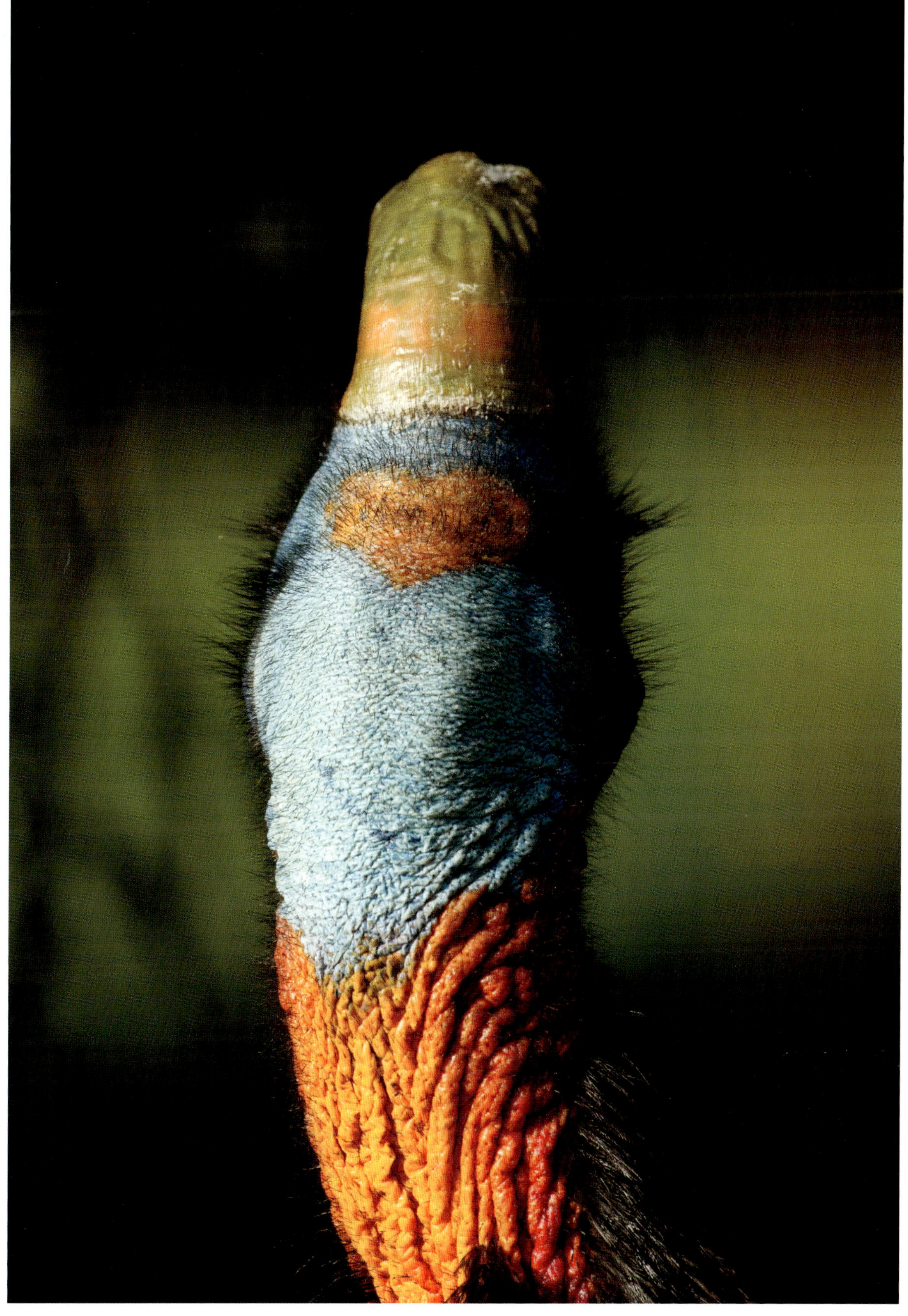

Birds on the Beach

Wonderful! Photographing birds on the beach is really great fun! Again, the most important rule is to take pictures at the subject's eye level, and in this case, that means getting all the way down to the sand (or pebbles)! If you're using a large telephoto lens, you'll need some sort of support because it'll be very difficult to hold the camera. A small bean bag or a floor tripod will do a good job. If you only have a regular tripod, spread its legs as far as you can to get the lowest possible angle. At times, I have also simply rested the lens on the back of my left hand, but it gets a bit uncomfortable after a while.

Many wading birds on the beach can be shy when you first approach them. It's best to stroll slowly and zigzag toward them, then crouch down as you get closer. This makes the rest of the approach a bit cumbersome, but the birds seem to feel less threatened by a low position. And even though I may still be quite a distance away at that point I often start taking pictures anyway.

Since wading birds usually walk up and down the beach, they often eventually return, even if they run away first. With a bit of patience, it's possible to get quite close to them.

Pied crow | Gambia | Observing birds on the beach always results in exciting motifs. This pied crow found a dead snake eel. | 600mm, aperture 11, 1/1000 s, ISO 1000

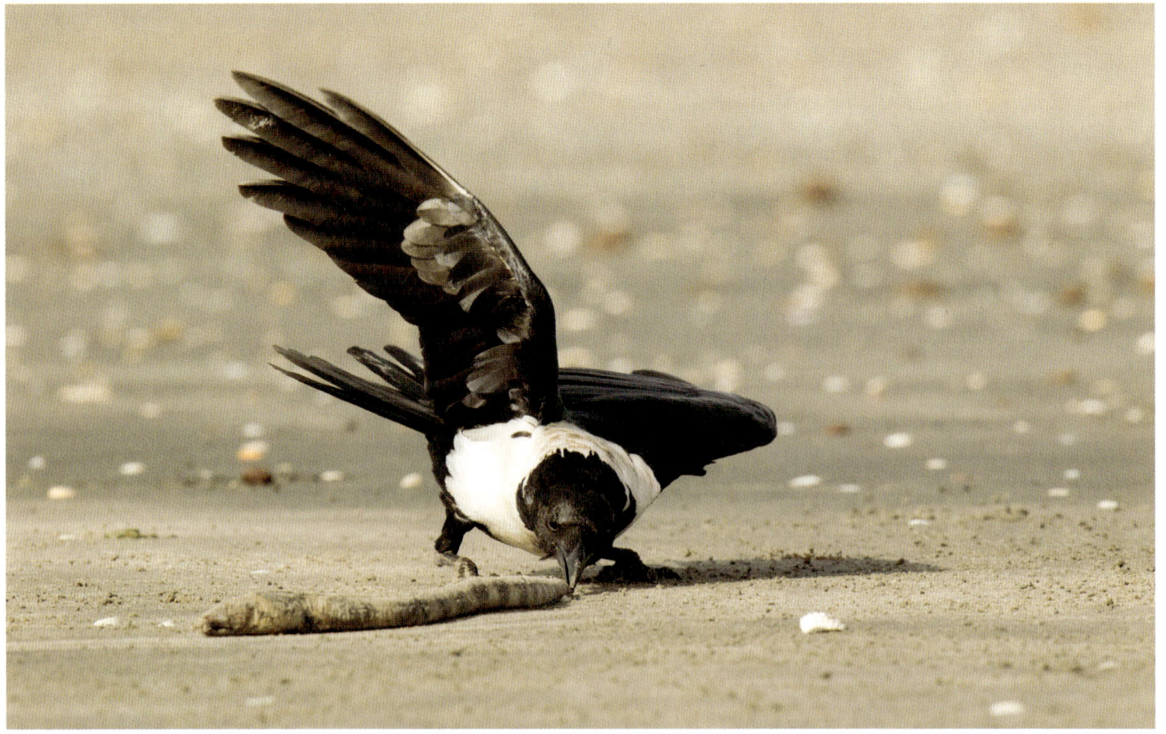

CHAPTER 4

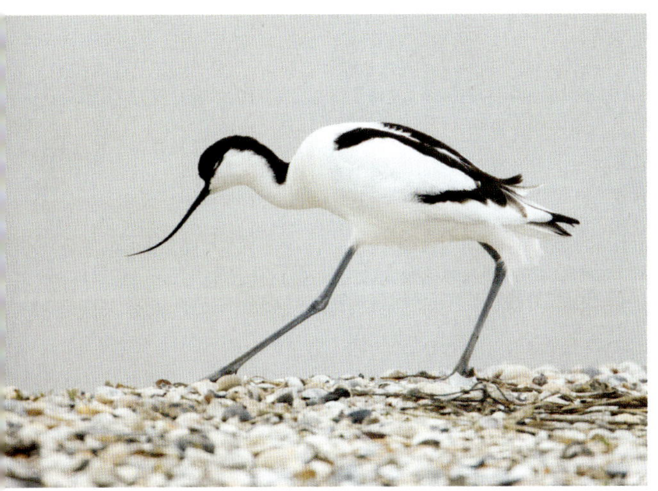

▲ 4-155

Pied avocet | Texel, The Netherlands |
Very important when photographing birds on
the beach: Go down to their eye level, even if
you must lie flat on your belly…. | 700mm (500mm
+ 1.4x converter), aperture 5.6, 1/1600 s,
ISO 640, +2/3 exposure compensation

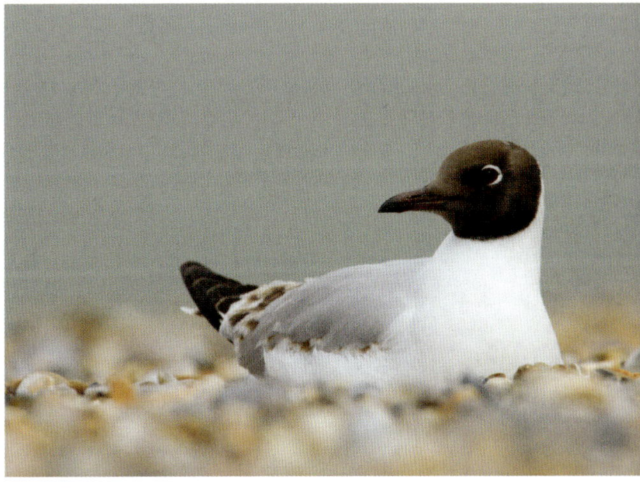

▲ 4-156

Black-headed gull | Wales | The water in the back-
ground has blurred to a soft blue, and the gull is
cleanly separated from it. | 700mm (500mm + 1.4x
converter), aperture 8.0, 1/1250 s, ISO 400, +1/3
exposure compensation

Bathing Birds

Many birds bathe every day, especially in hot and dry weather. You can
often spot whole flocks of sparrows or starlings bathing in shallow
puddles on roads or paths where there's little traffic.

At the zoo, it's mainly the ducks and geese that bathe regularly
and are relatively easy to photograph. Often, one animal starts and
more join in after a while. At lakes, too, you can observe bathing
geese and ducks but also coots and swans. However, probably nothing
beats visiting an observation deck that has been specifically set up at
a drinking and bathing spot. On a hot day at a well-frequented bathing site, you can probably take pictures of 20 to 30 different species
of birds bathing and drinking.

There are two different styles of photo that "work": First, you can
set the shutter speed so that every drop of water is sharp and every
movement practically frozen in time. The shutter speed will need to
be around 1/1250 s, sometimes even faster. Images like this are sharp
down to the tips of the feathers and show the bathing bird in clear
detail. However, not all the phases of a bird's bath are photogenic:
The best photos are those in which the head is clearly visible and the
wings are slightly stretched out. If the head is underwater or tucked
under a wing, the viewer can't make eye contact with the bird and the

Mute swan | Germany |
A fast shutter speed freezes the
birds' quick movements. In this
case, an exposure of 1/1250 s
was still too long to get everything up to the tips of the wing
sharp. | 700mm (500mm +
1.4x converter), aperture 11,
1/1250 s, ISO 1250

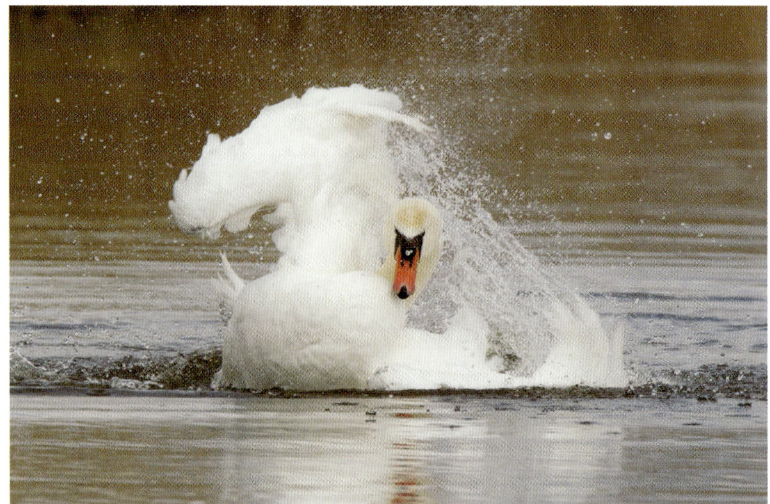

This dynamic photo of a bathing
swan was taken with a long
exposure. | 700mm (500mm +
1.4x converter), aperture 16,
1/50 s, ISO 100, +1/3 exposure
compensation

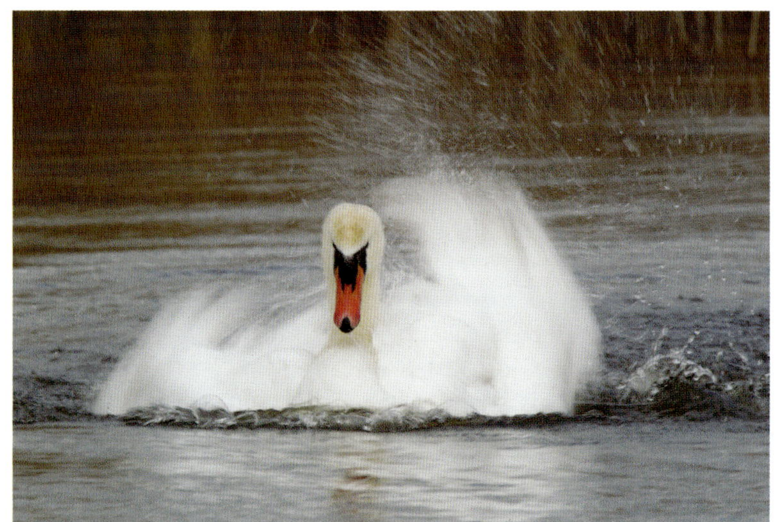

picture quickly becomes boring. The same is true if the bird assumes a
position during its bathing routine in which it is barely recognizable as
a bird at all. But another kind of image can also be very appealing: a
shot with a long exposure time! Especially against backlight and with
a dark background, it'll show the drops of water flying through the
air as elongated stripes that shine and sparkle in the sun. It's okay if
the wings are blurry with motion, but the head of the bird and especially the eye will need to be reasonably sharp for the image to work.
Shutter speeds of around 1/60 s to 1/200 s work best, depending on
the bird's "bathing speed."

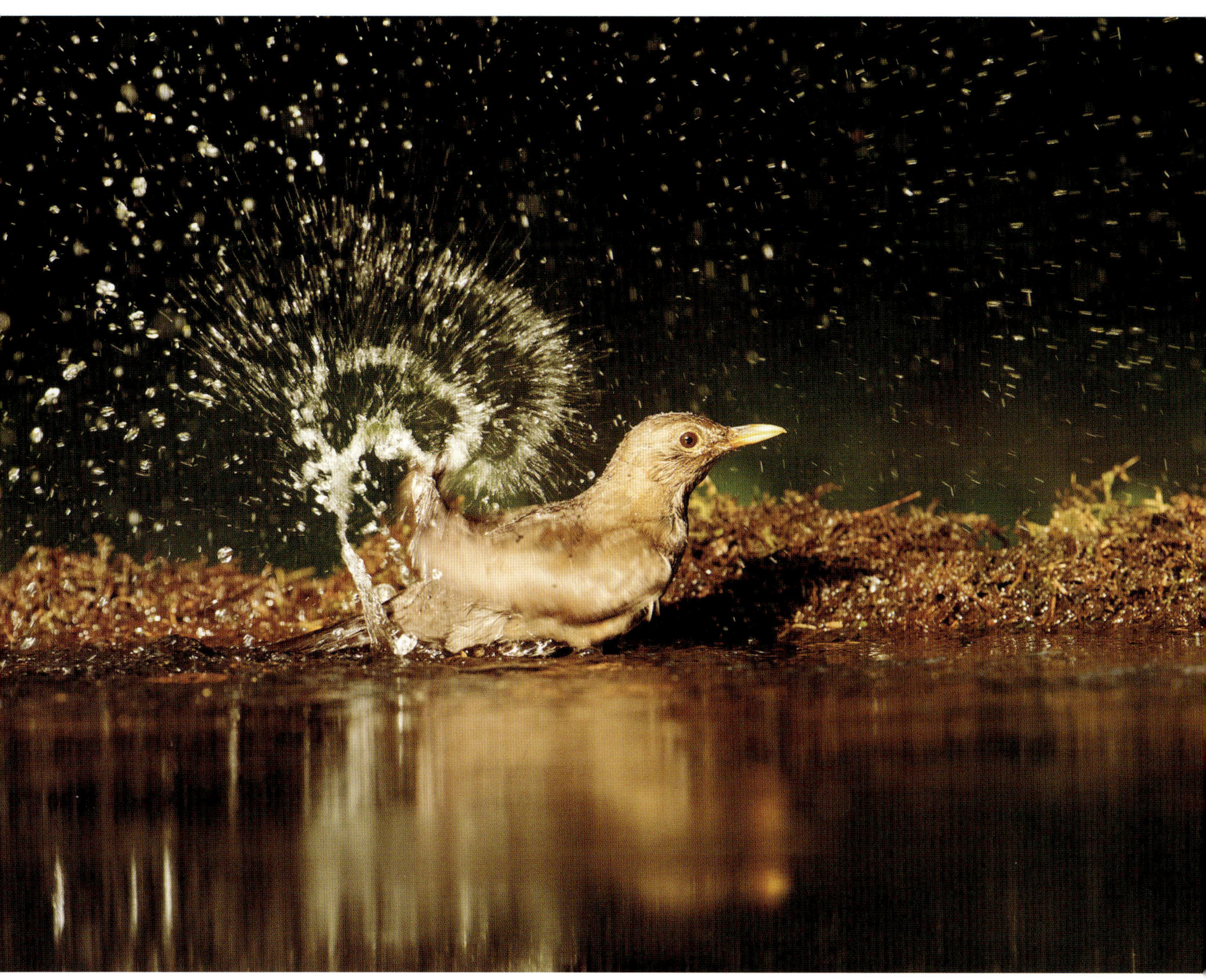

You can control the shutter speed by picking a shooting mode (time value, shutter priority) and selecting the time you want. The camera will then adjust the aperture accordingly. But another option is to open the aperture as wide as possible in the aperture priority mode, then adjust the shutter speed by setting the ISO value. If you choose a high ISO value, the shutter speed will be fast; a low ISO will result in pictures with a long exposure. Especially when photographing with a slow shutter speed you'll have to take many pictures because you'll produce a lot of unusable shots. But every successful long-exposure photo of a bathing bird will be a highlight in the portfolio!

▲ 4-159

Blackbird | Serbia | Splashing water looks particularly effective against a dark background. | 300mm, aperture 4.5, 1/640 s, ISO 1600, -1 1/3 exposure compensation

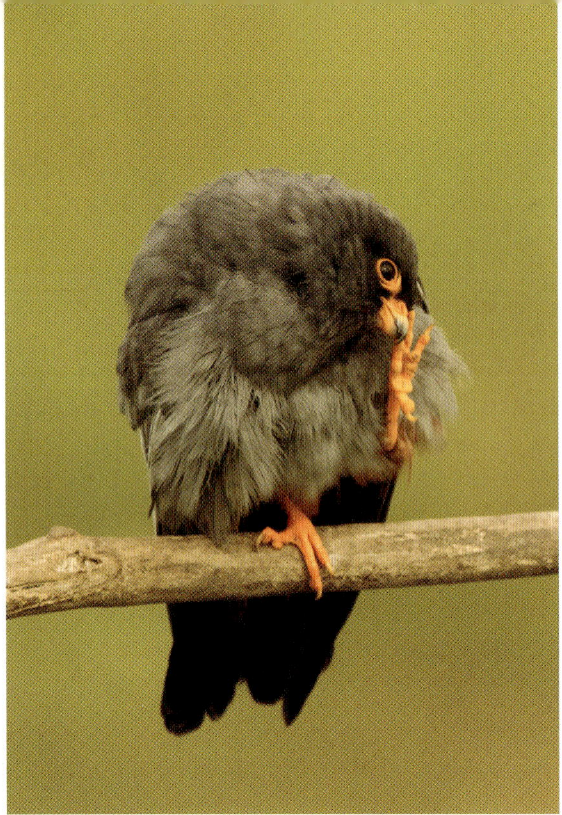

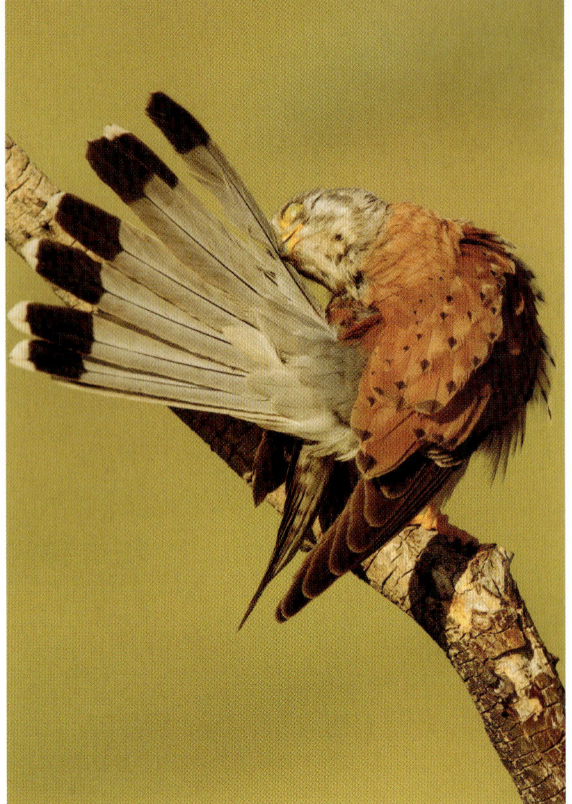

▲ 4-160
Red-footed falcon | Serbia | Birds often use their feet to preen in places they can't reach with their beaks. | 600mm, aperture 8.0, 1/250 s, ISO 800

▲ 4-161
Common kestrel | Serbia | The tail feathers are being pulled through the beak one by one. | 600mm, aperture 7.1, 1/800 s, ISO 500

Preening

Birds spend a lot of time preening. They need to maintain their feathers to keep them in the best shape for flying and to waterproof them. Preening is also good for the bird's well-being, especially when birds preen each other. A wild bird will only preen when it feels safe and unobserved, so your best chances for success come with photographing them from a tree stand or by using the car as camouflage.

Not all preening phases look good in a photograph. It's important that the bird's head is visible and, if possible, its eyes. The general rules of image composition still apply.

By the way, after an extensive preening session, birds will stretch and shake themselves vigorously. This behavior also works well in a photo!

4-162 ▶▶
Red-footed falcon | Serbia | After preening, the bird shakes itself vigorously, which always makes for a nice photo. | 600mm, aperture 8.0, 1/320 s, ISO 800

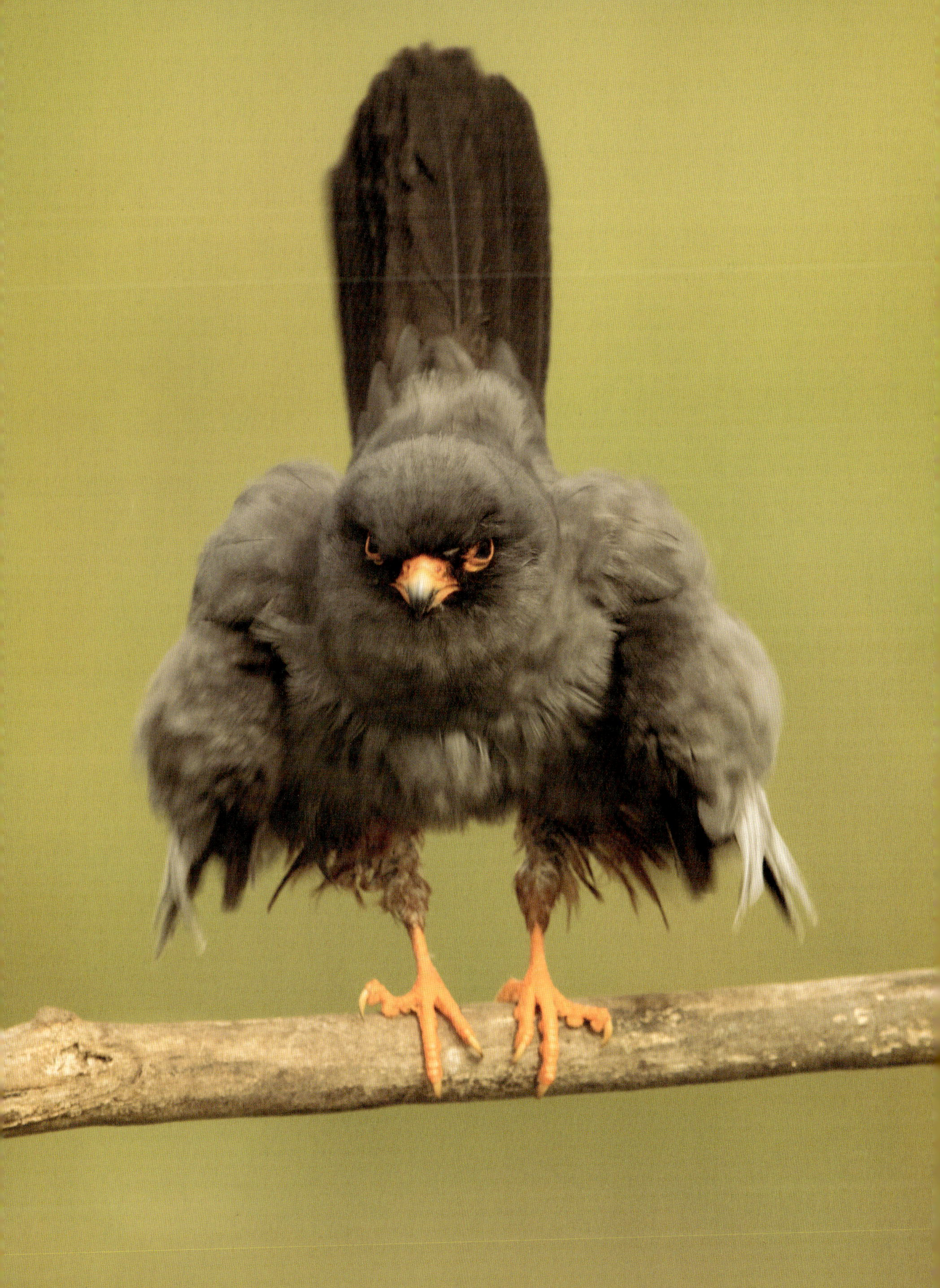

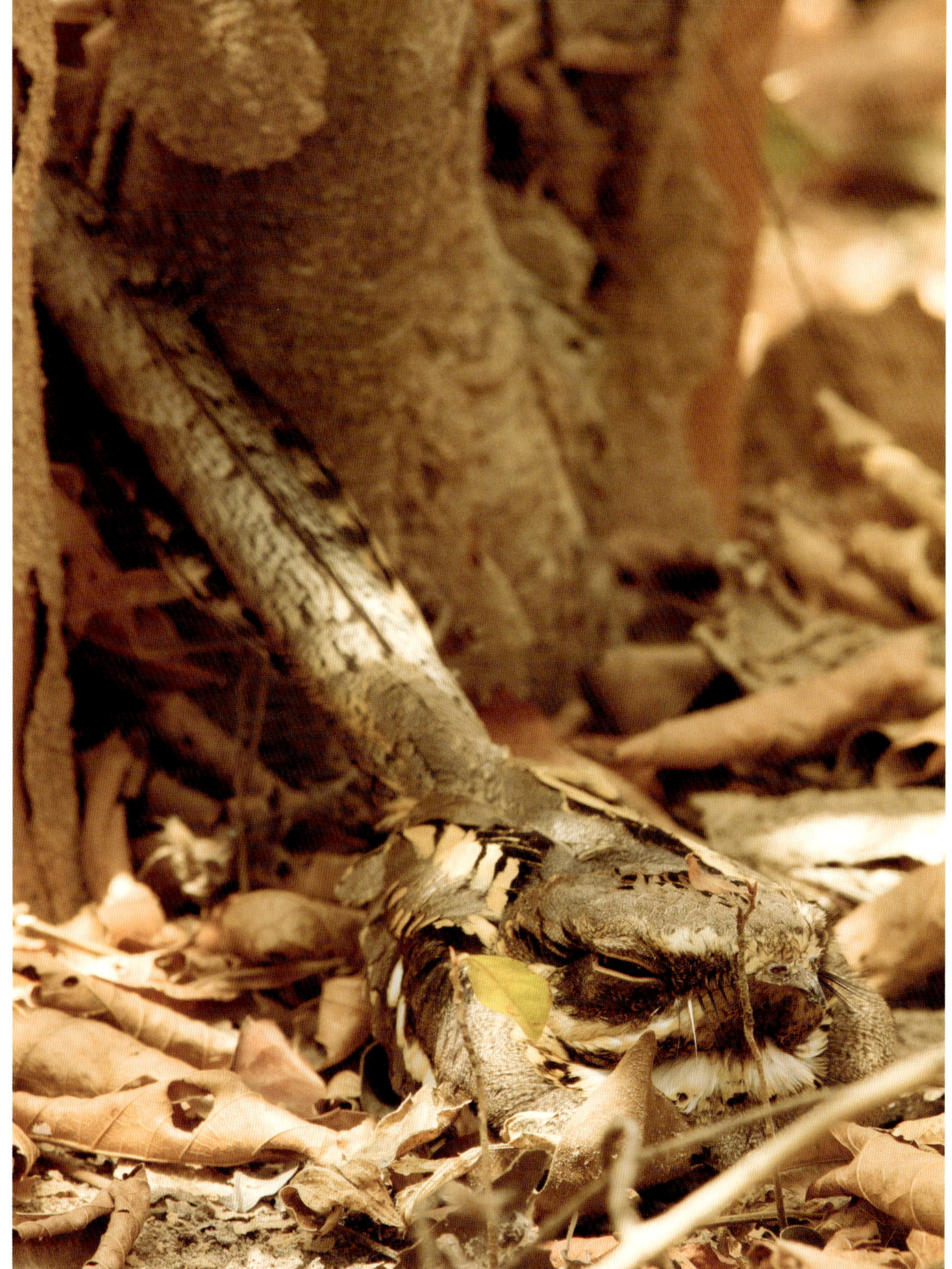

Long-tailed nightjar | Gambia | With the aperture closed to f/16, the bird's surroundings are sharp, emphasizing its camouflage. | 600mm, aperture 16, 1/60 s, ISO 800

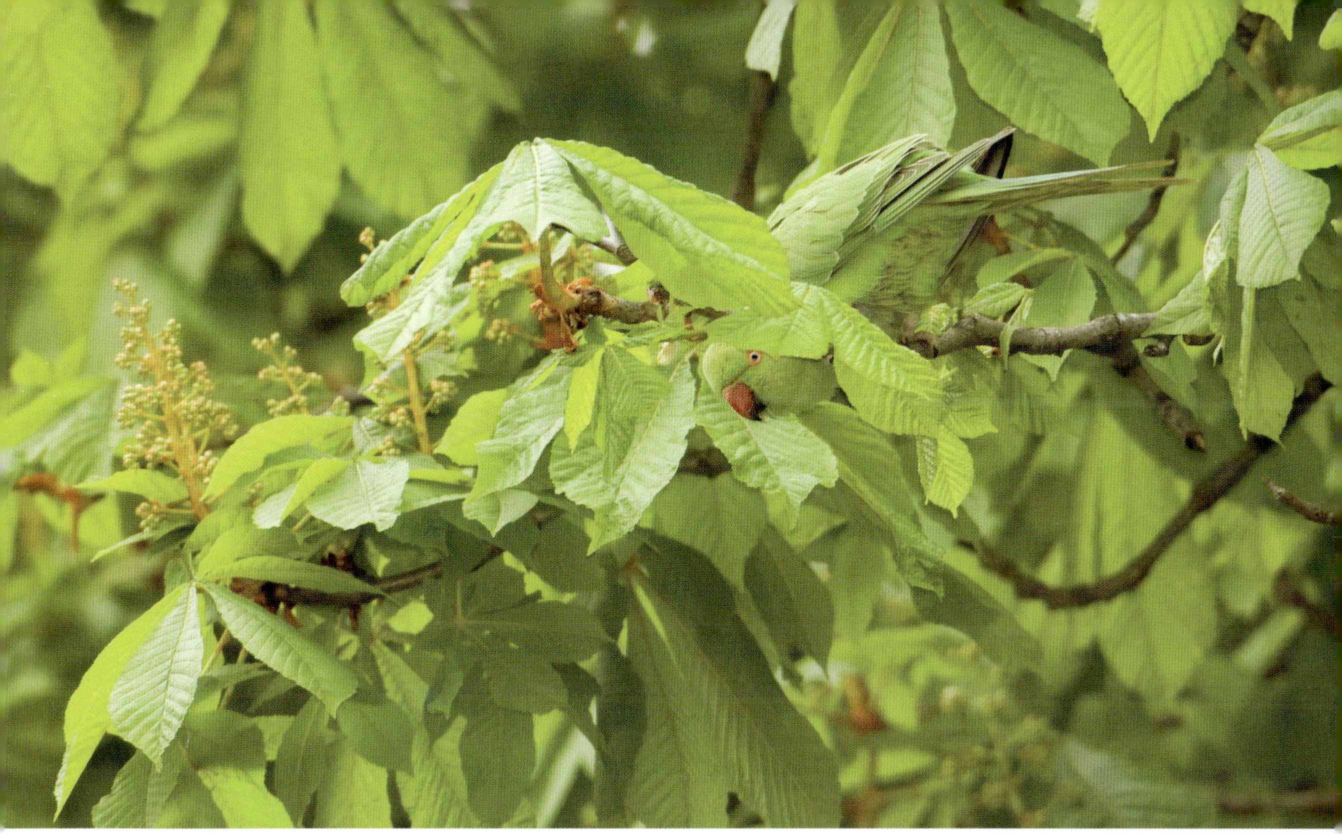

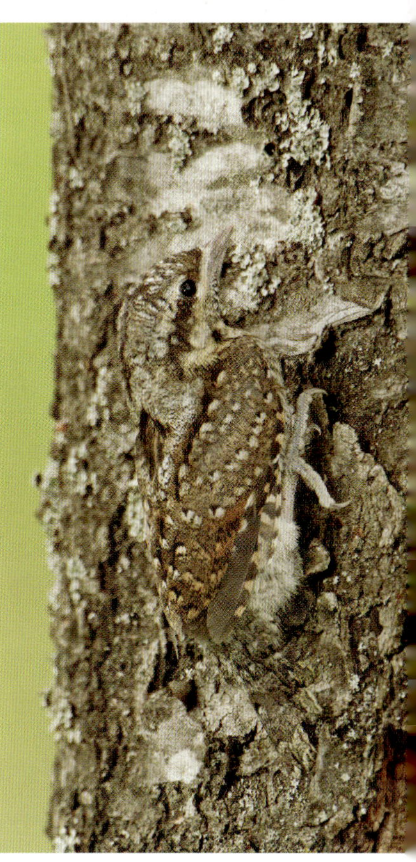

Rose-ringed parakeet | Wiesbaden | The parakeet is perfectly camouflaged in all that vibrant green! | 500mm, aperture 4.5, 1/300 s, ISO 1600

Well Camouflaged

Occasionally, you are lucky and spot a bird that is perfectly camouflaged. To showcase the camouflage in the image, part of the bird's surroundings must be visible, but not so much that the image becomes cluttered.

My goal with photos like this is to capture only the bird and those elements of its surroundings that provide camouflage. The image will be particularly effective if the bird and the surroundings are about the same level of sharpness, so close the aperture a bit to get a greater depth of field. If there's enough light, feel free to stop down to f/11. The greater depth of field will allow the outline of the bird to blend in even better with its surroundings than it would with a wide-open aperture.

4-165 ▶

Wryneck | Germany | The wryneck fledgling is barely visible against the tree trunk, that's how well it's camouflaged. | 500mm, aperture 5.6, 1/200 s, ISO 1600, -2/3 exposure compensation

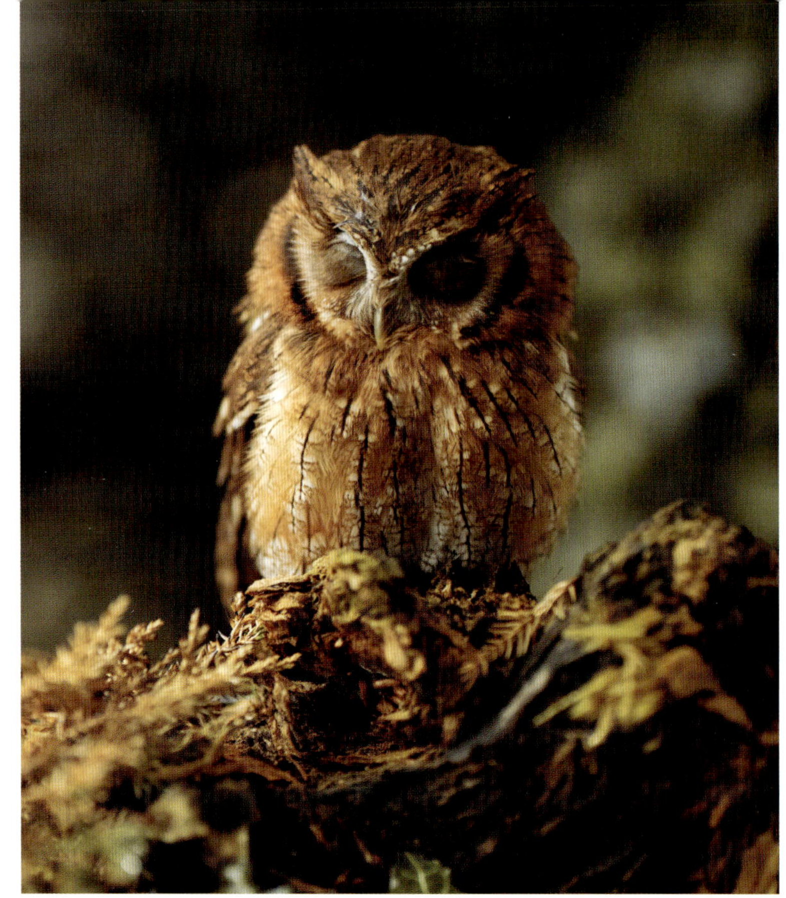

Tropical screech owl | Germany | Captured midblink, the owl appears to be sleeping…. | 135mm, aperture 2.2, 1/320 s, ISO 2000, -2/3 exposure compensation

The Bird is Sleeping

Birds need to sleep, too, and if you watch them long enough they may become so relaxed that they take a nap. You might assume that this is boring, but you'd be wrong. Even a sleeping bird can be an appealing subject.

Some birds, especially owls, blink quite frequently and if you capture it at just the right moment, it will look as if the bird is sleeping…. To catch the right moment, I recommend taking continuous shots of such birds, even if you are taking portraits!

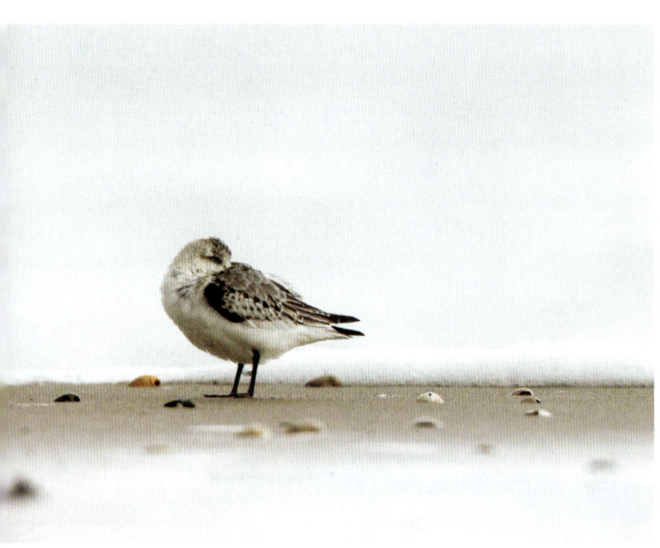

Sanderling | Texel, The Netherlands | I photographed a flock of sanderlings on the beach, and the birds were so relaxed that they started napping after a while. | 700mm (500mm + 1.4x converter), aperture 7.1, 1/1250 s, ISO 500, +1 exposure compensation

Photographing Singing Birds

Spring mating season is probably the best time to photograph birds. Many males position themselves on exposed singing perches and it's relatively easy to find and photograph them. Some are a bit less cautious during this time, which means that it's often less of a problem to get close than during the rest of the year.

It's also fairly easy to find the right moment since the bird will usually keep singing for quite some time, and you can wait until it opens its beak and starts its song before you release the shutter. A singing bird will always look more interesting than a photo of one with its beak closed.

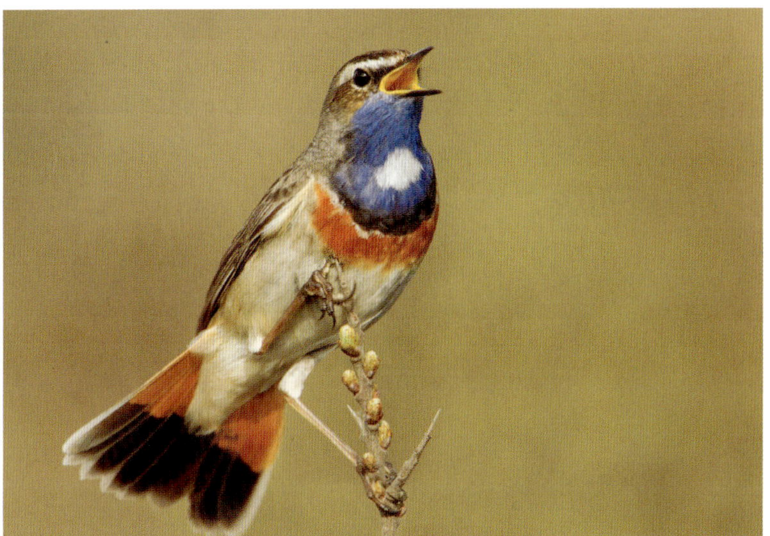

◄ 4-168

Bluethroat | Texel, The Netherlands | Fortunately, even with f/11, the bird is well separated from the background. | 700mm (500mm + 1.4x converter), aperture 11, 1/640 s, ISO 800

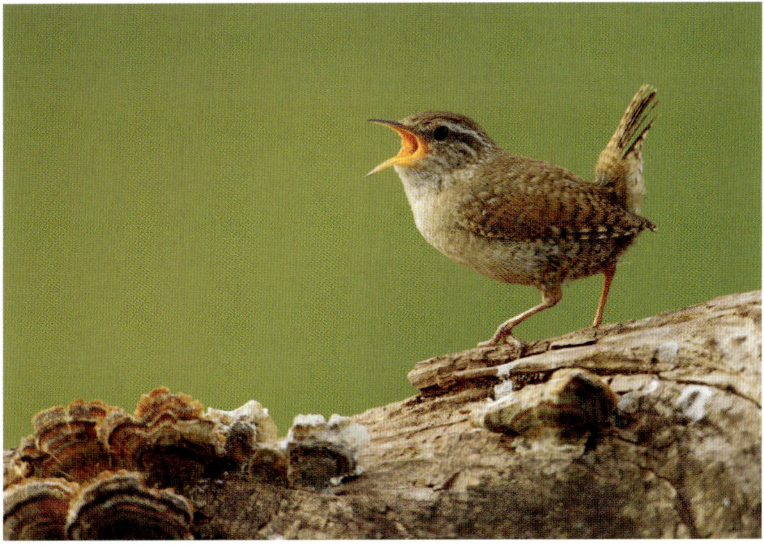

◄ 4-169

Wren | Germany | One of our smallest birds is also one of the biggest song artists. Often, you only see them because they sing so loudly. | 500mm, aperture 5.0, 1/250 s, ISO 1250, -2/3 exposure compensation

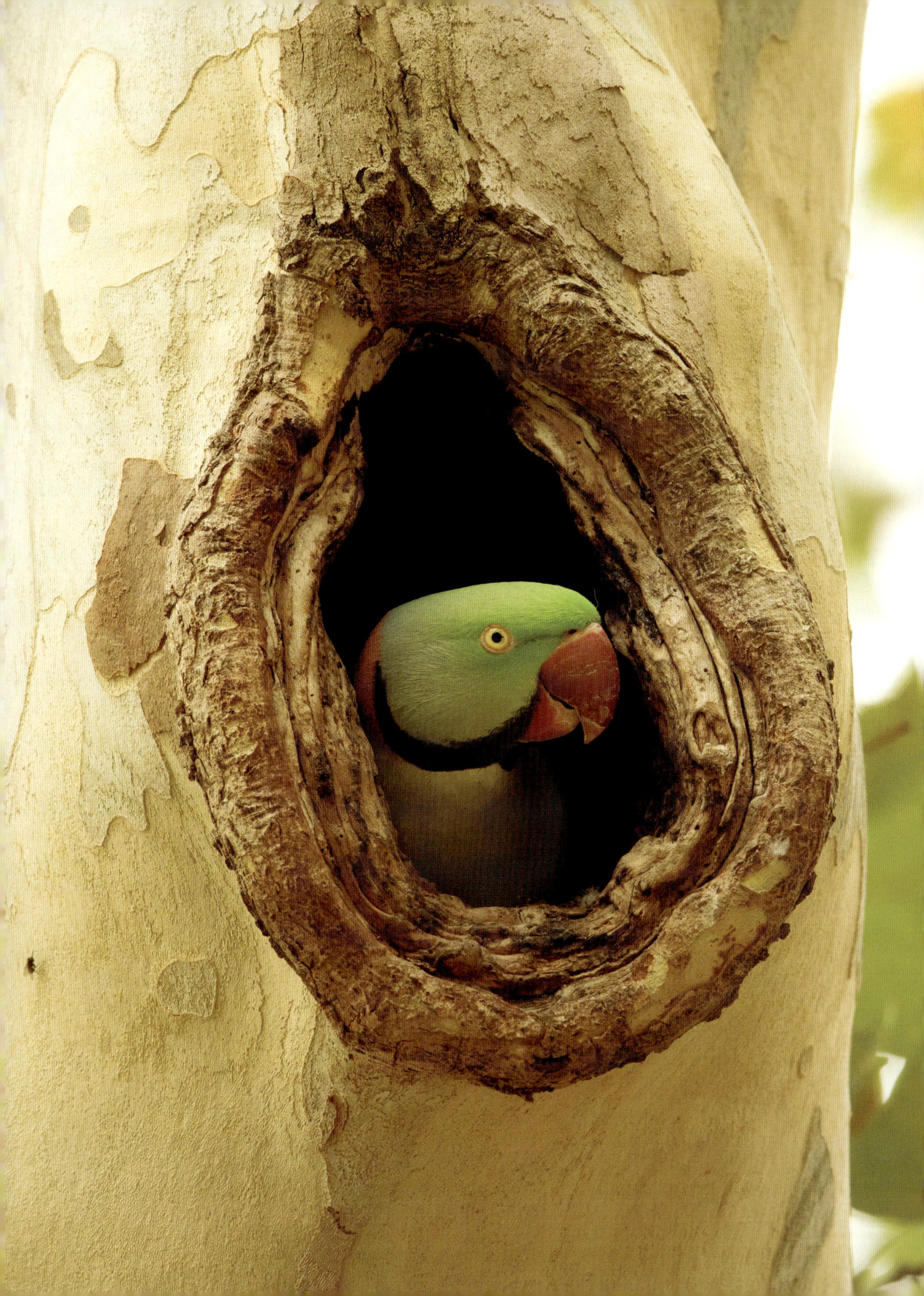

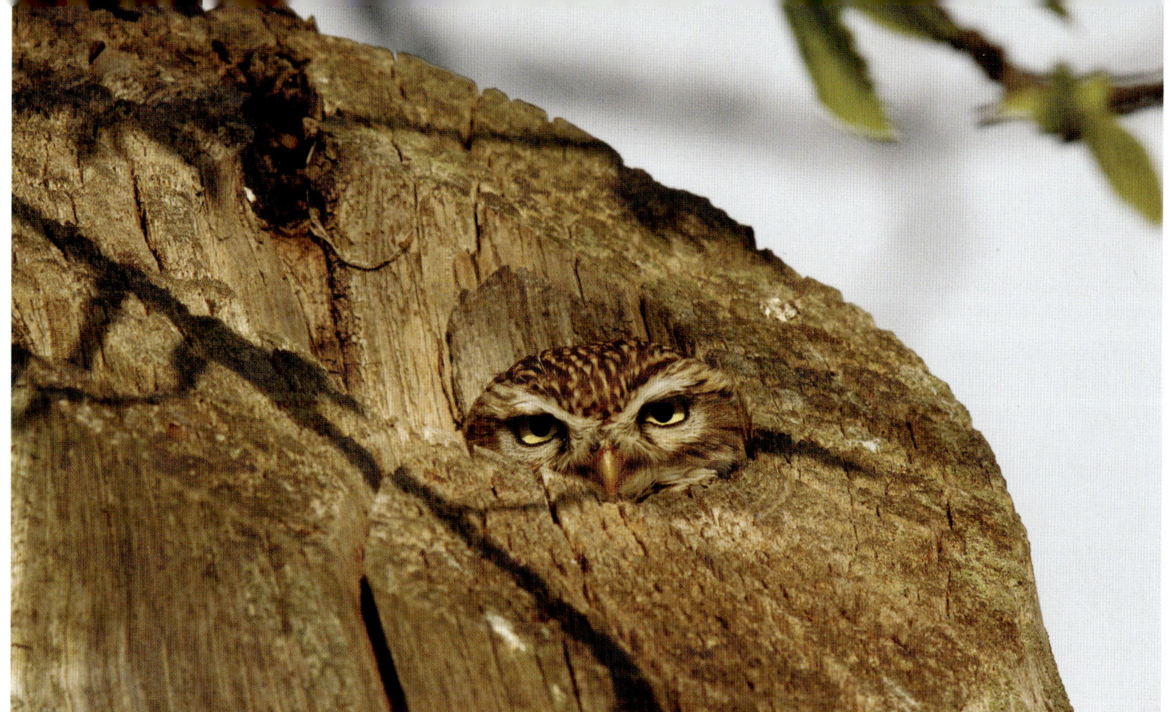

At the Cave

Many birds use tree caves for roosting. Owls even use theirs as resting places during the day, and since they like to stay close to "their" spots, you can often find them at their roosts. Surprisingly, they're often not very shy, which means that you can photograph them as they doze at the entrance of their caves. The most important thing if you're lucky enough to spot a bird at its roost, is that you don't disturb it. After all, we don't want to drive it away from its resting place. So act cautiously, don't get too close, and don't make noises or hasty movements.

Parks, zoos, or public green spaces are often places in which it is very easy to photograph roosting birds since they are used to humans.

It's important to put the focus on the bird's eye and not on the edge of the cave to make sure it's the bird and not the tree that will be sharp in the picture. Since the bird's head and the entrance of its cave are usually at different heights, the head would be on a different focal plane and out of focus.

▲ 4-171

Little owl | Germany | Many owls rest in tree caves during the day. Since they like to stay close to their spots, they can often be found there. | 840mm (600mm + 1.4x converter), aperture 8.0, 1/800s, ISO 640

◀ 4-170

Alexandrine parakeet | Wiesbaden | It's important to focus on the eye of the bird when taking these pictures, otherwise the autofocus will focus on the tree trunk. | 840mm (600mm + 1.4x converter), aperture 6.3, 1/640 s, ISO 1250

During Courtship

Birds display impressive courtship behavior and if you get to watch them, it's very special. The easiest way to do this is from a camouflage. Avoid disturbing the birds at all costs. Some birds, especially waterfowl, are easily observed during courtship and there's no reason to not take pictures as well. If you're photographing several birds at once, follow the rules described in the sections on this topic starting on page 68.

Be a Respectful Bird Photographer!

It's very important to me that the act of taking pictures should never disturb the birds! Especially during the sensitive periods when they mate and rear their young, but also at their roosting sites!

Keep a respectful distance, don't change the bird's environment, and retreat as soon as the bird shows any signs of distress!

No image is worth making a bird abandon its chicks or alerting a predator to its presence.

4-172 ▶

Mute swans | Germany | Some bird species are very easily observed during courtship. It's very important to not disturb them in any way! | 700mm, aperture 13, 1/1000 s, ISO 500

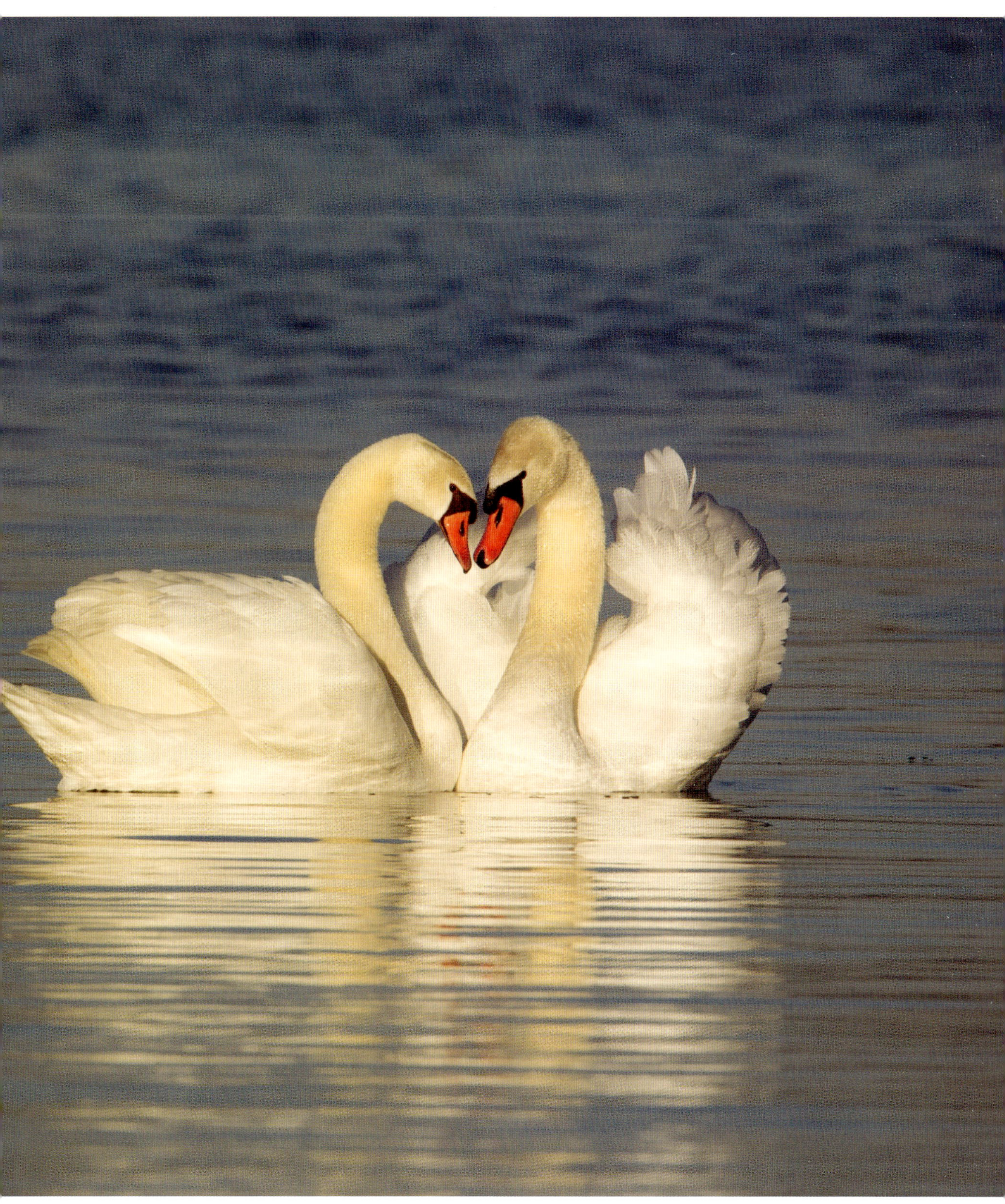

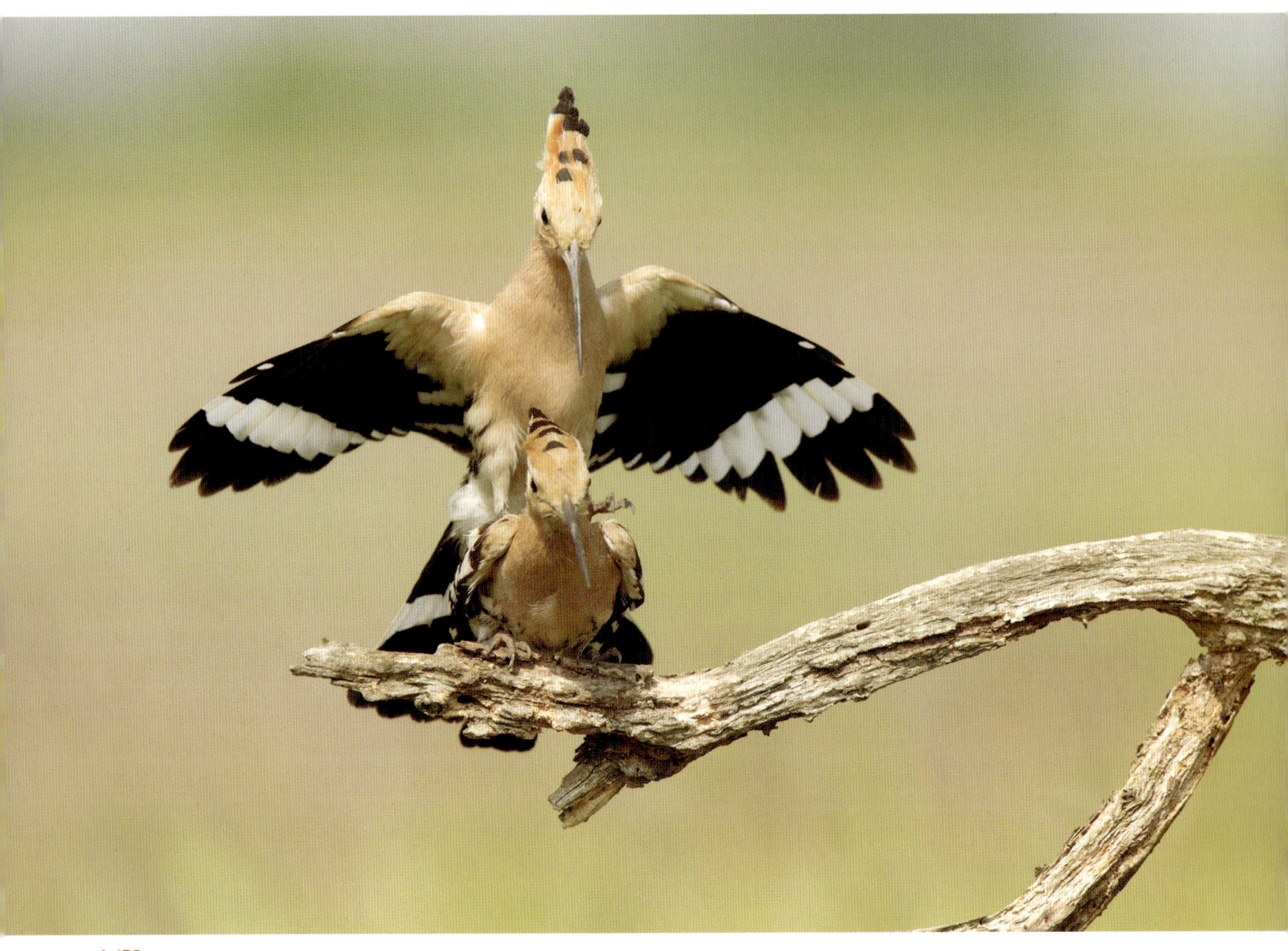

Hoopoes | Serbia | Photographed from a tree stand: The birds aren't aware of the observer and behave completely naturally. | 600mm, aperture 6.3, 1/2500 s, ISO 500, -1/3 exposure compensation

Mating

Helped by camouflage, you can sometimes even observe birds mating.

Again, it's important to not disturb the birds, since they'll only mate if they feel safe and unobserved. That's one reason why I like tree stands so much: The birds have grown used to the blind and don't realize that they're being watched. It makes it possible to take great pictures without disturbing the birds!

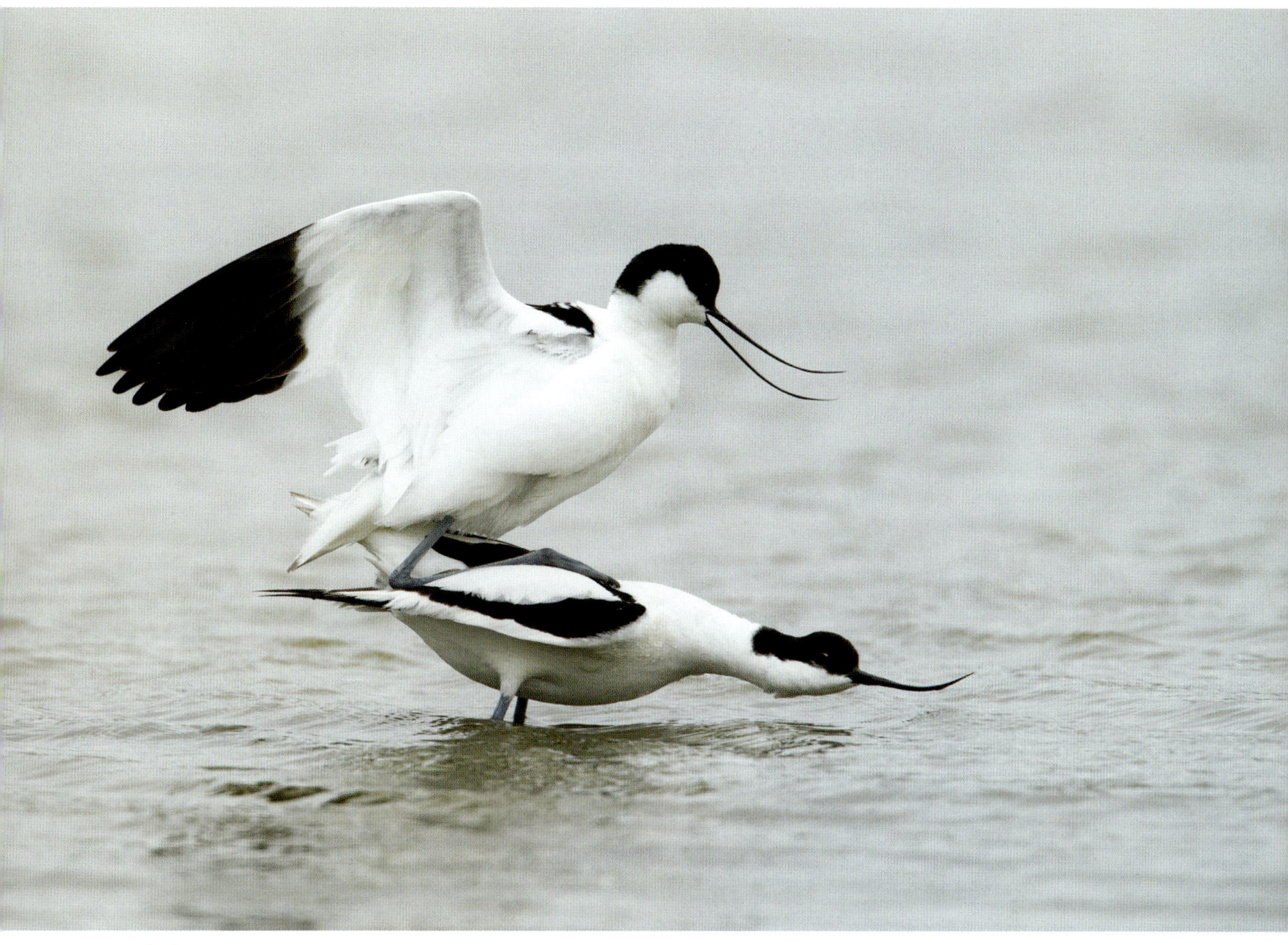

Pied avocets | Texel, The Netherlands | These two birds were used to the respectful photographers. A fixed sequence of movements announced that they were about to mate. | 700mm (500mm + 1.4x converter), aperture 7.1, 1/800 s, ISO 800, +2/3 exposure compensation

If you get the chance, observe birds closely during courtship and mating season. Usually, the different species have specific rituals that precede the act of mating. One of the birds might present food to the other or there's a special sequence of movements. Learning about the birds' behavior allows you to get the best photos.

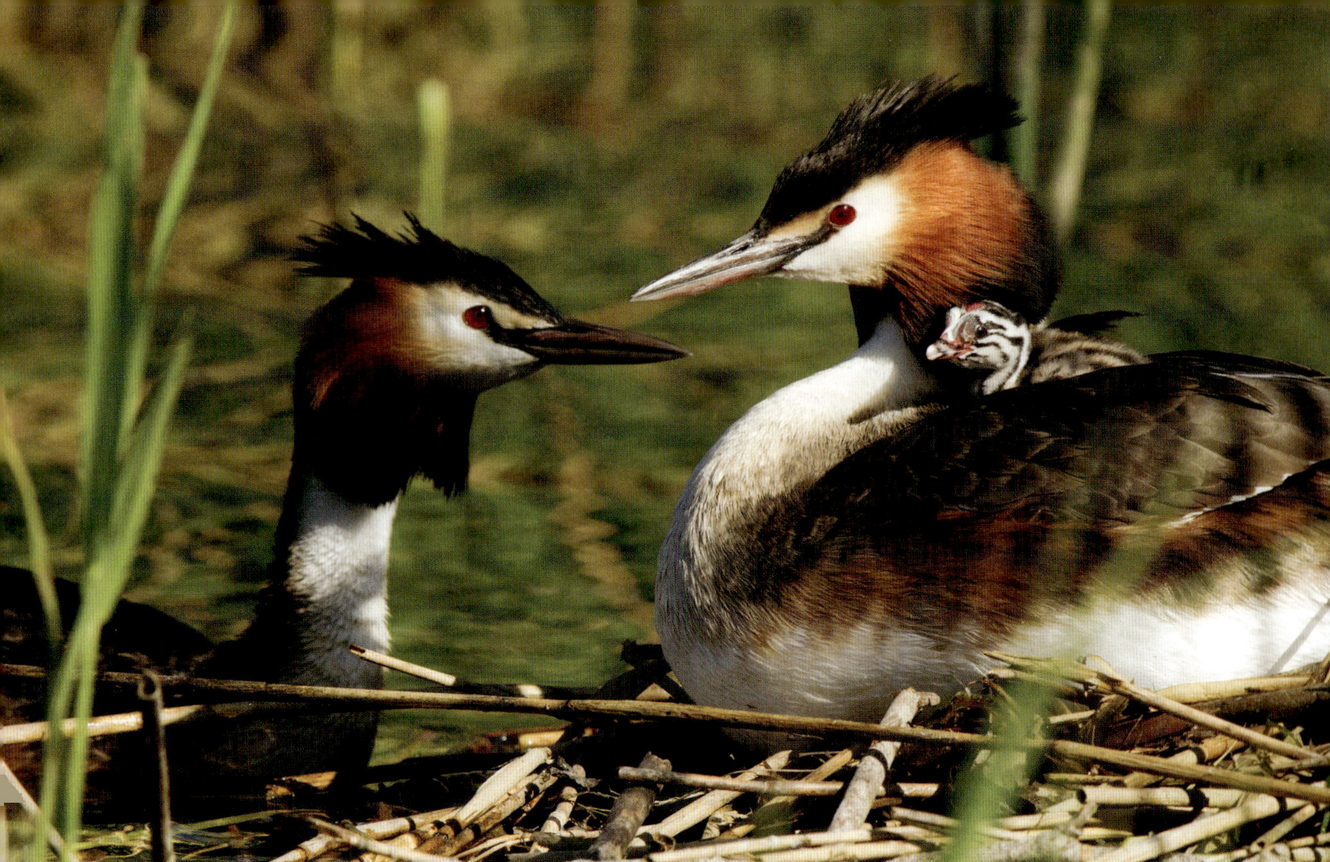

Great crested grebe | The Netherlands | This pair was nesting close to a public path at a small lake in a recreational area and wasn't bothered by the people who walked by every day. | 600mm, aperture 8.0, 1/1250 s, ISO 500

Nesting and Raising Chicks

This period is probably the most sensitive, and disturbances should be avoided at all costs. Do not, under any circumstances, change anything around the bird's nest. Do not move branches, for example, to get a better angle to photograph into a hedge! Nesting birds need all the protection they can get, and this is something you as a photographer must not violate under any circumstances. Even just observing a nest constitutes a disturbance and can lead to parent birds abandoning their eggs or neglecting to feed and warm their chicks.

However, there are situations in which birds have already become accustomed to the presence of humans and are not distressed by their presence when they raise their young. Waterfowl, such as ducks, geese, and swans, that are often quite easily photographed with their offspring.

You may also be able to use camouflage. But you can't just go and put up your camouflage tent next to a nest. The tent would most certainly frighten the birds at first and may cause them to neglect their parenting duties. Instead, use an established hide that the birds already know, or put up your tent in the vicinity early, before the birds start laying eggs so they have time to get used to it. Once they have, birds are usually quite tolerant of tents and don't mind them at all.

I can only appeal to everyone's sense of responsibility here. Just one thoughtless photographer can quickly bring disrepute to all nature photography enthusiasts. I think that we all take pictures because we are mesmerized by birds, not because we want to harm them. When in doubt, it's better to back off and give the birds their space!

▼ **4-176**

Common wood pigeons | Germany | Some birds even seek out humans. This wood pigeon fledgling landed on the railing of our balcony and begged for food. The picture was taken through the window. | 200mm, aperture 5.6, 1/320 s, ISO 1600

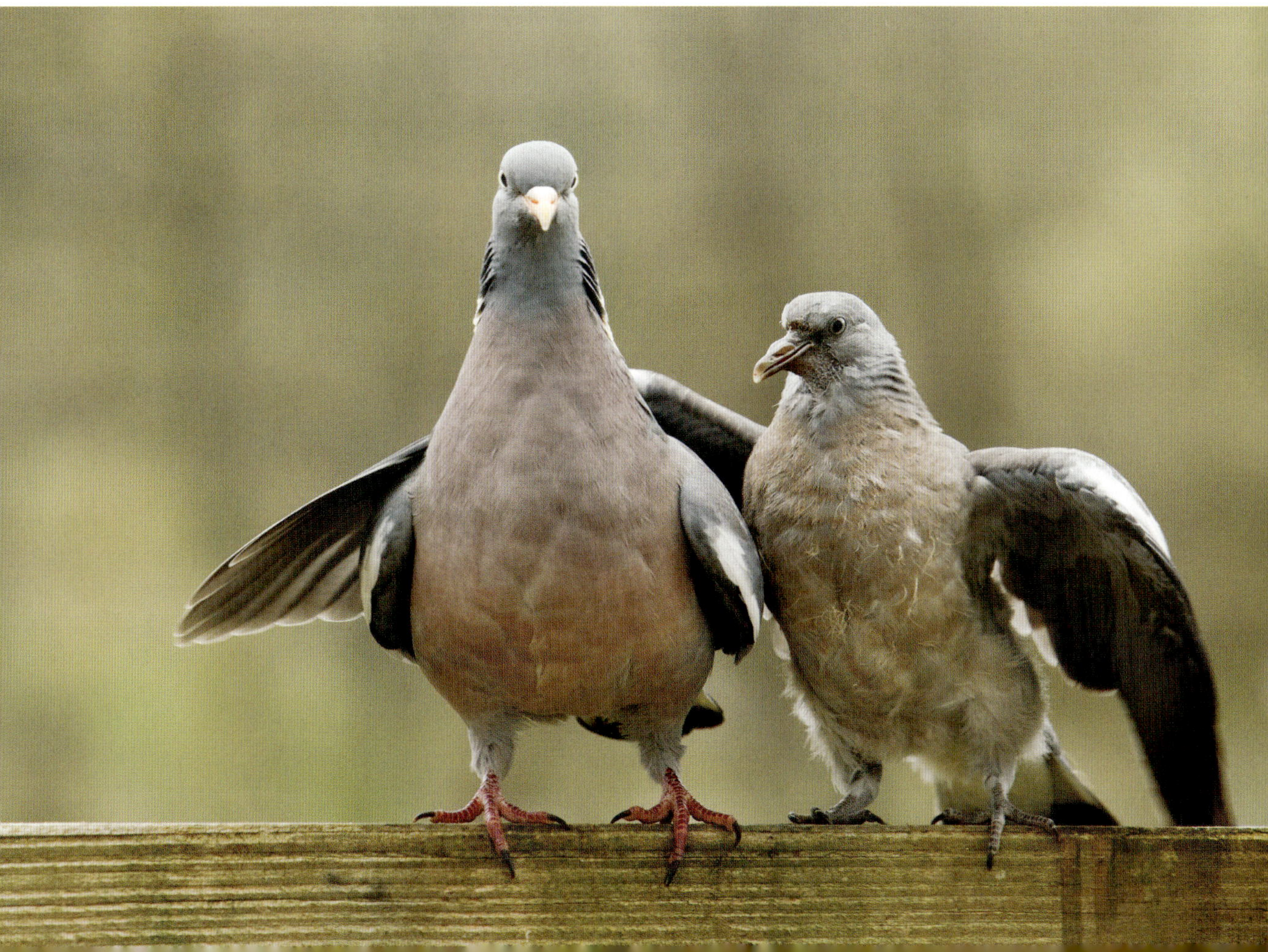

Squabbles

Sometimes squabbles happen, especially at the feeding station, and with a bit of luck, you might be able to capture them. But you'll need to avoid framing things too tightly. After all, birds in this situation require more space in the picture than an individual bird being portrayed.

When I'm working with a zoom lens, I'm able to adapt to the situation fairly quickly and adjust the zoom setting. With fixed focal lengths, I'm locked in as soon as I've selected the lens before the shoot. If I'm hoping for action shots, I deliberately choose a larger frame and concentrate on that kind of image.

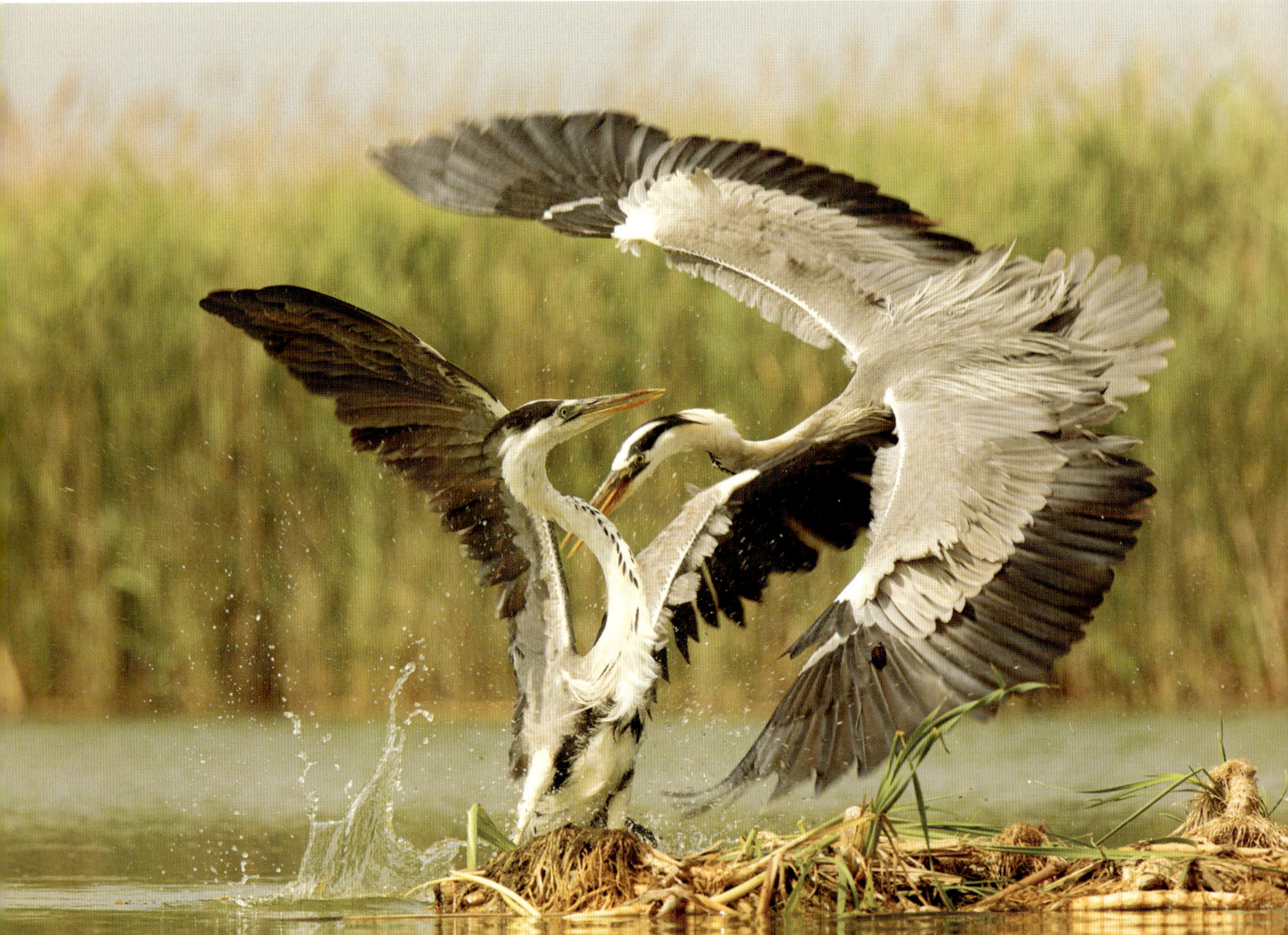

▲ 4-177

Gray heron | Serbia | Unfortunately, your focal length often ends up being too long in these situations and the frame too tight for two birds. Here I was lucky and neither bird is cut off. | 420mm (300mm + 1.4x converter), aperture 9.0, 1/640 s, ISO 800

CHAPTER 4

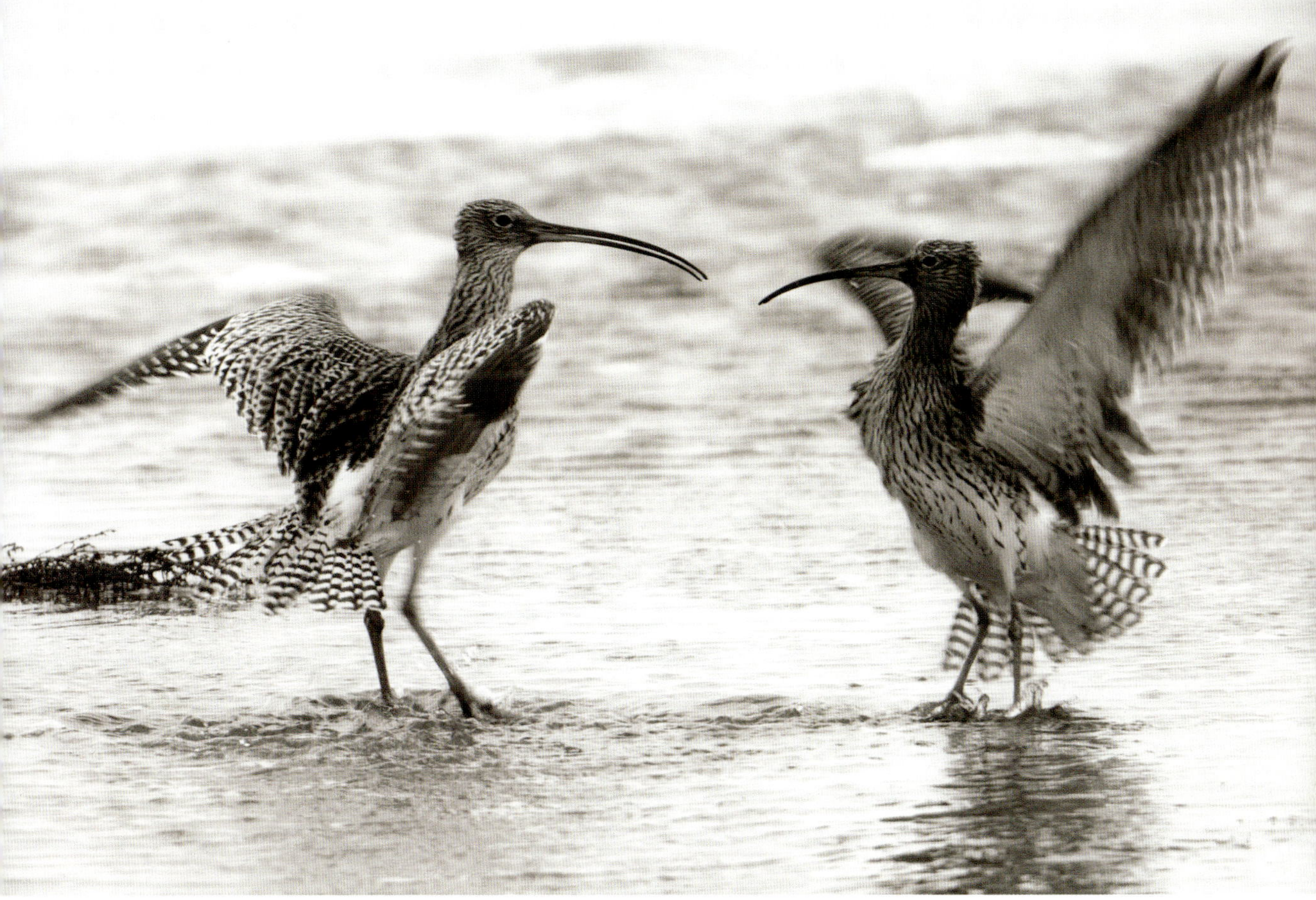

▲ **4-178**

Eurasian curlews | Texel, The Netherlands | Because of a long shutter time, the wings show some pronounced motion blur, which highlights the dynamic character of the scene. The sky was heavily overcast and the original image was tone-on-tone gray. Therefore, I decided to convert to black and white. | 700mm (500mm + 1.4x converter), aperture 5.6, 1/125 s, ISO 1000, +1 exposure compensation

If you want every detail of the squabble to show up sharp in your photo and freeze all motion down to the tips of the feathers, you'll need a very fast shutter speed of at least 1/2000 s, preferably even faster, especially for small songbirds. But sometimes, a bit of motion blur in the image can have its own appeal, provided the birds' heads are pretty sharp.

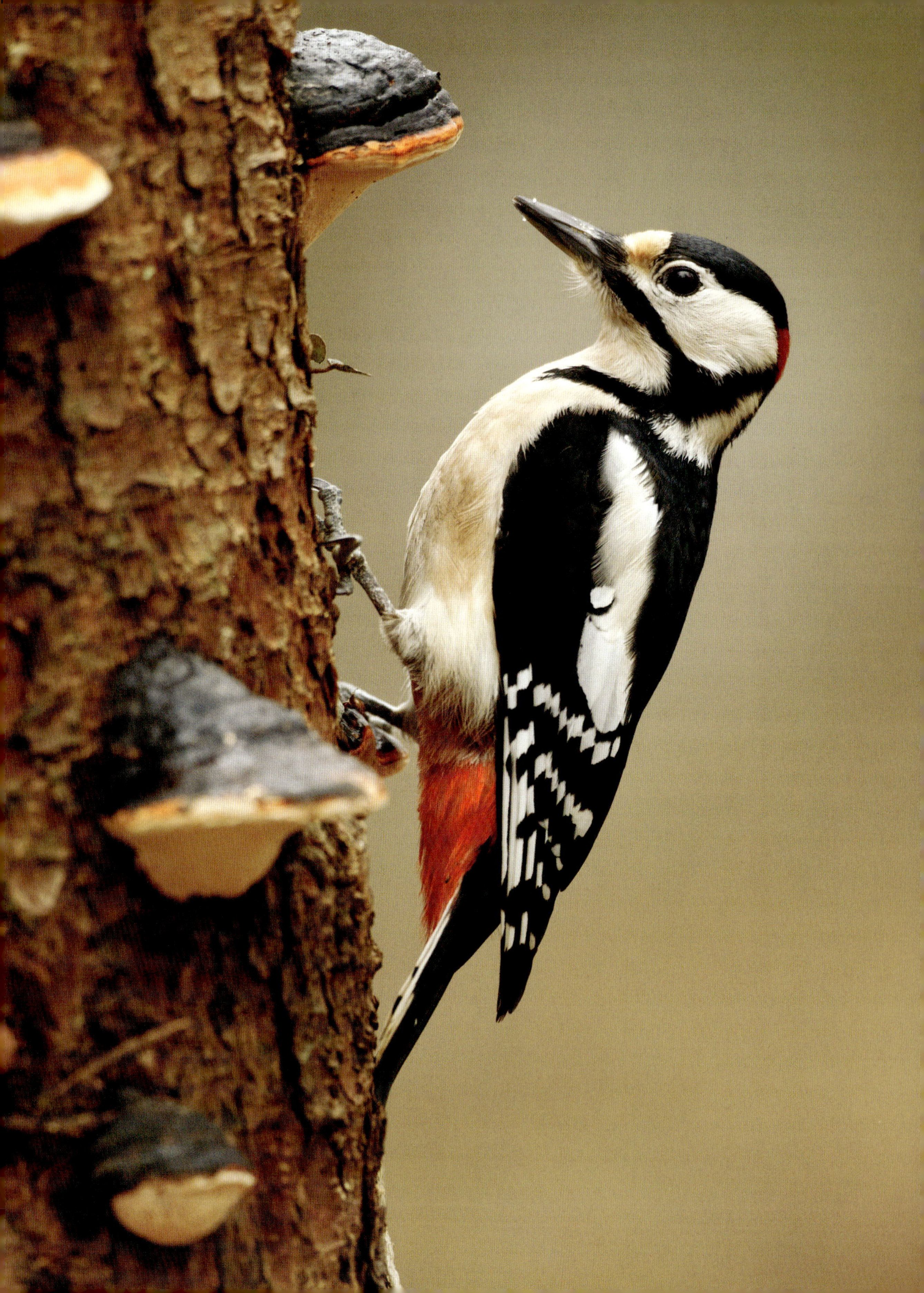

Birds at the Feeding Station

If you are fortunate enough to have your own backyard, you can easily set up a feeding station in the winter. You can even do this in a small front yard. I've also seen excellent photos that were taken at what was just a feeding station on a balcony. All you need is a bit of creativity to make the feeder attractive for the birds and the viewers alike. Use different kinds of feed: seeds for the seed-eaters like tits and bull-finches, fat balls and insects for woodpeckers, blackbirds, robins, and long-tailed tits. Keep an eye out for branches to add, and change things up at the feeding station from time to time. If you can, offer some water as well.

Put some thought into what kind of background the feeding station will have and position it in a place where the background will be as harmonious as possible for your pictures.

Personally, I don't like photos where you can see the feed. I drill holes into branches and hide the feed in them or hang up the fat balls on the backside of a tree trunk. Seeds can be tucked away in hollows in the wood. I've also filled a shallow bowl with feed and attached it to a branch for perching. Most birds land on the branch before eating from the feeder.

◀◀ 4-179
Great spotted woodpecker | Germany | With a bit of creativity, it's possible to take a wide variety of pictures at your own feeding station. | 500mm, aperture 5.0, 1/400 s, ISO 1600

▼ 4-180
Bullfinch | Germany | A quick stop on the way to the feeding station…. | 600mm, aperture 6.3, 1/800 s, ISO 1000

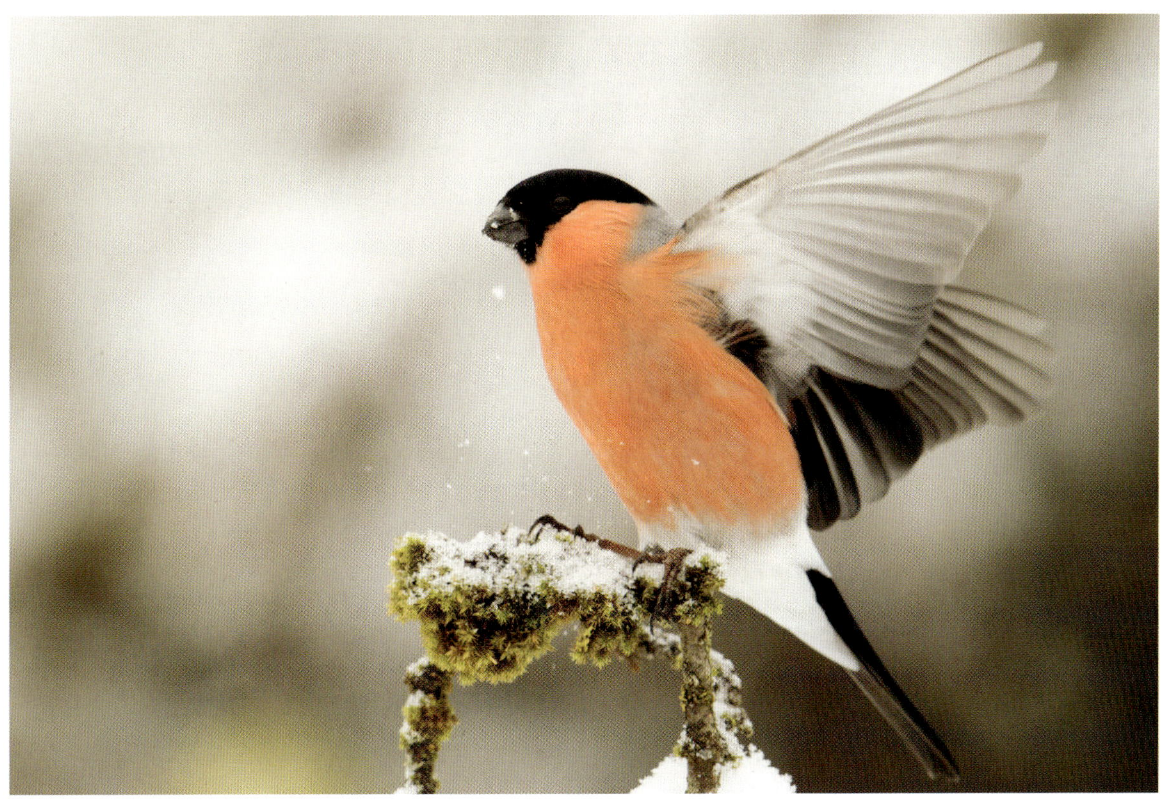

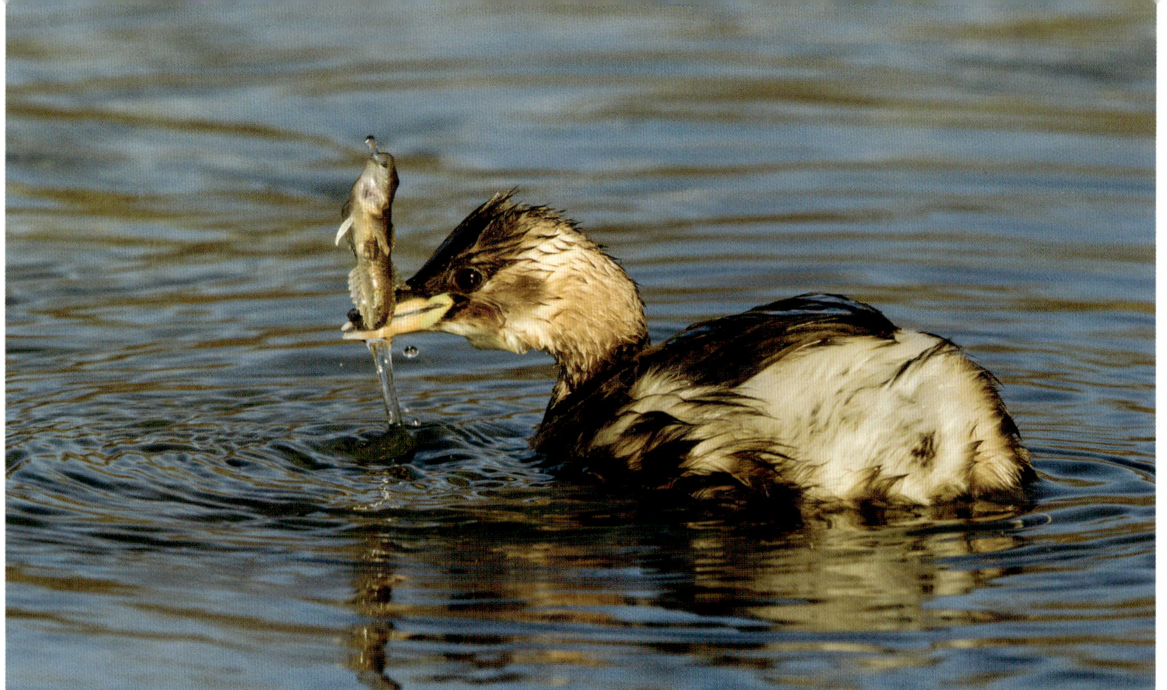

Little grebe | Germany |
I was watching a little grebe—
and suddenly it emerged with a
fish in its beak. With an aperture
of 10 I managed to keep both
sharp. | 600mm, aperture 10,
1/1000 s, ISO 640

Predators and Prey

The big birds of prey aren't the only accomplished predators. Even small birds catch amazing prey at times.

Little and great crested grebes, kingfishers, and gray herons hunt fish; bee-eaters, shrikes, and wagtails prey on insects, dragonflies, and butterflies; hoopoes and kestrels, among others, poach lizards. It's always exciting to capture these moments with your camera. And sometimes you'll get a big surprise later when you sit at your computer and discover what the bird had actually caught!

It's worth watching a gray heron for a while when it's wading through the water—quite likely it's searching for food and will strike sooner or later. Fundamentally, this is true whenever you observe a bird. For example, if I happen to spot a songbird from my car and it keeps returning to the same perch, I'll happily spend half or all day watching and photographing that one bird. Only patience will get you a steady supply of interesting photos!

There's nothing special you have to pay attention to in terms of camera settings. The depth of field must be large enough to get both the prey and the bird sharp, so it might be a good idea to close the aperture a bit. But I have also achieved good results with an open aperture. In some situations, you'll need a fast shutter speed, for example, if you want to photograph a bee-eater on the hunt or when a gray heron tosses a fish into its beak.

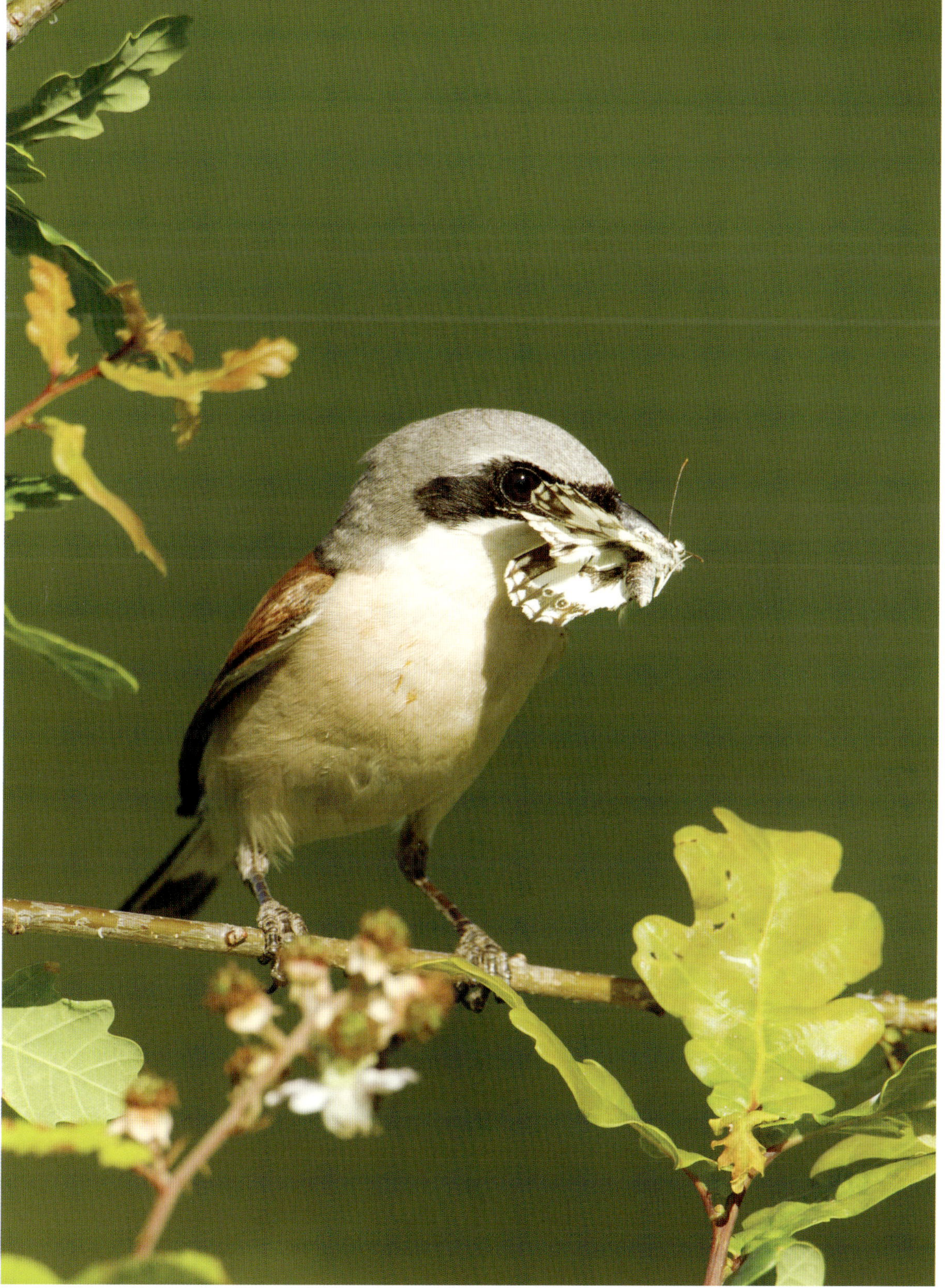

Red-backed shrike | Germany | The red-backed shrike kept returning to the same branch. One time, I got lucky and it brought a butterfly for its chicks. | 500mm, aperture 5.6, 1/1000 s, ISO 800

Big Birds Feeding on Carrion

You can rent observation stands at carrion feeding stations. These are locations that put out food for birds of prey at regular intervals. Please note that it might be forbidden to set up such a feedings station yourself without a permit, depending on where you live.

Buzzards, ravens, and—depending on the location—eagles are typical visitors at such stations. Gigrin Farm is a well-known farm in Wales where hundreds of red kites show up for feedings every day, accompanied by buzzards, magpies, crows, and ravens. Apart from the fact that it's a special experience to witness such feedings, it provides an opportunity to take some great pictures of these birds.

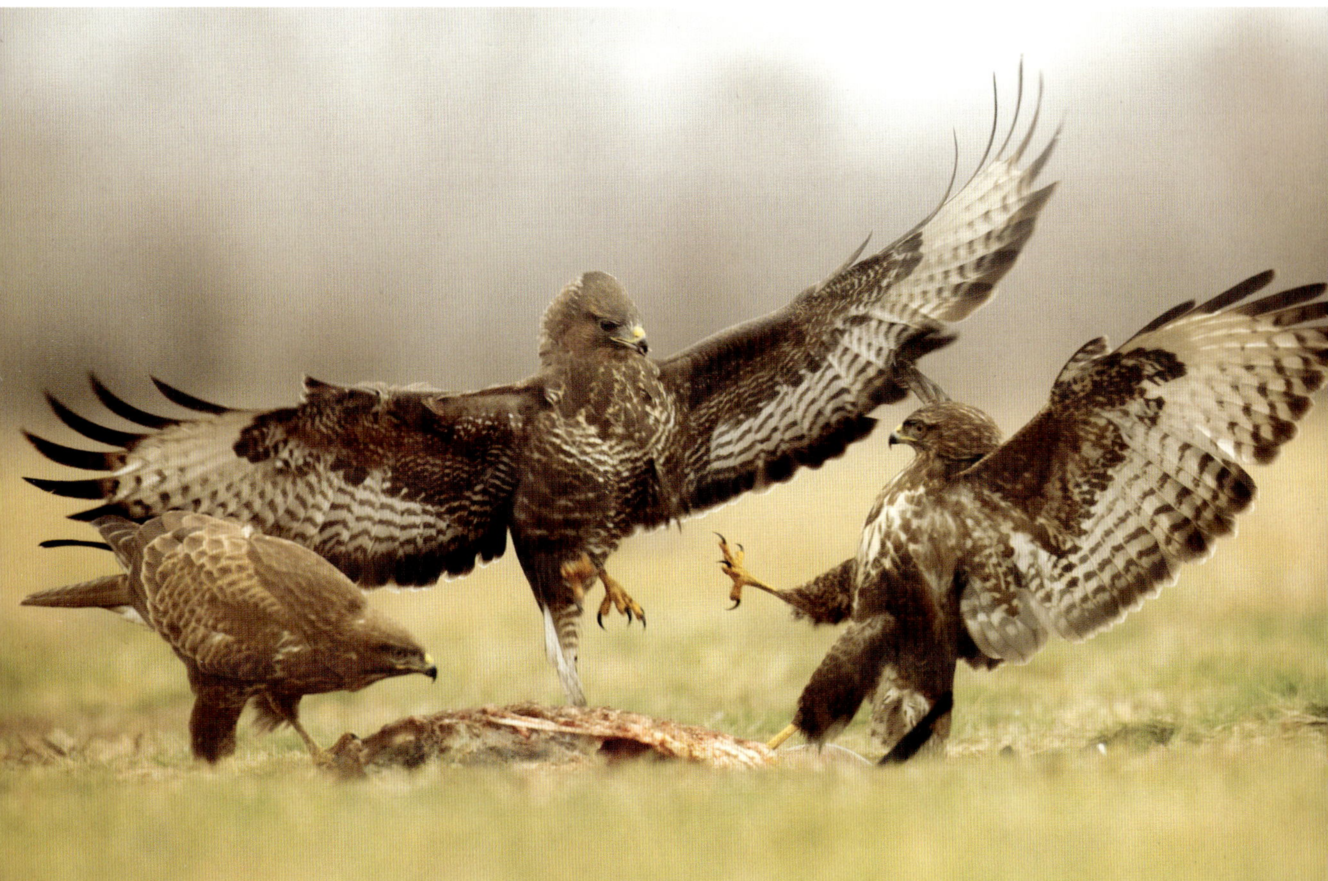

▲ 4-183

Buzzards | Serbia | For action shots like this you must keep the shutter time fast enough and the framing wide enough to accommodate all of the wings. | 500mm, aperture 5.0, 1/500 s, ISO 1600

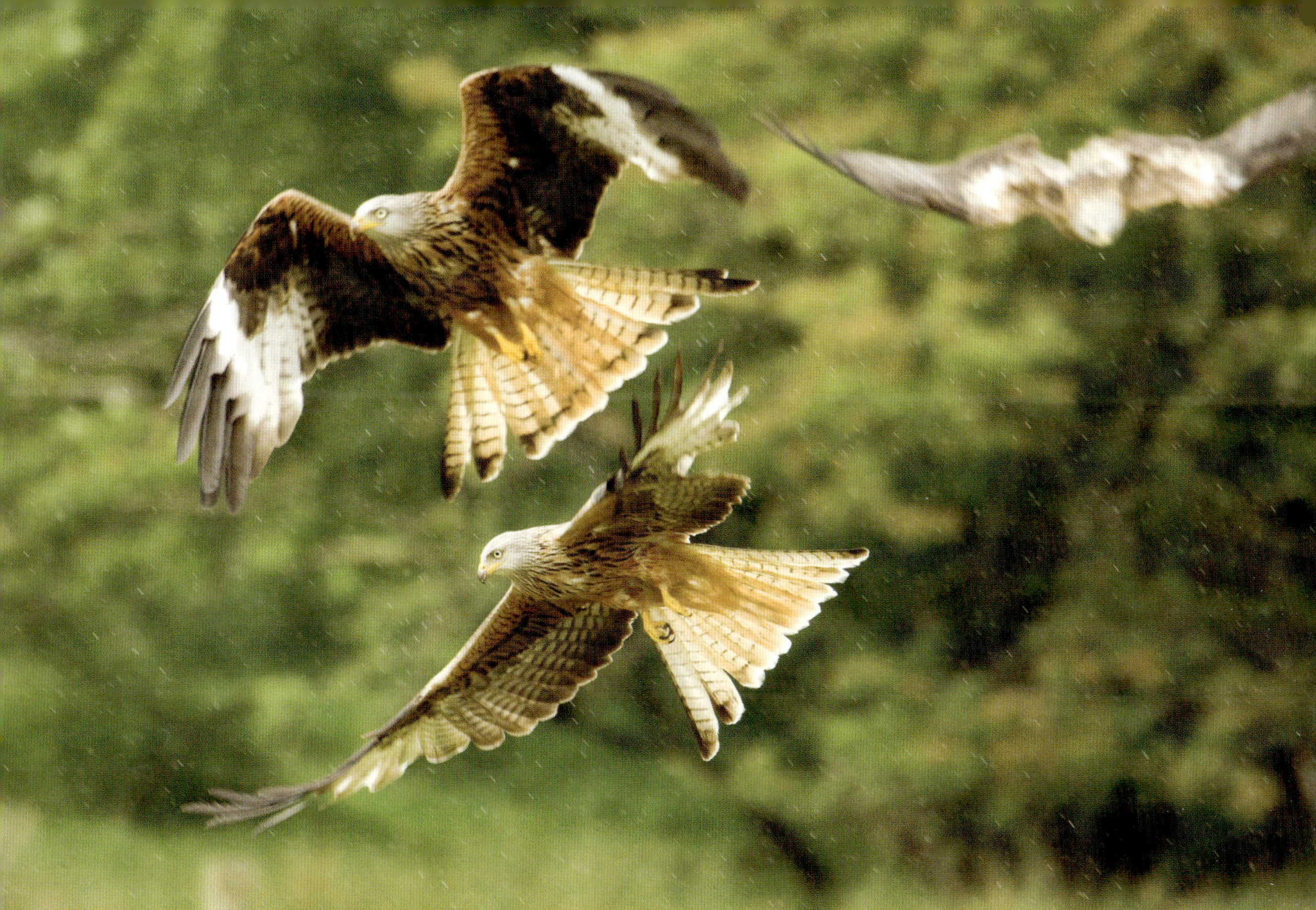

Red kites | Wales | The red kites at Gigrin Farm are well worth seeing! | 400mm, aperture 6.3, 1/800 s, ISO 1250

Unless the feedings are a tourist attraction like at Gigrin Farm, the birds that visit a carrion station tend to be quite shy and photographers have to follow a few rules. You often must be in the hide before sunrise and are not allowed to leave during the day. There will be a small camping toilet for personal needs—privacy is limited….

Some of the most extraordinary pictures come from birds that squabble about particularly desirable morsels of food—if more than one bird is feeding on a piece of carrion, you should always expect brawls to break out. Again, I recommend a focal length that isn't too long, so you can fit two of these birds with their wingspan into the frame.

4.7 The Changing of the Seasons

Spring Mood

Spring might be the best time to photograph birds. Most wear their prettiest plumage; they pick exposed perches to sing on—and everything around them is in bloom.

What's the best way to capture spring in a photo? Naturally, by keeping an eye out for blooming trees and by watching them closely to see if a magnificent male happens to pick that exact tree as his singing perch! Or you can do the opposite and listen for singing birds then look to see where they're perched. Don't hesitate to frame things a little more generously to include some blossoms in the picture.

Another springtime motif could be a bird gathering nesting material. You could put out some feathers from an old down pillow at your winter feeding station—the birds will be delighted to find them and you'll get some nice pictures when the feathers are being gathered up. Arguably, one could also include photos of chicks and fledglings in the spring repertoire.

▼ **4-185**

Egyptian goose | Germany | A young Egyptian goose explores the world. | 500mm, aperture 4.0, 1/300 s, ISO 400, -1/3 exposure compensation

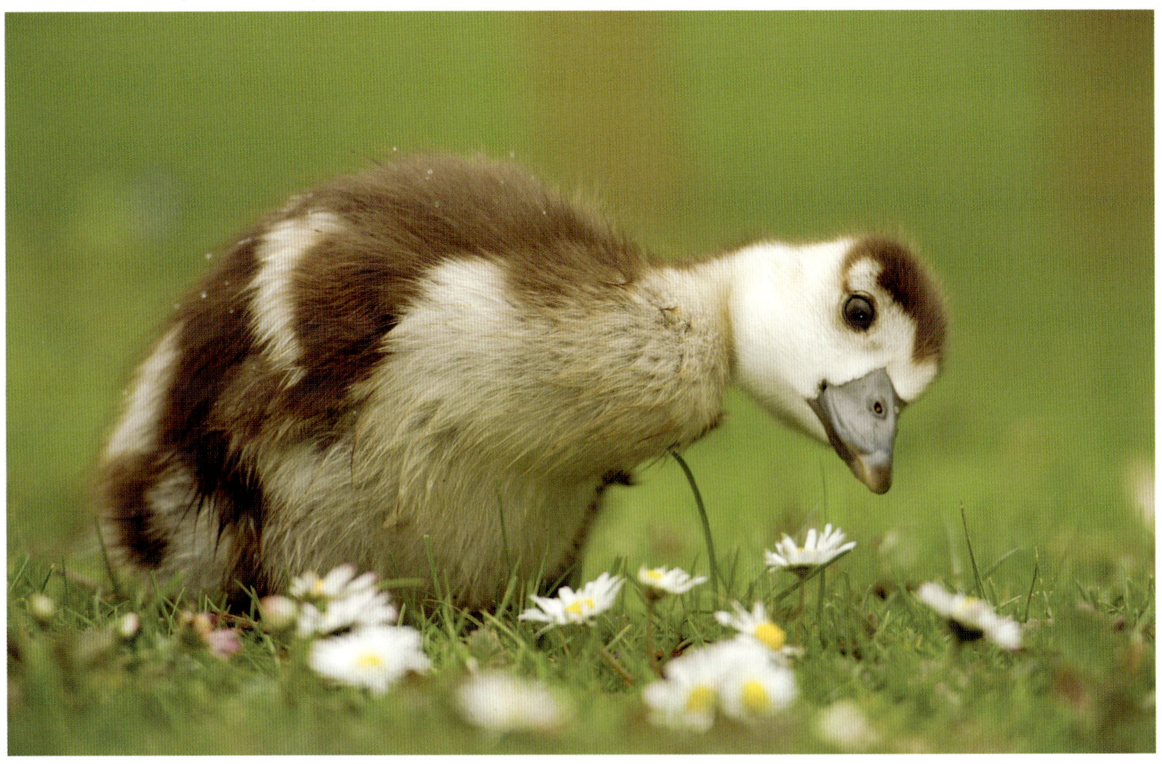

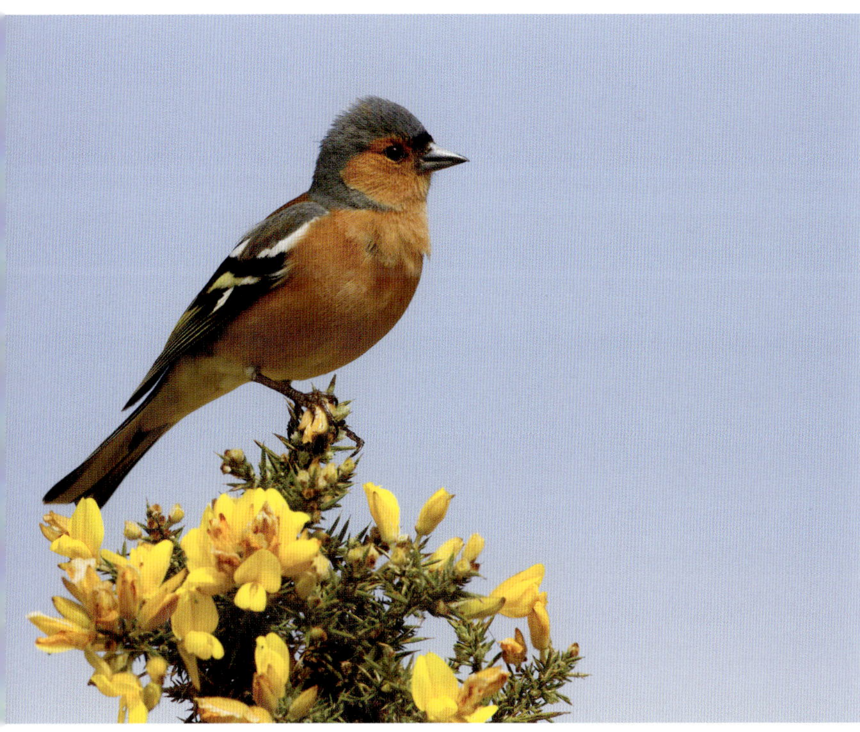

◀ **4-186**

Common chaffinch | Wales |
A typical spring photo: the male
chaffinch on his singing perch. |
500mm, aperture 8, 1/1600 s,
ISO 400

▼ **4-187**

Starling | Germany | The starling
is delighted to find the little
feather that will pad its nest. |
500mm | aperture 5.6, 1/500 s,
ISO 640

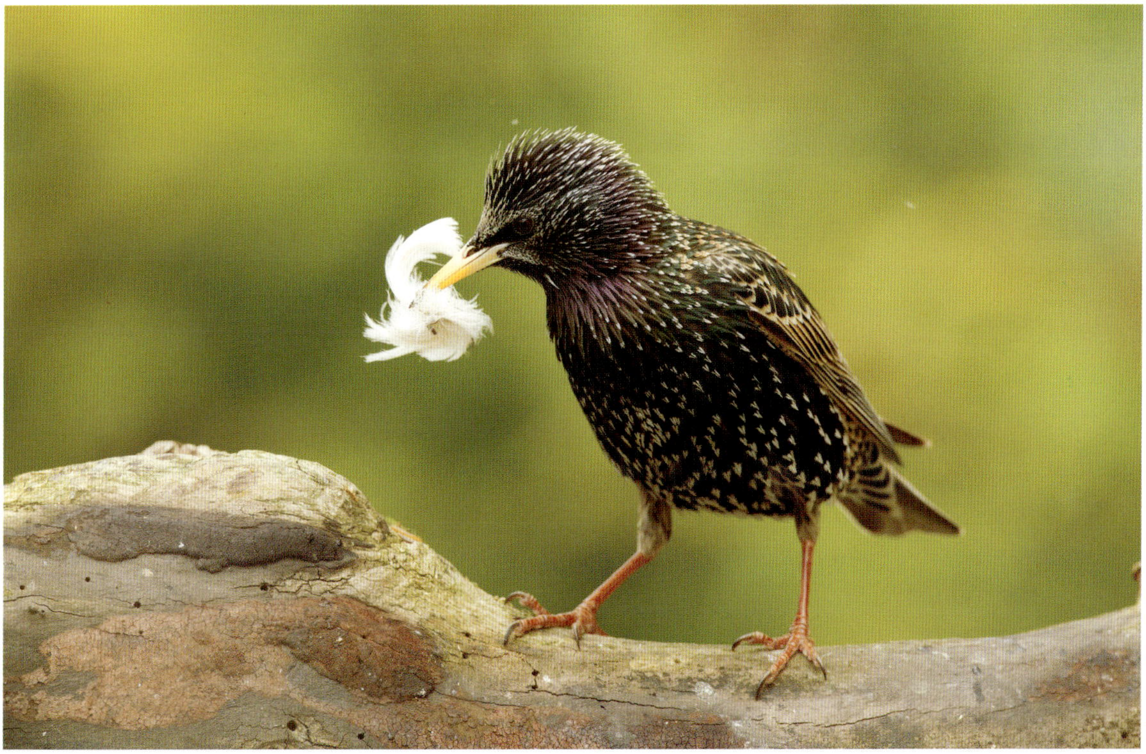

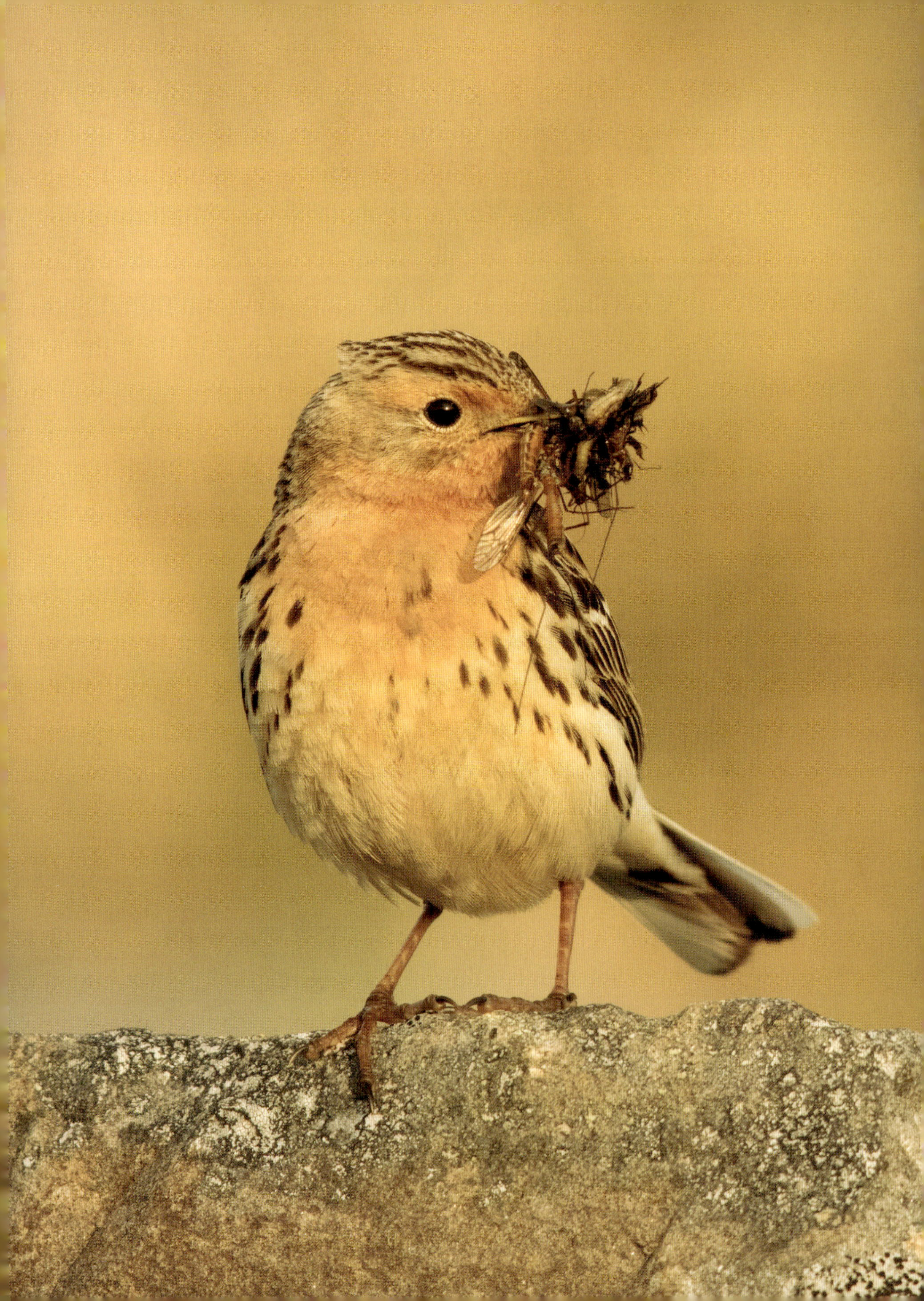

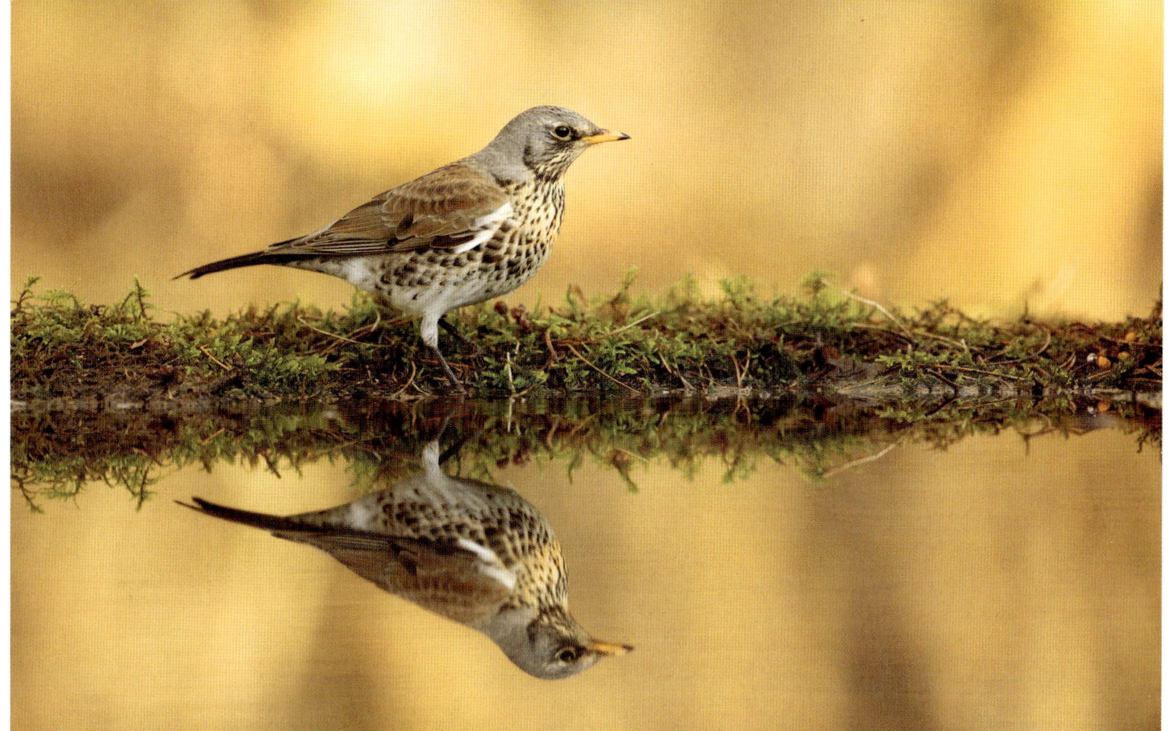

Summer Pictures

Hmm, what represents summer and how can summer be captured in a photo? For me, it's mostly about pictures with water. Birds drinking or taking a bath. Maybe you're able to create your own bathing spot for birds in the yard? Especially if there are no natural spots nearby where they can take a dip, they will certainly frequent such a drinking and bathing station.

Or perhaps a bird with its beak full of insects that it has collected for its young also says summer? Fledglings symbolize both summer and spring.

Basically, summer is a bit of a challenging season to photograph wild birds. Especially in late summer, when the chicks have fledged and are independent, and many birds are already preparing for their winter migration. They tend to be reclusive during this phase, and there are always summer days when I'll return from a photo outing with nothing much to show for it.

Red-throated pipit | Norway | In early summer, many parent birds are busy providing food for their chicks. | 840mm (600mm + 1.4x converter), aperture 6.3, 1/2000 s, ISO 1000

◀ 4-189

Fieldfare | Serbia | On hot, dry summer days, many birds frequent spots where they can drink and take a bath. | 300mm, aperture 3.2, 1/320 s, ISO 1000, -2/3 exposure compensation

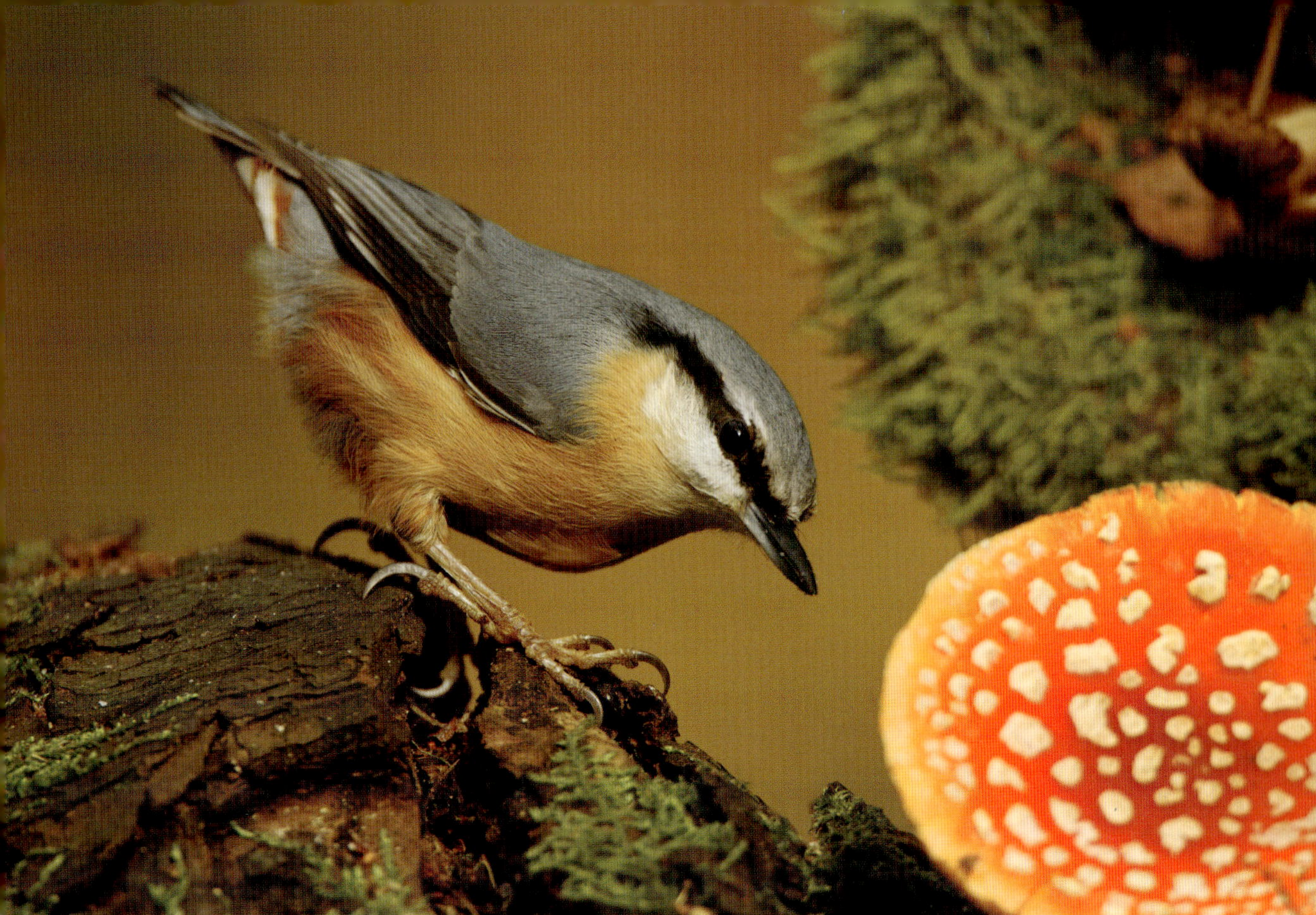

Nuthatch | Germany | In the fall, you can start taking your first pictures at the feeding place. | 700mm, (500mm + 1.4x converter), aperture 6.3, 1/500 s, ISO 640

Fall Impressions

Fall is a season that lends itself to being photographed. The wonderful colors of fall foliage, berries, and fruits—all symbolize fall. If you can't find enough motifs in nature, why not visit a zoo, bird park, or falconry and try to capture some of the fall colors there, combined with a bird, of course.

If you have your own yard, you can also start preparing your feeding station. This is the time when you can find lots of pretty branches with berries or fruit in nature that can be used to embellish a feeding station.

4-191 ▶

White-faced owl | Germany | Also use the fall to visit zoos and falconries to capture some autumnal atmosphere. | 135mm, f/2.2, 1/8000 s, ISO 1600, -1/3 exposure compensation

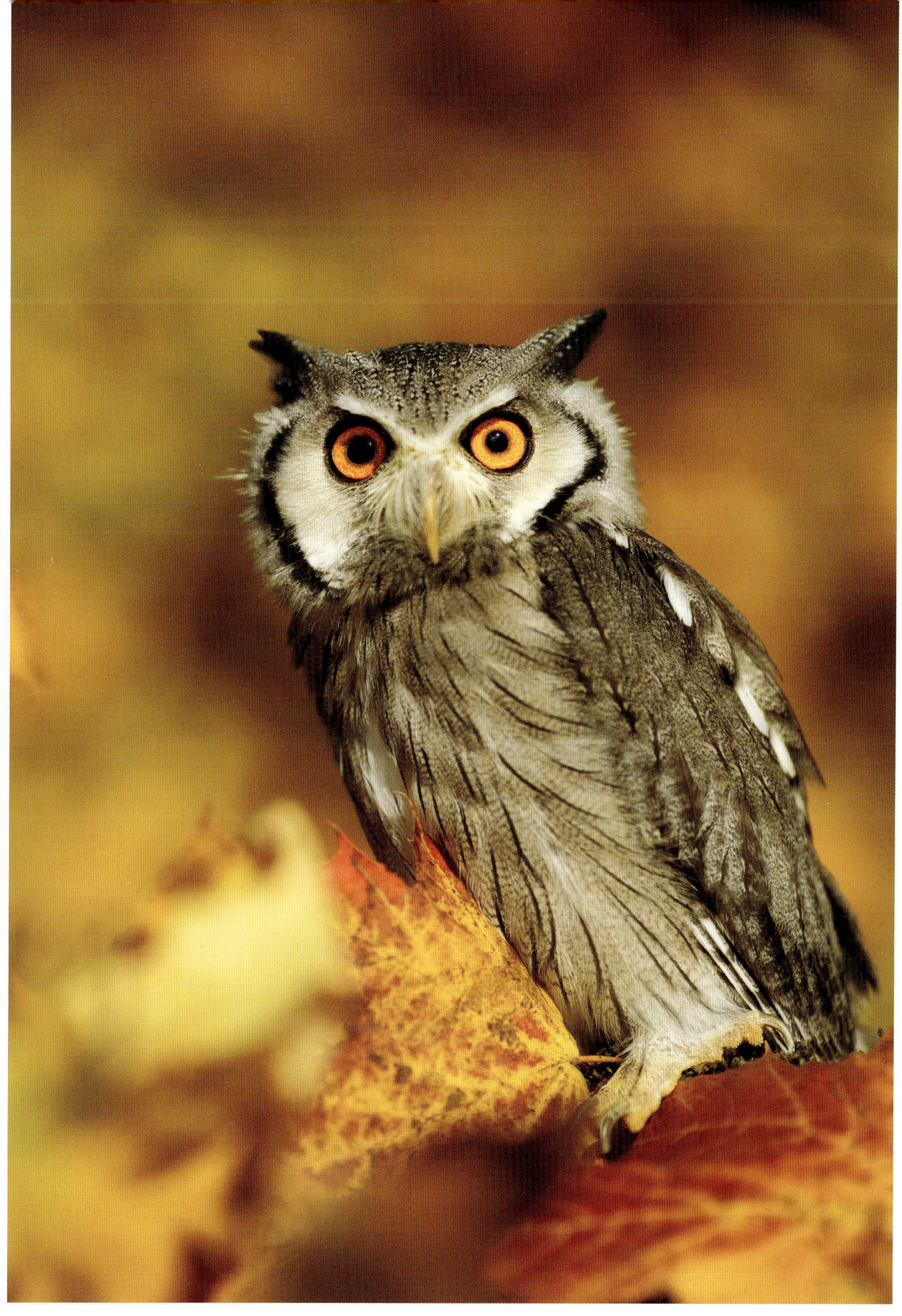

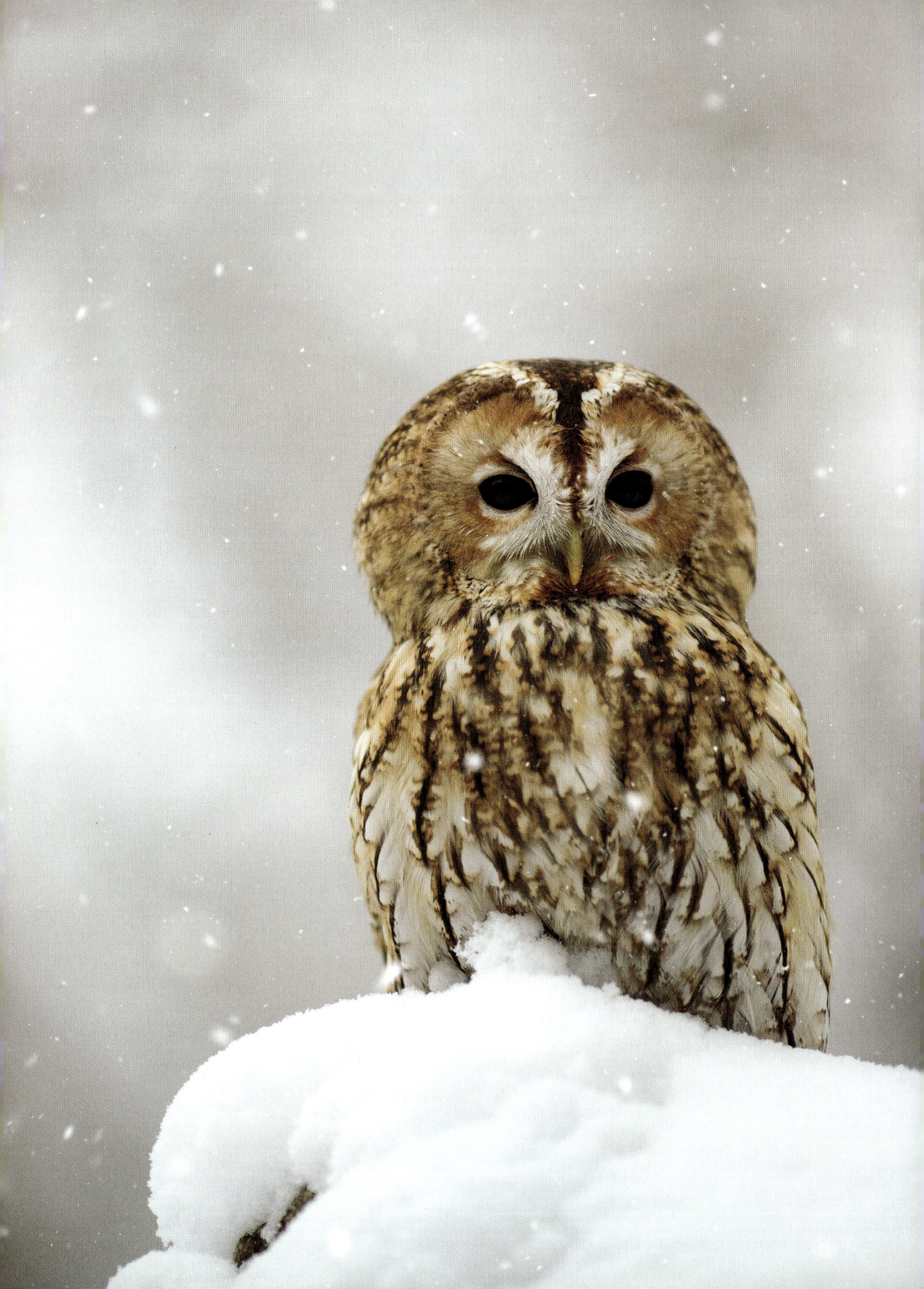

Winter Feeling

Almost every feeding site will get lots of visitors, and if you dress warm enough, you can take wonderful photos. Should you plan to do some intense photographing at your own feeding site, it may even be worth building a small hide or at least using a mobile camouflage tent. These tents are very affordable and a worthwhile purchase if you are hoping to photograph some of the more shy birds at your feeding station. A snow day in winter spent at the feeding station may be cold, but you'll be rewarded!

There's plenty to photograph in nature, too. At lakes, it's easy to observe waterfowl. There are often spots where they have become accustomed to visitors and you can get quite close to them.

Other than snow, colors in the cool temperature range also express the winter atmosphere well. Pay attention to getting the white balance right. Use RAW files so that you can still adjust the white balance in each photo later. If there's a lot of snow in the image, you'll also need to think about exposure compensation. Auto exposure will turn the snow gray so dial a positive exposure compensation!

◀◀ 4-192

Tawny Owl | Germany |
A snowy winter day is perfect for capturing the season's mood. |
135mm, aperture 2.0, 1/8000 s, ISO 1000

▼ 4-193

Mute swan | Germany | It was freezing that morning and the swans pushed their way through the ice. | 500mm, aperture 10, 1/1000 s, ISO 1250, +1/3 exposure compensation

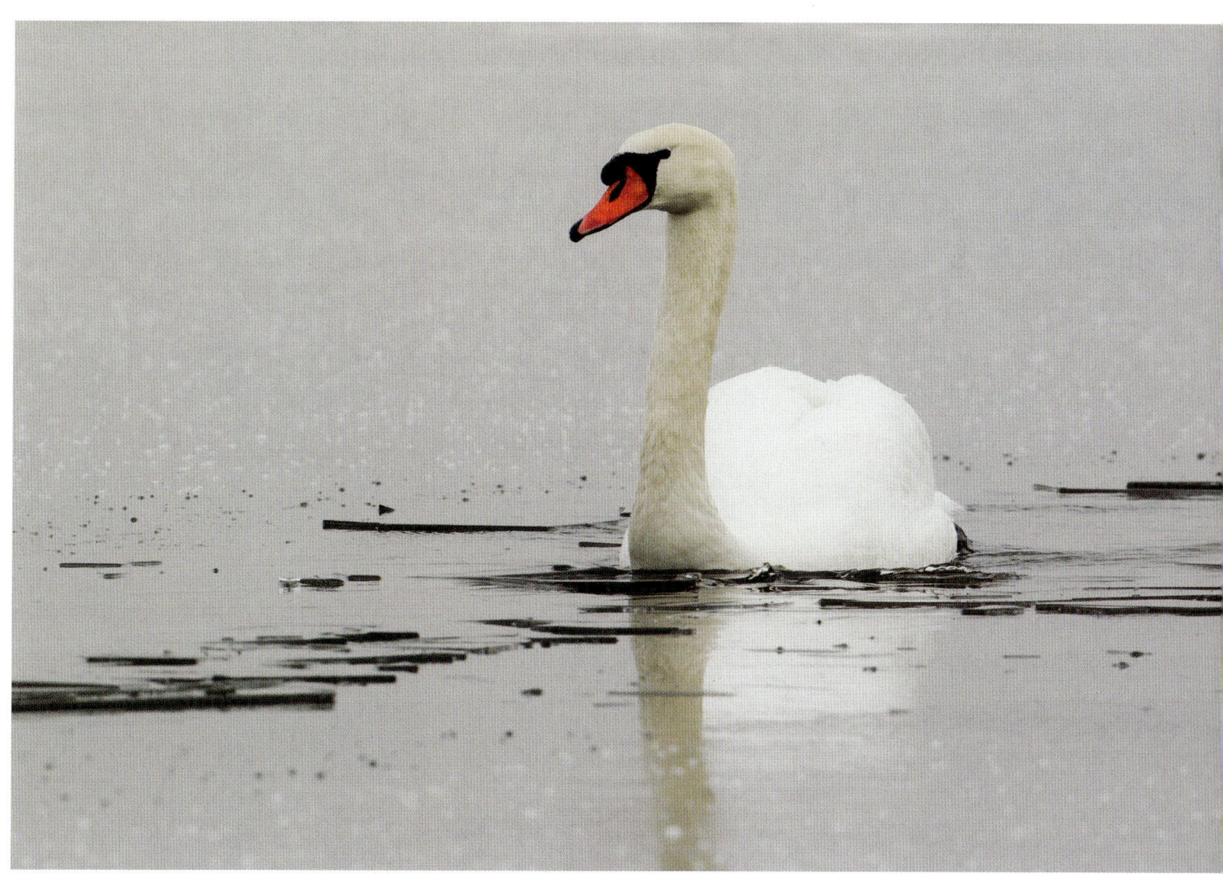

4.8 Evoking Emotions

I might just as well have started the book with this because it's the most important tip: A really great photo must evoke emotions, and you may break every rule of image composition to achieve this!

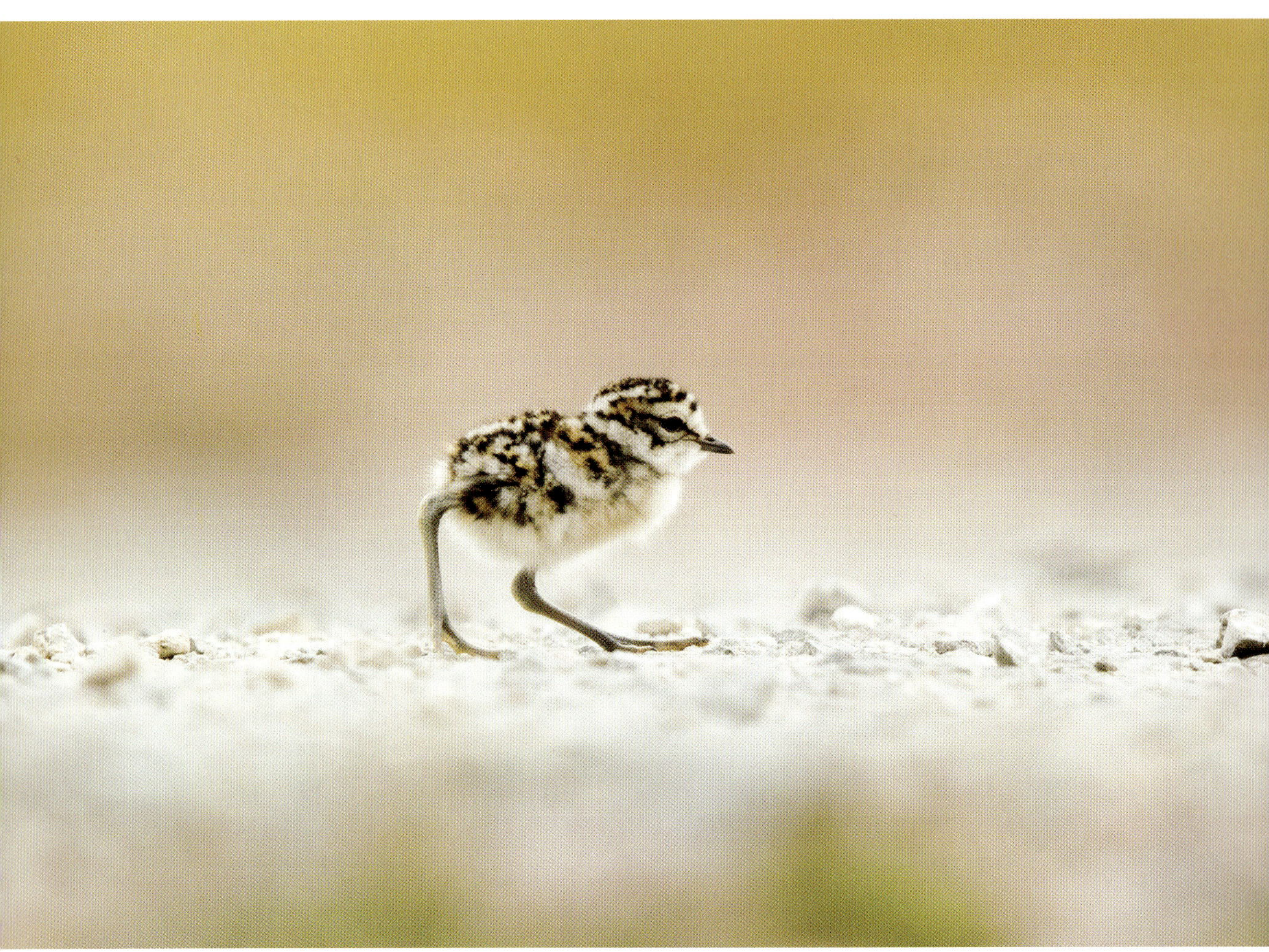

▲ 4-194

Eurasian dotterel | Norway | I managed to photograph a dotterel with its baby chicks as they crossed a gravel road. This one was the last in the group and hurried to catch up with the others. | 840mm (600mm + 1.4x converter), aperture 6.3, 1/1250 s, ISO 1000, +2/3 exposure compensation

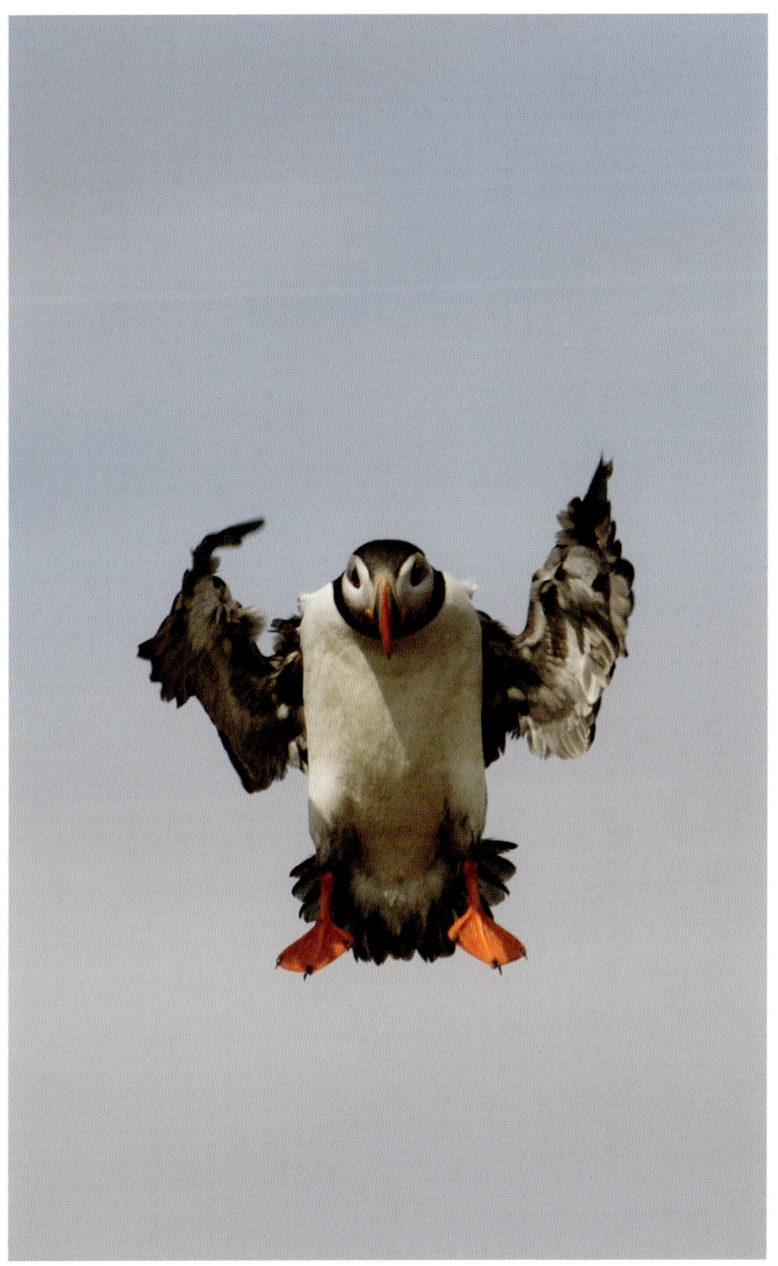

Puffin | Farne Islands | The light is too harsh, yet the picture of this clumsy-looking bird makes most viewers smile…. | 400mm, aperture 8.0, 1/2000 s, ISO 400

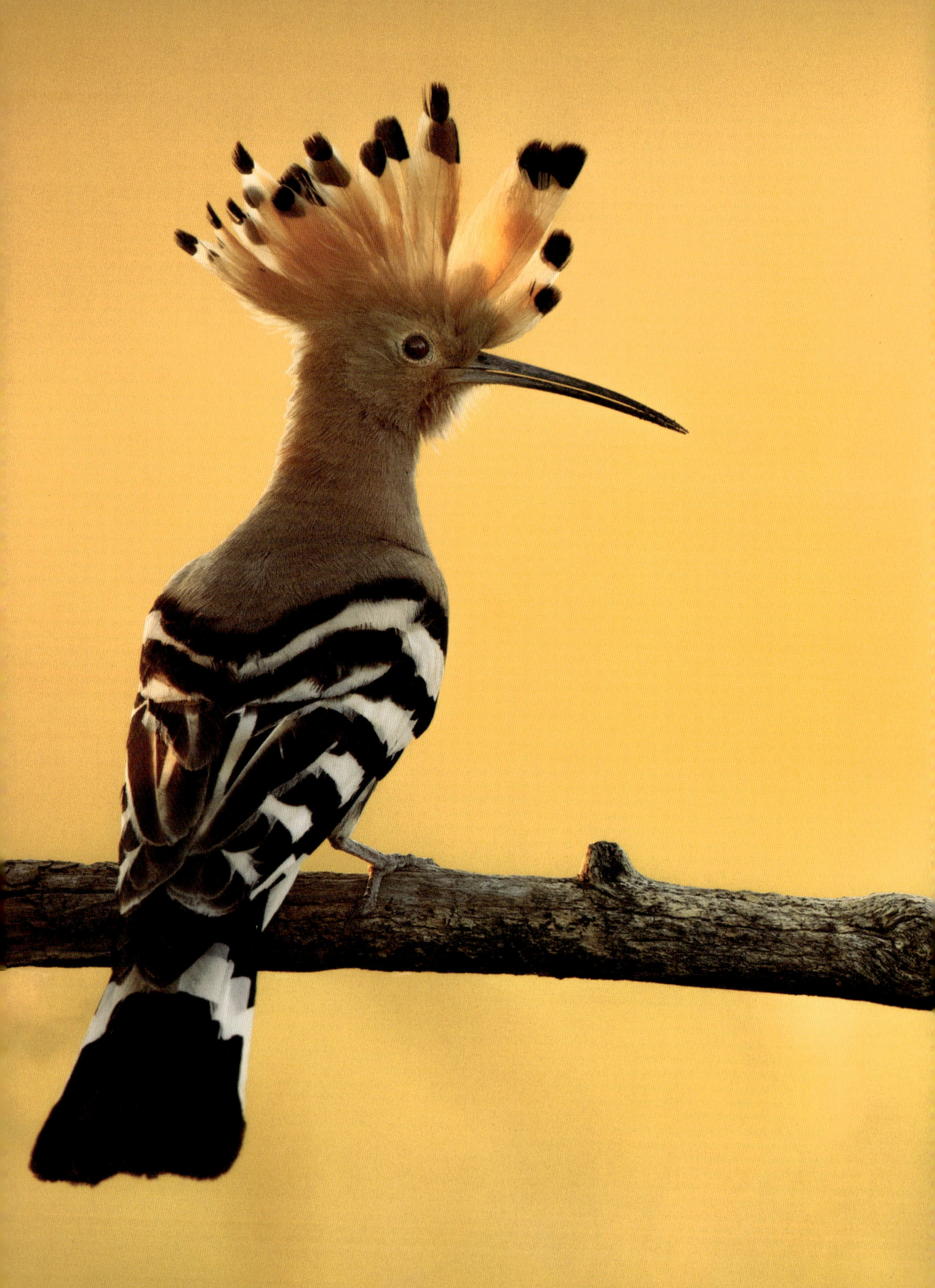

5 THE MAKING OF 25 SUCCESSFUL PHOTOGRAPHS

What do I mean by a successful photograph? The ones in this compilation are either pictures that have sold well through my stock photo agency or ones I really like myself.

I want to share a bit about how some of these images came to be, because it shows how complicated and time-consuming it can sometimes be to take a successful photo.

And finally, I'll discuss some of the things we've covered in the previous chapters—you can analyze photos yourself using your eye and knowledge.

◀

Hoopoe | Serbia | A wonderful, simple subject: the hoopoe against the evening backlight with its crown raised. | 600mm, aperture 5.0, 1/640 s, ISO 1250

5.1 A Delicate Beauty

These barn owls in Norfolk, England, usually hunt in the darkest hours of the night, but when they raise their chicks they extend their hunting to the early morning and late evening hours—when there's still daylight to take pictures. A pair of these owls was nesting in the barn of a farm. A friend of mine was able to set up a camouflage tent in the farm's sheep pasture, which is where these barn owls hunted.

I flew to England to use the camo tent for five days and sat in it every day from 4:30 to 9:00 a.m. and 5:30 to 9:30 p.m., waiting for the owls. The tent was set up in a nice spot; there was a harmonious background and a bush with white flowers that would have worked well in a picture—or so I thought…. Alas, as the days went by, I waited in vain. The only times I spotted the barn owls, they were either behind me or flying past at a great distance. For days, I didn't get a single picture of them. But on the very last day, I got lucky: One of the owls flew toward me and as it did, it came close enough for a shot. When I later checked the few photographs that I managed to take, I found this picture: The wing position is perfect and the flowers complement the warm colors of the owl, which adds to the composition.

Barn owl | Norfolk | 700mm (500mm + 1.4x converter),
aperture 5.6, 1/500 s, ISO 1250

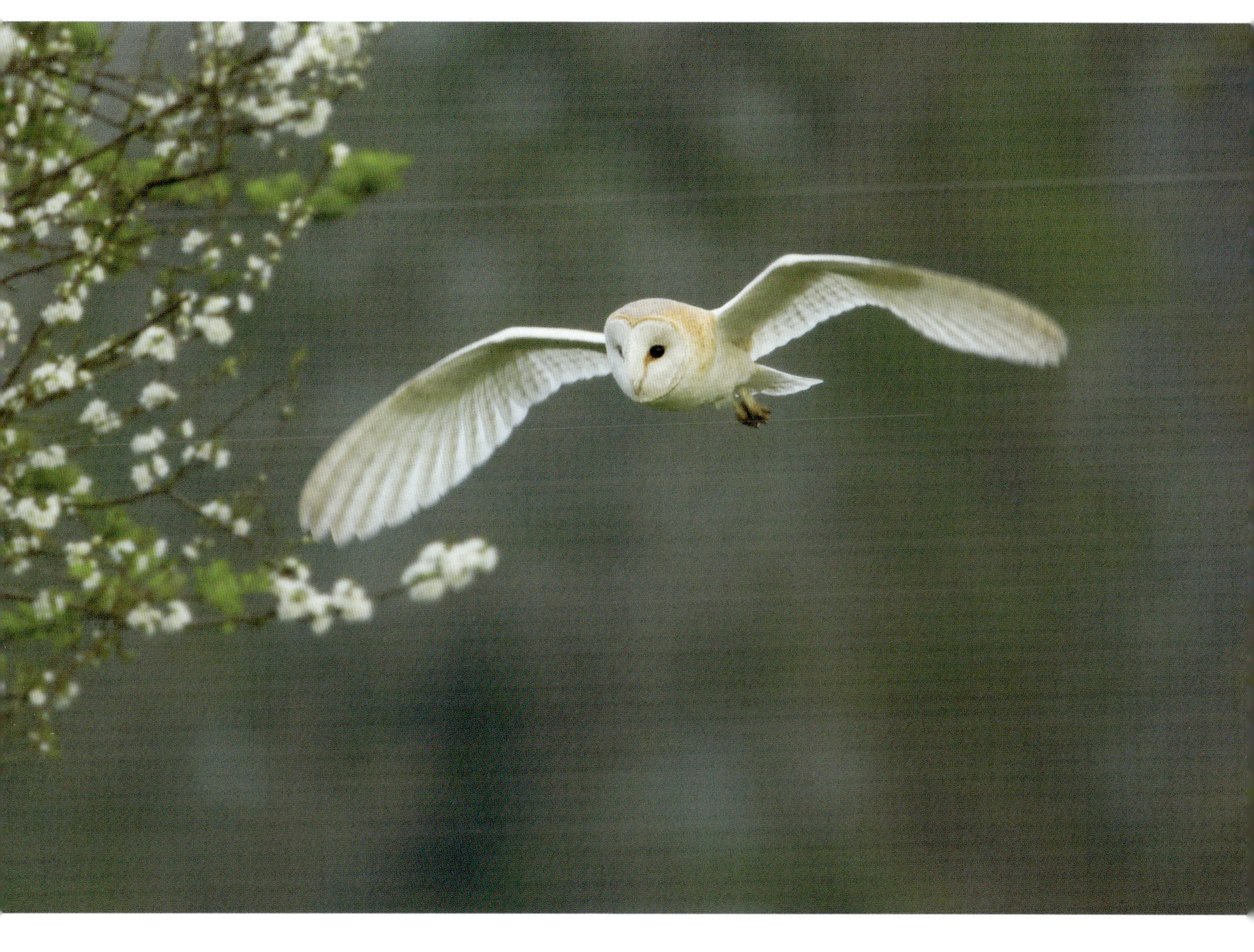

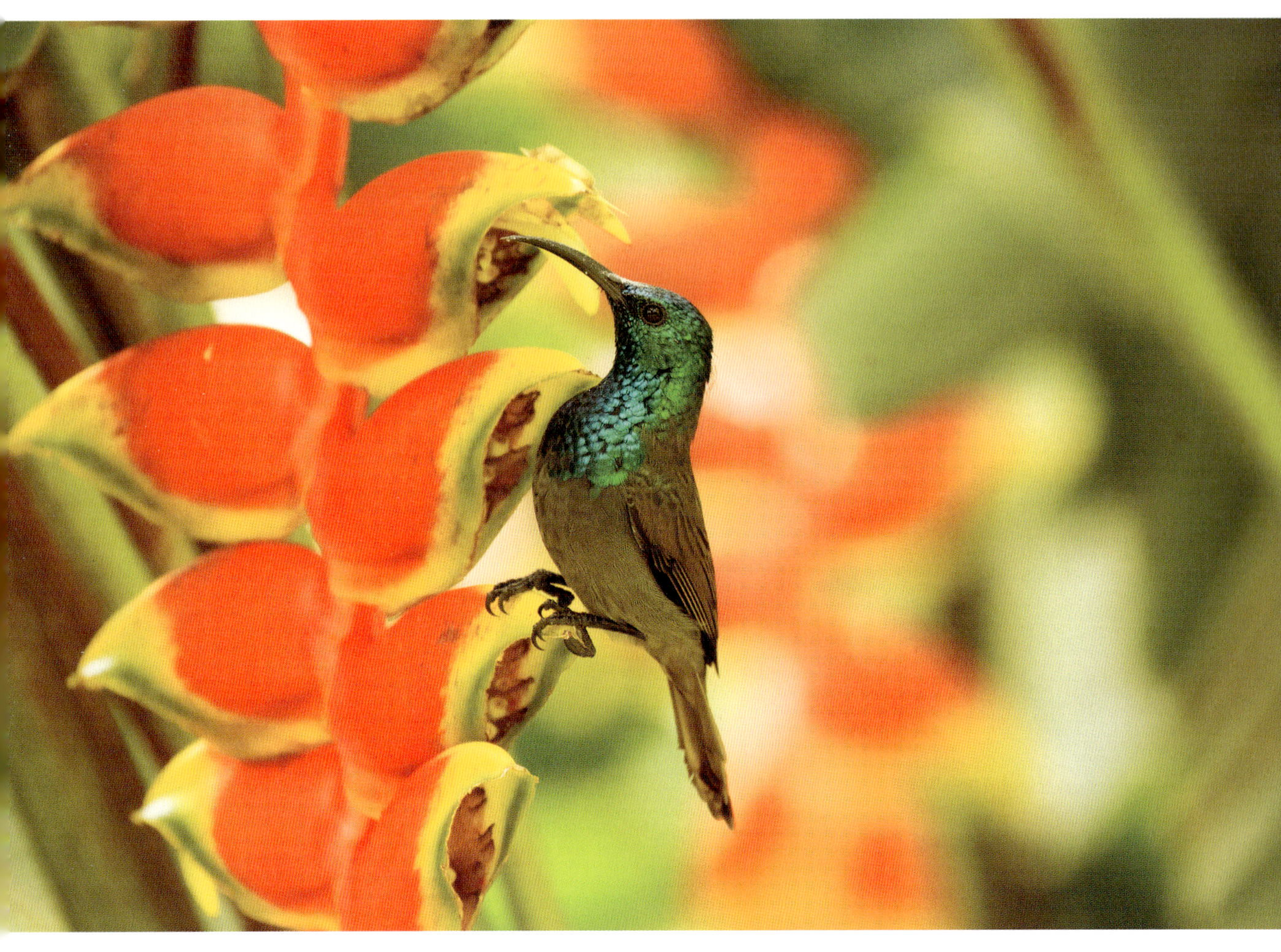

5.2 Floral Splendor

I spotted this pretty green-headed sunbird in the garden of a hotel in Kenya. It darted from plant to plant, drinking nectar from the flowers. Photographing it was tricky because it was constantly moving and very fast, too. I stalked it with my camera and eventually, it sat on these colorful flowers, which provided a wonderful contrast to the bird's iridescent green feathers. Fortunately, it paused just long enough for me to snap this picture. It works mostly because of the magnificent colors. The flowers, which also form the blurry background, add to the composition. I'm not too fond of the diagonal line on the right, but unfortunately, it couldn't be avoided in the moment of shooting.

Green-headed sunbird | Kenya | 400mm, aperture 5.6,
1/250 s, ISO 1250

5.3 Snow Flurries?

The British Farne Islands are a mecca for puffin lovers. The islands are protected and access to them is strictly regulated—you can reach them by boat, waves permitting. Once on the islands, you have about three hours until the boat picks you up again. On that day, I spent quite a bit of time with this one puffin that was lingering at the edge of the cliffs. I got down to the bird's eye level—it was rather unafraid—and started taking pictures.

The dark rocks and the light-blue sea in the background make for a serene composition. The camera frames the puffin with enough space in front of it. Suddenly, a high breaker crashed against the cliff, and water sprayed over the edge. The puffin looks at the flying droplets as if astonished; to me, the drops look like snow flurries.

Puffin | Farne Islands | 500mm, aperture 9.0, 1/1250 s, ISO 1000, +1/3 exposure compensation

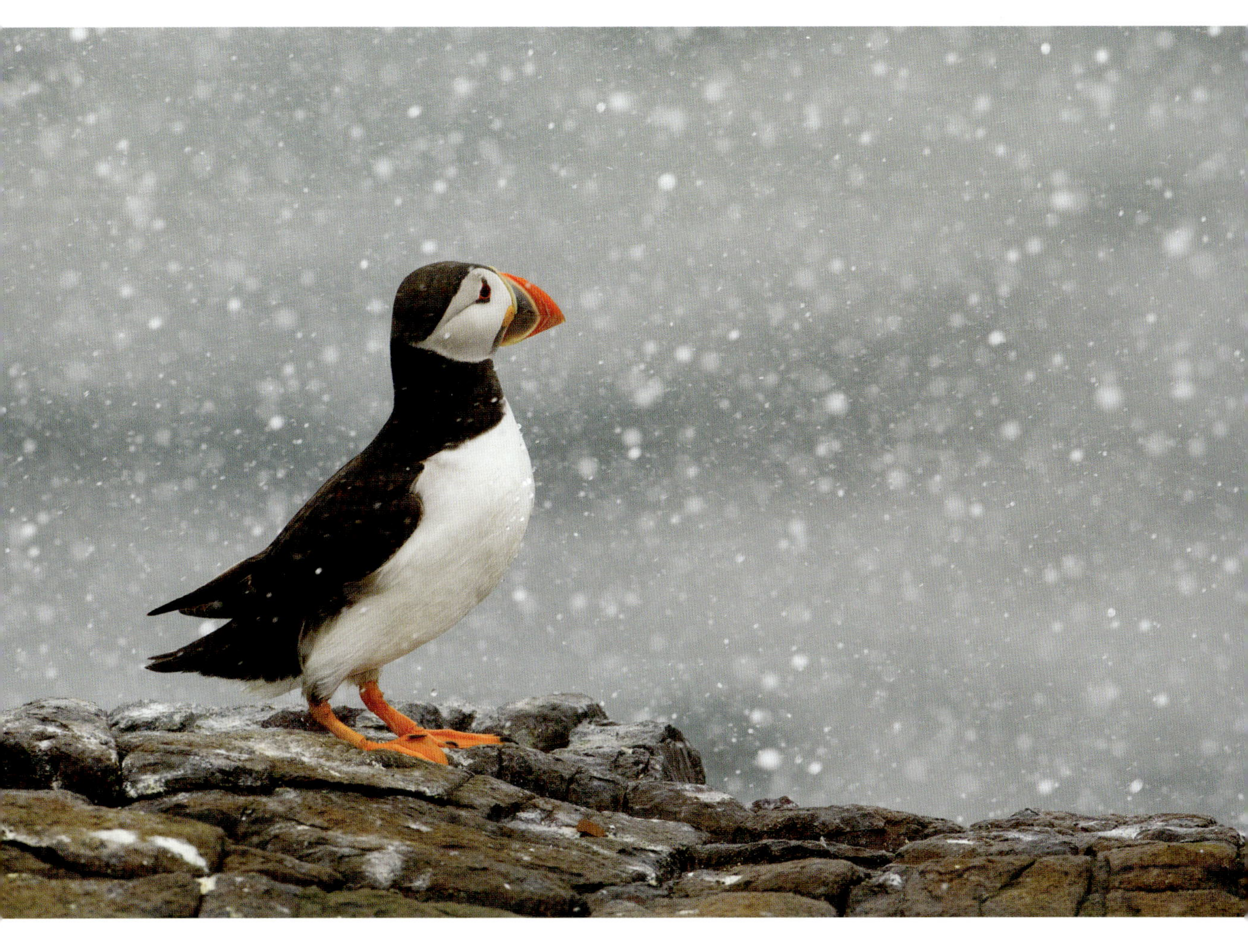

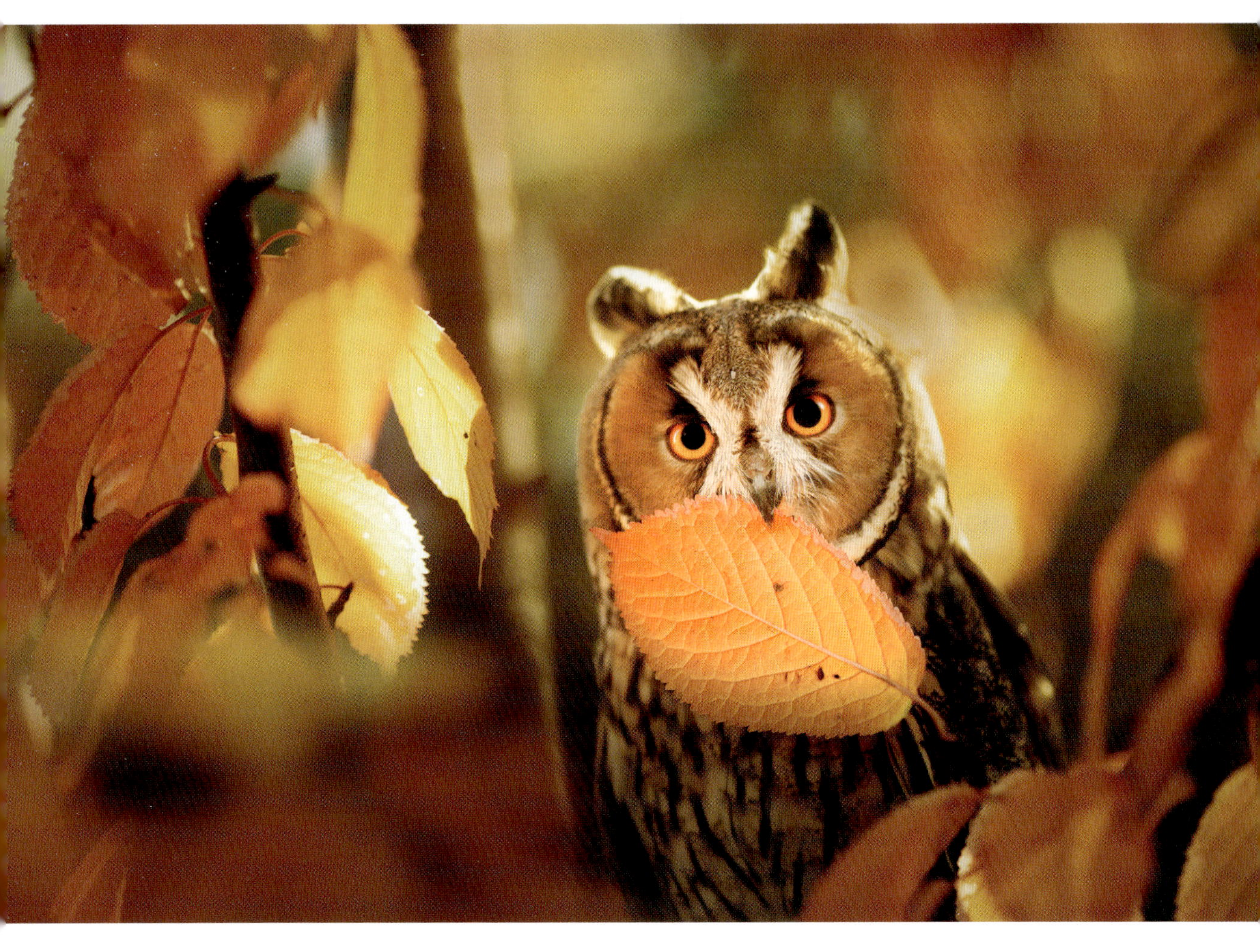

CHAPTER 5

5.4 Picking a Leaf

I was out for a walk with a friend and her long-eared owl, named Walter, to take photos with the fall foliage. We hadn't walked far when we discovered a good spot in a tree where we placed Walter.

We found a good angle to take a picture so that the branches and leaves framed Walter. His plumage harmonized wonderfully with the foliage, and I already liked the motif quite a bit. Walter got curious and plucked a leaf, which he held in his beak for a few moments. I knew immediately that this would be my favorite picture of the day!

Long-eared owl | Germany | 135mm, aperture 2.0, 1/3200 s, ISO 500

5.5 Shadow Bird

While photographing a pair of peregrine falcons against a rock wall in Germany, I noticed a small wallcreeper that was also flitting along the wall. It was too far away to get a decent shot. But I couldn't resist and started photographing the pretty bird.

It was partly climbing, partly flying along the wall so I tried to get some in-flight pictures, too. It wasn't until I got home that I realized that while this photo doesn't show much of the wallcreeper itself, it perfectly captures its shadow. I like the colors, the pattern of the rock, and the angled lines of the crevices in this picture. The shadow cast by the wallcreeper catches the eye, even though you can barely make out the bird itself.

Wallcreeper | Germany | 500mm, aperture 6.3, 1/1000 s, ISO 1250, -2/3 exposure compensation

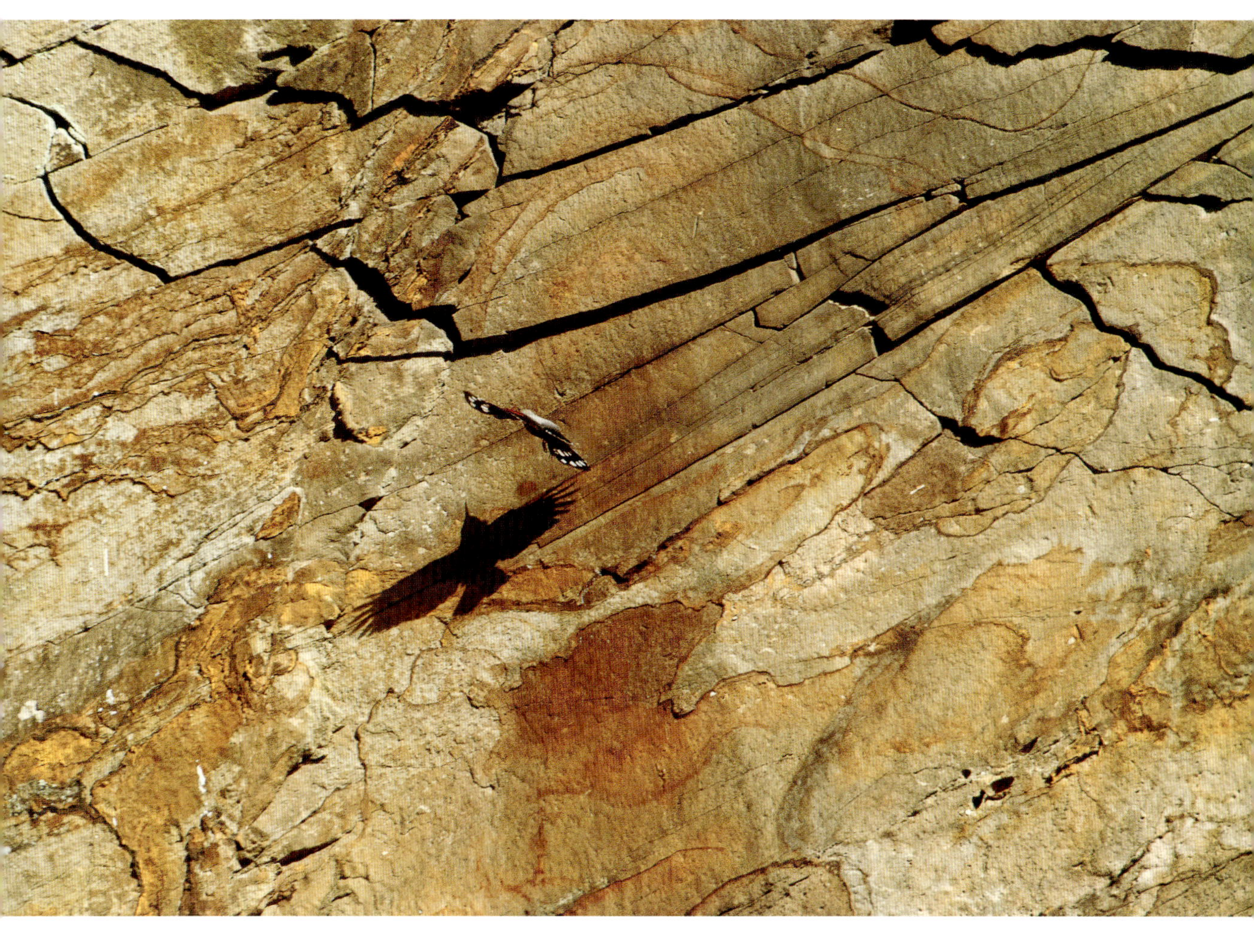

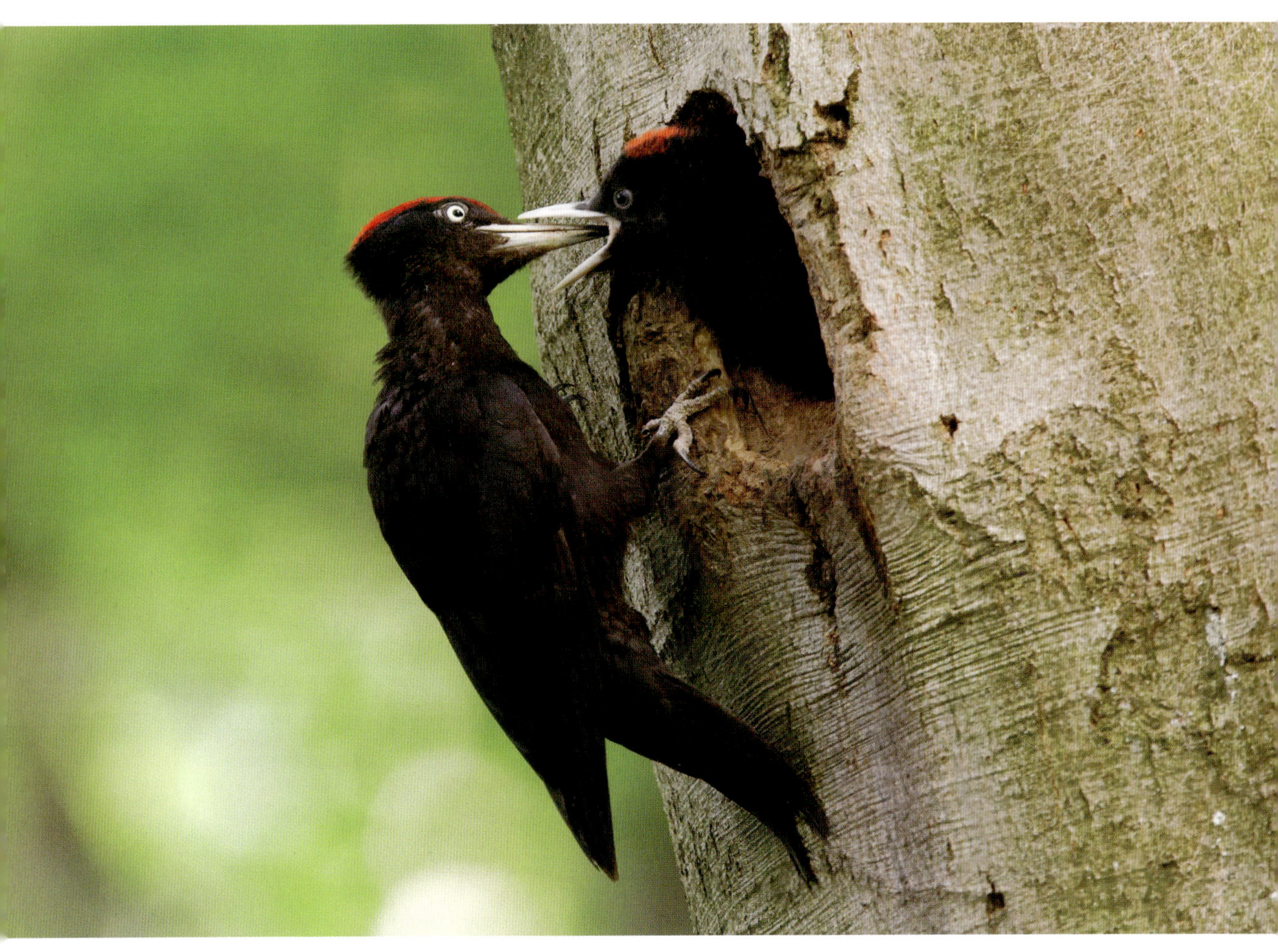

CHAPTER 5

5.6 In Lofty Heights

I had kept my eye on this tree cave belonging to a pair of black wood-peckers for a long time. Again and again, I rode past it on my horse and watched the parent birds fly up to it. Eventually, the chicks grew larger and appeared at the entrance during feedings.

Spontaneously, I decided that I wanted to be at eye level with the birds! I asked my local forestry department for permission to climb a beech tree about 50 feet away to take pictures of the black wood-peckers from there. Unfortunately, I don't have a lot of tree-climbing experience, but friends of mine do. A friend was happy to meet me and help me climb up the beech tree to a height of a good 30 feet. I settled down in the fork of a branch and kept completely quiet while my assistant left. Shortly after, the parent birds returned to feed their young and I managed to take this picture. Three hours later, I was helped down again because getting down a tree is tricky if you don't know what you're doing. Anyway, I'll never forget how this series of photos came to be!

Black woodpeckers | Germany | 700mm (500mm + 1.4x converter), aperture 5.6, 1/200 s, ISO 1600, -2/3 exposure compensation

5.7 Green, Green, Green

When the redstart became Germany's Bird of the Year in 2011 this photo was included in the Bird of the Year campaign initiated by the Nature and Biodiversity Conservation Union (NABU) and its partner conservation groups. What makes the image very effective are the various shades of green from the foreground and background foliage, the caterpillar in the redstart's beak, and the cherries on the branch below it. The greens make the bold orange of the male redstart's breast stand out. Everything about the bird works; it has ample space in the direction of its gaze, and its eye is clear and sharp with a nice catchlight. The background blurs harmoniously, and the leaves on the left provide a bit of an anchor.

Redstart | Germany | 500mm, aperture 5.6, 1/160 s, ISO 1250

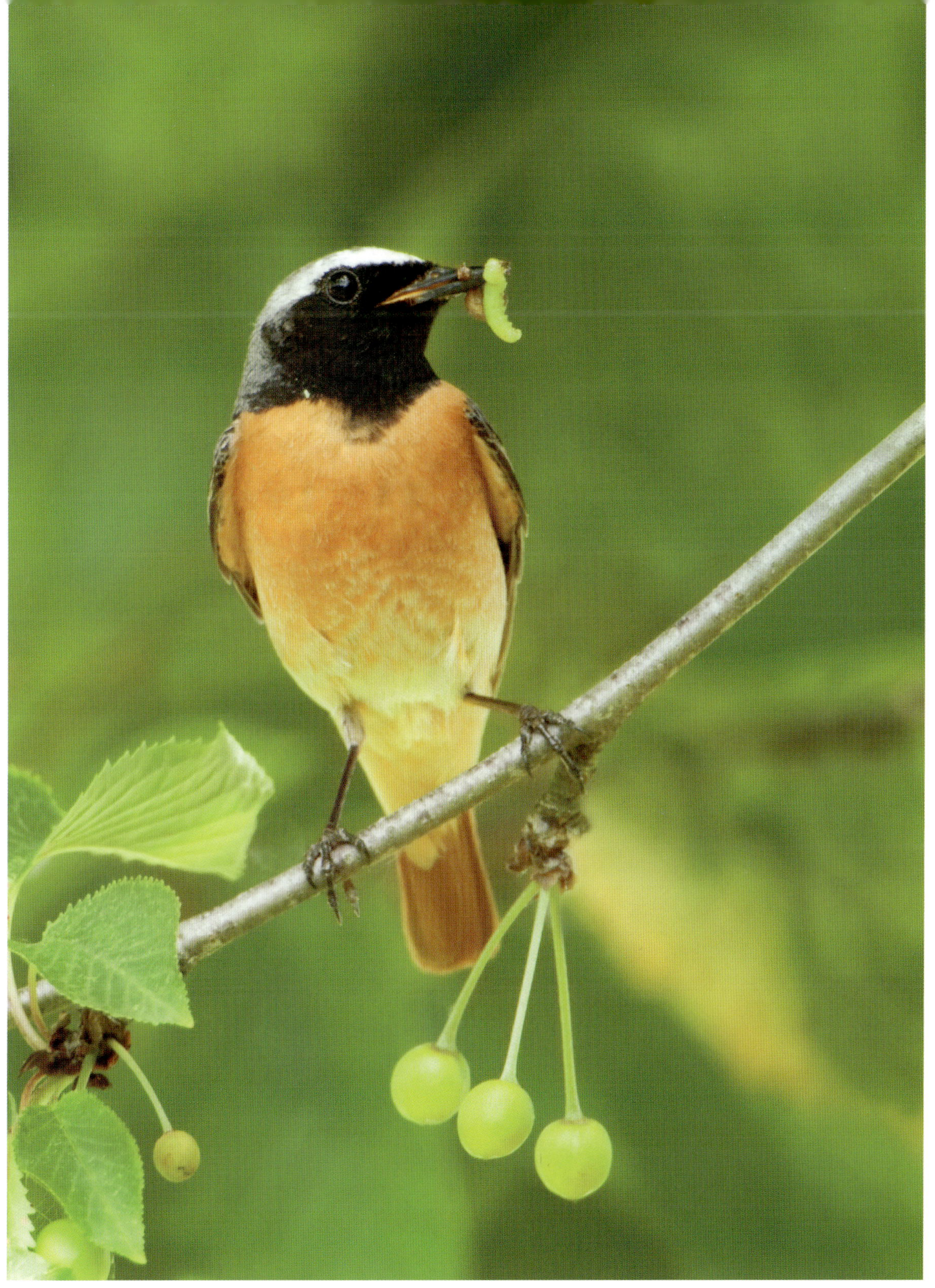

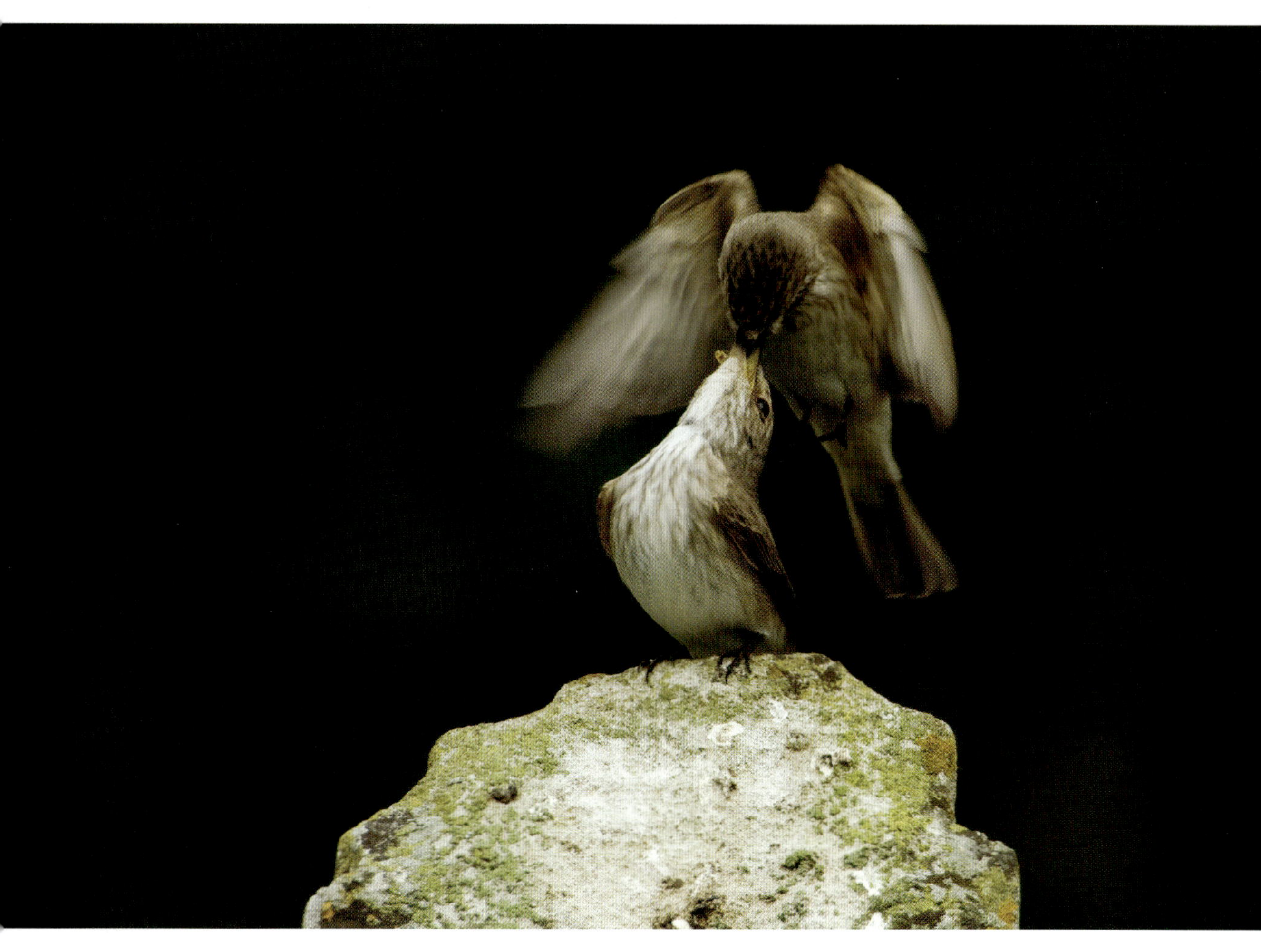

5.8 Food Transfer

I was sitting in my car and taking pictures of a female spotted flycatcher that was perched on a reasonably attractive stone pillar, preening herself. The pictures turned out quite nice. Spotted flycatchers are not all that common and I was quite pleased with the results I had gotten thus far. I had framed the bird well in the photo, although I would have liked it to fill the frame a bit more. But I couldn't get any closer. As it turns out, this was my luck because then the photo would have cut off the male that appeared quite suddenly. He hovered over the female, passed her some food from the air, and was gone again in a heartbeat.

The dark background required some negative exposure compensation and since I had only planned to take portrait shots, I had not set a particularly fast shutter speed. As a result, the wings are blurred, but I think that this fits in nicely with the image's story about a quick transfer of food.

Spotted flycatcher | Wales | 500mm, aperture 5.0, 1/400 s,
ISO 1000, -2 exposure compensation

5.9 Tongue Acrobatics

In the summer of 2010, I lucked out and discovered the territory of a pair of wrynecks in a wild orchard. It was close to where I live, which enabled me to spend quite a bit of time there. I was taking pictures from the car and had noticed an apple tree to which the wryneck kept returning. I parked my car nearby and was delighted to find that this gave me a wonderfully colored background. Then I waited patiently for the wryneck to approach its perch. Luckily, it returned soon after and was so relaxed that it started preening. One thing you need to know is that wrynecks have very long, sticky tongues that they use to catch ants. During preening, the bird also cleans its tongue by literally flinging it out of its beak. I had seen this behavior many times before but had never managed to catch it on camera. With this picture, I finally did.

Wryneck | Germany | 500mm, aperture 5.0, 1/125 s, ISO 1600

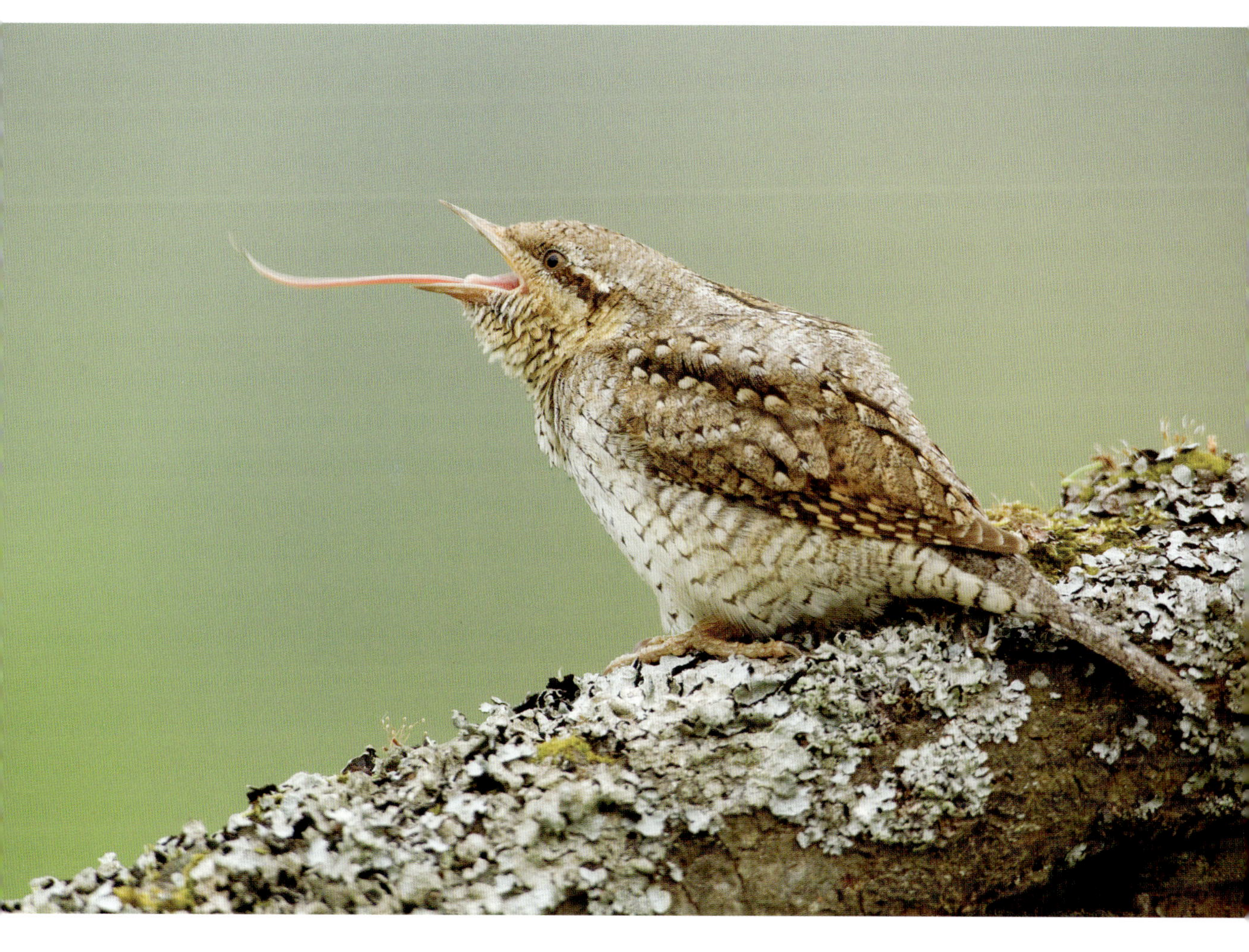

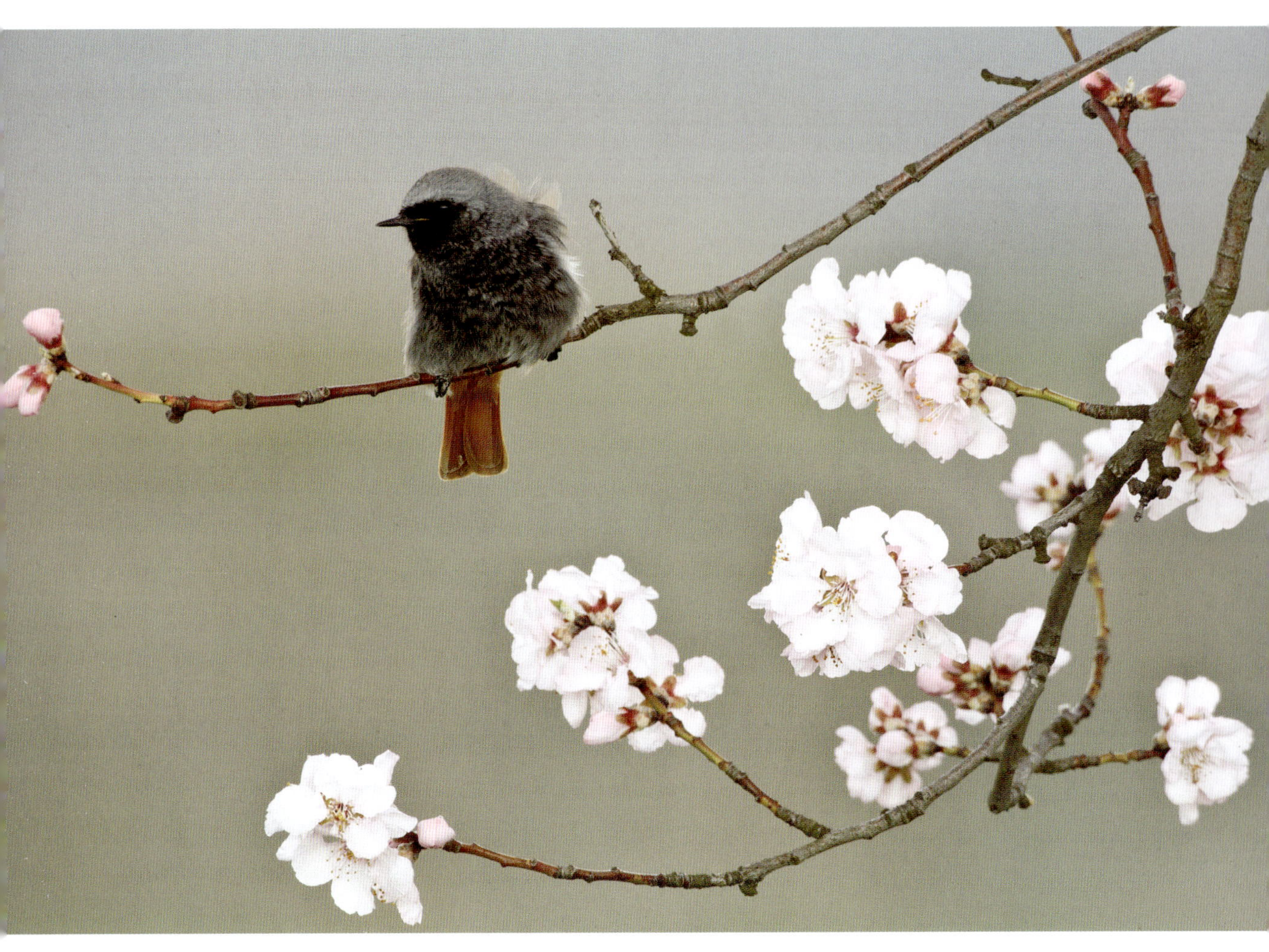

CHAPTER 5

5.10 Like a Japanese Painting

One day in the spring, I was out and about in my part of Germany to photograph woodlarks, yellowhammers, and cirl buntings when I came across an almond tree in bloom. I heard a black redstart singing nearby, so I decided to spend some time and wait near the almond tree, hoping the black redstart might pick a perch amid its blossoms. I waited several hours. Now and then, the bird flew into the tree, but never in a way that would have allowed for a harmonious composition.

Finally, it humored me and perched on some branches right next to my car. I searched for the right way to frame it to avoid cutting off the lower branch. This meant that the redstart got repositioned into the upper-left corner. In this photo, the bird looks toward the left, which I don't really like because it means it's looking at the edge of the frame instead of toward the center. I do have another photo of it looking to the right, but despite what all the rule books say, it looks better in this shot. Sometimes you just have to break the rules….The photo reminds me a bit of a Japanese painting.

Black redstart | Germany | 500mm, aperture 7.1, 1/80 s, ISO 640

5.11 Interesting Prey

I spent a day on the beach of Ijmuiden, in the Netherlands, watching herring gulls. That's when I noticed that some of the birds kept returning from the water with some kind of prey. Initially, I couldn't tell what they were pulling from the sea, because as soon as one gull had caught something the other gulls went into wild pursuit to take it the prey away.

I slowly worked my way closer to the gulls and realized that they were preying on starfish—what a great motif! Now all I needed was for a seagull with a starfish to come close enough to photograph. After a while, I got lucky and a seagull even came a tad too close, which unfortunately meant that I had to cut off a tiny bit of its wing. I like the warm side light in this picture, which accentuates the texture of the starfish. The splashing water adds another nice element to the story the image tells.

Herring gull | The Netherlands | 840mm (600mm + 1.4x converter), aperture 5.6, 1/4000 s, ISO 1250

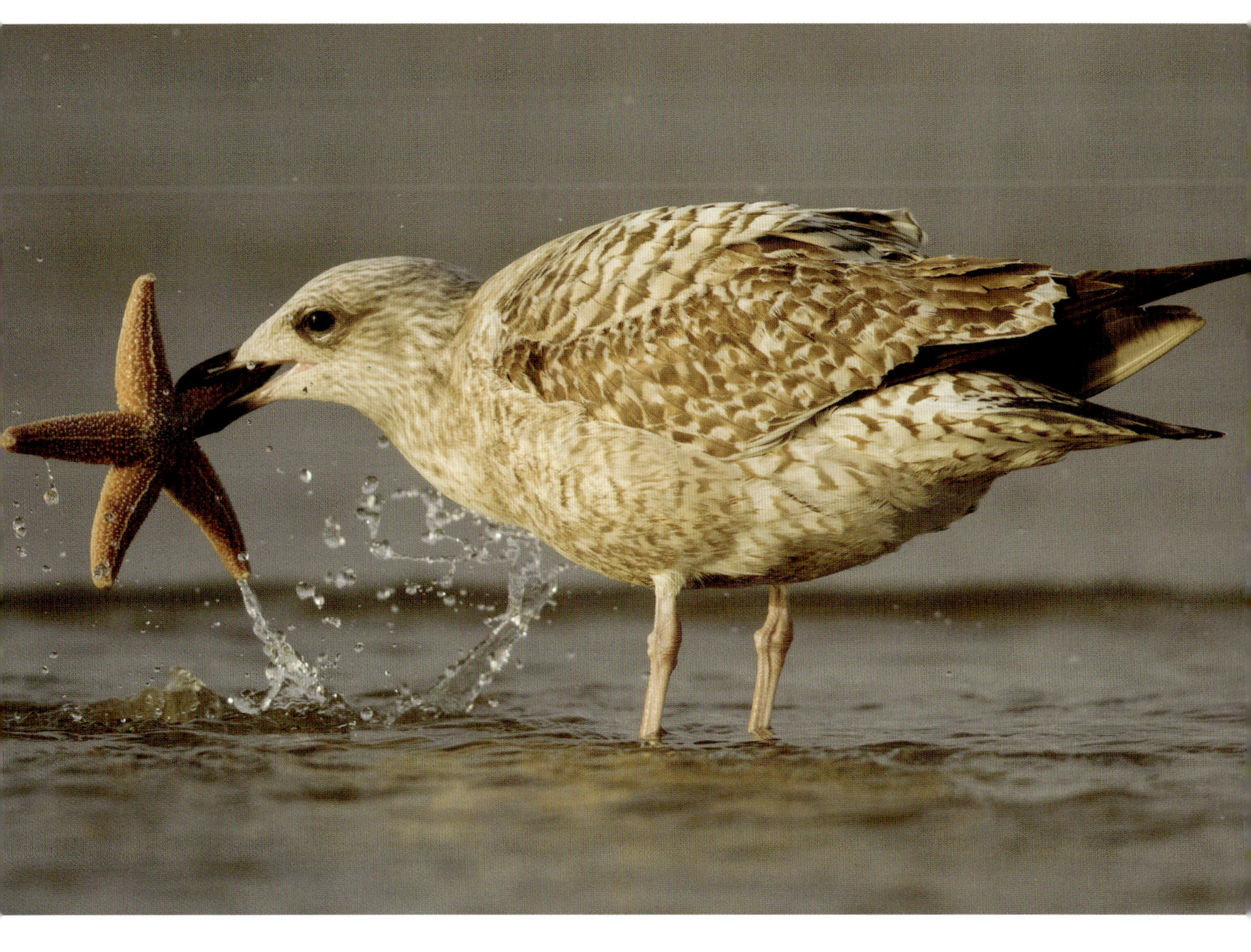

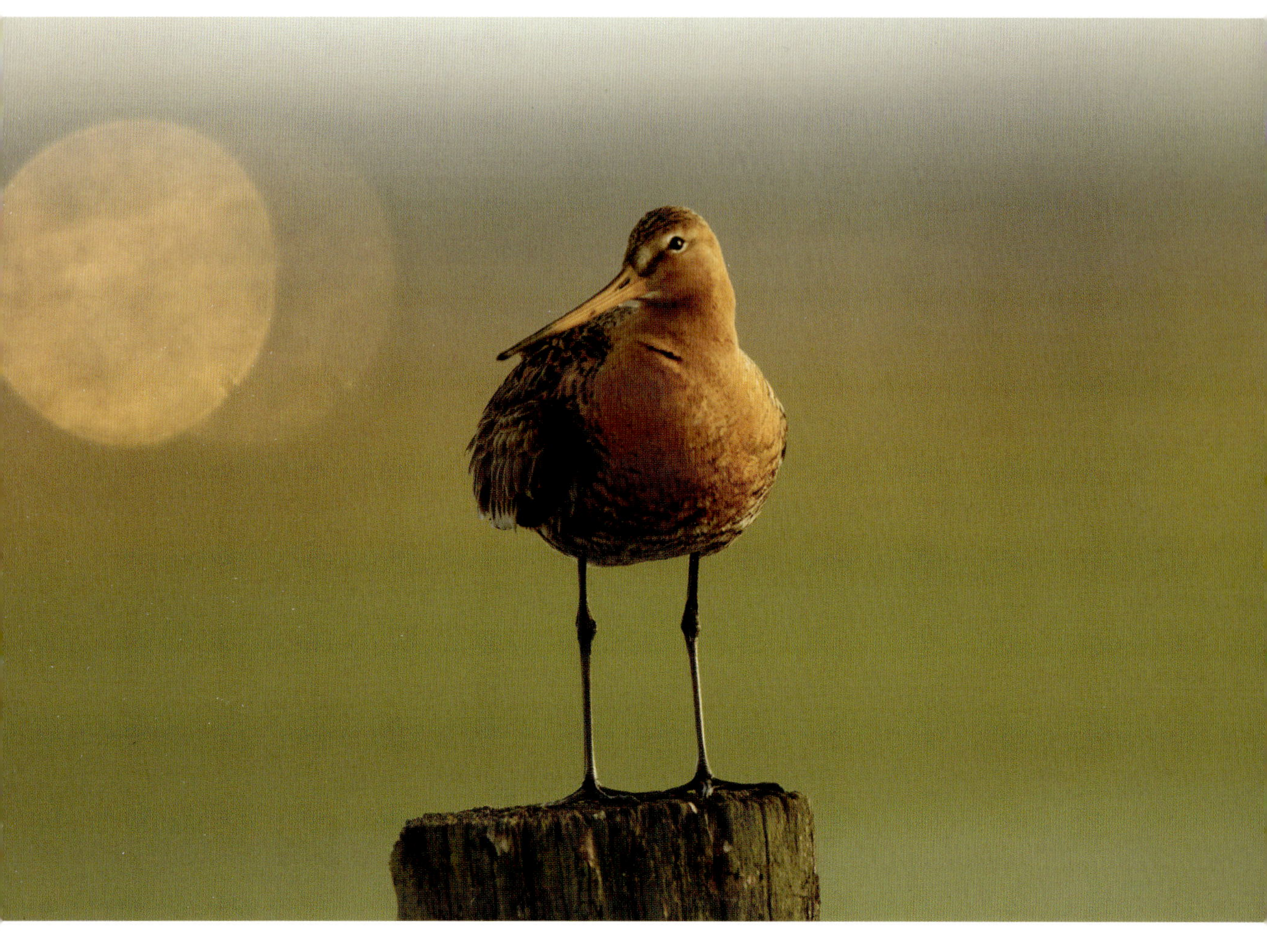

CHAPTER 5

5.12 Black-Tailed Godwit in the Moonlight

In spring, it's possible to see ruffs, northern lapwings, common redshanks, greylag geese, and black-tailed godwits at some flood meadows near a lake in Germany called Dümmersee. The black-tailed godwits in particular are quite trusting, and if you move around by car and use it as camouflage, you can take great pictures since they often perch on fence posts, which puts them at your eye level.

But for this picture, I wanted to do something different: I saw a godwit perch on a very low post, and since I was on foot, I sat down on the ground and photographed it. As I did, I noticed the road in the background on which cars were passing from time to time. Since it was getting late in the afternoon, the cars already had their headlights on and that's when an image was created in my mind. I only needed to shift my position slightly and wait for the right moment to have exactly one headlight in the picture. The light almost makes it look like the godwit is posing before a softly lit moon.

Black-tailed godwit | Germany | 840mm (600mm + 1.4x converter), aperture 5.6, 1/1250 s, ISO 800

5.13 Portrait of a Thick-Billed Lark

We were traveling in Morocco and I wanted to see and, of course, photograph a thick-billed lark. From reading books, I knew that there was an area in which it was worth searching for it. But what my books hadn't mentioned was that this area was a huge dumping ground for the entire region. There were plastics, old bottles, stinky garbage bags, and other kinds of trash everywhere. The smell was horrible, and tons of flies were swarming around us. But there were a lot of birds, too, so we toughed it out and went looking for the thick-billed lark.

After some searching, we found a small flock of thick-billed larks, and this handsome male was amenable to being photographed in a quite attractive and almost trash-free setting. What I like best about this photo is how nicely the foreground blends with the background and how everything is tone on tone. You can clearly see the thick bill that is typical for this lark.

Thick-billed lark | Morocco | 700mm (500mm + 1.4x converter), aperture 8.0, 1/3200 s, ISO 640

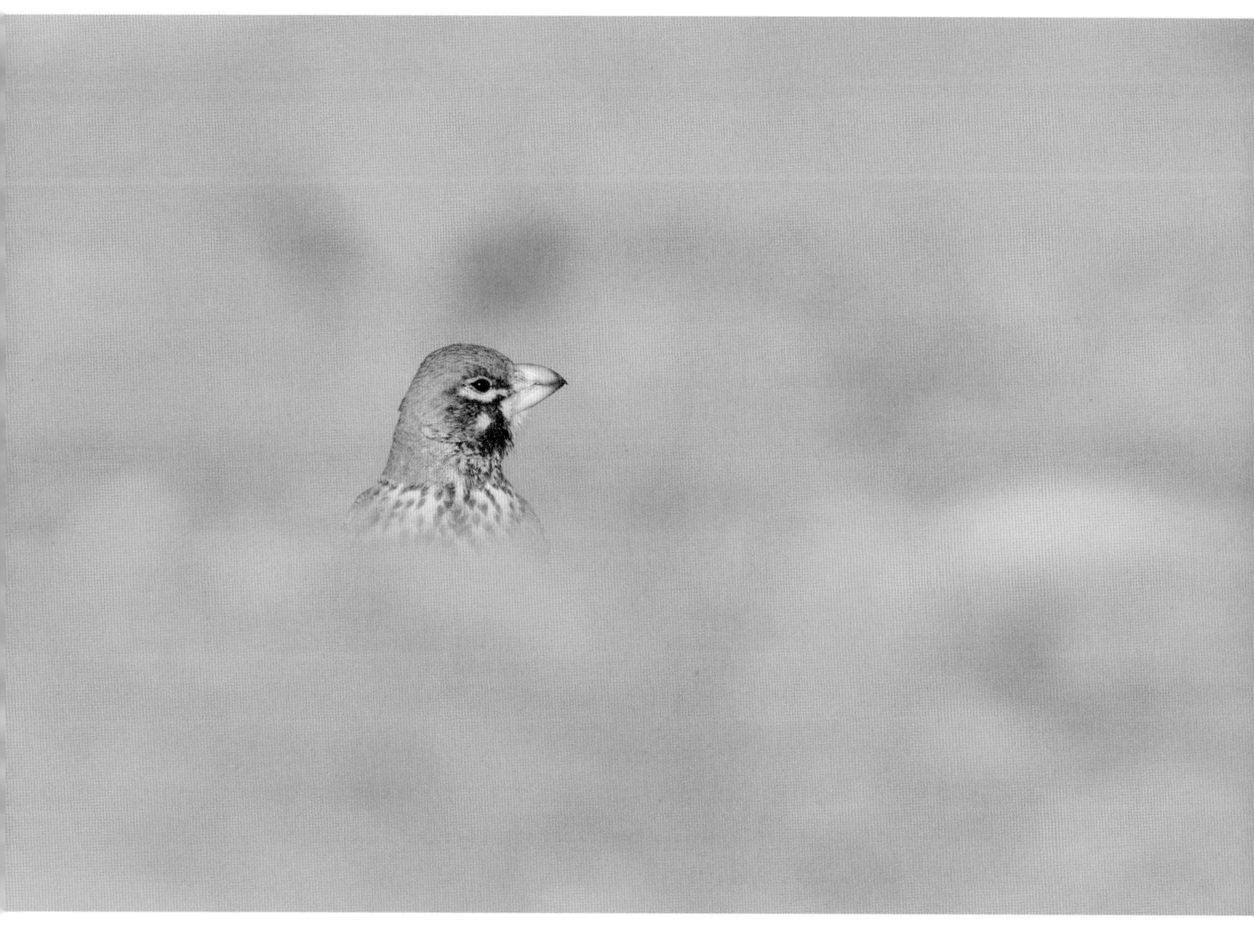

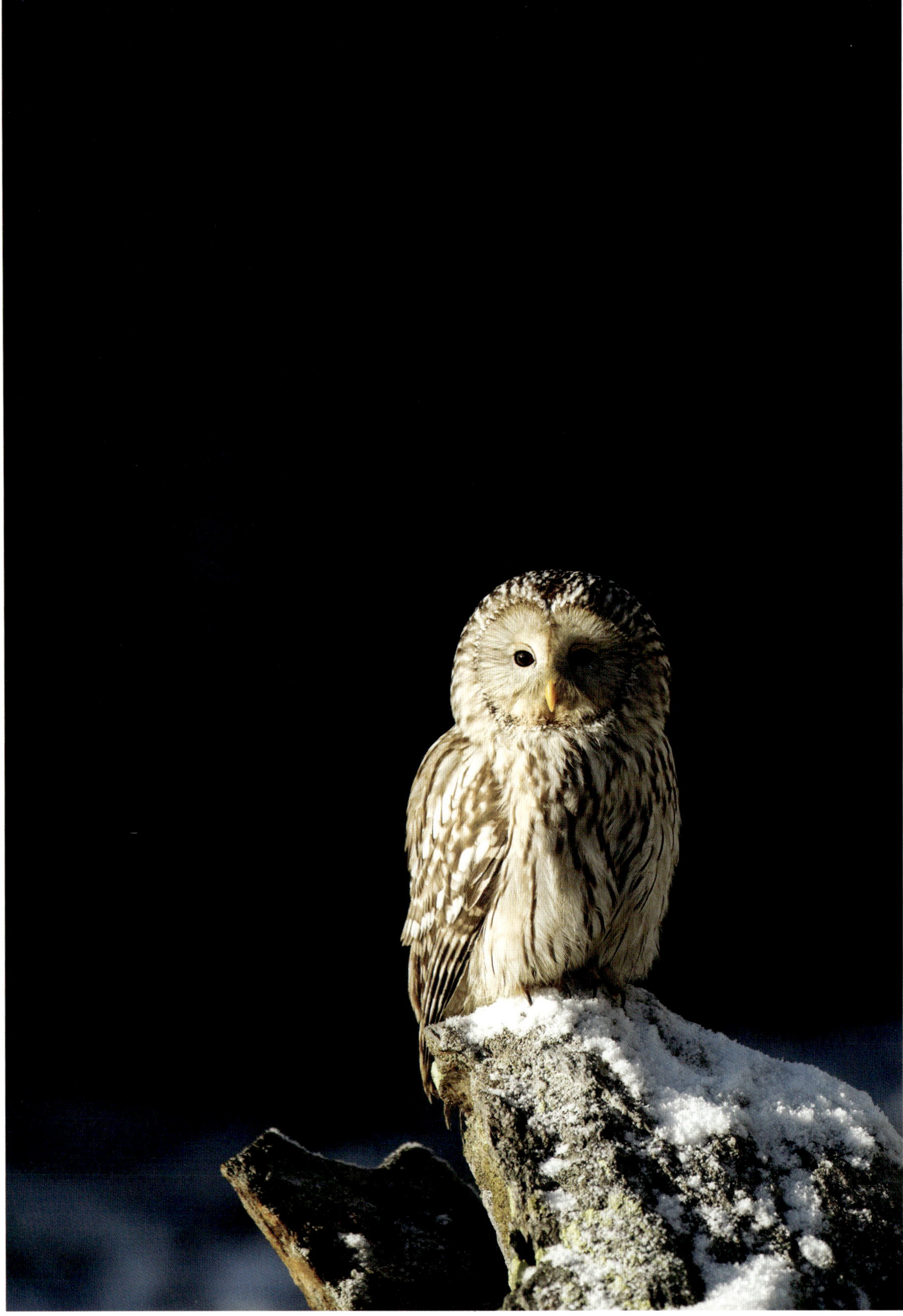

CHAPTER 5

5.14 Winter Scene

The morning was very cold and snow had fallen overnight. I had made an appointment for a photo shoot and one of the birds we photographed was this ural owl. We had already taken a few pictures at another location when we noticed a rock bathed in sunlight. The owl was quite agreeable to sitting on it and very relaxed about having its picture taken.

I like how the light-colored plumage and the snow contrast with the dark trees in the background. You can still make out a branch on the left lightly dusted with snow. I might like this picture even more if both sides of the bird were evenly lit. As it is, one half of the face is in the shade and somewhat darker than the other. On the other hand, the side light has its own charm….

Ural owl | Germany | 300mm, aperture 2.8, 1/8000 s, ISO 1000, -1 2/3 exposure compensation

5.15 Burrowing Owl with Delicate Flowers

I'm a big owl lover so it's hardly surprising that I was eager to see burrowing owls, some of which live in parks right in the middle of cities in Florida. Burrowing owls breed in underground dens and can often be found sitting on the ground nearby. People mark the burrows with small wooden posts or crosses to keep lawnmowers away. Supposedly land with burrowing owl dens is protected from development—at least that's what I've been told….

The owls are accustomed to people and are not particularly shy, and I was super happy that I could lie down on my belly and take pictures of these beautiful birds. For this image, I wanted to work with a shallow depth of field to put the owl and two of the flowers in focus, while blurring the rest of the flowers. They fill the negative space in the image and it results in a harmonious composition.

But I do have some criticism as well: The picture would be even more harmonious if there was a bit more space below the owl. Unfortunately, I couldn't achieve that without cutting off the top of the flowers. Since I was working with a fixed focal length, I'd have had to move a little farther back.

Burrowing owl | Florida | 500mm, aperture 4.5, 1/800 s, ISO 800

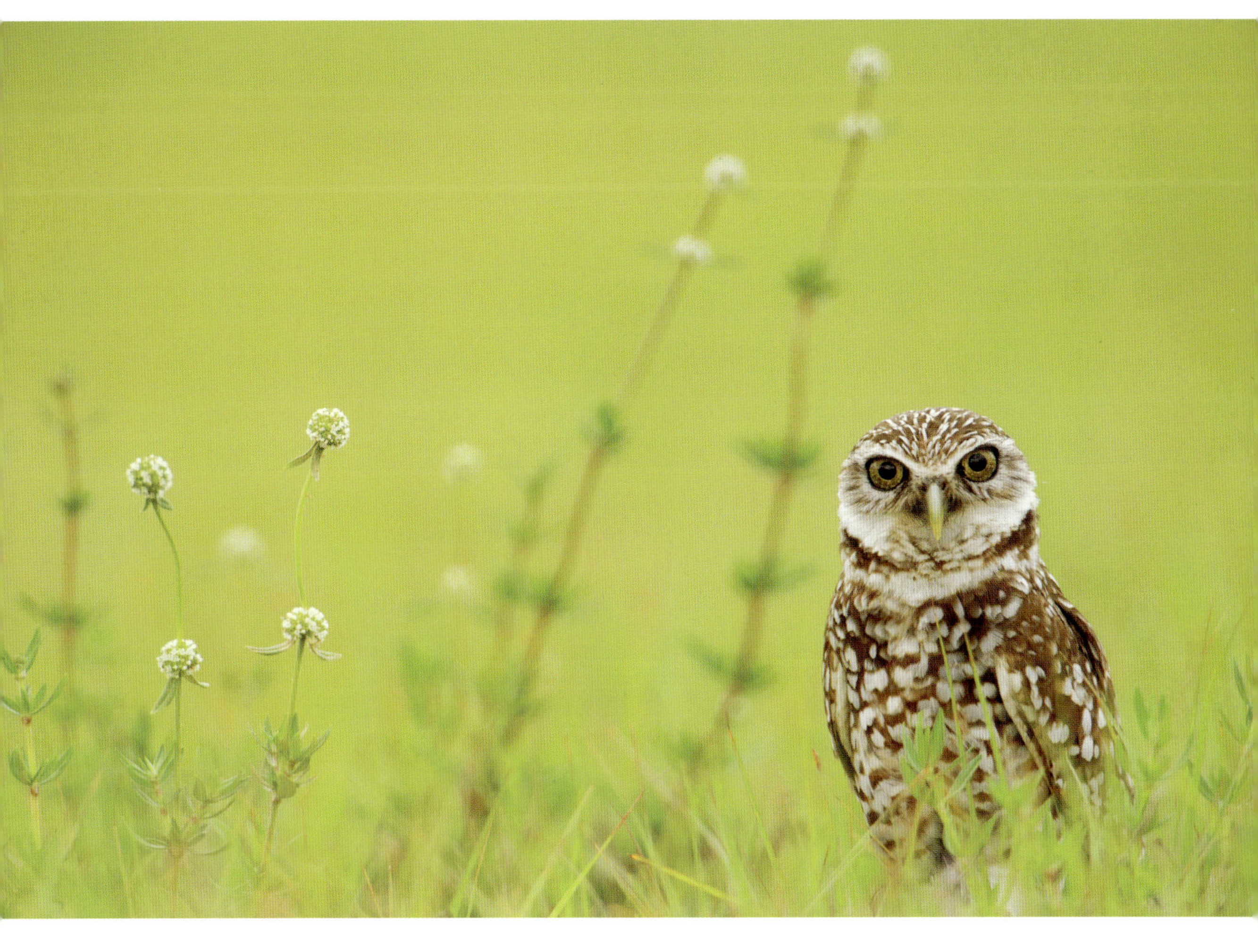

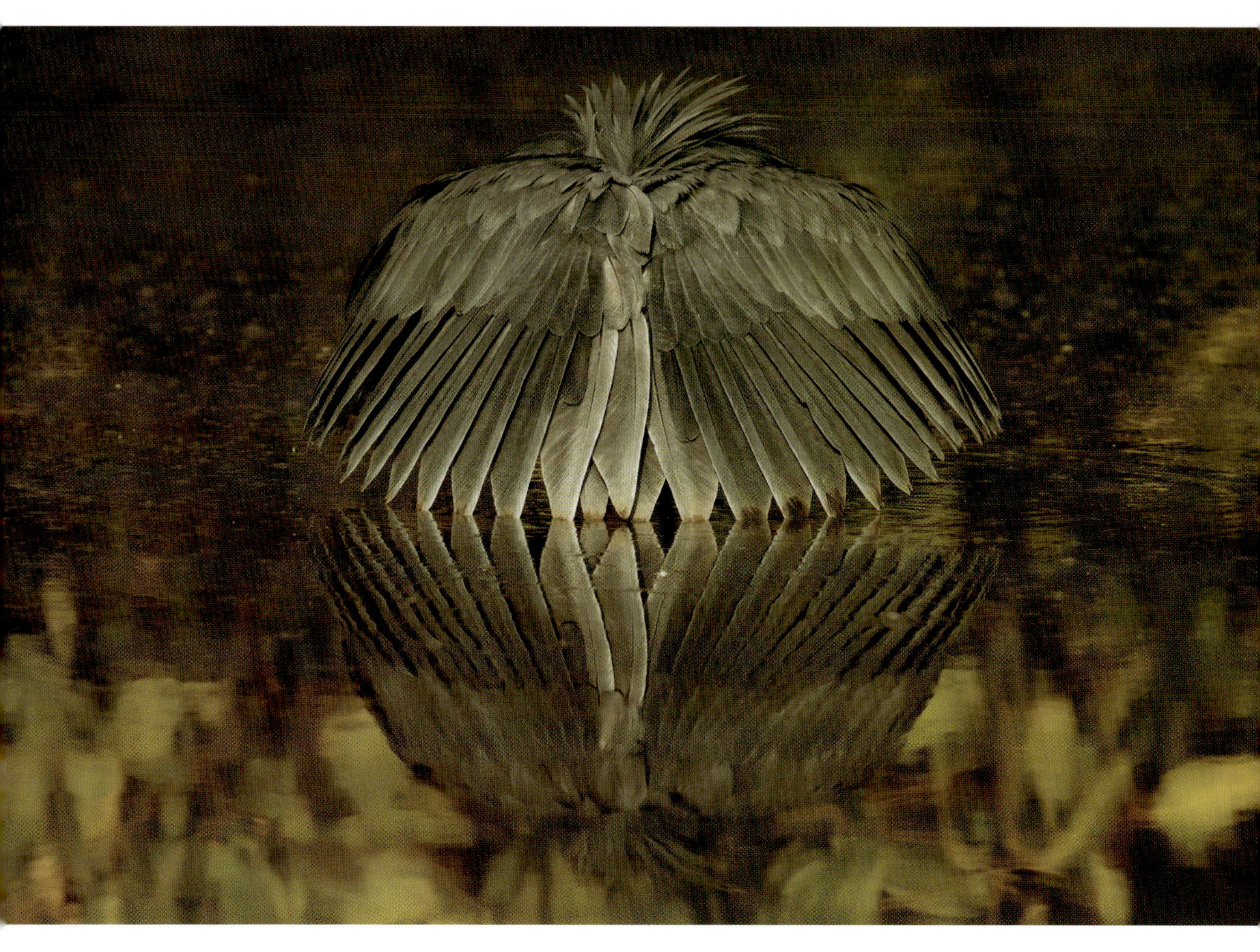

CHAPTER 5

5.16 The Exotic Fisher

I once saw a TV documentary that showed footage of a black heron catching a fish. The heron is a darkly colored, medium-sized bird that has developed a very special hunting technique. It slowly wades through the water, occasionally unfolding its wings around its head like an umbrella. This blocks out the reflection of the sun on the surface of the water and enables the bird to see better—plus, the sudden shadow confuses the fish.

I was so happy when this black heron approached my tree stand at a small mangrove pond in Gambia! It kept unfolding its wings to form an umbrella and I managed to take many photos. I had time to think about composition, so I decided to close the aperture to f/11 to get all of the feathers as well as the reflection sharp. I also wanted to capture the moment in which the wing umbrella was unfolded as perfectly as possible and the reflection in the water clear. Since the background was a bit dark, I dialed a negative exposure compensation of 1/3 stop. I got exactly the image I had hoped for.

Black heron | Gambia | 840mm (600mm + 1.4x converter),
aperture 11, 1/1000 s, ISO 1000, -1/3 exposure compensation

5.17 A Big Catch

I am fortunate in that I'm able to take a photo trip to Serbia every year to observe the magnificent birds in that country. My favorite is the hoopoe and there's a tree stand that provides fantastic opportunities to photograph them so they don't notice. During this particular stay, I was taking pictures of a pair that was busy bringing food to their young. Mostly, they carried caterpillars and maggots in their beaks. But all of a sudden, I saw one of the parent birds approach the tree cave with something long. I couldn't tell what it was right away. Luckily, I was all set up for taking approach shots. I had dialed the exposure down to f/8 and with an ISO of 1000 managed to get a fast shutter time of 1/3200 s.

Since the bird is about to land at the tree cave on the right side of the picture, its wings are optimally fanned out for deceleration and you can see the wonderful pattern on its underside. Only when I looked at the picture on the display did I realize that it was a lizard that the hoopoe had brought to feed its young!

Hoopoe | Serbia | 500mm, aperture 8.0, 1/3200 s, ISO 1000, -1 1/3 exposure compensation

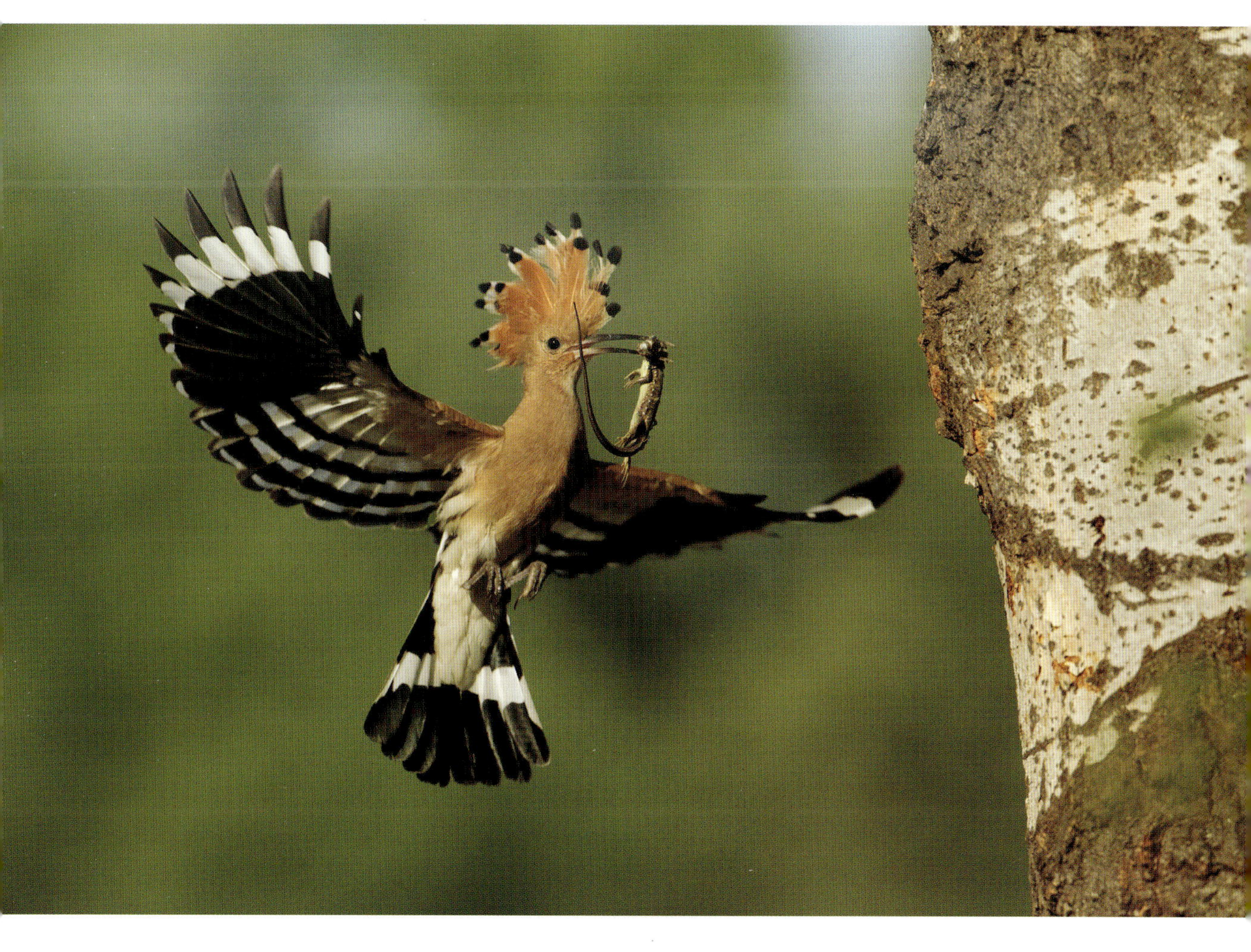

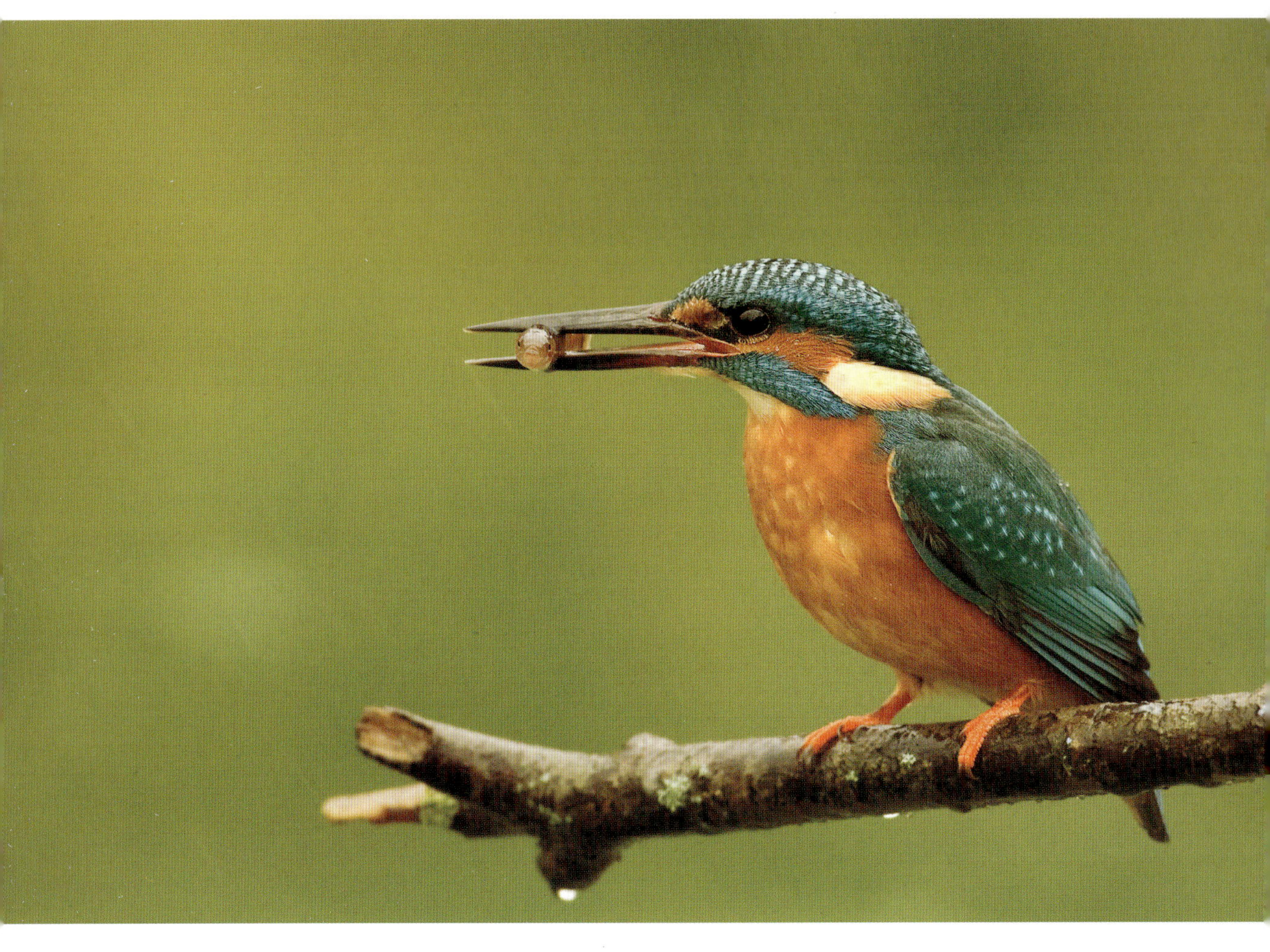

CHAPTER 5

5.18 Rainy Day View

Many years ago, a great dream of mine came true when I could take a trip to Lower Saxony to photograph a kingfisher from a tree stand. It also allowed me to try out a 500mm lens for the first time. Two great experiences!

Unfortunately, both days of the photo shoot were quite rainy. But the hungry kingfisher didn't care. Because of the dull light, the shutter time was a quite slow 1/200 s, despite an ISO of 1600. It made the raindrops show up as elongated stripes in the image. The gorgeous colors sparkle and are nicely complemented by the uncluttered green background. But what makes this photo stand out for me is the look on the poor fish's face. One thing I don't like very much is the branch on which the bird perches. With its two broken edges, it's a bit unattractive.

Kingfisher | Germany | 500mm, aperture 6.3, 1/200 s, ISO 1600

5.19 The "V"

I wanted to photograph a crested tit at least once, so I visited a friend in The Netherlands, who had a tree stand near a feeding spot of these birds. The day was beautiful and cold; there was even some frost on the branches.

The crested tits showed up now and then and I got the photos I had longed for. But in the end, I also really liked this simple shot of a marsh tit. The tit displays such a quiet beauty and the curved branch on which it perches adds an exciting line to the composition.

Marsh tit | The Netherlands | 500mm, aperture 7.1, 1/400 s, ISO 1250, -2/3 exposure compensation

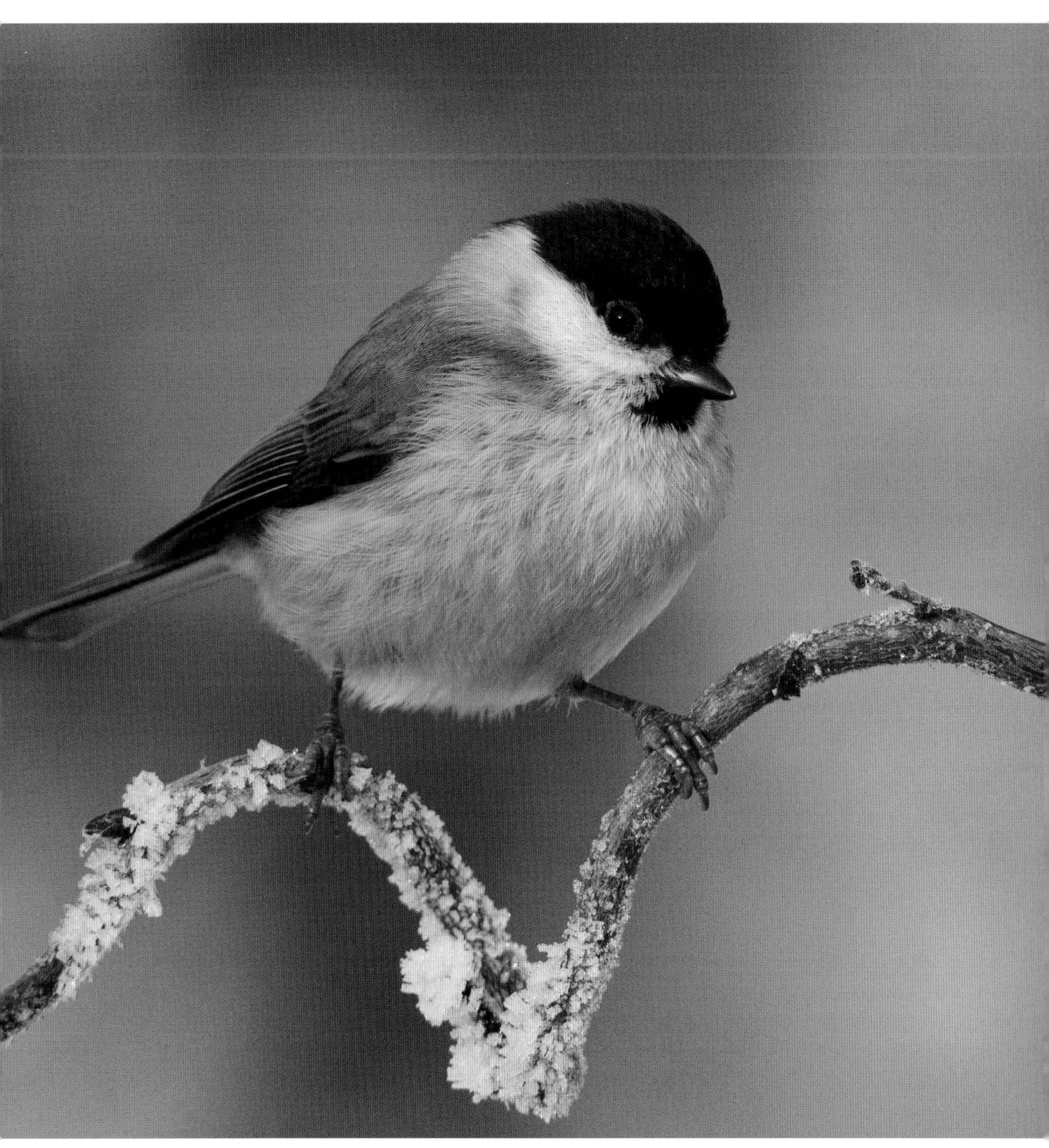

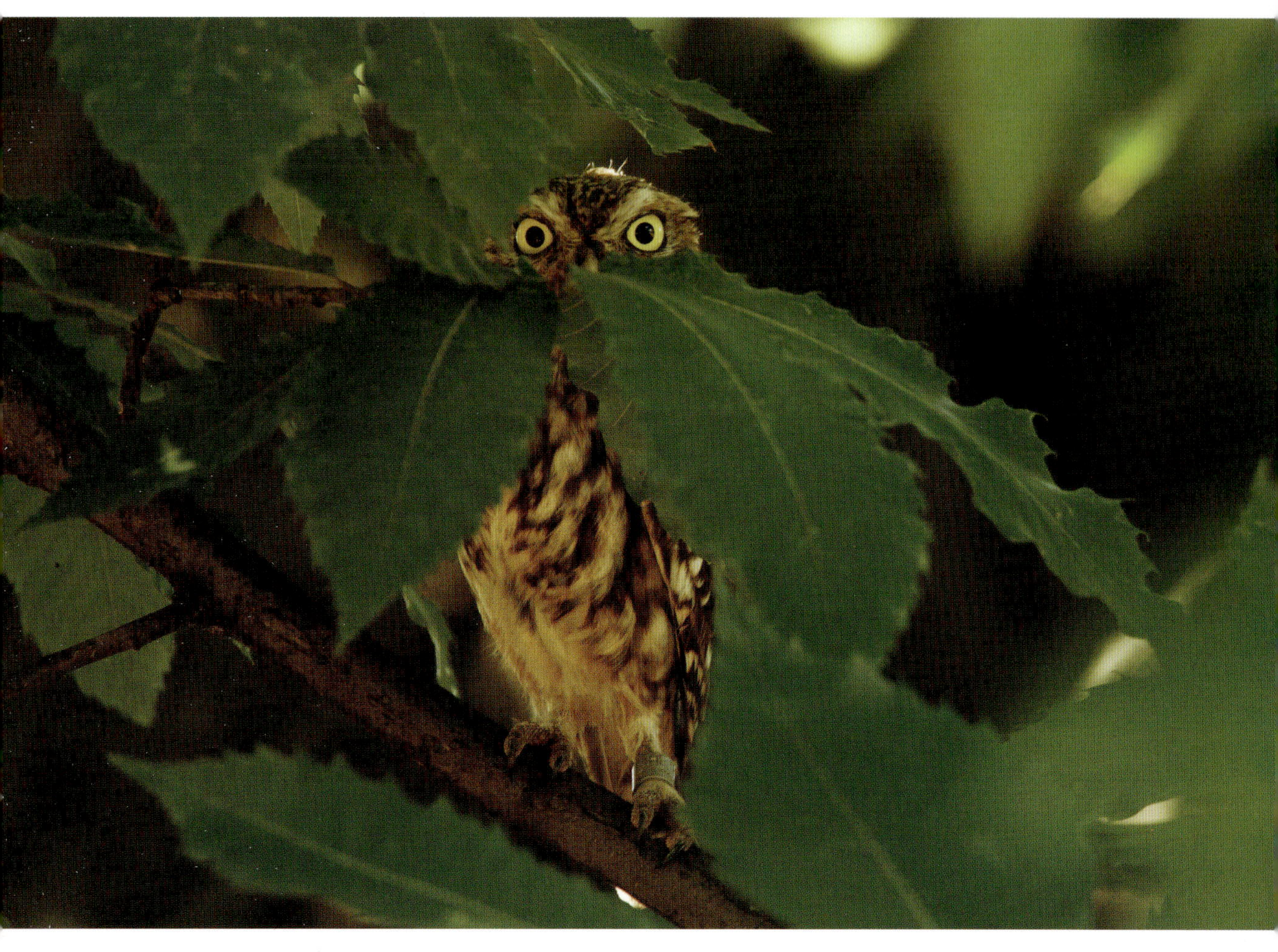

5.20 Eye Contact

I know a small meadow in the Palatinate region of Germany where some quite mature trees grow. A pair of little owls has been breeding there for years in a nesting box that was installed for that purpose. I've visited these two little owls many times. With a bit of luck, you can find them outside their cave in the late afternoon.

This photo of the little owl was taken on such a day. It looks as though it's peeking curiously at the viewer from behind some leaves. You actually can't see very much of the bird at all. But there's such intense eye contact that I almost feel like I'm getting pulled into the picture.

Little owl | Germany | 700mm (500mm + 1.4x converter), aperture 5.6, 1/250 s, ISO 1000, -2/3 exposure compensation

5.21 Black Background

I have some tame owls that you've already met a few times throughout this book. For one project, I wanted to photograph them individually against a black background. I prepared a very simple setup in the living room: A black canvas served as the background, a root as a perch, and a photo lamp mounted on a tripod provided light.

From this series, I chose the image of my tawny owl lady Fynja. Tawny owls are nocturnal, which means that the photo shows her in an almost natural setting that just happens to be inside a studio. I like this photo with its mystical atmosphere quite a bit.

Tawny owl | Germany | 135mm, aperture 4.5, 1/320 s, ISO 1600, -2 exposure compensation

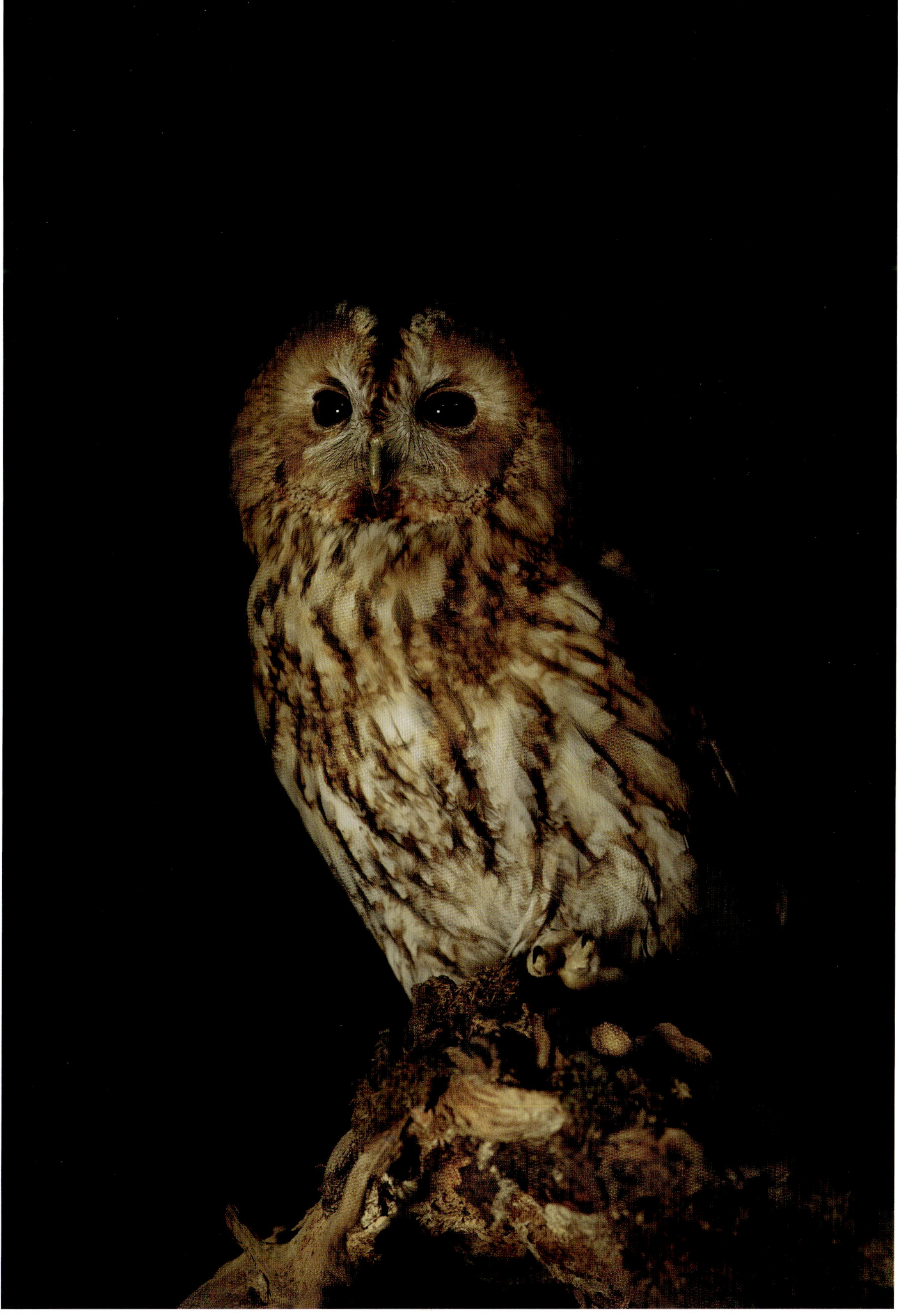

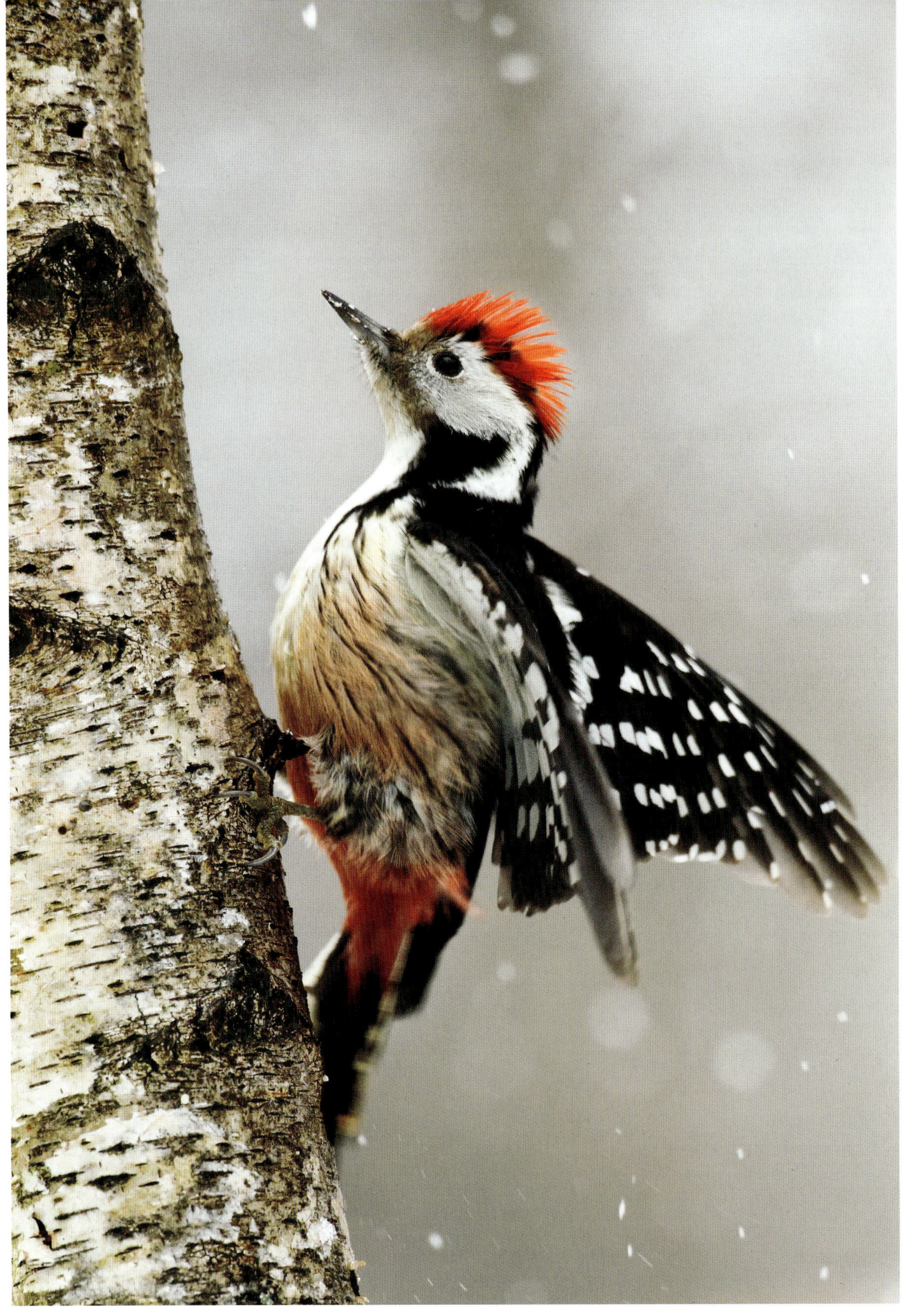

5.22 The Punk

It was a cold winter day and I spent it in my tree stand. Many different birds came to the feeder and I had already taken some nice shots. Even the rare middle spotted woodpecker stopped by to help itself to some much-needed energy from the suet in the feeder. I was watching it when a great spotted woodpecker also approached the trunk of the birch. The middle spotted woodpecker responded by adopting this imposing defensive posture. It fanned out its wings to appear larger and raised its red head feathers into a magnificent crown. The strong red provides an interesting accent of color in a picture that is otherwise dominated by shades of black, white, and gray.

Middle spotted woodpecker | Germany | 500mm, aperture 5.6, 1/640 s, ISO 1250, +2/3 exposure compensation

5.23 Mirror Image

We have set up a place for birds to bathe in our yard. During the winter we provide food nearby, and from my stand I can see both the feeding and the bathing area. Many birds, especially the seed-eaters, like to take a sip of water between feedings, and this always makes for good photo opportunities.

Marsh tits are usually very restless and always on the move. It's not that easy to get a picture of them standing still. But in this case, the little tit paused briefly on a stone on its way to the water and I managed to snap this picture. I'm particularly fond of it because of the beautiful reflection. The warm, uniform colors further enhance the harmonic effect.

Marsh tit | Germany | 600mm, aperture 5.6, 1/2000 s, ISO 1250, -1/3 exposure compensation

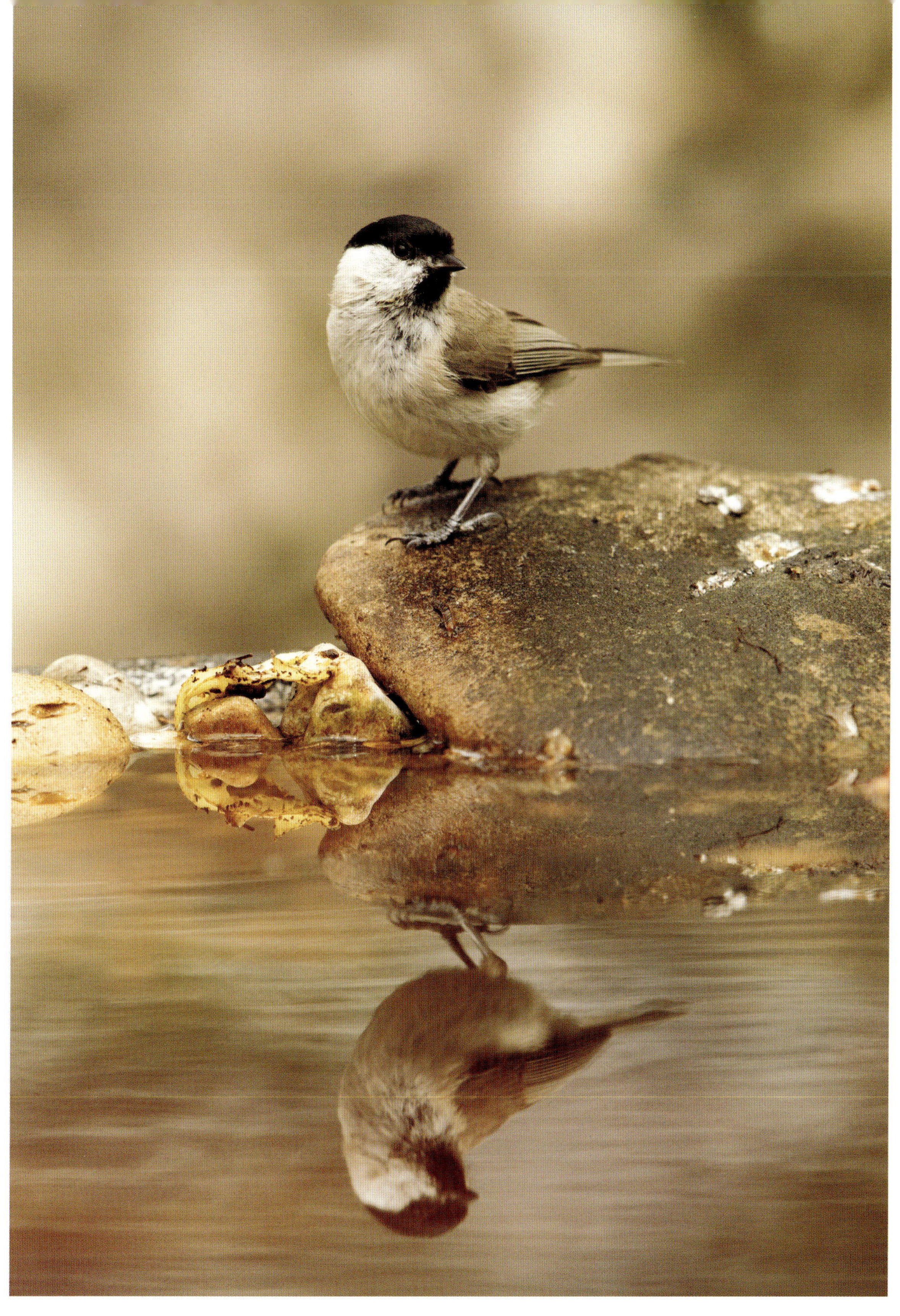

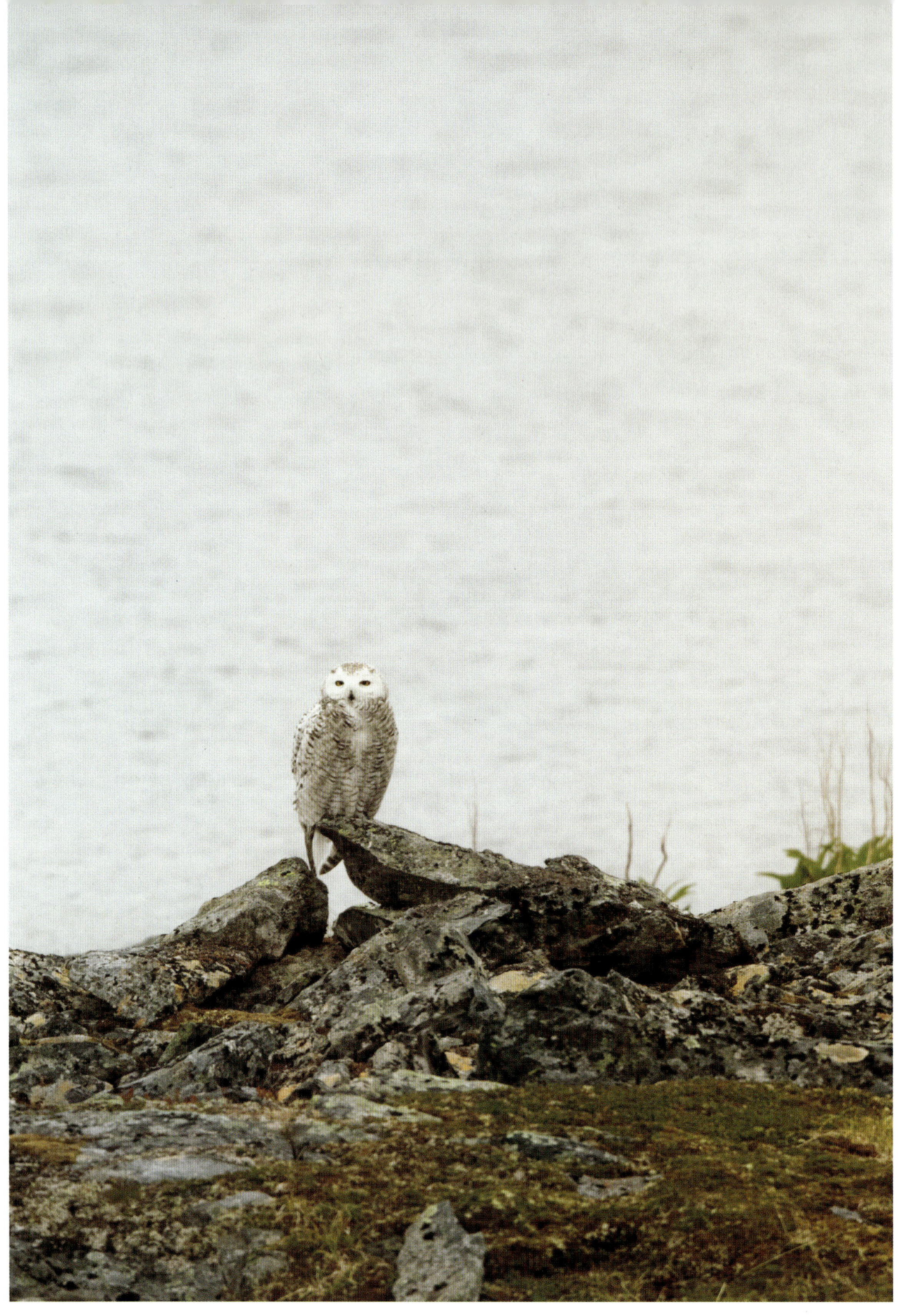

5.24 Seek and You Shall Find

I was traveling in Norway and watching a white-tailed eagle on a beach when a Norwegian approached me and wanted to chat about the various bird species that could be found in the area. Finally, he asked if I'd ever seen wild snowy owls. When I said no, he tipped me off about an area in which a family of these beautiful owls was said to be living at the time.

Unfortunately, the place was almost 200 miles away. I decided to go there anyway to try my luck.

I took off the same afternoon. He had described a road along a small lake with a large rocky area behind it where the owls were supposedly living. I arrived in the evening and combed the area. For a long time, I searched in vain and got back into my car several times to switch locations. From my car, I suddenly spotted this snowy owl sitting on a rock on the other side of the lake. Unfortunately, it was very far away. Nevertheless, I got out of the car and carefully crept closer. I got some pictures that show the owl, albeit quite small. Suddenly, it took off and I figured that this had been it with the photos. But no, it flew across the lake, bringing it quite a bit closer to me. That's how this picture came about, in the middle of the night, shortly after 3 a.m. when a long search came to a happy end.

Snowy owl | Norway | 840mm (600mm + 1.4x converter), aperture 7.1, 1/400 s, ISO 1250, +1 1/3 exposure compensation

5.25 Splendid Colors

My two white-faced owls have already made several appearances in this book, but this image is one of the most delightful.

We had bought some beautiful blooming heather for our flower bed and, of course, I wanted to use the plants for a photo shoot. However, on this day, my little owl didn't feel like looking at the camera. I snapped several photos of the owl looking either to the right or left. But it didn't want to look at me at all.

Initially, I was a bit disappointed, until I got a good view of my pictures later on the computer and realized that this slight sideways glance works just beautifully. The gorgeous flowers frame the pretty owl and with its misty background, it's a colorful yet tranquil shot.

White-faced owl | Germany | 13mm, aperture 2.8, 1/2000 s, ISO 800

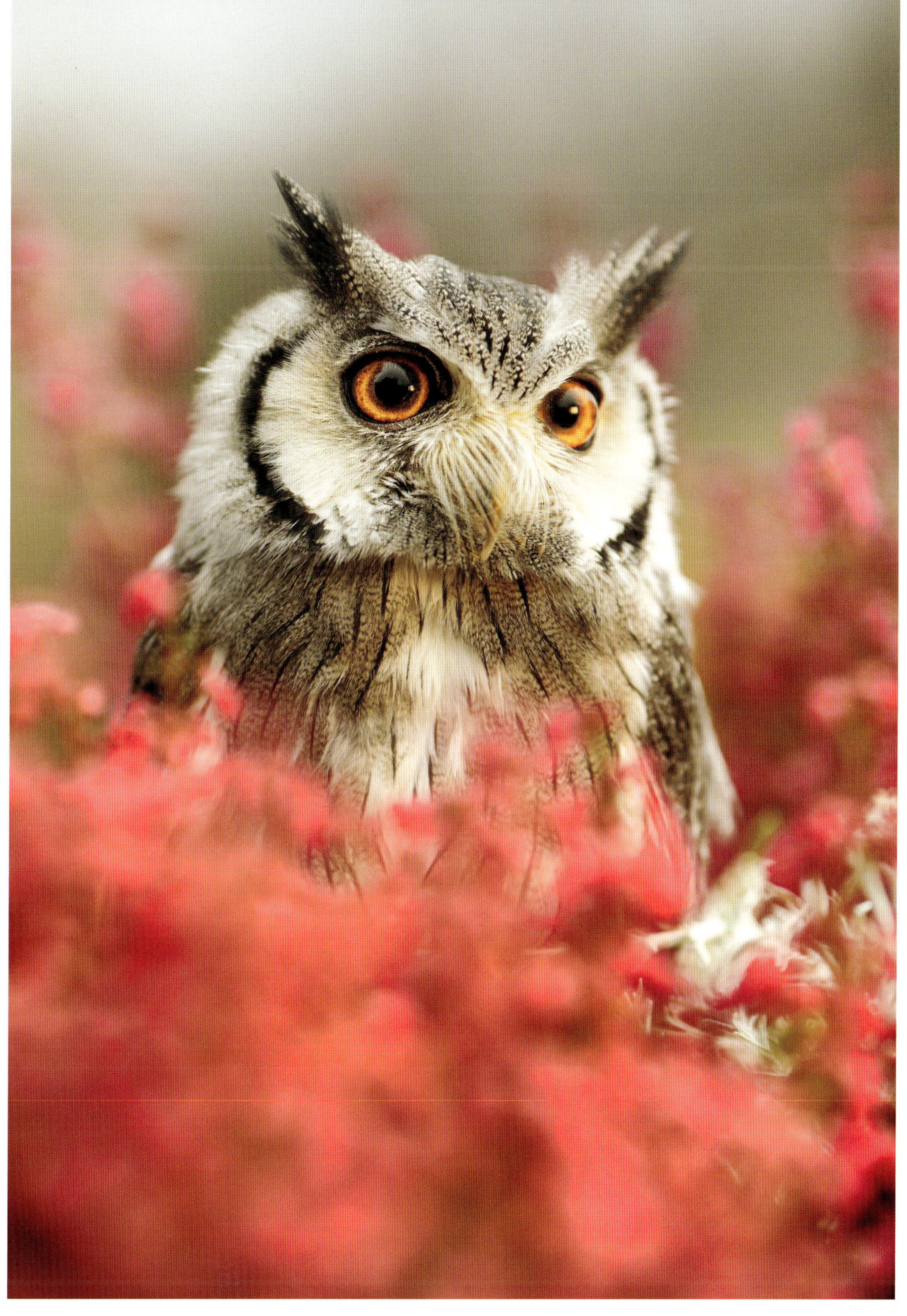

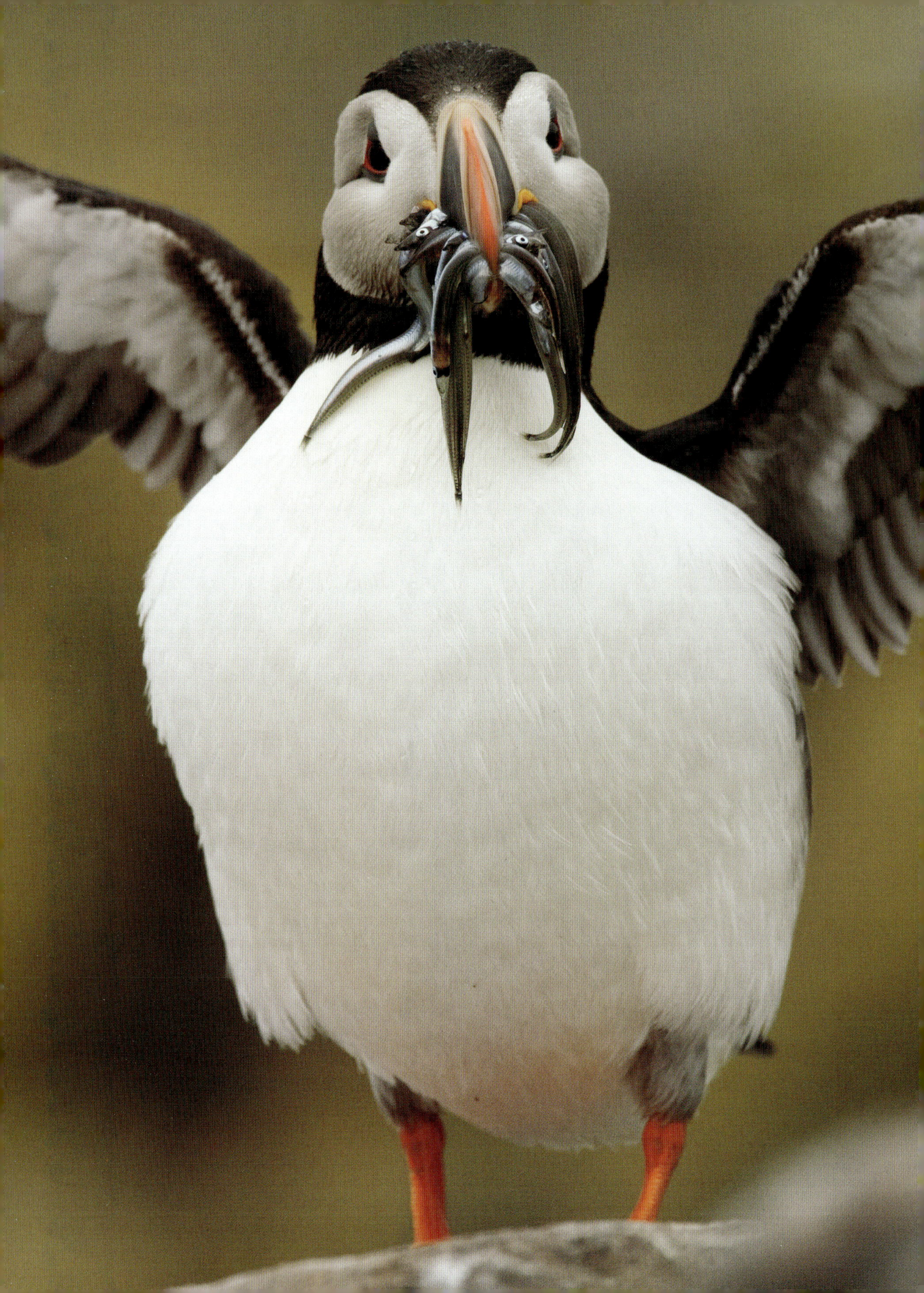

THANK YOU

Now go and have fun taking pictures! I hope this book has helped you to understand the fascination of bird photography and that you walk away with some valuable knowledge about how to take great shots and analyze pictures.

At this point, I would like to thank a few people. First of all, a big thank you to my partner Jürgen; without him, I could not devote so much time to my animals and my photography. I also want to thank my father for having supported my ideas over so many years and for reading a draft of this book. More thanks go to the team of the German Raptor Research Center at Guttenberg Castle. Many of the pictures wouldn't exist without them and they always support me when I need advice or assistance with my own owls!

I would also like to thank the Walsrode Bird Park, the Cologne Zoo, the Zoological Gardens Karlsruhe, the Alpine Zoo Innsbruck, the Wilhelma Stuttgart, the Heidelberg Zoo, and the Hagenbeck Zoo Hamburg for their kind permission to publish the pictures I took there. And finally, I want to thank Ms. Karin Wempe for the copyediting of this book, and my editor Mr. Rudolf Krahm, who always supported me and believed in this project from the start.

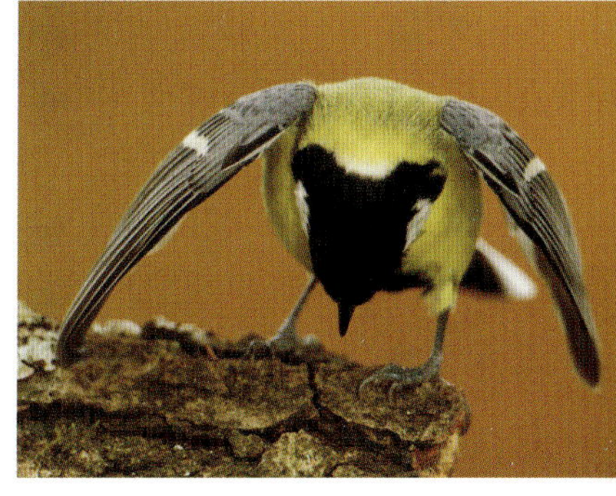

Great tit | Germany | 500mm, aperture 4.5, 1/160 s, ISO 1000

Puffins | Farne Islands | Other than the people listed I also want to thank all the wonderful birds that I've already had the pleasure of photographing…. | 700mm (500mm + 1.4x converter), aperture 9.0, 1/500 s, ISO 1000

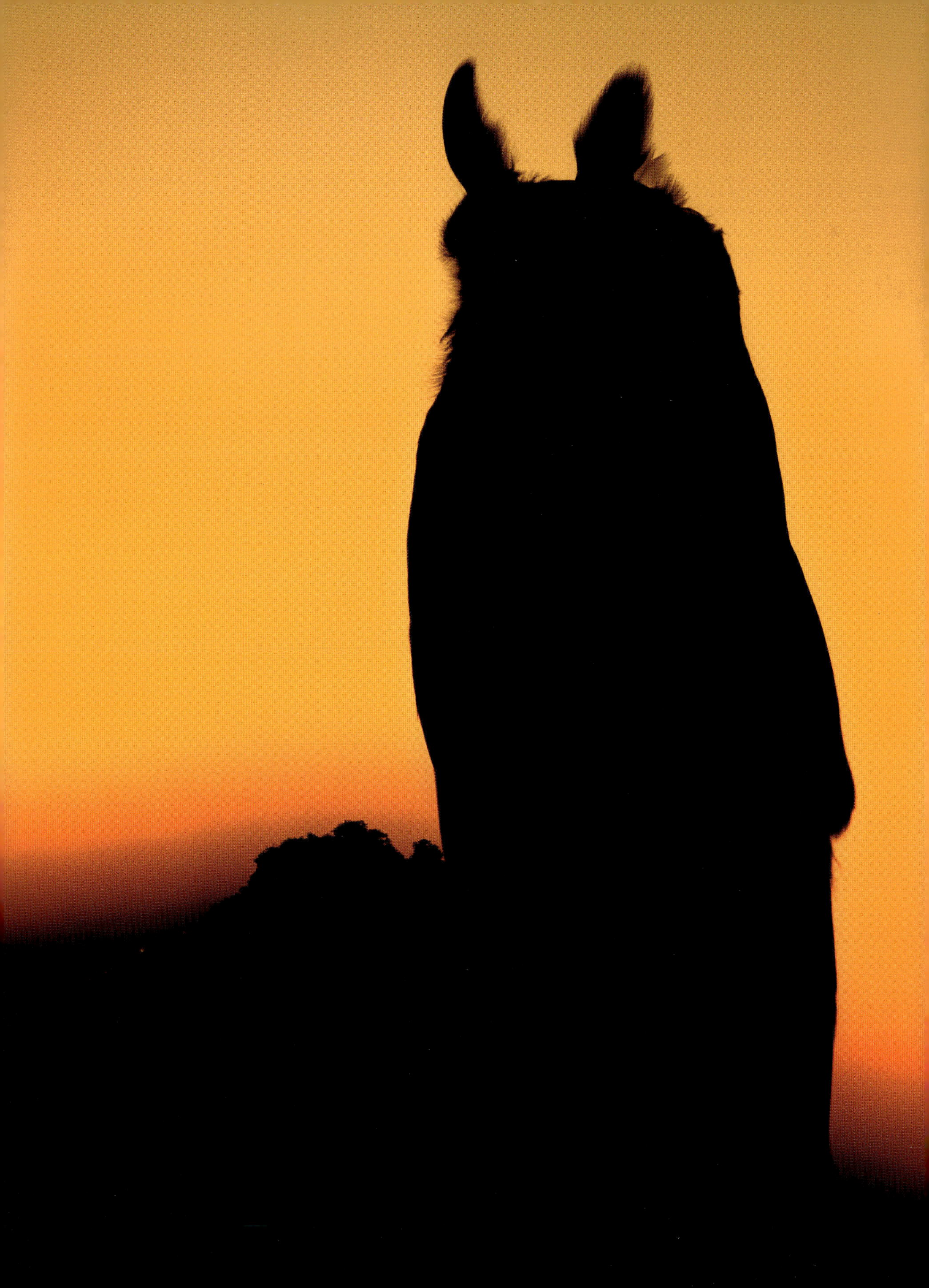